Lecture Notes in Computer Science 16144

Founding Editors

Gerhard Goos
Juris Hartmanis

Editorial Board Members

Elisa Bertino, *Purdue University, West Lafayette, IN, USA*
Wen Gao, *Peking University, Beijing, China*
Bernhard Steffen ⓘ, *TU Dortmund University, Dortmund, Germany*
Moti Yung ⓘ, *Columbia University, New York, NY, USA*

The series Lecture Notes in Computer Science (LNCS), including its subseries Lecture Notes in Artificial Intelligence (LNAI) and Lecture Notes in Bioinformatics (LNBI), has established itself as a medium for the publication of new developments in computer science and information technology research, teaching, and education.

LNCS enjoys close cooperation with the computer science R & D community, the series counts many renowned academics among its volume editors and paper authors, and collaborates with prestigious societies. Its mission is to serve this international community by providing an invaluable service, mainly focused on the publication of conference and workshop proceedings and postproceedings. LNCS commenced publication in 1973.

Aidan Hogan · Ken Satoh · Hasan Dağ ·
Anni-Yasmin Turhan · Dumitru Roman ·
Ahmet Soylu
Editors

Rules and Reasoning

9th International Joint Conference, RuleML+RR 2025
Istanbul, Turkey, September 22–24, 2025
Proceedings

 Springer

Editors
Aidan Hogan
DCC, Universidad de Chile
Santiago, Chile

Ken Satoh
Center for Juris-informatics, ROIS
Tokyo, Japan

Hasan Dağ
Kadir Has University
Istanbul, Türkiye

Anni-Yasmin Turhan
Paderborn University
Paderborn, Germany

Dumitru Roman
SINTEF AS
Oslo, Norway

Ahmet Soylu
Kristiania University of Applied Sciences
Oslo, Norway

OsloMet – Oslo Metropolitan University
Oslo, Norway

ISSN 0302-9743   ISSN 1611-3349 (electronic)
Lecture Notes in Computer Science
ISBN 978-3-032-08886-4   ISBN 978-3-032-08887-1 (eBook)
https://doi.org/10.1007/978-3-032-08887-1

© The Editor(s) (if applicable) and The Author(s), under exclusive license to Springer Nature Switzerland AG 2026

This work is subject to copyright. All rights are solely and exclusively licensed by the Publisher, whether the whole or part of the material is concerned, specifically the rights of translation, reprinting, reuse of illustrations, recitation, broadcasting, reproduction on microfilms or in any other physical way, and transmission or information storage and retrieval, electronic adaptation, computer software, or by similar or dissimilar methodology now known or hereafter developed.
The use of general descriptive names, registered names, trademarks, service marks, etc. in this publication does not imply, even in the absence of a specific statement, that such names are exempt from the relevant protective laws and regulations and therefore free for general use.
The publisher, the authors and the editors are safe to assume that the advice and information in this book are believed to be true and accurate at the date of publication. Neither the publisher nor the authors or the editors give a warranty, expressed or implied, with respect to the material contained herein or for any errors or omissions that may have been made. The publisher remains neutral with regard to jurisdictional claims in published maps and institutional affiliations.

This Springer imprint is published by the registered company Springer Nature Switzerland AG
The registered company address is: Gewerbestrasse 11, 6330 Cham, Switzerland

If disposing of this product, please recycle the paper.

Preface

These are the proceedings of the 9th International Joint Conference on Rules and Reasoning (RuleML+RR). RuleML+RR joined the efforts of two well-established conference series: the International Web Rule Symposia (RuleML) and the Web Reasoning and Rule Systems (RR) conferences.

The RuleML symposia have been held since 2002 and the RR conferences since 2007. The RR conferences were a forum for discussion and dissemination of new results on Web Reasoning and Rule Systems, with an emphasis on rule-based approaches and languages. The RuleML symposia were devoted to disseminating research, applications, languages, and standards for rule technologies, with attention to both theoretical and practical developments, as well as challenging new ideas and industrial applications. Building on the tradition of both RuleML and RR, the joint conference series RuleML+RR aims to bridge academia and industry in the field of rules, and to foster cross-fertilization between the different communities focused on the research, development, and applications of rule-based systems. RuleML+RR aims to be the leading conference series for all subjects concerning theoretical advances, novel technologies, and innovative applications relating to knowledge representation and reasoning with rules.

To leverage these ambitions, RuleML+RR 2025 was organized as part of the event *Declarative AI 2025: Rules, Reasoning, Decisions, and Explanations*, which was held between the 22nd and the 24th of September 2025. This event was hosted by Kadir Has University, Türkiye. With its general topic *"Declarative Artificial Intelligence,"* a core objective of the event was to present the latest advancements in AI and rules, reasoning, decisions, and explanations and their adoption in IT systems towards improving key fields such as environment, health, and societies. To this end, *Declarative AI 2025* brought together co-located events with related interests. In addition to RuleML+RR, this included the Reasoning Web Summer School (RW 2025) and DecisionCAMP 2025.

The RuleML+RR conference moreover included several subevents:

1. *Doctoral Consortium* – an initiative to attract and promote student research in rules and reasoning, with the opportunity for students to present and discuss their ideas, and benefit from close contact with leading experts in the field.
2. *International Rule Challenge* – an initiative to provide competition among work in progress and new visionary ideas concerning innovative rule-oriented applications, aimed at both research and industry.
3. *Industry Track* – an initiative to present work from all areas of rules- and reasoning-based technologies specifically for solving real industry problems.
4. *Project Networking Session* – an initiative to bring together relevant projects working in the area of data and AI with particular focus on, but not limited to, the event topics: rules, reasoning, decisions, and explanations

The program of the main track of RuleML+RR 2025 included the presentation of 12 full research papers and 2 short papers. These contributions were carefully selected by the Program Committee from 31 full paper submissions, and 3 short paper submissions; thus 34 submissions were sent for review. Each paper was carefully single-blindly reviewed by at least 3 reviewers and all borderline papers were discussed in detail. The technical program was then enriched with the additional contributions from its subevents as well as from DecisionCAMP 2025, an event aimed at practitioners which was virtual this year.

At RuleML+RR 2025, three keynote speakers were invited:

- Robert Kowalski, Imperial College London (UK): *Two Kinds of Rules: Goal Rules and Belief Rules*
- Boris Motik, University of Oxford (UK): *RDFox: The Journey From Research To Commercialisation*
- Esra Erdem, Sabanci University (Turkey): *Applications of Answer Set Programming in Robotic Construction*

The chairs sincerely thank the keynote speakers for their contribution to the success of the event; these proceedings also include an extended invited paper from Robert Kowalski, and keynote abstracts from Boris Motik and Esra Edrem. The chairs also thank the Program Committee members and the additional reviewers for their hard work in the careful assessment of the submitted papers. Further thanks go to all authors of contributed papers for their efforts in the preparation of their submissions and the camera-ready versions within the established schedule. Sincere thanks are also due to the chairs of the Doctoral Consortium, Rule Challenge, Industry Track, Project Networking Session, and to the chairs of all co-located Declarative AI 2025 events. The chairs finally thank the entire organization team including the Publicity, Proceedings, and Sponsorship Chairs, who actively contributed to the organization and the success of the event.

A special thanks goes to all the sponsors of RuleML+RR 2025 and Declarative AI 2025: Springer, Kadir Has University, Paderborn University, Kristiania University of Applied Sciences, RuleML Inc, and RR Association. A special thanks also goes to the publisher, Springer, for their cooperation in editing this volume and publication of the proceedings. We are grateful to the sponsors of RuleML+RR 2025 as they also contributed towards the awards: RuleML+RR Harold Boley Distinguished Paper award, and RuleML+RR Best Student Paper award, RuleML+RR Best Rule Challenge paper award, and RuleML+RR Best Doctoral Consortium Paper award

August 2025

Aidan Hogan
Ken Satoh
Hasan Dağ
Anni-Yasmin Turhan
Dumitru Roman
Ahmet Soylu

Organization

General Chairs

Hasan Dağ	Kadir Has University, Türkiye
Anni-Yasmin Turhan	Paderborn University, Germany
Ahmet Soylu	Kristiania University of Applied Sciences, Norway

Program Chairs

Aidan Hogan	University of Chile, Chile
Ken Satoh	National Institute of Informatics, Japan

Rule Challenge Chairs

Alessandro Margara	Politecnico di Milano, Italy
Tomáš Kliegr	Prague University of Economics and Business, Czechia
Ognjen Savkovic	Free University of Bozen-Bolzano, Italy

Doctoral Consortium

Shqiponja Ahmetaj	TU Wien, Austria
Riccardo Tommasini	INSA Lyon, France

Industry Track Chairs

Luigi Bellomarini	Banca d'Italia, Italy
Evgeny Kharlamov	Bosch Center for Artificial Intelligence, Germany
Ioana Georgiana Ciuciu	Babeș-Bolyai University, Romania

Networking Session Chairs

Dumitru Roman	SINTEF AS/Oslo Metropolitan University, Norway
George Konstantinidis	University of Southampton, UK
Emanuel Sallinger	Vienna University of Technology, Austria

Proceedings Chairs

Dumitru Roman	SINTEF AS/Oslo Metropolitan University, Norway
Ahmet Soylu	Kristiania University College, Norway

Publicity Chairs

Kai Sauerwald	FernUniversität in Hagen, Germany
Tor-Morten Grønli	Kristiania University of Applied Sciences, Norway
Romuald Esdras Wandji	Umeå University, Sweden

Local Chair

Mehmet Nafiz Aydin	Boğaziçi University, Türkiye

Local Team

E. Fatih Yetkin	Kadir Has University, Türkiye
Tuğçe Ballı	Kadir Has University, Türkiye
Mert İlhan Ecevit	Kadir Has University, Türkiye
Elif Özgüngör Kozak	Kadir Has University, Türkiye
Judi Sekban	Kadir Has University, Türkiye
Gönül Sılav Tuzlu	Kadir Has University, Türkiye

Web Chair

Ahmet Soylu Kristiania University of Applied Sciences, Norway

Finance Chair

Mehmet Nafiz Aydin Kadir Has University, Türkiye

Program Committee

Adrian Paschke Freie Universität Berlin, Germany
Albin Ahmeti Semantic Web Company, TU Wien, Austria
Alisa Kovtunova TU Dresden, Germany
Andrea Cimmino Arriaga Universidad Politécnica de Madrid, Spain
Andrea Mazzullo Free University of Bozen-Bolzano, Italy
Andreas Pieris University of Edinburgh, UK
Anisa Rula University of Brescia, Italy
Anni-Yasmin Turhan Paderborn University, Germany
Antonino Rotolo University of Bologna, Italy
Antonis Bikakis University College London, UK
Bernardo Cuenca Grau University of Oxford, UK
Cecilia Di Florio University of Bologna, Italy
Chang Sun Maastricht University, Netherlands
Claudia D'Amato University of Bari, Italy
Cristina Feier Technical University of Cluj-Napoca, Romania
Daniel Hernandez University of Stuttgart, Germany
Davide Sottara Mayo Clinic, USA
Diego Calvanese Free University of Bozen-Bolzano, Italy
Diego Torres Universidad Nacional de La Plata, Argentina
Doerthe Arndt TU Dresden, Germany
Domenico Lembo Sapienza University of Rome, Italy
Egor V. Kostylev University of Oslo, Norway
Erman Acar University of Amsterdam, Netherlands
Federico Ulliana University of Montpellier, France
Francesca Alessandra Lisi Università degli Studi di Bari "Aldo Moro", Italy
Francesco Ricca University of Calabria, Italy
Francesco Santini University of Perugia, Italy
Francesco M. Donini Universita' della Tuscia, Italy
George Konstantinidis University of Southampton, UK

Giorgos Flouris	ICS-FORTH, Greece
Giuseppe Mazzotta	University of Calabria, Italy
Gong Cheng	Nanjing University, China
Guido Governatori	Central Queensland University, Australia
Horatiu Cirstea	Loria, France
Jan Rauch	Prague University of Economics and Business, Czechia
Jan Van den Bussche	Hasselt University, Belgium
Jesse Heyninck	Open Universiteit, The Netherlands
Jessica Zangari	University of Calabria, Italy
Jia-Huai You	University of Alberta, Canada
João Paulo Almeida	Federal University of Espírito Santo, Brazil
Johannes Fürnkranz	Johannes Kepler University Linz, Austria
Joost Vennekens	Vrije Universiteit Brussel, Belgium
Juan Reutter	Pontificia Universidad Católica de Chile, Chile
Julian Padget	University of Bath, UK
Juliana Bowles	University of St Andrews, UK
Julien Corman	Free University of Bozen-Bolzano, Italy
Kia Teymourian	University of Texas at Austin, USA
Konstantin Schekotihin	Alpen-Adria Universität Klagenfurt, Austria
Kouji Kozaki	Osaka Electro-Communication University, Japan
Leopoldo Bertossi	SKEMA Business School Canada, Canada
Livio Robaldo	University of Swansea, UK
Loris Bozzato	Fondazione Bruno Kessler, Italy
Luca Geatti	University of Udine, Italy
Marcin Przybyłko	University of Leipzig, Germany
Marco Manna	University of Calabria, Italy
Marco Maratea	University of Genoa, Italy
María Poveda-Villalón	Universidad Politécnica de Madrid, Spain
Maria Vanina Martinez	Artificial Intelligence Research Institute (IIIA - CSIC), Spain
Marina De Vos	University of Bath, UK
Markus Krötzsch	TU Dresden, Germany
Martin Giese	University of Oslo, Norway
Maxime Jakubowski	TU Wien, Austria
Meghyn Bienvenu	CNRS, University of Bordeaux, France
Michaël Thomazo	Inria, France
Mihai Pomarlan	University of Bremen, Germany
Nico Potyka	Cardiff University, UK
Nicoletta Fornara	Università della Svizzera italiana, Switzerland
Ognjen Savkovic	Free University of Bozen-Bolzano, Italy
Oshani Seneviratne	Rensselaer Polytechnic Institute, USA

Paul Krause	University of Surrey, UK
Peter Patel-Schneider	independent, USA
Piero Bonatti	University of Naples Federico II, Italy
Pierre Bisquert	University of Montpellier, France
Rafael Peñaloza	University of Milano-Bicocca, Italy
Roman Kontchakov	Birkbeck, University of London, UK
Ryutaro Ichise	Tokyo Institute of Technology, Japan
Sebastian Rudolph	TU Dresden, Germany
Serena Villata	CNRS - Laboratoire d'Informatique, Signaux et Systèmes de Sophia-AntipolisFrance
Sergio Tessaris	Free University of Bozen - Bolzano, Italy
Shqiponja Ahmetaj	Vienna University of Technology, Austria
Simon Vandevelde	Katholieke Universiteit Leuven, Belgium
Theresa Swift	Johns Hopkins Applied Physics Lab, USA
Thomas Meyer	University of Cape Town and CAIR, South Africa
Timotheus Kampik	Umeå University, Sweden
Tomas Kliegr	Prague University of Economics and Business, Czechia
Umberto Straccia	ISTI-CNR, Italy
Umutcan Serles	University of Innsbruck, Austria
Veruska Zamborlini	Federal University of Espírito Santo, Brazil
Werner Nutt	Free University of Bozen-Bolzano, Italy

Additional Reviewers

Cyprien Michel-Delétie	ENS de Lyon, France
Gioacchino Sterlicchio	Polytechnic University of Bari, Italy
Jingcheng Wu	Universität Stuttgart, Germany
Sofiane Elguendouze	CNRS, INRIA, I3S - Université Côte d'Azur, France
Yi Wang	Universität Stuttgart, Germany

RuleML+RR 2025 Sponsors

Keynotes

RDFox: The Journey From Research To Commercialisation

Boris Motik

Department of Computer Science, University of Oxford Wolfson Building, Parks Road, OX1 3QD Oxford,

> **Abstract.** RDFox[1] is a Datalog-enabled RDF management system that originated in the Knowledge Representation & Reasoning at the University of Oxford. Its development started in 2009, at a time when commodity computers started routinely offering large amounts of RAM and several CPUs. RDFox was thus conceived as a in-memory RDF database, and it was developed around efficient data structures and algorithms that support effective parallelisation. It uses the *materialisation* approach to Datalog reasoning—that is, it precomputes all consequences of an RDF dataset and a set of rules in a preprocessing step. Once materialisation is complete, SPARQL queries can be evaluated directly, without any further reference to the rules. RDFox was used as a testbed for the development of a number of different techniques, including
>
> - data structures and algorithms for parallel materialisation [5],
> - efficient reasoning and query answering over datasets with equality (i.e., *owl:sameAs*) [2], and
> - incremental materialisation maintenance for programs without [3,4] and with [1] equality.

The combination of RAM-based storage and highly optimised algorithms allowed RDFox to outperform similar systems by a considerably margin, which lead to considerable commercial interest. In order to further develop and use the system in an industrial setting, Ian Horrocks, Bernardo Cuenca Grau, Adam Parr, and I founded Oxford Semantic Technologies in December 2016 as a spinout of Oxford University. In January 2018, Peter Crocker joined the founders' team as the company's CEO. In the following years, RDFox was developed from a research prototype to a robust and commercially viable system. This involved almost completely reengineering the original system, developing extensive APIs for programmatic access, developing new algorithms for query answering, providing tools for analysing the system's performance, implementing transaction isolation mechanisms, introducing a robust durability layer, supporting common enterprise-level features such as high availability and security, and porting the system to several platforms.

The system was commercially successful and was successfully applied in use cases such as product compatibility in manufacturing, financial crime monitoring in banking, and product recommendation in retail. What made RDFox stand out in virtually all such engagements is its consistently high performance of reasoning and query answering,

---

[1] https://www.oxfordsemantic.tech/rdfox

correctness and adherence to the standards, and robustness in a wide range of scenarios. Samsung Electronics recognised the potential of RDFox and acquired Oxford Semantic Technologies in July 2024. The system has been embedded into Samsung's software offering on their S25 Galaxy range of smartphones and is currently used to offer personalised experiences while holding users' data privately on the device.

In my talk, I will outline our journey of taking the basic research idea and bringing it into practice. Specifically, I will present an overview of the data structures and algorithms that sparked the development of RDFox. I will further discuss the work that was needed to make the product commercially viable. I will particularly focus on my experience and difficulties in guaranteeing the system's quality in the face of rising complexity. I will also discuss my experience in implementing the standards underpinning RDFox (i.e., RDF, OWL, SHACL, and so on). Finally, I will discuss several use cases that clearly demonstrate the benefits of symbolic reasoning in practice.

References

1. Motik, B., Nenov, Y., Piro, R., Horrocks, I.: Combining rewriting and incremental materialisation maintenance for Datalog programs with equality. In: Proceedings of the 24th International Joint Conference on Artificial Intelligence (IJCAI 2015), pp. 3127–3133. AAAI Press, Buenos Aires, Argentina, 25–31 July 2015
2. Motik, B., Nenov, Y., Piro, R., Horrocks, I.: Handling owl:sameAs via rewriting. In: Proceedings of the 29th AAAI Conference on Artificial Intelligence (AAAI 2015), pp. 231–237. AAAI Press, Austin, TX, USA, 25–30 January 2015
3. Motik, B., Nenov, Y., Piro, R., Horrocks, I.: Incremental update of Datalog materialisation: the backward/forward algorithm. In: Proceedings of the 29th AAAI Conference on Artificial Intelligence (AAAI 2015), pp. 1560–1568. AAAI Press, Austin, TX, USA (January 25–30 2015)
4. Motik, B., Nenov, Y., Piro, R., Horrocks, I.: Maintenance of Datalog materialisations revisited. Artif. Intell. **269**, 76–136 (2019)
5. Motik, B., Nenov, Y., Piro, R., Horrocks, I., Olteanu, D.: Parallel materialisation of Datalog programs in centralised, main-memory RDF systems. In: Proceedings of the 28th AAAI Conference on Artificial Intelligence (AAAI 2014), pp. 129–137. AAAI Press, Québec City, Québec, Canada, 27–31 July 2014

Applications of Answer Set Programming in Robotic Construction

Esra Erdem

Computer Science and Engineering, Sabancı University, İstanbul, Türkiye
esra.erdem@sabanciuniv.edu

In robot construction problems, multiple robots rearrange stacks of prefabricated blocks to build stable structures. In these problems, the input consists of an initial configuration of blocks of different sizes on a table, some goal conditions, and an upper bound on a makespan. The objective is to find a stable configuration of blocks stacked on each other that satisfy the specified goal conditions, and a feasible stack rearrangement plan to obtain this goal configuration from a specified initial configuration of the blocks.

In these problems, it is desirable that the goal conditions and the rearrangements plans make sense in the spirit of [4], so the goal conditions may involve abstract specifications (e.g., a bridge or an overhang), and the plans may involve subassembly construction and manipulation (instead of manipulating one block at a time), temporary counterweight and scaffolding (for stability of intermediate configurations), and concurrency.

For example, consider the robot construction problem instance (Scenario 13 of [1]), where the initial state is specified as in the left figure below, and the goal is to build a bridge in at most 7 time steps.

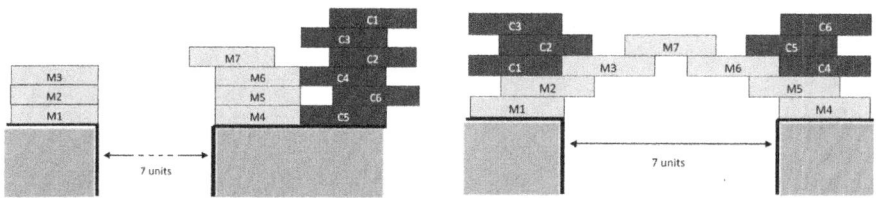

A solution of this problem instance consists of a possible goal state, as depicted in the right figure above, and a plan of length 7 to reach it. In this plan, a bimanual robot concurrently picks and places subassemblies of blocks using its left and right manipulators. First, it concurrently picks the towers with the base blocks $M2$ and $M5$ with its left and right manipulators, respectively, and then places these towers on top of blocks $M1$ and $M4$, respectively, so that $M2$ and $M5$ gets closer to each other. After building the left and right sides of the bridge, the robot places the block $M7$ on top of the blocks $M7$ and $M6$ so that both sides of the bridge are connected.

As can be seen from this example, robot construction problems involve challenges from the perspective of planning, knowledge representation and reasoning, and robotics. These challenges include representation of sophisticated ramifications of actions, reasoning about global constraints to eliminate spurious structures during planning, integrating low-level feasibility checks into planning to ensure stability of constructions and feasibility of plan executions, and an elaboration tolerant representation of variations of robot construction problems.

For instance, in the example above, consider the last action of placing the block $M7$ on the block $M6$. As a direct effect of this action, the right part of $M7$ becomes on $M6$. As a ramification of this action, the left part of $M7$ becomes located on the block $M3$ while the middle part of $M7$ is not located on any blocks. Representing such positive and negative ramifications require concepts (e.g., global positions of parts of blocks relative to a reference frame, transitive closure of "being immediately on top of another block or the table") that are recursively defined. Representing such ramifications is challenging [6].

In a robotic construction plan, all the actions must be feasible for the robot in that the robot can reach, grasp, pick, carry and place the subassemblies without colliding with any objects or itself. In all the world states (including the computed goal state, i.e., a bridge construct), both the subassemblies that the robot is carrying or constructing, and the rest of the blocks should be stable without any falls or collapses. Therefore, robot construction problems necessitate a proper use of feasibility checks together with the planner. Combining task planning with feasibility checks is challenging [3,5].

In this talk, we will discuss such challenges of robotic construction planning over a wide range of construction problems (e.g., building bridges, overhangs, tallest towers), and present a general elaboration tolerant method to address them. Our method is hybrid: it is based on the knowledge representation and reasoning paradigm of Answer Set Programming with external atoms [2] (i.e., semantic attachments [7]), and it utilizes the state-of-the-art feasibility checkers and physics engines. It is proven to be sound and complete, and shown to be applicable with real robots in dynamic simulations and physical implementations.

This is work joint with Faseeh Ahmad (Lund University, Sweden) and Volkan Patoglu (Sabancı University, Turkey), presented in our article [1].

References

1. Ahmad, F., Patoglu, V., Erdem, E.: Hybrid planning for challenging construction problems: an answer set programming approach. Artif. Intell. **319**, 103–902 (2023)
2. Eiter, T., Ianni, G., Schindlauer, R., Tompits, H.: A uniform integration of higher order reasoning and external evaluations in answer-set programming. In: Proceedings of IJCAI, pp. 90–96 (2005)
3. Erdem, E., Haspalamutgil, K., Palaz, C., Patoglu, V., Uras, T.: Combining high level causal reasoning with low-level geometric reasoning and motion planning for robotic manipulation. In: Proceedings of ICRA, pp. 4575–4581 (2011)
4. Fahlman, S.E.: A planning system for robot construction tasks. Artif. Intell. **5**(1), 149 (1974)
5. Nouman, A., Patoglu, V., Erdem, E.: Hybrid conditional planning for robotic applications. Int. J. Robot. Res. **40**(2-3) (2021)

6. Thiébaux, S., Hoffmann, J., Nebel, B.: In defense of PDDL axioms. Artif. Intell. **168**(12), 38 69 (2005) 7. Weyhrauch, R.W.: Prolegomena to a theory of mechanized formal reasoning. Artif. Intell. **13**(1), 133 170 (1980)

Contents

Two Kinds of Rules: *Goal Rules* and *Belief Rules* 1
   Robert Kowalski

Specifying an Obligation Taxonomy in the Non-Markovian Situation
Calculus 18
   Kalonji Kalala, Iluju Kiringa, and Tet Yeap

A Novel Concept Induction Approach for Explainable Quality 4.0 36
   Léa Charbonnier, Franco Giustozzi, Julien Saunier,
   and Cecilia Zanni-Merk

An Optimized Framework for DSPG Synthesis and Trust Network
Analysis with Subjective Logic 54
   Koffi Ismael Ouattara, Ana Petrovska, Ioannis Krontiris,
   Theo Dimitrakos, and Frank Kargl

When Does Naïve Evaluation Work for Datalog? 72
   Heng Liu and Eugenia Ternovska

Scalable Evaluation of Rule-Based Recommender Systems: Algorithms
and Benchmarks 90
   Len Feremans and Bart Goethals

Rule2Text: Natural Language Explanation of Logical Rules in Knowledge
Graphs 108
   Nasim Shirvani-Mahdavi, Devin Wingfield, Amin Ghasemi,
   and Chengkai Li

Minimizing Side-Effects in Virtual Knowledge Graph Updates 119
   Romuald Esdras Wandji and Diego Calvanese

Rule Extraction and Interaction-Aware Explainability for AI-Driven
Malware Detection 137
   Peter Anthony, Kefas Rimamnuskeb Galadima, Zekeri Adams,
   Monday Onoja, Daniel Arp, Martin Homola, and Štefan Balogh

Probabilistic Answer Set Programming Driven Ranking of Dynamic
Space-Time Belief Models 156
   Julius Monsen, Jakob Suchan, and Mehul Bhatt

Learning Interpretable Probabilistic Models and Schema Axioms
for Knowledge Graphs 176
  Ivan Diliso, Nicola Fanizzi, and Claudia d'Amato

Integrating Environmental Regulations into Autonomous Agricultural
Robotics: A Case for Waterbody-Aware Fertilization 194
  *Guillaume Perution-Khili, Ahmad Kadi, Nikolas Müller,
  Akira Charoensit, David Carral, Pierre Bisquert, Federico Ulliana,
  Ansgar Bernardi, and Marie-Laure Mugnier*

SPARQL in N3: SPARQL CONSTRUCT as a Rule Language for the Semantic
Web 209
  Dörthe Arndt, William Van Woensel, and Dominik Tomaszuk

Positioning LLM-Enabled Agents as Legal Compliance Aides for Data
Pipelines 227
  *Adela Nedisan Videsjorden, Nikolay Nikolov, Carl-Henrik Lien,
  Arda Goknil, Sagar Sen, Hui Song, Ahmet Soylu, and Dumitru Roman*

Learning to Contest Argumentative Claims 237
  Emanuele De Angelis, Maurizio Proietti, and Francesca Toni

Author Index 257

Two Kinds of Rules: *Goal Rules* and *Belief Rules*

Robert Kowalski

Imperial College London, London, UK
r.kowalski@imperial.ac.uk

Abstract. It is generally agreed that there are two kinds of if-then rules: logic-based rules, in which *if-then* has a logical semantics, and reactive rules, in which *if-then* represents change of state without a logical semantics. I will argue that reactive rules have an implicit logical semantics, as *goals* that need to be satisfied by generating a model that makes the goals true.

The logical semantics of reactive rules can be made explicit by making change of state explicit, and by understanding the rules as meaning that if some conditions are true at a time, then some actions are performed at a future time. This is the approach taken by the modal logic MetateM. The same approach can be used with a non-modal logic, such as the situation calculus or event calculus. However, all these logics use frame axioms to reason that if a fact is true in a state, then it remains true in the next state, unless it is terminated by the change of state.

Reasoning by means of frame axioms is intolerably inefficient, compared with destructive change of state in conventional reactive systems. I will argue that this inefficiency can be avoided in logic-based systems by using destructive change of state, with frame axioms becoming an emergent property.

But giving a logical semantics to reactive rules leaves open the relationship of reactive rules with ordinary logic-based rules. I will argue that ordinary logic-based rules can be understood as *beliefs* that help an agent satisfy its goals.

Keywords: reactive rules · logic programs · goals and beliefs · LPS

1 Introduction

The distinction between two kinds of rules is widely recognized in the AI and Semantic Web communities: *logic-based rules*, which have a logical semantics, and *reactive rules*, which represent change of state without a logical semantics [15]. Despite this dissimilarity, the two kinds of rules are often confused with one another. Even when a clear distinction is made between them, their relationship can remain unclear.

In [16–21], we presented a language, LPS (Logic-based Production System), which combines logic programs, representing an agent's *beliefs* with reactive rules, representing an agent's *goals*. LPS gives a logical semantics to reactive rules, by treating them as sentences that need to be satisfied by generating a model that makes them true. This semantics of reactive rules in LPS is like the semantics of programs in MetateM [4, 12]. However, MetateM does not have a separate representation for logic programs. LPS, on the other hand, uses the model-theoretic semantics of logic programs to define the space of candidate models that can be generated to make reactive rules true. The resulting combination of reactive rules and logic programs in LPS is similar in spirit to the homogeneous Event-Condition-Action Logic Programming language (ECA-LP) [29].

The distinction in LPS between *goal rules*, which are reactive rules, and *belief rules*, which are logic programs, is similar to other distinctions made in other areas. It is related, for example, to the distinctions between:

- Integrity constraints and derivation rules in database systems [26];
- Regulative and constitutive norms in normative systems [5];
- Operative rules and structural rules in the operation of an enterprise [27];
- Reactive systems and transformational systems in "software engineering, programming languages, and system and hardware design" [13].
- Beliefs and desires in the belief-desire-intention (BDI) model of intelligent agents [7, 10, 11].

History. The origins of LPS go back to our work on combining integrity constraints with logic programming rules in deductive databases [32]. This contributed to our subsequent work on abductive logic programming (ALP) [14], using logic programs to generate abductive explanations and using integrity constraints to eliminate unacceptable candidate explanations. Later, we embedded ALP into an agent cycle, using integrity constraints both to generate reactive behaviour and to serve as higher-level maintenance goals [16]. We developed LPS, as a scaled-down variant of ALP agents, to combine the functionality of both production rules and logic programming rules, together with destructive change of state for the sake of efficiency [17].

During these developments, we were aware of MetateM, but we did not understand how it related to our work. We were also aware of the BDI agent model [7]. However, in both cases, I was dissuaded by their use of modal logic, which seemed unnecessarily complicated and conceptually questionable.

In the case of MetateM, I eventually realized that its use of modal logic for representing time is a relatively minor difference from our use of explicit timestamps. Moreover, I was encouraged to discover that we came to the same conclusion of viewing computation as model generation, coming from opposite directions.

The relationship between LPS and BDI is more complicated. On the one hand, BDI overlaps with LPS and ALP with its distinction and focus on goals and beliefs. But on the other hand, the early BDI agent systems were specified in multi-modal logics, with separate modal operators for goals, beliefs and intentions. However, the practical implementations of BDI agents bore little resemblance to their logical specifications.

Following the lead of AgentSpeak [31], most BDI agent implementation languages abandoned their modal specifications and their logical semantics, and they represented beliefs, desires, and intentions as "data structures" [10, 11, 31]. In AgentSpeak, the main data structure is a *plan*, which has the rule-like form: *triggering event: beliefs ← goals or actions*. The arrow is written in the backward direction because of its resemblance to a logic program rule. However, unlike a logic program rule, the invocation of a plan can be "both data-directed (using addition/deletion of beliefs) and goal-directed (using addition/deletion of goals)" [31]. As a consequence, plans in BDI languages of the AgentSpeak variety do not have a logical semantics.

In this paper, I will explore:

- How the logical semantics of LPS and MetateM can be used to give a logical semantics to other reactive rule languages;
- How the use of destructive change of state in LPS can be used to improve the efficiency of other logic-based languages;
- How the incorporation of logic programs in LPS can be used to improve the level of abstraction in other reactive rule languages; and
- How the combination of goal rules and belief rules in LPS can be viewed as a scaled-down model of human thinking.

The paper is deliberately written in an informal style, to make it more accessible to readers without an extensive background in logic and computing. More rigorous treatments can be found in the references.

2 Reactive Systems

Reactive systems include a wide range of programming, database and AI systems [28]. Not all these systems are rule-based, but they all treat computation as generating a sequence of states to maintain a desired relationship with a changing environment. Production systems are possibly the simplest example of such a reactive rule system.

Production Systems. A *production system* [9] consists of:

- A *working memory*, represented as a set of facts;
- *Production rules* of the form *if conditions then actions*;
- An *"inference engine"*, which uses "forward chaining" to match conditions of rules with facts in the working memory, and derives candidate actions;
- *Conflict resolution*, which selects candidate actions for execution; and
- *Action execution*, which adds, deletes or modifies facts, updating the current state of the working memory.

As Paul Thagard remarks in his Introduction to Cognitive Science [35], production rules "are very similar to" logical conditionals, "but they have different representational and computational properties". In this paper, I will show how LPS reformulates production rules as logical conditionals and combines them with logic programs.

MetateM. To a first approximation, computation with reactive rules in LPS is like computation in MetateM. Computation in MetateM uses *reactive rules*, to maintain a *current history of states* and a current collection of *commitments*, where:

- The *current history of states*, including the present state and all past states, is represented by a set of facts.
- *Reactive rules* have the form *if antecedent then consequent*.
- *Computation* uses forward reasoning with reactive rules to generate a *complete history* of states.

- *Forward reasoning* identifies any instances of the *antecedents* of rules that are true in the current history. For each such rule, it derives the *consequent* of the rule as a *commitment* to be made true in the next state or in the future.
- Given the complete collection of all previous and new commitments, a *choice* is made between different actions needed to make the commitments true.
- The chosen commitments and any external events are executed, updating the current history by *adding facts* that are true in the next state.

The *logical semantics* of the reactive kernel of LPS, KELPS [20], is similar to the logical semantics of MetateM. In both cases, reactive rules represent *goals*, and computation generates a complete history to try to make the goals true.

Reactive rules in MetateM generalize production system rules. Whereas antecedents of rules in production systems can only express conditions about the current state of the working memory, antecedents in MetateM can refer to any states or events in the current history. Whereas consequents of rules in production systems can only refer to actions to be performed immediately, consequents in MetateM can express commitments about any states or actions in the future.

As a consequence of this greater generality, MetateM needs to store the complete history of previous states, and not only the current state. Moreover, it needs to store the complete collection of all present and future commitments, whereas production systems do not need to store any commitments at all.[1]

MetateM is a modal temporal logic, with a possible world semantics, in which individual states are models, and the history of all individual states is itself a model. Unlike the sequence of states in production systems, the history is constructed by adding facts, without deleting any facts.

By treating computation as model generation, MetateM provides a simple and elegant, logical interpretation of *conflict resolution*, as a choice between alternative ways of making the goals true. This choice creates a natural opportunity to employ decision theory and game theory, to aid in the choice of alternatives [3].

Example. Given the production rules:

If hungry then eat. If sleepy then sleep.

and a current state in which hungry and sleepy are both true, a production system would need to perform conflict resolution, to decide whether to eat or sleep (and to do so immediately), assuming it is not possible to eat and sleep at the same time. This means that the production rules cannot be treated as logical implications, because taken literally there is no model in which both rules are true.

In MetateM, the same rules would be written in the form:

If hungry then ◊ eat. If sleepy then ◊ sleep.

where ◊ is a temporal modal operator, which means "at some time in the future".

---

[1] However, in practice, production systems (and BDI implementations) often add "goal facts" to working memory, both to represent future commitments and to simulate goal reduction rules.

Moreover, it is also necessary to state explicitly the *constraint* that eat and sleep cannot both be true at the same time. This constraint can be expressed by the rule:

If ● true then not eat or not sleep.

where ● means "at the last time", and ● true is always true in the previous state, and therefore not eat or not sleep is true in all states.

To satisfy the rules, MetateM needs to reason with "frame axioms", which express that if a fact is true at a time and the fact is not terminated by an action or external event that occurs at the time, then the fact continues to be true at the next time. For example:

If hungry and not eat then ○ hungry.
If sleepy and not sleep then ○ sleepy.

where ○ is a modal operator, which means "in the next state".

Given a current state in which hungry and sleepy are both true, there are infinitely many models that satisfy the goals, depending on how far into the future the commitments ◊ eat and ◊ sleep are made true. Among other decision-making strategies, the MetateM interpreter chooses models that make commitments true as soon as possible.

Brief Comparison with Reactive Rules and Constraints in LPS. Reactive rules in LPS are like rules in MetateM. In both cases, antecedents of reactive rules can refer to any states or events in the current history, and consequents can express commitments about any states or actions in the future.

The semantics of reactive rules in LPS is also like the semantics of rules in MetateM. In both cases, reactive rules are treated as goals, which need to be made true in the complete history of all states and state-changing events. But, whereas MetateM is a modal temporal logic, in which a complete history is a collection of models, one for each state, LPS is a non-modal logic in which a complete history is a single model in which facts whose truth values can change with the passage of time are timestamped.

In LPS, because all times in the consequent of a reactive rule are later than or equal to the latest time in the antecedent, and because the conditions in both the antecedent and consequent can be written in temporal order, time variables can often be suppressed, as in:

if hungry then eat. if sleepy then sleep.

Written with explicit time variables, these sentences become:

If hungry at any time T1 then eat from some time T2, where $T1 \leq T2$.
If sleepy at any time T1 then sleep from some time T2, where $T1 \leq T2$.

Time variables can also be suppressed if a constraint has only one time variable. For example, using LPS syntax:

false if sleep, eat.

which means: For all times T, it is not the case that: eat from T and sleep from T.

In general, reactive rules generate candidate actions, and constraints eliminate candidate actions. This combination of reactive rule goals and constraint goals is like the combination of obligations and prohibitions in deontic logic. The possibility that obligations can be violated, resulting in a suboptimal situation can be understood as some models being better than others [22].

The same combination of reactive rules and constraints is also like the combination of liveness and safety properties in model checking of concurrent and distributed systems. In model checking, liveness and safety need to be verified as *emergent properties* of a program. However, in model generation, as in MetateM and LPS (and potentially in production systems), liveness and safety are built into the program, and execution of the program is designed to ensure that liveness and safety are true by design.

In the next section, we will explore the relationship between the use of frame axioms to generate state transitions, as in MetateM, with the use of destructive updates, as in production systems and LPS. In the following sections, we will:

- present KELPS, which is the reactive kernel of LPS,
- show how logic programs can be used in conjunction with reactive rules, and
- discuss the potential of LPS as a scaled-down model of human thinking.

3 Representing and Reasoning About Change of State

In production systems and many other reactive rule languages, actions are normally bookkeeping operations that add, delete or modify facts in working memory. In logic-based systems, actions and other events represent events in the problem domain.

Frame Axioms. In logic-based systems, the standard approach for dealing with change is to use a causal theory [33], in which times, states or situations are reified and are represented explicitly as arguments of predicates. Many of these approaches distinguish between *fluents*, which are facts that hold true at time points (or over time intervals), and *events*, which occur between time points. Events include both *external events*, generated by the environment, and *actions*, generated by the system. Change of state can be defined by two meta-level axioms, the second of which is a *frame axiom*:

If the events that occur between T and T+1 initiate a fluent,
then the fluent is true at T+1.

If a fluent is true at T
and the fluent is not terminated by the events that occur between T and T+1,
then the fluent is true at T+1.

To apply these axioms in a specific domain, the initiation and termination predicates need to be defined by *causal laws*, such as:

eat initiates eating. eat terminates hungry.
sleep initiates sleeping. sleep terminates sleepy.

Forward reasoning with such axioms means that, when a state transition occurs from time (or state) T to T + 1, all the fluents that are initiated and all the fluents that are already true at time T, but not terminated, are added to the new state with the new timestamp T + 1. If a fluent is terminated, it is not deleted, but simply not added to the new state with a new timestamp. This approach respects the logic of change of state, but it does so at the cost of copying every fluent that is not terminated, from one state to the next. This is certainly not practical for even a moderately large number of fluents.

Destructive Change of State. Most practical computer languages, including production systems, reason with change of state by storing only a single current state, which can be regarded as a database of facts that are true in that state. These facts are stored without timestamps, and are updated destructively, by adding any facts that are initiated and deleting any facts that are terminated. Any facts that are not terminated are left unchanged, without reasoning that the facts are unchanged. This practical approach is very efficient, but it raises the problem of how to reconcile such destructive change of state with logic-based representations that employ frame axioms.

Reconciling Frame Axioms with Destructive Change of State. The solution of the problem can be found in the way that the real world exists only in its current state, changing state by destroying its past and unfolding its future. But in its totality, the real world is the complete history of all its states and events, past, present and future. The frame axiom is true in this history, but it is not used to generate change of state.

The implementation of LPS employs a similar approach: It maintains a single current state in which facts are represented without explicit times or states. As a result, facts that are not terminated by a state transition can be left unchanged without using frame axioms to reason that they are unchanged. However, in the complete history, fluents and events are timestamped, and the frame axiom is true as an emergent property.

The LPS approach can also be used to implement and justify destructive change of state in other logic-based languages, such as MetateM. Conversely, the LPS approach might be used to give a logical semantics to suitably modified production systems and other reactive rule languages. For this purpose, facts need to be associated with the times at which they hold, and reactive rules need to be understood as rewritten with explicit times. In addition, constraints need to be written explicitly, and they need to be enforced to prevent untimely choice of actions. Moreover, conflict resolution needs to be restricted to strategies that have a logical interpretation, such as specifying preferences between different models.

4 The Reactive Kernel of LPS (KELPS)

The kernel of LPS (KELPS), which consists of a current state, reactive rules, constraints and causal laws, is a reactive system language in its own right [20]. It combines the efficiency of destructive change of state in production systems with the expressive power and logical semantics of MetateM.

Compared with production systems, the greater expressive power of KELPS and MetateM comes from the more general antecedents and consequents of their reactive rules. KELPS deals with these more general consequents, in the same way as MetateM, by maintaining a separate collection of all present and future commitments.

The problem of dealing with more general antecedents is more difficult. MetateM deals with this problem by maintaining the entire current history of states and events, to identify any instances of antecedents that are true in the current history. But this current history is not available in KELPS, which maintains only the current state. KELPS deals with the problem by partially evaluating the antecedents of rules in the current state, and generating the partially evaluated rules as additional rules to be evaluated further in future current states.

For example, consider a rule expressing that if an item is ordered, and the item is not delivered two days later, then the order is cancelled.

If order(Item, OrderId, Day1), Day1 + 2 = Day2, not delivered(Item, Day2).
then cancel(OrderId, Day2).

When an event, say order(newBed, ord0017, 01/04/2026) occurs, LPS unifies the event with the first condition of the rule, evaluates the second condition of the rule and adds the *resolvent* as a new reactive rule to be monitored in the future:

If not delivered(newBed, 03/04/2026) then cancel(ord0017, 03/04/2026).

In general, KELPS uses *causal laws* and *constraints* to maintain a *current state*, a current collection of *commitments*, and a current collection of *reactive rules*, where:

- The *current state* is represented by a set of facts, called *fluents*, which are represented without timestamps.
- *Reactive rules* have the form *if antecedent then consequent*, where all variables (including time variables) in the *antecedent* are universally quantified with scope the entire rule, and all variables in the *consequent* that are not in the *antecedent* are existentially quantified with scope the consequent of the rule. All times in the *consequent* are later than or equal to the latest time in the *antecedent*.
- *Causal laws* represent the postconditions of events. They have the form *events initiate fluents* and *events terminate fluents*, where all variables are universally quantified, and all variables in the *fluents* occur in the *events*.[2]
- *Constraints* represent the preconditions of actions. They have the form *false if actions and conditions*, where all variables are universally quantified with scope the entire constraint.
- At any time that any events occur, including any actions that may have been chosen to be performed at that time, the causal laws are used to update the current state, *adding any fluents* that are initiated by the events and *deleting any fluents* that are terminated by the events.

---

[2] Note that *initiate* and *terminate* are meta-predicates, which express a relationship between ordinary object-level predicates.

- *Forward reasoning* identifies any instances of conditions (including events) in the *antecedents* of rules that are true at the current time. For each such rule, it derives the *resolvent* as a *new reactive rule* to be made true in the future. If there are no remaining antecedents in the rule, it derives the instantiated *consequent* of the rule as an additional commitment.
- Given the updated collection of all commitments, a *choice* of actions is made, selecting the actions from among alternative ways of making the commitments true. The choice needs to satisfy all the constraints.

In the *logical semantics* of KELPS, reactive rules and constraints are *goals*, and computation attempts to make these goals true in the complete history of all states and events. For this purpose, all fluents, external events and actions in the history are represented with timestamps.

In generating the history, the causal laws, the external events and the fluents belonging to the initial state all serve as *beliefs*, which determine the search space of histories that can be generated. In addition, as soon as an action is performed and becomes true, it also becomes a belief, as do all the fluents that then belong to the resulting state.

In full LPS, beliefs can be defined more generally by logic programs.

5 Combining Goals and Beliefs in LPS

Logic Programming (LP). A logic program consists of:

- A set of *facts*[3], represented by atomic sentences; and
- A set of *rules* of the form *conclusion if conditions*, where the *conclusion* is an atomic formula, possibly containing variables, and the *conditions* are a conjunction of atomic formulas and negations of atomic formulas. All variables are universally quantified, with scope the entire rule.[4]

Negative conditions are interpreted, by *negation as failure*, where not p means that p cannot be shown. Negation as failure can be understood as exploiting the *closed world assumption* that the logic program contains all the information about its subject matter. For example, it is natural to assume that a railway timetable contains all the information about train journeys within its geographical area. So, if it cannot be shown that there is a train connection between two places at a time, then there is no train connection between the two places at the time.

In LPS, negation needs to be stratified (or locally stratified [30]). This excludes rules, such as p if not p, where the conclusion of the rule depends negatively on itself. Logic programs conforming to this restriction have a unique minimal model, whose true facts

---

[3] In this paper, facts do not contain variables. So, for example sleep(P) initiates sleeping(P), where P is a variable, would not be a fact, but would be a rule without any conditions. This contrasts with the usual convention in LP that rules without conditions are called "facts".

[4] Or, equivalently, all variables in the conclusion are universally quantified with scope the entire rule, and all variables in the conditions that are not in the conclusion are existentially quantified with scope the conditions of the rule.

coincide with the facts that are true in all the models of the program. This model can be understood as the intended model defined by the logic program.

Logic Programs in LPS. In LPS, logic programs are used to define:

- *Extensional fluents*, which are defined by facts and *intensional fluents*, which are defined by rules.
- *Causal laws*, in which the fluents that are initiated and terminated by events depend on fluents that are true in the current state.
- *Composite events*, which include multiple, simpler events, combined in logical and temporal relationships, and which include plans of actions.
- *Timeless auxiliary predicates*, including arithmetic predicates, which do not depend upon time.

Fluents. In LPS, there are two kinds of fluents: *Extensional fluents*, which represent "ground truths" or concrete facts, are defined by LP facts. *Intensional fluents*, which represent abstract concepts or other consequences of the concrete facts, are defined by LP rules. Extensional fluents are stored explicitly in the current state and are updated when they are initiated and terminated by events. Intensional fluents are not stored explicitly but are derived as ramifications of changes to the extensional fluents.

For example, the balance in a bank account might be stored in an extensional fluent, and the interest in the account might be represented by an intensional fluent:

balance(bobAccount, 100).
interestRate(Account, 0) if balance(Account, Amount), Amount < 1000.

If the balance in bobAccount changes due to any bank transfers, then any necessary changes to the interest rate will take place automatically.

Ironically, the same kind of automatic updating of an intensional fluent as the result of updating an extensional fluent is called *reactivity* in "reactive programming" [2].

Causal Laws. Causal laws with variables in KELPS are actually LP rules without any conditions. They are not expressive enough for realistic examples. Here is an example that shows the use of conditions in causal laws:

transferTo(Account, Amount) initiates balance(Account, NewBalance).
if balance(Account, OldBalance), NewBalance = OldBalance + Amount.

transferTo(Account, Amount) terminates balance(Account, OldBalance).

Composite Events. Similarly to the way that intensional fluents provide an abstract, higher-level view of concrete, extensional fluents, composite events provide an abstract, higher-level view of simple events, including plans of actions.

For example, in formal grammar, a non-terminal symbol can be understood as a composite event, defined in terms of terminal symbols and other non-terminals. Terminal symbols are simple events, which cannot be decomposed into other events. For example, here saying is a composite event, and say is a simple event:

saying(Agent, sentence) from T1 to T3
if saying(Agent, nounphrase) from T1 to T2, saying(Agent, verbphrase) from T2 to T3.

saying(Agent, nounphrase) from T1 to T2
if saying(Agent, noun) from T1 to T2.

saying(Agent, verbphrase3) from T1 to T3
if saying(Agent, verb) from T1 to T2, saying(Agent, nounphrase) from T2 to T3.

saying(Agent, noun) from T1 to T2 if say(Agent, donna) from T1 to T2.
saying(Agent, noun) from T1 to T2 if say(Agent, logic) from T1 to T2.
saying(Agent, verb) from T1 to T2 if say(Agent, likes) from T1 to T2.

The definition of saying in terms of say can be used both to recognize sentences and to generate sentences. A silly example can be found and executed online at https://demo.logicalcontracts.com/example/turingTest.pl.

Important examples of the use of logic programs to define composite events are Golog [25], Openlog [8] and Transaction Logic [6]. Golog and Openlog both use frame axioms, Golog uses the situation calculus, whereas Openlog employs a procedural syntax with a semantics and interpreter based on abductive logic programming. Transaction Logic uses destructive change of state with a possible world semantics.

The Dining Philosophers. The problem of the dining philosophers illustrates the combination of logic programs, constraints and reactive rules to solve a classic problem in concurrent systems. The solution in LPS presented here can be found and executed online at https://demo.logicalcontracts.com/p/new%20dining%20philosophers.pl. Similar solutions can be implemented in other reactive rule languages, such as MetateM, suitably extended with logic programs, as suggested above.

There are five philosophers, sitting in a circle around a table with one fork to the left and one fork to the right of each philosopher. For simplicity, being a philosopher and sitting at the table with a pair of adjacent forks are both represented by timeless predicates. They could equally well be represented by fluents that are true initially and never terminated. Here there is only one fluent, representing that a fork is on the table, available to be picked up by one or other of the two adjacent philosophers:

philosopher(donna). philosopher(bob). philosopher(dania).
philosopher(tania). philosopher(nina).

adjacent(fork1, donna, fork2). adjacent(fork2, bob, fork3).
adjacent(fork3, dania, fork4). adjacent(fork4, tania, fork5).
adjacent(fork5, nina, fork1).

initially: available(fork1), available(fork2), available(fork3),
            available(fork4), available(fork5).

The goal is represented by a reactive rule expressing that all philosophers must eventually dine, and the constraints that a fork cannot be picked up if it is not available and that two philosophers cannot pick up the same fork at the same time:

if philosopher(P) then dine(P).

false if pickup(P, F), not available(F).
false if pickup(P1, F), pickup(P2, F), P1 \= P2.

Dining is defined by an LP rule as a composite event (or plan) of picking up two adjacent forks simultaneously, eating, and putting down the two forks simultaneously:

dine(P) from T1 to T4 if adjacent(F1, P, F2), pickup(P, F1) from T1 to T2, pickup(P, F2) from T1 to T2, eat(P) from T2 to T3, putdown(P, F1) from T3 to T4, putdown(P, F2) from T3 to T4.

The causal laws defining change of state, namely that putting down a fork initiates its availability, and picking up a fork terminates its availability, are also expressed in LP:

putdown(P, F) initiates available(F). pickup(P, F) terminates available(F).

LPS solves the goal by generating the following sequence of actions:

Time 1 to 2: nina and dania pick up their adjacent forks.
Time 2 to 3: nina and dania eat.
Time 3 to 4: nina and dania put down their forks.
Time 4 to 5: tania and donna pick up their adjacent forks.
Time 5 to 6: tania and donna eat.
Time 6 to 7: tania and donna put down their forks.
Time 7 to 8: bob picks up his adjacent forks.
Time 8 to 9: bob eats.
Time 9 to 10: bob puts down his forks.

Reasoning with Logic Programs. In general, logic programs can be used to reason either *forwards (or bottom-up)* to derive new facts from existing facts, or *backwards (or top-down)* to reduce goals to subgoals. Most Datalog systems reason forwards, and all Prolog systems reason backwards. Like Prolog, LPS also reasons backwards, both to evaluate the truth of conditions in the antecedents of reactive rules, and to reduce goals to subgoals in the consequents of reactive rules.

However, the logical semantics of LPS is compatible with other reasoning strategies. In particular, the integrity checking method of [32] could be used to trigger reactive rules by reasoning forwards from updates and deriving facts or new rules whose conclusions unify with conditions of reactive rules.

6 Combining Goals and Beliefs in Human Thinking

I have argued that the distinction between goals and beliefs is a useful way to look at rule-based computer systems. It is also possible to argue that a similar combination of goals and beliefs can serve as a cognitive model of human thinking. The plausibility of the argument relies in part on the success of production systems in such cognitive models as Soar [24] and Act-R [1].

The argument is complicated by the fact that it is easy to confuse different kinds of rules. The most famous example is probably the confusion about the meaning of conditionals in the Wason selection task.

The Wason Selection Task. In the standard version of the task, participants are given four cards lying on a table, with numbers showing on one side of the cards and letters showing on the other side. Participants are also given the rule:

> if a card has a vowel on one side, then it has an even number on the other side.

The task is to determine which cards need to be turned over to test whether the rule is true or false. Typically, only 10% of the participants reason correctly with the conditional as a material implication in classical logic [36].

Cognitive psychologists have proposed a wide variety of explanations for human performance on the Wason task, including the explanation that human reasoning is performed by domain-specific methods as opposed to general-purpose, logical reasoning. Arguably, a better explanation is that conditionals can represent goals or beliefs, and that different logical reasoning methods apply, depending on whether a conditional is interpreted as a goal or as a belief [23, 34].

Stenning and van Lambalgen [34], in particular, argue that the response of most participants in the selection task is consistent with their interpreting the conditional descriptively as a logic program rule: Participants correctly turn over the card showing a vowel, to make sure that the card has an even number on the other side. They also turn over the card showing an even number, which is consistent with the closed world assumption, but unnecessary with the open world assumption of classical logic. Moreover, they do not turn over the card showing an odd number, because this involves reasoning with negation in ways that are not common with logic program rules, even though it is necessary when reasoning with material implications in classical logic.

Stenning and van Lambalgen argue that most participants in the selection task reason in accordance with classical logic if the conditional has a natural interpretation as a prescription. For example, given a scenario involving people drinking in a bar, most participants in the selection task will interpret the following conditional prescriptively; and they will reason with it correctly as a material implication:

> If a person is drinking alcohol in a bar, then the person is over eighteen.

They will not only check whether a person drinking alcohol is over eighteen, but they will also check whether a person who is under eighteen is drinking alcohol. They will not check what a person over eighteen is drinking. Nor will they check the age of a person drinking tap water.

LPS as a Cognitive Model. These arguments about the two interpretations of conditionals in psychological experiments support the view of LPS as a cognitive model, which combines beliefs, which are descriptive, with goals, which are prescriptive. However, they also show that LPS does not fully support the complete range of human thinking associated with satisfying goals as material implications.

LPS and other reactive rule languages can only make goals of the form if p then q true *reactively*, by making q true when p becomes true. They cannot make goals true *proactively*, by making q true before p becomes true. Nor can they make goals true *preventatively*, by making p false. For example, consider the goal:

If you leave home then the front door is locked.

Given LP rules that initiate the fact that the door is locked by generating an action of locking the front door, LPS will make the goal true reactively, by performing the action of locking the door when leaving home. However, LPS will not attempt to make the goal true proactively, by locking the door before leaving home. Nor will it attempt to make the goal true preventatively, by not leaving home.

LPS has been deliberately scaled down to eliminate these kinds of reasoning, to make it more efficient for routine computational activities. However, routine computation and other kinds of more intelligent reasoning are possible in abductive logic programming (ALP) agents [17].

ALP Agents. ALP agents perform abductive reasoning, to generate hypotheses to make goals true in a model determined by the agents' beliefs. Abductive reasoning in ALP includes both the generation of hypothetical actions, as in LPS, as well as the generation of hypothetical events, to explain observations of facts that are true in the environment.

Beliefs in ALP are used reason backwards to reduce goals to subgoals. They are also used to reason forwards to derive logical consequences, both from given facts and from hypothetical facts. In particular, more generally than in LPS, beliefs are used to reason forwards from hypothetical actions to determine their logical consequences, and to determine whether they might violate constraints or have other noteworthy side effects. This use of forward reasoning, together with estimates of the probability of circumstances that are outside the agent's control, can help an agent to make better decisions and obtain better solutions for its goals.

7 Conclusions

The web-based implementation of LPS on SWISH [37] at https://demo.logicalcontracts.com/ includes a variety of runnable and editable examples. These include the dining philosophers, the prisoner's dilemma, rock-paper-scissors, sorting, map colouring, toy blocks worlds, Conway's game of life, self-driving cars and bank account transactions. The implementation includes a declarative Prolog-based sublanguage for associating images with fluents, animating the history computed by the program.

The implementation is still only a proof of concept, which needs to be developed further to make it viable for realistic applications. In particular, further work is needed to improve the strategy for choosing between alternatives, when there is a choice of different actions to satisfy the same goals.

Improving the current implementation is only one direction for future work. It might also be useful to explore other directions, including how to use some of the features of

LPS in other computer languages. For example, the way in which LPS (and MetateM) gives a logical semantics to reactive rules could also be used to give a logical semantics to suitably modified versions of other reactive rule languages. Moreover, the combination of goals and beliefs in LPS might also suggest ways in which reactive languages can be extended to include logic program beliefs, and ways in which LP languages might be extended to include constraint goals and reactive rule goals.

Acknowledgments. Although the opinions expressed in this paper are my own, Fariba Sadri was an equal contributor to all the technical work. Miguel Calejo and Jacinto Dávila also made important contributions. Fariba, Veronica Dahl, Dov Gabbay, Daniel Harris, Aidan Hogan, Ken Satoh and Mario Wenzel made helpful comments on an early draft of the paper. The implementation of LPS at https://demo.logicalcontracts.com/ was supported by an EPSRC Pathways to Impact research grant.

Disclosure of Interests. The author has no competing interests to declare that are relevant to the content of this article.

References

1. Anderson, J.R.: The architecture of cognition. Psychology Press (2013)
2. Bainomugisha, E., Carreton, A.L., Cutsem, T.V., Mostinckx, S., Meuter, W.D.: A survey on reactive programming. ACM Computing Surveys (CSUR) (2013)
3. Baron, J.: Thinking and Deciding. Cambridge University Press (2023)
4. Barringer, H., Fisher, M., Gabbay, D., Owens, R., Reynolds, M. (eds.): The Imperative Future: Principles of Executable Temporal Logic. John Wiley & Sons, Inc. (1996)
5. Boella, G., van der Torre, L.: Regulative and constitutive norms in normative multiagent systems. In: Ninth International Conference Principles of Knowledge Representation and Reasoning, pp. 255–265. Whistler, Canada (2004)
6. Bonner, A.J., Kifer, M.: An overview of transaction logic. Theoret. Comput. Sci. **133**(2), 205–265 (1994)
7. Bratman, M. E.: Intentions, Plans, and Practical Reason. Harvard University Press (1987)
8. Dávila, J.A.: OPENLOG: a logic programming language based on abduction. In: International Conference on Principles and Practice of Declarative Programming, pp. 278–293. Springer, Berlin, Heidelberg (1999)
9. Davis, R., King, J.: An overview of production systems. Technical Report, STAN-CS-75-524, AIM-27, Stanford University (1975)
10. Dennis, L.A., Farwer, B., Bordini, R.H., Fisher, M., Wooldridge, M.: A common semantic basis for BDI languages. In: International Workshop on Programming Multi-Agent Systems, pp. 124–139. Springer, Berlin, Heidelberg (2007)
11. De Silva, L., Meneguzzi, F.R., Logan, B.: BDI agent architectures: A survey. In: Proceedings of the 29th International Joint Conference on Artificial Intelligence (IJCAI) (2020)
12. Gabbay, D.: The declarative past and imperative future. In: Barringer, H. (ed.) Proceedings of the Colloquium on Temporal Logic and Specifications, pp. 409–448, vol. 398 of LNCS, Springer Verlag (1989)
13. Harel, D.: Statecharts: a visual formalism for complex systems. Sci. Comput. Program. **8**, 231–274 (1987)
14. Kakas, A.C., Kowalski, R.A., Toni, F.: Abductive logic programming. J. Log. Comput. **2**(6), 719–770 (1992)

15. Kifer, M.: Rule interchange format: The framework. In: International Conference on Web Reasoning and Rule Systems, pp. 1–11. Springer, Berlin, Heidelberg (2008)
16. Kowalski, R., Sadri, F.: Towards a unified agent architecture that combines rationality with reactivity. In: Proceedings of International Workshop on Logic in Databases, pp. 131–150. Springer-Verlag, LNCS 1154 (1996)
17. Kowalski, R., Sadri, F.: Abductive logic programming agents with destructive databases. Ann. Math. Artif. Intell. **62**(1), 129–158 (2011)
18. Kowalski, R., Sadri, F.: A logic-based framework for reactive systems. In: RuleML 2012. LNCS 7438, pp. 1–15. Springer, Heidelberg (2012)
19. Kowalski, R., Sadri, F.: Reactive computing as model generation. N. Gener. Comput. **33**(1), 33–67 (2015)
20. Kowalski, R., Sadri, F.: Programming in logic without logic programming. TPLP **16**, 269–295 (2016)
21. Kowalski, R., Sadri, F., Calejo, M., Dávila, J.: Combining logic programming and imperative programming in LPS. In: Prolog: The Next 50 Years, pp. 210–223. Springer Nature, Switzerland, Cham (2023)
22. Kowalski, R., Satoh, K.: Obligations as optimal goal satisfaction. J. Philos. Log. **47**(4), 579–609 (2018)
23. Kowalski, R.: Computational Logic and Human Thinking: How to be Artificially Intelligent. Cambridge University Press (2011)
24. Laird, J.E., Newell, A., Rosenbloom, P.S.: Soar: an architecture for general intelligence. Artif. Intell. **33**(1), 1–64 (1987)
25. Levesque, H.J., Reiter, R., Lesperance, Y., Lin, F., Scherl, R.B.: GOLOG: a logic programming language for dynamic domains. J. Logic Program. **31**(1), 59–83 (1997)
26. Nicolas, J.M., Gallaire, H.: Database: theory vs. interpretation. In: Gallaire, H., Minker, J. (eds.) Logic and Databases, Plenum, New York (1978)
27. Object Management Group: Semantics of Business Vocabulary and Business Rules SBVR™ 1.5 2019. https://www.omg.org/spec/SBVR
28. Paschke, A., Kozlenkov, A.: Rule-based event processing and reaction rules. In: International Workshop on Rules and Rule Markup Languages for the Semantic Web, pp. 53–66. Springer, Berlin, Heidelberg (2009)
29. Paschke, A.: ECA-LP/ECA-RuleML: A homogeneous event-condition-action logic programming language, In: International Conference on Rules and Rule Markup Languages for the Semantic Web (RuleML'06) (2006)
30. Przymusinski, T.: On the declarative semantics of stratified deductive databases and logic programs. In: Foundations of Deductive Databases and Logic Programming, Morgan Kaufmann, J. Minker (Ed.) 193 – 216. (1987)
31. Rao, A.S.: AgentSpeak (L): BDI agents speak out in a logical computable language. In: European Workshop on Modelling Autonomous Agents in a Multi-agent World, pp. 42–55. Springer, Berlin, Heidelberg (1996)
32. Sadri, F., Kowalski, R.: A theorem-proving approach to database integrity. In: Foundations of Deductive Databases and Logic Programming, pp. 313–362. Morgan Kaufmann (1988)
33. Shanahan, M.: Solving the Frame Problem: A Mathematical Investigation of the Common Sense Law of Inertia. MIT Press (1997)
34. Stenning, K., van Lambalgen, M.: Human Reasoning and Cognitive Science. MIT Press (2012)
35. Thagard, P.: Mind: Introduction to Cognitive Science. Second Edition. MIT Press (2005)

36. Wason, P.C.: Reasoning about a rule. Q. J. Exp. Psychol. **20**(3), 273–281 (1968)
37. Wielemaker, J., Riguzzi, F., Kowalski, R.A., Lager, T., Sadri, F., Calejo, M.: Using SWISH to realize interactive web-based tutorials for logic-based languages. Theory Pract. Logic Program. **19**(2), 229–261 (2019)

Specifying an Obligation Taxonomy in the Non-Markovian Situation Calculus

Kalonji Kalala[✉], Iluju Kiringa, and Tet Yeap

University of Ottawa, Ottawa, ON K1N 1A2, Canada
{hkalo081,iluju.kiringa,tyeap}@uottawa.ca
https://www.uottawa.ca/faculty-engineering/

Abstract. Over more than three decades, the Situation Calculus has established itself as an elegant, powerful, and concise formalism for specifying dynamical domains as well as for reasoning about the effects of actions of those domains both in the world and in the mental state of the modelled agents. Moreover, it has also been established that the preconditions of a given action and its effects may be determined entirely by the current situation alone, or they may be determined by past situations as well. When past situations are involved in determining action preconditions and effects, resulting theories are non-Markovian. Assuming a specification of actions that produce obligations, we consider using non-Markovian control in the Situation Calculus to specify different notions of obligations found in the literature. These notions have been specified using Event Calculus; but, as far as we know, they have never been specified using the Situation Calculus. The specifications in this paper yield intuitive properties that ensure the correctness of the whole endeavour.

Keywords: Obligations · Obligation Types · Situation Calculus · Reasoning · Actions · Non-Markovian · Legal norms

1 Introduction

The Situation Calculus is a pre-eminent logical language that has been used in artificial intelligence for specifying and reasoning about dynamical systems such as robotics, database updates, control systems, simulated software agents, and computer agents. One specifies these systems by providing axioms in the language of the Situation Calculus to capture the prerequisites of actions of the domain and the effects of these actions both on the external world around the specified system as well as on the internal mental state of the dynamic agent that is being modelled. Typically, the effects of actions are captured by fluents, predicates whose truth values are changed as the result of performing actions. In this context, it is necessary to provide axioms that state which fluents remain unchanged during action performance. The number of such axioms is large: this is known as the frame problem in artificial intelligence. In his seminal work in [9], Raymond Reiter has proposed the so-called successor state axioms as a solution to the frame problem [20] for actions that change the external world.

Reiter's solution to the frame problem relies on the Markov property, that is: the preconditions and the effects of an action are solely determined by the current situation in which the action is executed. In [26], Gabaldon has extended the original Reiter's solution to the Situation Calculus with the non-Markovian property; that is, the preconditions and the effects of an action may be determined by one or more of the past situations preceding the one in which the action is executed. This extended Situation Calculus is most appropriate to specify a variety of dynamic domains that clearly showcase the non-Markovian property such as database transactions [27, 28], semantics of dynamics integrity constraints [29], and decision-theoretic planning with reward functions that look back in the past [25].

In [8], Scherl and Levesque extend Reiter's solution to the frame problem to actions that result in changing the state of knowledge of the reasoning agent; these actions are called *knowledge-producing actions*. Scherl and Levesque's solution still uses the Markovian theories to capture knowledge.

Even more sophisticated domains are emerging nowadays which require the ability to specify them using non-Markovian theories in order to reason about them accurately. One such domain is smart contracts that have emerged in cyber physical systems as a way of enforcing formal agreements between entities that constitute these systems. A contract is a legally enforceable agreement that contains requirements for different parties to engage in a business transaction. Those requirements are made of **obligations to be fulfilled** by the parties. In the last decade, a considerable amount of research was conducted to represent a legal contract electronically [21, 22]. Such electronically codified contracts are meant to be executed automatically by the involved parties (contracting agents). The execution of legal contracts must be monitored to make sure that the dealings of all parties comply with the requirements of the contract.

Any formal specification of the smart contracts mentioned above clearly calls for a explicit formal account of obligations. In [37], authors extend the Situation Calculus account of knowledge by Scherl and Levesque to the concept of obligation.

This paper uses the Situation Calculus account of obligations in the Situation Calculus presented in [37] to provide a Situation Calculus account of the taxonomy of obligations given in [31]: we use non-Markovian theories of the Situation Calculus to model the various type of obligations in that taxonomy.

The paper is organized as follows. In the next Sect. 2, we introduce the sequential temporal Situation Calculus along with deontic logic notions; here, we introduce a running example used throughout the paper in Subsect. 2.3. The formalization of the obligation modality in the Situation Calculus given in [37] is summarized in Sect. 3. Section 4 spells out the details of the formalization of the obligation types in the Situation Calculus. Furthermore, in Sect. 5, we state and prove some properties of the obligation types in the Situation Calculus. We discuss the issue of the interaction between obligation violation and compensation of violated obligation in Sect. 6. Section 7 discusses related work. Finally, we conclude and indicate avenues for future work in Sect. 8.

2 Situation Calculus with Non-Markovian Control

The Situation Calculus [34,36] is a logical framework that has been successfully employed in the formalization of a wide variety of dynamical systems. In Subsect. 2.1, we give an overview of the Situation Calculus as formulated by Reiter [34]. In Subsect. 2.2, we complete the summary of Situation Calculus with non-Markovian control first introduced in [38].

2.1 Sequential and Temporal Situation Calculus

The sequential and temporal Situation Calculus is a many-sorted second order logic with four sorts: actions, situations, time, and objects other than the first three sorts. Actions are first order terms that consist of an action function symbol and several arguments, the last of which is a time [11]. Situations represent finite sequences of actions that are responsible for all the changes in the world or, in the case of obligations, in the mental state of the modelled agent. Fluents are properties of the world that change from situation to situation as a result of the execution of actions.

In addition to variables of the aforementioned sorts, the language includes a finite number of function symbols called action functions such as $unlock(d,t)$ to represent the actions of unlocking the door d at time t, functions such as $do(unlock(d,t),s)$ to denote the situation resulting from the execution of the action $unlock(d,t)$ in the situation s, and predicates for representing fluents such as $open(d,s)$, meaning that the door d is open in the situation s. In addition to predicate fluents, there are functional fluents that denote values that vary from situation to situation as a consequence of executions of actions. Furthermore, the languages includes a finite number of situation independent predicates and functions. The initial situation is denoted by the constant S_0. The function $do(a,s)$ denotes the non-empty history of actions that have been executed up to and including action a. Situation S_0 represents the starting empty history. Finally, the language also includes special predicates $Poss$, and $\sqsubset$; $Poss(a,s)$ means that the action a is possible in the situation s, and $s \sqsubset s'$ states that the situation s' is reachable from s by performing some sequence of actions.

Notice that the introduction of time calls for a way of specifying times of actions as well as start times of situations that results from actions. To achieve this, first a function symbol $time(\alpha)$ to specify occurrence times of actions is introduced [30]; thus, for each given action $A(\boldsymbol{x},t)$, the axiomatization of the domain must include an axiom that specifies the occurrence time of that action as follows: $time(A(\boldsymbol{x},t)) = t$. Second, foundational axioms must include one that states that the situation $do(a,s)$ starts at the time of the action a, that is, $start(do(a,s)) = time(a)$.

Finally, by convention in this paper, a free variable will always be implicitly bound by a prenex universal quantifier. For a complete formal description see [5,34].

A term $do(a_k, do(a_{k-1}, \ldots, do(a_1, \sigma) \ldots))$ is said to be *rooted at σ* if σ is S_0 or a situation variable and is the only (if any) subterm of sort situation occurring in $a_1, \ldots, a_k$. We will use the shorthand notation $do([a_1, \ldots, a_k], \sigma)$ to denote the situation term $do(a_k, do(a_{k-1}, \ldots do(a_1, \sigma) \ldots))$.

A Situation Calculus axiomatization of a domain, includes the following set of axioms:

1. For each action function $A(\mathbf{x})$, an *action precondition axiom* of the form: $Poss(A(x_1, \ldots, x_n), s) \equiv \Pi_A(x_1, \ldots, x_n, s)$ where s is the only term of sort situation in $\Pi_A(x_1, \ldots, x_n, s)$.
2. For each fluent $F(\mathbf{x}, s)$, a *successor state axiom* of the form:

$$F(x_1, \ldots, x_n, do(a, s)) \equiv \Phi_F(x_1, \ldots, x_n, a, s)$$

where s is the only term of sort situation in $\Phi_F(x_1, \ldots, x_n, a, s)$.
3. Unique names axioms for actions. For instance: $lock(d, t) \neq unlock(d, t)$.
4. Axioms describing the initial situation, e.g. the initial database: a finite set of sentences whose only situation term is the constant S_0.

Successor state axioms are a solution to the so-called frame problem, namely the problem of providing for a small and efficient set of axioms that accounts for what is changing and what is not changing as the result of the execution of actions. A set of these axioms above, together with the following set of domain independent foundational axioms denoted by Σ,

$$do(a_1, s_1) = do(a_2, s_2) \supset a_1 = a_2 \wedge s_1 = s_2,$$
$$(\forall P).P(S_0) \wedge (\forall a, s)[P(s) \supset P(do(a, s))] \supset (\forall s)P(s),$$
$$\neg s \sqsubset S_0,$$
$$s \sqsubset do(a, s') \equiv s \sqsubset s' \vee s = s',$$

is called a (Markovian) *basic action theory*. Note that the foundational axioms include a characterization of the relation $\sqsubset$. For two situations s_1, s_2, $s_1 \sqsubset s_2$ intuitively means that s_1 is a situation that precedes s_2, i.e., in terms of sequences of actions, the sequence s_1 is a prefix of s_2; moreover, no situation precedes S_0.

2.2 Non-Markovian Control in Situation Calculus

For a basic action theory without the Markov assumption, we need some preliminary definitions. These are based on those in [38]. First, we need to introduce the following obvious abbreviations:

$$(\exists s).\sigma' \sim \sigma'' \sim \sigma \wedge W \stackrel{def}{=} (\exists s)[\sigma' \sim \sigma'' \wedge \sigma'' \sim \sigma \wedge W] \tag{1}$$
$$(\forall s).\sigma' \sim \sigma'' \sim \sigma \supset W \stackrel{def}{=} (\forall s)[(\sigma' \sim \sigma'' \wedge \sigma'' \sim \sigma) \supset W]$$

where $\sim$ stands for $\sqsubset, =$ or $\sqsubseteq$, and variable s appears in σ''. If σ' is S_0 then we may write $(\exists s : \sigma'' \sim \sigma)W$ and $(\forall s : \sigma'' \sim \sigma)W$ instead.

Definition 1 (Bounded Formulas). *For $n \geq 0$, let σ be a term $do([\alpha_1, \ldots, \alpha_n], \lambda)$ rooted at λ. The formulas of the Situation Calculus bounded by σ are the smallest set of formulas such that:*

1. *If W is an atom whose situation terms are all rooted at λ, then W is bounded by σ.*
2. *If W', W'' are formulas bounded by situation terms rooted at s and λ, respectively, then $(\exists s).\sigma' \sim \sigma'' \sim \sigma \wedge W$ and $(\forall s).\sigma' \sim \sigma'' \sim \sigma \supset W$ are formulas bounded by σ, where σ'' is rooted at s and $W = (\neg)(W' \wedge W'')$.*
3. *If W_1, W_2 are formulas bounded by situation terms rooted at λ, then $\neg W_1$, $W_1 \wedge W_2$ and $(\exists v) W_1$, where v is of sort action or object, are formulas bounded by σ.*

The set of formulas *strictly bounded* by σ is similarly defined by requiring in item (1) above that all situation terms of W be subterms of σ, in item (2) that W' be strictly bounded by a subterm of σ'' and W'' by a subterm of σ; and in item (3) that W_1, W_2 be strictly bounded by subterms of σ.

Non-Markovian basic action theories differ from Markovian ones by using action preconditions and successor state axioms in which preconditions and effects of actions may depend on past situations, and not only on the current one.

Formally, this means that the formula $\Pi_A(x_1, \ldots, x_n, s)$ which is the right hand side of an action precondition axiom will be a formula bounded by the situation term s in which $Poss$ is not mentioned and that may refer to past situations of the kind given in abbreviations (1). Moreover, this means also that the formula $\Phi_F(x_1, \ldots, x_n, a, s)$, which is the right hand side of a successor state axioms, will be a formula strictly bounded by s.

For basic action theories with the Markov assumption, Pirri & Reiter [5] define a *regression* mechanism that takes a non-Markovian Situation Calculus sentence and, under certain restrictions on the form of this sentence, compiles it into an equivalent sentence that mentions no other situation term than S_0. This allows proving sentences without appealing to the foundational axioms Σ. This regression operator was generalized for non-Markovian theories in [38]. For the sequel of this paper which does not include reasoning, we do not need caring about the regression mechanism.

2.3 Running Example: Opening a Door

Consider a door opening domain where the agent is opening a door. Agents open and close the door depending on whether certain conditions are met. To start, we enumerate some of the actions and fluents and situation independent predicate and functions of the domain. **Primitive actions** are: $unlock(d, t)$, $pressButton(d, c, t)$, $lock(d, t)$, $moveTo(d)$, and $notify(m, t)$. As for **Fluents**, we have: $open(d, s)$, $locked(d, s)$, $notifiedManager(s)$, and $at(d, s)$. Finally, **situation independent predicates and function** are: $manager(m)$, and $door(d)$. All these actions, fluents, functions, and predicates are intuitively understandable, except the following:

Primitive Actions.

- $pressButton(d, E, t)$: press the button to open the door d with credential E at time t; E is a constant meaning "Employee".
- $notify(m, t)$: notify the manager m of the locking of the door at time t.

Fluents.

- $notifiedManager(s)$: functional fluent meaning the manager has been notified of the locking of the door.
- $at(d, s)$: the agent is at the door d in situation s.

Action Precondition Axioms. There is one for each action function $A(\boldsymbol{x}, t)$ listed above:

$$Poss(unlock(d, t), s) \equiv door(d) \wedge at(d, s) \wedge locked(d, s), \quad (2)$$
$$Poss(lock(d, t), s) \equiv open(d, s) \wedge at(d, s) \wedge door(d), \quad (3)$$
$$Poss(moveTo(d, t), s) \equiv true, \quad (4)$$
$$Poss(pressButton(d, c, t), s) \equiv at(d, s) \wedge door(d) \wedge c = E. \quad (5)$$
$$Poss(notify(m, t), s) \equiv true. \quad (6)$$

Successor State Axioms. There is one such axiom for each $(n+1)$-ary relational fluent F, and there is one for each $(n+1)$-ary functional fluent f:

$$open(d, do(a, s)) \equiv (\exists t, c).a = pressButton(d, c, t) \vee$$
$$open(d, s) \wedge a \neq lock(d, t), \quad (7)$$
$$locked(d, do(a, s)) \equiv (\exists t)a = lock(d, t) \vee (locked(d, s) \wedge$$
$$\neg(\exists t', c)(c = E \wedge a = pressButton(d, c, t'))), \quad (8)$$
$$at(d, do(a, s)) \equiv$$
$$(\exists t)a = moveTo(d, t) \vee at(d, s) \wedge \neg(\exists d', t')moveTo(d', t'), \quad (9)$$
$$notifiedManager(do(a, s)) = m \equiv$$
$$(\exists t)(manager(m) \wedge a = notify(m, t)) \vee notifiedManager(s) = m. \quad (10)$$

Assume that we have successor state axioms for the other fluents listed earlier as well.

3 Obligations in the Situation Calculus

3.1 A Deontic Fluent for Expressing Obligations

Before expressing any taxonomy of obligation types such the one provided in [31] in the Situation Calculus, one must have already expressed the obligation modality in the Situation Calculus. That is, we must assume a solution for an embedding of the obligation modality in the Situation Calculus. In the sequel, we want to summarize an embedding proposed in [37].

The idea of using the Situation Calculus to specify obligations has been floated by a previous source: in [4], Demolombe and Herzig give the first formulation of Deontic Logic in the Situation Calculus to capture an agent's set of obligations [3]. They use Scherl and Levesque's approach [8] of not directly resorting to some modal logic and by introducing modal logic possible worlds as the situations of the Situation Calculus. This allows one to represent obligations directly in the language of the Situation Calculus by using an appropriate first-order representation of the accessibility relation of semantics of modal logics: this accessibility relation is captured as a fluent $O(s', s)$ to be read as: "s' is deontically accessible from s".

In [37], authors go a step further than in [4] by combining Deontic modalities with time in the Situation Calculus to give an account of actions that produce obligations and extend Reiter's regression mechanism to the new obligation setting. Thus, the authors of [37] account for the extension of Reiter's solution to the frame problem for "world" actions of an application domain to actions that change the state of an agent's obligations.

Like in [4], the following proposal is used in [37] to represent that, in situation s, an agent is obliged to bring about ϕ:

$$(\forall s'). O(s', s) \supset \phi[s'], \tag{11}$$

where $\phi[s']$ represents the formula ϕ with situation arguments added recursively to fluents that occur in ϕ. So, to express that it is obligatory to have the *door* locked by an agent, we will write:

$$(\forall s'). O(s', s) \supset locked(d, s'). \tag{12}$$

In representing the obligation modality, the notation $\mathbf{Oblg}(\phi, s)$ is used to capture the fact that, in situation s, it is obligatory to the modelled agent that ϕ is true:

$$\mathbf{Oblg}(\phi, s) \stackrel{\text{def}}{=} (\forall s'). O(s', s) \supset \phi[s']. \tag{13}$$

The formula ϕ used in the abbreviation $\mathbf{Oblg}(\phi, s)$ represents a formula obtained from a Situation Calculus formula by recursively suppressing its situation arguments. Conversely, $\phi[s]$ represents a Situation Calculus formula obtained by recursively restoring its suppressed situation arguments.

This definition (13) as well as the formula (12) are based on the semantic condition $(C.O^+)$ given in [7] as Kripke semantics for the obligation modality. For example, $\mathbf{Oblg}(locked(d), s)$ expands as follows:

$$\mathbf{Oblg}(locked(d), s) \stackrel{\text{def}}{=} (\forall s'). O(s', s) \supset locked(d, s'). \tag{14}$$

3.2 Obligation-Producing Actions

With a formal concept of obligation in the Situation Calculus in hand, we can now link obligations with actions performed by agents. Among these, some do affect what is happening in the world and some others do not, but rather do affect an agent's state of obligations. We call the later obligation-producing actions, by reference to knowledge-producing actions introduced by Scherl and Levesque in [8]. At the atomic level, obligation-producing actions are of two kinds: those actions whose effect is to make some (atomic) formula obligatory, and those whose effects is to make the denotation of some term obligatory.

As an example of the first kind of obligation-producing actions, the ground action $unlock(D, 10)$ executed by the agent in situation S_0 makes the ground atomic formula $locked(D, do(unlock(D, 10), S_0))$ obligatory. In other words, the sentence **Oblg**$(locked(D), do(unlock(D, 10), S_0))$ is made true by the execution of the action $unlock(D, 10)$. In our running example, $unlock(d, t)$ is an obligation-producing action that creates the obligation for the agent to subsequently get the door locked. That is, by executing the action $unlock(D, 10)$ in situation S_0, the agent has the obligation to make sure that in some situation S following the situation $do(unlock(D, 10), S_0)$, the formula $locked(D, S)$ is true by virtue of an action executed by the agent to make $locked(D, S)$ true.

In general, we assume that there is a provision of (finitely many) obligation-producing actions $a_{F_i}(\boldsymbol{x}_i, s)$ where $i = 1 \ldots m$, and that for each one of them, there is a fluent $F_i(\boldsymbol{x}_i, s)$, $i = 1 \ldots m$, of the domain that is made obligatory in situation $do(a_{F_i}(\boldsymbol{x}_i), s)$ upon the execution of $a_{F_i}(\boldsymbol{x}_i, s)$ in situation s.

For the second kind of obligation-producing actions, we assume that there is a provision of (finitely many) such actions $a_{f_j}(\boldsymbol{x}_j)$ where $j = 1 \ldots n$, and that for each one of them, there is a functional fluent $f_j(\boldsymbol{x}_j)$, $j = 1 \ldots n$, of the domain whose denotation is made obligatory to the agent.

3.3 The Frame Problem for Obligation-Producing Actions

Suppose the agent executes the action $set(E, 20)$ in S_0 where no obligation holds and the door is $locked(D, S_0)$ is true. Then, $credential(E, do(set(E, 20), S_0))$ holds, and no new obligation is introduced. Now, if $unlock(D, 30)$ is executed, the sentence $open(D, do(unlock(D, 30), do(set(E, 20), S_0)))$ holds and the agent has the obligation of subsequently locking the door. Finally, the execution of the action $lock(D, 40)$ will stop the obligation for the agent to get the door locked.

What the above consideration shows is that we have three sorts of actions. The first sort is made of a provision of ordinary actions that do not produce any obligation with respect to the agent and do not defeat any existing obligations. The second sort is made of ordinary actions that do not produce any obligation, but they stop existing obligation. Finally, the third sort is made of obligation-producing actions.

To start, suppose that a deontic agent is located in a situation s. We can imagine several other infinitely many situations $s'_1, s'_2, s'_3, \ldots$, which are deontic alternatives to s. Furthermore, suppose that the deontic agent performs some action a in s and therefore lands in the successor situation $do(a, s)$. We now wonder what are the deontic alternatives to $do(a, s)$, and how these alternatives are related to the situations $s'_1, s'_2, s'_3, \ldots$. We must come up with successor state axioms for the three sorts of actions identified above by spelling out how an action a affects the fluent O. Proposals for such successor state axioms are given in [4], and in [37]: we refer the reader to these works for details.

4 Obligation Types in the Situation Calculus

In [2] [1], the author has proposed a taxonomy of obligation types which the authors of [31] have revisited and modelled in the Event Calculus [12,16,18,19]. The modelled obligation types are: punctual, persistent (with maintenance and achievement variants), perdurant, and compensated.

In each of the subsections in the sequel of this section, we first introduce a given obligation type by providing its definition taken from the work in [31]. Then we provide abbreviations that model these various types in the non-Markovian Situation Calculus.

To start, we introduce two functions that are used in the definitions of the obligation types. Suppose that $\mathcal{L}$ is the language of the Situation Calculus. A **State** is defined as a function $\mathbb{N} \mapsto 2^{\mathcal{L}}$, such that, for a given time point t, $State(t)$ is the set of all formulas that are valid at time t. That is, $\textbf{State}(t) = \{\phi(s) : \phi(s) \text{ and } time(s) = t\}$. Furthermore, an obligation is said to be in force at time t if $\textbf{Oblg}(\phi, s)$ and $start(s) = t$. Thus, **Force** is defined as a function $\mathbb{N} \mapsto 2^{\mathcal{L}}$ such that, for a given time point t, $Force(t)$ is the set of all obligations that are valid at time t. That is, $\textbf{Force}(t) = \{\phi(s) : \textbf{Oblg}(\phi, s) \text{ and } time(s) = t\}$.

4.1 Punctual Obligation

An obligation ϕ is punctual at a time point $t \in \mathbb{N}$, if and only if we have: for time point $t-1$, $\phi \notin \textbf{Force}(t-1)$; for time point $t+1$, $\phi \notin \textbf{Force}(t+1)$; and $\phi \in \textbf{Force}(t)$. The abbreviation below expresses the punctual obligation in the Situation Calculus in terms of situations.

$$\textbf{OblgAt}(\phi, s) \stackrel{\text{def}}{=} (\forall s', a_1)\,[s = do(a_1, s') \supset \neg\textbf{Oblg}(\phi, s')] \land$$
$$(\forall s'', a_2)\,[s'' = do(a_2, s) \supset \neg\textbf{Oblg}(\phi, s'')] \land \textbf{Oblg}(\phi, s). \quad (15)$$

Intuitively, $\textbf{OblgAt}(\phi, s)$ in the abbreviation (15) means that the formula ϕ is obligatory at the situation s if and only if ϕ is obligatory at the situation s; moreover, ϕ is neither obligatory at the situation immediately before the situation s, nor at the situation immediately after s.

A punctual obligation that is not fulfilled exactly at situation s is said to be violated. A violation of a punctual obligation ϕ in situation s means that at s, ϕ is not true; formally, this means that we have: $\neg\phi[s]$. To specify the fact that a given obligation ϕ is violated in situation s, we need a predicate $violatedType(\phi, s)$, where the substring $Type$ encodes the type of the the obligation being violated; $violatedType(\phi, s)$ abbreviates an appropriate formula that formally spells out the conditions under which the violation occurs. The following abbreviation spells out the violation condition for the punctual obligations:

$$violatedAt(\phi, s) \stackrel{\text{def}}{=} \neg\phi[s]. \quad (16)$$

The specification 15 above is given in terms of situations. We can easily translate it into a specification in terms of time points as follows:

$$\mathbf{OblgAt}(\phi, t) \stackrel{\text{def}}{=}$$
$$(\exists s)[\mathbf{Oblg}(\phi, s) \land start(s) = t \land$$
$$(\forall s', a_1)\,[s = do(a_1, s') \supset \neg \mathbf{Oblg}(\phi, s')] \land$$
$$(\forall s'', a_2)\,[s'' = do(a_2, s) \supset \neg \mathbf{Oblg}(\phi, s'')]]. \tag{17}$$

Intuitively, $\mathbf{OblgAt}(\phi, t)$ in the abbreviation (17) means that the formula ϕ is obligatory at time t if and only if ϕ is obligatory at some situation s whose start time is t; furthermore, ϕ is neither obligatory at the situation immediately before the situation s, nor at the situation immediately after s.

4.2 Persistent Obligation

An obligation ϕ is persistent between time points $t_1 \in \mathbb{N}$ and $t_2 \in \mathbb{N}$, if and only if we have: $t_1 < t_2$; for $t' = t_1 - 1$, $\phi \notin \mathbf{Force}(t')$; for $t'' = t_2 + 1$, $\phi \notin \mathbf{Force}(t'')$; and for all time points t''' such that $t_1 \leq t''' \leq t_2$, $\phi \in \mathbf{Force}(t''')$. A persistent obligation that is not fulfilled at least one of the points in the interval $[t_1, \ldots, t_2]$ is said to be violated. The Situation Calculus specification of the persistent obligation in terms of situations is expressed in the following abbreviation:

$$\mathbf{OblgPersist}(\phi, s_1, s_2) \stackrel{\text{def}}{=}$$
$$(\forall s', a_1)\,[s_1 = do(a_1, s') \supset \neg \mathbf{Oblg}(\phi, s')] \land$$
$$(\forall s'', a_2)\,[s'' = do(a_2, s_2) \supset \neg \mathbf{Oblg}(\phi, s'')] \land$$
$$(\forall s''')\,[(s_1 \sqsubseteq s''' \sqsubseteq s_2) \supset \mathbf{Oblg}(\phi, s''')] \tag{18}$$

In the abbreviation (18), $\mathbf{OblgPersist}(\phi, s_1, s_2)$ means that the formula ϕ is obligatory between situations s_1 and s_2 if and only if ϕ is obligatory between situations s_1 and s_2 inclusively; moreover, ϕ is neither obligatory at the situation immediately before the situation s_1, nor at the situation immediately after s_2.

In terms of time points, we have the following specification:

$$\mathbf{OblgPersist}(\phi, t_1, t_2) \stackrel{\text{def}}{=}$$
$$(\exists s_1, s_2)[(\forall s')[s_1 = do(a_1, s') \land start(s_1) = t_1 \supset \neg \mathbf{Oblg}(\phi, s')] \land$$
$$(\forall s'')[s'' = do(a_2, s_2) \land start(s_2) = t_2 \supset \neg \mathbf{Oblg}(\phi, s'')] \land$$
$$(\forall s''')[((s_1 \sqsubseteq s''') \land (s''' \sqsubseteq s_2) \land$$
$$start(s_1) = t_1 \land start(s_2) = t_2) \supset \mathbf{Oblg}(\phi, s''')]] \tag{19}$$

Intuitively, $\mathbf{OblgPersist}(\phi, t_1, t_2)$ in the abbreviation (19) is to be read in a manner similar to the reading of the abbreviation (17), mutatis mutandis.

Achievement Obligation. Persistent obligations have two variants, namely achievement and maintenance obligations. This section specifies the achievement obligations and the next one deals with maintenance obligations.

A formula ϕ is an achievement obligation between time points $t_1 \in \mathbb{N}$ and $t_2 \in \mathbb{N}$, if and only if we have: $t_1 < t_2$; and for all time points t' such that $t_1 \leq t' \leq t_2$, $\phi \in \textbf{Force}(t')$. The following abbreviation captures achievement obligations in the Situation Calculus in terms of situations:

$$\textbf{OblgAchieve}(\phi, s_1, s_2) \stackrel{\text{def}}{=} (\forall s')\,[(s_1 \sqsubseteq s' \sqsubseteq s_2) \supset \textbf{Oblg}(\phi, s')] \quad (20)$$

There are two sub-variants of achievement obligations. The first sub-variant is called pre-emptive obligation; intuitively, the latter is an achievement obligation that can be fulfilled before it becomes in force in the interval $[t_1, t_2]$; that is, we have at least a t_3 such that $t_3 \leq t_2$, and $\phi \in \textbf{State}(t_3)$. The abbreviation (21) captures pre-emptive achievement obligations in the Situation Calculus in terms of situations.

$$\textbf{OblgPreemptive}(\phi, s_1, s_2) \stackrel{\text{def}}{=}$$
$$(\forall s')\,[(s_1 \sqsubseteq s' \sqsubseteq s_2) \supset \textbf{Oblg}(\phi, s')] \wedge$$
$$(\forall s'')(\exists s_3)\,[s'' \sqsubseteq s_3 \sqsubseteq s_2 \wedge \phi[s_3]] \quad (21)$$

The second sub-variant of achievement obligations is called non pre-emptive obligation. Intuitively, the latter is an achievement obligation that needs not be fulfilled before it is in force in the interval $[t_1, t_2]$. The specification of non pre-emptive obligations in terms of situations is as follows:

$$\textbf{OblgNonPreemptive}(\phi, s_1, s_2) \stackrel{\text{def}}{=}$$
$$(\forall s')\,[(s_1 \sqsubseteq s' \sqsubseteq s_2) \supset \textbf{Oblg}(\phi, s')] \wedge$$
$$(\exists s_3)\,[s_1 \sqsubseteq s_3 \sqsubseteq s_2 \wedge \phi[s_3]] \quad (22)$$

We now turn to abbreviations that spell out violation conditions for the various types of obligations. Consider a preemptive obligation ϕ to be fulfilled in the interval $[s_1, \ldots, s_2]$. The following abbreviation spells out the violation condition for preemptive obligations:

$$\textbf{violatedPreemptive}(\phi, s_1, s_2) \stackrel{\text{def}}{=} (\forall s)[s \sqsubseteq s_1 \sqsubseteq s_2 \wedge \neg\phi[s]]. \quad (23)$$

Informally, the abbreviation (23) stipulates that a preemptive obligation ϕ is said to be violated iff it is not fulfilled at least one of the situations in the interval $[s_1, \ldots, s_2]$.

Consider a non-preemptive obligation ϕ to be fulfilled in the interval $[s_1, \ldots, s_2]$. The violation condition for non-preemptive obligations is given as follows:

$$\textbf{violatedNonPreemptive}(\phi, s_1, s_2) \stackrel{\text{def}}{=} (\forall s)[s_1 \sqsubseteq s \sqsubseteq s_2 \wedge \neg\phi[s]]. \quad (24)$$

Maintenance Obligation. We now turn our attention to the maintenance obligation. A formula ϕ is a maintenance obligation between time points $t_1 \in \mathbb{N}$ and $t_2 \in \mathbb{N}$, if and only if we have: $t_1 < t_2$; and for all time points t' such that $t_1 \leq t' \leq t_2$, $\phi \in \mathbf{Force}(t')$ and $\phi \in \mathbf{State}(t')$. The following abbreviation captures maintenance obligations in the Situation Calculus in terms of situations:

$$\mathbf{OblgMaintenance}(\phi, s_1, s_2) \stackrel{\text{def}}{=}$$
$$(\forall s')[(s_1 \sqsubseteq s' \sqsubseteq s_2) \supset [\mathbf{Oblg}(\phi, s') \land \phi[s']]] \quad (25)$$

The following abbreviation specifies the violation condition for a maintenance obligation ϕ in the interval $[s_1, \ldots, s_2]$:

$$\mathbf{violatedMaintenance}(\phi, s_1, s_2) \stackrel{\text{def}}{=} (\exists s)[s \sqsubseteq s_1 \sqsubseteq s_2 \land \neg \phi[s]]. \quad (26)$$

4.3 Perdurant Obligation

We finally deal with the perdurant obligation. A formula ϕ is a perdurant obligation with deadline d between time points $t_1 \in \mathbb{N}$ and $t_2 \in \mathbb{N}$, if and only if we have: $t_1 < d < t_2$; and for all t' such that $t_1 \leq t' \leq t_2$, $\phi \in \mathbf{Force}(t')$. The following abbreviation captures perdurant obligations in the Situation Calculus in terms of situations:

$$\mathbf{OblgPerdurant}(\phi, s_1, d, s_2) \stackrel{\text{def}}{=} (\forall s)[(s_1 \sqsubseteq d \sqsubseteq s \sqsubseteq s_2) \supset \mathbf{Oblg}(\phi, s)] \quad (27)$$

The violation condition for a perdurant obligation ϕ in the interval $[s_1, \ldots, s_2]$ with deadline d is expressed in the following:

$$\mathbf{violatedPerdurance}(\phi, s_1, d, s_2) \stackrel{\text{def}}{=} (\forall s)[s_1 \sqsubseteq s \sqsubseteq d \sqsubseteq s_2 \supset \neg \phi[s]]. \quad (28)$$

5 Correctness

This section turns to the correctness of the formalization of the obligation types that were modelled in the Situation Calculus in Sect. 4. For each one of the obligation types, we modelled the obligation itself as well as its violation. Therefore, for each obligation type, we need to show that the right-hand sides of the abbreviations that model the obligations and their violations indeed do reflect the informal definitions of the obligations and their violations. In the proofs, we need to relate the main predicates used in the formalization to the functions *Force* and *State* as follows:

- (R1): $\mathbf{Oblg}(\phi, t)$ holds $\iff \phi \in \mathbf{Force}(t)$
- (R2): $\neg \mathbf{Oblg}(\phi, t)$ holds $\iff \phi \notin \mathbf{Force}(t)$
- (R3): $\phi[t]$ holds $\iff \phi \in \mathbf{State}(t)$

Note that these correlations can be expressed in terms of situations as well, e.g.,

- (R1): $\mathbf{Oblg}(\phi, s)$ holds $\iff \phi \in \mathbf{Force}(s)$.

Lemma 1. *(Punctual Obligation)* If **OblgAt**(ϕ, t) is true, then ϕ is a punctual obligation in force at time t, not in force neither at time $t-1$ nor at time $t+1$; that is, $\phi \in$ **Force**(t), $\phi \notin$ *Force*$(t-1)$, and $\phi \notin$ **Force**$(t+1)$.

Proof. Assume the semantics of punctual obligations, which is provided by the combination of the following conditions : **(1)**: $\phi \in$ **Force**(n); **(2)**: $\phi \notin$ **Force**$(n-1)$; and **(3)**: $\phi \notin$ **Force**$(n+1)$. Now suppose that, for a fixed formula Φ and a fixed time point T, **OblgAt**(Φ, T) holds. From the right hand side of the abbreviation (17), with appropriate substitutions and skolemization, we get the following conjunction:

$$[\textbf{Oblg}(\Phi, S) \wedge start(S) = T] \wedge$$
$$(\forall s', a_1) [S = do(a_1, s') \supset \neg \textbf{Oblg}(\Phi, s')] \wedge$$
$$(\forall s'', a_2) [s'' = do(a_2, S) \supset \neg \textbf{Oblg}(\Phi, s'')]]. \qquad (29)$$

We must show that the three conditions **(1)**, **(2)**, and **(3)** hold.
Condition **(1)**: From the first conjunct in the formula 29 we get that **Oblg**(Φ, S) and $start(S) = T$ hold; therefore, by the correlation R.(1), we have $\Phi(S) \in$ **Force**(S).
Condition **(2)**: From the second conjunct in the formula (29) and by fixing a_1 and s_1, we get that $[S = do(A_1, S') \supset \neg \textbf{Oblg}(\Phi, S')]$. That is, suppose we have $S = do(A_1, S')$, that is, we have the immediate predecessor situation S' of S; then we conclude that $\neg \textbf{Oblg}(\Phi, S')$. Hence, by (R2), we have that $\Phi \notin$ **Force**(S').
Condition **(3)**: By a similar argument as for Condition **(2)**, The third conjunct in the formula 29) yields $[S'' = do(A_2, S) \supset \neg \textbf{Oblg}(\Phi, S'')]$, and, from there, $\Phi \notin$ **Force**(S''). $\square$

Lemma 2. *(Violation of Punctual Obligation)* If *violatedAt*(ϕ, s) is true, then ϕ is a punctual obligation in force at situation s, that is, $\phi \in$ **Force**(s), and $\phi \notin$ **State**(s).

Proof. For the violation of the punctual obligation, the right hand side of the abbreviation (16) implies that ϕ is not *true*; that is, $\neg \phi[s]$. Hence, by the correlation (R3), we have $\phi \notin$ **State**(s). $\square$

Lemma 3. *(Perdurant Obligation)* If **OblgPerdurant**(ϕ, s_1, d, s_2) holds, then ϕ is a perdurant obligation in force in all situations s in the interval $[s_1 \ldots s_2]$, that is, for all $s \in [s_1 \ldots s_2]$, $\phi \in$ **Force**(s).

Proof. The semantics of perdurant obligations is as follows : for $s \in [s_1 \ldots d \ldots s_2]$, we have the condition: **(A)** $\phi \in Force(s)$. Now suppose that, for a fixed formula Φ and fixed situations $S_1, \ldots, D, \ldots D_2$, **OblgPerdurant**$(\Phi, S_1, D, S_2)$ holds. From the right hand side of the abbreviation (27), with appropriate substitutions, we get:

$$(\forall s)[(S_1 \sqsubseteq D \sqsubseteq s \sqsubseteq S_2) \supset \textbf{Oblg}(\Phi, s)].$$

Suppose that for a fixed S, we have $(S_1 \sqsubseteq D \sqsubseteq S \sqsubseteq S_2$. Then, by the correlation (R1), $S \in$ **Force**. Henceforth, the condition **(A)** is satisfied. $\square$

Lemma 4. *(Violation of Perdurant Obligation) If the violation predicate* ***violatedPerdurant***(ϕ, s_1, d, s_2) *holds, then ϕ is a perdurant obligation in force in all situations s in the interval $[s_1 \ldots d]$, that is, for all $s \in [s_1 \ldots d]$, $\phi \in$* ***Force***(s), *and $\phi \notin$* ***State***(s).

Proof. For the violation of the perdurant obligation, from right hand side of the abbreviation (28), ϕ is not *true*, meaning that $\phi \in$ **Force**(s) but $\phi \notin$ **State**(s). □

6 Obligation Violation and Compensation

6.1 Compensation

We first need to introduce the notion of compensation. Obligations that are violated are meant as penalty to be compensated by the violator. Intuitively, a compensation of a violation is a set of measures that the violator must take to make amend for the violation. Formally, a compensation **Comp** is defined as a function $\mathcal{L} \mapsto 2^{\mathcal{L}}$, such that, for a given obligation ϕ, **Comp**(ϕ) is the set of all obligations ϕ', called compensation obligations, that come in force after ϕ has been violated. That is, **Comp**$(\phi) \in 2^{\mathcal{L}}$.

An obligation ϕ is compensable if and only if **Comp**$(\phi) \neq \emptyset$, and for all $\phi' \in$ **Comp**(ϕ), there is a $t \in \mathbb{N}$ such that $\phi' \in$ **Force**(t); that is, a compensable obligation is associated with a non empty set of obligations that are in force at least any one time point.

Finally, an obligation ϕ is compensated if and only if ϕ is violated and every $\phi' \in$ **Comp**(ϕ) is either not violated or compensated. To keep matters simple, we assume that compensation obligations are never violated, thus avoiding (for now) the possibility of recursive compensation.

6.2 Compensation Action

An obligation violation must be countered by a compensation action that must be executed whenever it is possible, which is when an obligation violation has occurred; that is, when *violatedType*() is true. This is done in a manner similar to natural actions of Reiter [35] that are forced to happen whenever their preconditions are met. We introduce a compensation action *execComp*(t) which is similar to natural actions, and whose effect is to compensate violated obligations. Next, like for any action, we must provide an action precondition axiom for the newly introduced compensation action as follows:

$$\begin{aligned}
Poss(execComp(\phi, t)) \equiv \\
&(\exists s)[violatedAt(\phi, s) \wedge start(s) = t] \vee \\
&(\exists s_1, s_2, t_1, t_2)[violatedPreemptive(\phi, s_1, s_2) \wedge start(s_1) = t_1 \wedge \\
&\quad start(s_2) = t_2 \wedge t \leq t_2] \vee \\
&(\exists s_1, s_2)[violatedNonPreemptive(\phi, s_1, s_2) \wedge start(s_1) = t_1 \wedge \\
&\quad start(s_2) = t_2 \wedge (t_1 \leq t \leq t_2)] \vee \\
&(\exists s_1, s_2)[violatedMaintenance(\phi, s_1, s_2) \wedge start(s_1) = t_1 \wedge \\
&\quad start(s_2) = t_2 \wedge t \leq t_2] \vee \\
&(\exists s_1, d, s_2)[violatedPerdurant(\phi, s_1, d, s_2) \wedge start(s_1) = t_1 \wedge \\
&\quad start(s_2) = t_2 \wedge (t_1 \leq t \leq d \leq t_2)].
\end{aligned} \quad (30)$$

Furthermore, we introduce a fluent $compensated(\phi_1, \phi_2, s)$ whose truth value is affected by the compensation action $execComp(t)$ and which intuitively means that the obligation ϕ_2 compensates the obligation ϕ_1 in situation s. Finally, we extend Reiter's notion of executability of situations to those situations that include the compensation action as follows:

$$\begin{aligned}
executable(s) \stackrel{\text{def}}{=} \\
&(\forall a, s')[do(a, s') \sqsubseteq s \supset Poss(a, s') \wedge start(s') \leq time(a)] \wedge \\
&(\forall a', s'', t)[Poss(execComp(\phi, t), s'') \wedge do(a', s'') \sqsubseteq s \supset time(a') < t].
\end{aligned} \quad (31)$$

The axiom 31 expresses in its first conjunct of the right-hand side the condition for the executability of non-natural actions, while the second conjunct adds an additional condition that characterizes the executability of the $execComp(\phi, t)$ action.

7 Related Work

Our obligation-producing actions in the Situation Calculus are similar to and a substantial modification of those that were first introduced in [23] and in [4], where the deontic accessibility relationship O was introduced. In [23] and [4], authors ranked deontic alternatives in terms of their levels of ideality; they subsequently define the obligatory sentences as those that are true in all alternative situations with maximal ideality; and, finally, they give a successor state axiom for the fluent O. By contrast, our work simplifies the formalization by removing any use of situation idealities and by solely embedding the possible world semantics for SDL from [7] in the Situation Calculus. Furthermore, we expand Reiter's regression to reason about obligation-producing actions.

Another approach for incorporating deontic notions into the Situation Calculus is presented by Classen and Delgrande in [32]. In [32], deontic assertions and modalities are expressed as constraints that subsequently compiled into a

Situation Calculus action theory which are used to reason about obligations. We differ from this approach by expressing obligations directly in the Situation Calculus so that there is no need of an extra compilation step.

In [6], authors have proposed a contract ontology called *Symboleo* to systematically organize the main concepts of typical legal contracts. These concepts include: contract, asset, role, power, obligation, party, and event. The structure of the contract ontology that is made of these concepts is summarized by the authors of [6] in a meta-model. Symboleo is a language for specifying smart contracts and reasoning about them using statecharts and Event Calculus. There is a striking difference between the Symboleo framework and the framework that this paper presents: Symboleo models the obligation modality without conceptualising the kind of obligation types that this paper pursues.

Event Calculus may also be used for specifying obligations [31]. The Situation Calculus, however, enjoys the key advantage of the existence of GOLOG [13], a Situation Calculus-based programming language for defining complex actions in terms of a set of primitive actions axiomatized in the Situation Calculus.

8 Conclusion and Future Work

This paper used the Situation Calculus account of obligations in the Situation Calculus presented in [37] to provide a Situation Calculus formal account of the taxonomy of obligations given in [31]. Our formalization of this taxonomy used non-Markovian theories of the Situation Calculus to model the various types of obligations. We showed the correctness of the formalization and we mentioned related work pertaining to the formalisms used to give a formal account of obligations.

This paper has introduced obligation-producing actions into the temporal Situation Calculus. The ensuing formalism allows us to enlarge the scope of dynamic domains that can be specified in the language of the Situation Calculus.

One avenue for future work will be to construct logical theories called *basic contractual theories* to formalize legal contracts along the tradition set by [14]. Those basic contractual theories provide the formal semantics of the corresponding legal contracts.

Another avenue for future work will be to represent legal contracts as processes in the Situation Calculus; such processes lead to states where desirable properties holds that logically follow from the basic contractual theory representing those legal contracts. Our approach will provide one with an implementable specification, thus allowing one to automatically check many properties of the specification using an interpreter. The later will be GOLOG [13], a Situation Calculus-based programming language for defining complex actions in terms of a set of primitive actions axiomatized in the Situation Calculus. We will use GOLOG to develop a framework for obligation-based programming which we will apply to smart contracts.

References

1. Hashmi, M., Governatori, G., Wynn, M.: Normative requirements for business process compliance. In: Australian Symposium On Service Research And Innovation, pp. 100–116 (2013)
2. Governatori, G.: An Abstract Normative Framework for Business Process Compliance. Inf. Technol. **55**, 231–238 (2013)
3. Demolombe, R., Parra, P.: Integrating state constraints and obligations in situation calculus. Inteligencia Artif. **13**, 54–63 (2009)
4. Demolombe, R., Herzig, A.: Obligation change in dependence logic and situation calculus. In: International Workshop on Deontic Logic in Computer Science, pp. 57–73 (2004)
5. Pirri, F., Reiter, R.: Some contributions to the metatheory of the situation calculus. J. ACM (JACM). **46**, 325–361 (1999)
6. Parvizimosaed, A.: Towards the specification and verification of legal contracts. In: 28th IEEE International Requirements Engineering Conference (RE'20). IEEE CS. (2020)
7. Hintikka, J.: some main problems of deontic logic. In: Deontic Logic: Introductory and Systematic Readinds, pp. 59–104 (1970)
8. Scherl, R., Levesque, H.: The frame problem and knowledge-producing actions. In: Proceedings of the 11th National Conference on Artificial Intelligence. Washington, DC, USA, July 11–15, 1993, pp. 689–695 (1993)
9. DD Reiter, R.: The frame problem in the situation calculus: a simple solution (sometimes) and a completeness result for goal regression. In: Artificial and Mathematical Theory of Computation, Papers in Honor of John Mccarthy on the Occasion of His Sixty-fourth Birthday, pp. 359–380 (1991)
10. Pinto, J., Reiter, R.: Reasoning about time in the Situation Calculus. Ann. Math. Artif. Intell. **14**, 251–268 (1995)
11. Pinto, J., Reiter, R.: Temporal reasoning in logic programming: a case for the Situation Calculus. In: Logic Programming, Proceedings of the Tenth International Conference on Logic Programming, June 21-25, 1993, pp. 203–221 (1993)
12. Kowalski, R., Sadri, F.: The Situation Calculus and Event Calculus Compared. In: Logic Programming, Proceedings of the 1994 International Symposium, pp. 539–553 (1994)
13. Levesque, H., Reiter, R., Lespérance, Y., Lin, F., Scherl, R.: GOLOG: a logic programming language for dynamic domains. J. Log. Program. **31**, 59–83 (1997)
14. Reiter, R.: Knowledge in action: logical foundations for specifying and implementing dynamical systems by Raymond Reiter, MIT Press, 0-262-18218-1, 448 pp. Knowl. Eng. Rev. **20**, 431–432 (2005)
15. Levesque, H., Pirri, F., Reiter, R.: Foundations for the Situation Calculus. Electron. Trans. Artif. Intell. **2**, 159–178 (1998)
16. Kowalski, R., Sergot, M.: A logic-based calculus of events. In: Foundations Of Knowledge Base Management, pp. 23–55 (1989)
17. Delgrande, J., Schaub, T., Jackson, W.: Alternative approaches to default logic. Artif. Intell. **70**, 167–237 (1994)
18. Shanahan, M.: The event calculus explained. Artif. Intell. Today: Recent Trends Develop. **1600**, 409–430 (1999)
19. Mueller, E.: The event calculus. In: Commonsense Reasoning, pp. 19–46 (2015)
20. McDermott, D.: AI, logic, and the frame problem. In: The Frame Problem In Artificial Intelligence. pp. 105–118 (1987)

21. MacLeod, W.: Complexity and contract. In: SRN Electronic J. 0-25 (2005)
22. De Kruijff, J., Weigand, H.: Ontologies for commitment-based smart contracts. In: OTM Confederated International Conference "On The Move To Meaningful Internet System", pp. 383–398 (2017)
23. Demolombe, R.: From belief change to obligation change in the Situation Calculus. In: Proceedings of the 16th Eureopean Conference on Artificial Intelligence, ECAI'2004, Including Prestigious Applicants of Intelligent Systems, PAIS 2004, pp. 991–992 (2004)
24. Reiter, R.: Foundations for knowledge-based systems (Invited Paper). In: Information Processing 86, Proceedings of the IFIP 10th World Computer Congress, pp. 663–668 (1986)
25. Bacchus, F., Boutilier, C., Grove, A.: Rewarding behaviors. In: Proceedings of the National Conference on Artificial Intelligence, pp. 1160–1167 (1996)
26. Gabaldon, A.: Non-Markovian Control in the Situation Calculus. In: Proceedings of the Eighteenth National Conference on Artificial Intelligence and Fourteenth Conference on Innovative Applications of Artificial Intelligence, pp. 519–525 (2002)
27. Kiringa, I., Gabaldon, A.: Synthesizing advanced transaction models using the Situation Calculus. J. Intell. Inf. Syst. **35**, 157–212 (2010)
28. Kiringa, I., Gabaldon, A.: Expressing transactions with savepoints as non-Markovian theories of actions. In: Proceedings of the 10th International Workshop On Knowledge Representation Meets Databases (KRDB 2003), vol. 79 (2003)
29. Chomicki, J.: Efficient checking of temporal integrity constraints using bounded history encoding. ACM Trans. Database Syst. **20**, 149–186 (1995)
30. Reiter, R.: Sequential, Temporal GOLOG. In: Proceedings of the Sixth International Conference on Principles of Knowledge Representation And Reasoning (KR'98), pp. 547–556 (1998)
31. Hashmi, M., Governatori, G., Wynn, M.: Modeling obligations with event-calculus. In: Rules on the Web. From Theory To Applications - 8th International Symposium, RuleML, vol. 8620, pp. 296–310 (2014)
32. Claßen, J., Delgrande, J.: Dyadic obligations over complex actions as deontic constraints in the situation calculus. In: Proceedings of the 17th International Conference on Principles of Knowledge Representation and Reasoning. pp. 253-263 (2020)
33. Delgrande, J.: a preference-based approach to defeasible deontic inference. In: Proceedings of The 17th International Conference on Principles of Knowledge Representation and Reasoning, pp. 326–335 (2020)
34. Reiter, R.: On knowledge-based programming with sensing in the Situation Calculus. ACM Trans. Comput. Log. **2**, 433–457 (2001)
35. Raymond, R.: Natural actions, concurrency and continuous time in the Situation Calculus. In: Proceedings of the Fifth International Conference on Principles of Knowledge Representation and Reasoning November 5–8 (1996)
36. McCarthy, J.: Situations, Actions, and Causal Laws. Stanford Univ, Dept of Computer Science (1963)
37. Kalonji, K., Kiringa, I., Yeap, T.: The frame problem and obligation-producing actions. (University of Ottawa,2024)
38. Gabaldon, A.: Non-Markovian control in the Situation Calculus. Artif. Intell. **175**, 25–48 (2011)

A Novel Concept Induction Approach for Explainable Quality 4.0

Léa Charbonnier[1(✉)], Franco Giustozzi[2], Julien Saunier[1], and Cecilia Zanni-Merk[1]

[1] INSA Rouen Normandie, Univ Rouen Normandie, Université Le Havre Normandie, Normandie Univ, LITIS UR 4108, 76000 Rouen, France
`{lea.charbonnier,julien.saunier,cecilia.zanni-merk}@insa-rouen.fr`
[2] INSA Strasbourg, University of Strasbourg, ICube laboratory, CNRS (UMR 7357), 67000 Strasbourg, France
`franco.giustozzi@insa-strasbourg.fr`

Abstract. Quality 4.0 integrates Industry 4.0 technologies into quality management by analyzing machine sensor data with intelligent systems to predict and identify failures and quality issues. This paper presents a method for diagnosing the causes of product quality problems using sensor data and quality control outcomes. It employs the Concept Induction framework to derive precise, explanatory concepts that distinguish compliant from non-compliant products. A new evaluation metric, combining instance coverage, classification precision, and hierarchical relevance, is proposed to identify the most informative concepts. The approach is validated using a synthetic Predictive Maintenance dataset simulating a milling machine, linking sensor data with quality outcomes via an ontology. Results show improved concept induction and accurate identification of factors related to defective products.

Keywords: Concept Induction · Quality Assurance and Industry 4.0 (Quality 4.0) · Ontology · Quality issues detection

1 Introduction

A key challenge for the industry is promptly detecting anomalies and identifying their root causes to minimize the economic and ecological repercussions [27]. In this context, Quality 4.0 integrates intelligent systems to enhance quality management. It is an extension of Industry 4.0 that uses smart technologies in quality assurance processes, i.e., procedures aimed at ensuring products meet predefined standards. The goal is to detect and explain quality issues using production data. Root Cause Analysis (RCA) is commonly used to trace defects or process disruptions. Many quality control efforts are based on data-driven approaches using machine learning, deep learning, and computer vision algorithms. While these techniques use data such as time series and product images to verify quality compliance [23], their dependency on extensive labeled data and their lack of transparency make root cause analysis particularly difficult.

Another line of research for condition monitoring relies on symbolic and logical models, such as ontologies and rule-based approaches [13]. These models can be applied to real-time data when combined with approaches such as stream reasoning [6], enabling dynamic analysis of evolving environments. Previous works have employed these techniques to identify unusual situations in manufacturing processes [5,12]. While these methods support formal, interpretable reasoning, they presuppose known abnormal situations, and encoding them into the ontology is often cumbersome.

To tackle this issue, concept induction or concept learning, a sub-problem of ontology learning, facilitates the automatic extraction of well-defined concepts in description logic [25,32]. Formally, this problem consists of a knowledge base $\mathcal{O} = (\mathcal{T}, \mathcal{A})$ made up of a TBox $\mathcal{T}$ and an Abox $\mathcal{A}$, and two disjoint sets of individuals P and N, considered respectively as positive and negative examples. The goal is to find a class expressions C over a description logic $\mathcal{L}$ such that $\mathcal{O} \models C(a)$ for all $a \in P$, and $\mathcal{O} \not\models C(b)$ for all $b \in N$. In this work, the knowledge base $\mathcal{O}$ is an ontology that models products, machines, and their associations with machine failures occurring during production. The set of individuals P corresponds to products that failed quality control (i.e., defective products), while N includes those that passed. The objective is to derive a class expression C that characterizes defective products, thereby providing insights into the potential causes of quality issues. Concept induction algorithms may, at times, produce class expressions that inadequately separate the sets P and N. This can be attributed to an incomplete conceptual representation within the knowledge base. Furthermore, since these algorithms often rely only on coverage as a ranking criterion, they tend to favor overly general expressions that obscure the distinction between defective and compliant products, thus hindering root cause analysis.

This work introduces a novel concept induction method to formalize complex class expressions within the framework of Quality 4.0. These expressions aim to capture potential root causes, thus improving the ontological representation of quality-related phenomena. To support the identification of the most relevant classes (those that accurately cover defective products), a new ranking metric is proposed, incorporating coverage, precision, and concept hierarchy. Evaluation on the Predictive Maintenance dataset [20] shows that the proposed metrics yield more precise and representative concepts for failed product identification.

The paper is organized as follows: Sect. 2 reviews Root Cause Analysis and Concept Induction; Sect. 3 introduces our approach to explainable Quality 4.0; Sect. 4 presents its evaluation on the Predictive Maintenance dataset; and Sect. 5 concludes with a discussion of future work.

2 Related Work

The advent of Industry 4.0 facilitates the integration of novel technologies in quality management. In this context, the deployment of industrial sensors enables the systematic collection and utilization of machine and process data to identify and explain quality-related issues [26]. Explaining a quality issue requires identifying its root causes, that is, the fundamental factors leading to defects, such as equipment malfunctions or component failures. This data-driven approach often leverages sensor readings and production monitoring data to uncover underlying causes [22]. In this study, we focus on two Root Cause Analysis (RCA) approaches that are most applicable to our context.

- The **Factors $\implies$ Root Cause (RC)** techniques aim to link physical factors to specific root causes through a classification task, where root causes act as target labels. This approach relies on labeled datasets and commonly uses traditional or deep learning methods (Sect. 2.1).
- The **Factors $\implies$ Problem** techniques link various factors extracted from sensor data to specific machine failures, with a focus on providing explanations for the identified problems (Sect. 2.2).

2.1 Machine Learning Approaches for Root Cause Classification

Among existing methods for detecting anomalies in manufacturing and industrial processes, we can cite machine learning approaches. Methods such as KNN, ABOD, and isolation forests often achieve high accuracy (AUROC up to 0.99) [1]. For the root cause analysis, statistical process control and Pareto charts are used, revealing that a small number of causes account for the majority of issues. This contributes to a substantial reduction in rejection rates across assembly machines. Nevertheless, achieving this reduction relies on properly tuning the specification limits associated with the identified causes of rejection for each product series. Autoencoders and SHAP approaches are also used to detect and explain early anomalies [34]. The results obtained are consistent with the on-site inspection. However, while increasing model complexity tends to improve performance, it also significantly raises the demand for training data and computational resources, factors that can negatively affect the overall outcome. Another approach employs a hierarchical neural network to detect anomalies in complex, multivariate time-series data [16]. Deep learning is leveraged to capture intricate relationships among variables, with saliency maps providing a degree of interpretability. However, the method does not always assign the highest scores to the actual root causes, raising concerns about the explanations trustworthiness and reliability.

While classification-based methods offer effective solutions for identifying known root causes, they often require large labeled datasets and rely on complex models whose decision processes are challenging to interpret. These techniques are typically focused on accuracy over explainability, which can hinder their adoption in industrial contexts where understanding the reasoning behind a diagnosis is critical. Moreover, they are less suited to exploring new or evolving faults where root causes are unknown or labels are unavailable. This limitation motivates a shift toward approaches that associate factors directly with observed problems, enabling the extraction of interpretable patterns that can reveal potential causes without requiring explicit root cause annotations.

2.2 Enhancing Interpretability and Usability in Root Cause Analysis

Decision trees are commonly employed in both anomaly detection and root cause analysis owing to their interpretability and computational efficiency. In domains such as manufacturing and quality management, interactive decision trees enable analysts to swiftly identify product attributes most strongly associated with defects, facilitating expert-driven interpretation and rapid root cause identification [8]. However, as the number of variables and decision paths increases, the clarity and interpretability of decision trees can deteriorate significantly.

To address these limitations, alternative approaches, such as causal discovery, have been proposed. These methods aim at identifying the underlying structural relationships between sensor readings and failure events, providing a more principled framework for uncovering cause-and-effect dependencies in complex industrial processes. Rehak et al. [24] combine anomaly detection with causal graphs to perform root cause analysis (RCA) in industrial contexts, with a focus on robotic gripping. Their method employs counterfactual reasoning within a causal framework, enabling interpretable and causally grounded diagnoses. While this approach offers strong explanatory capabilities, counterfactual analysis using causal graphs is largely centered on individual anomaly cases. It assesses which hypothetical changes to variables could have prevented a specific fault. Consequently, the resulting explanations are tailored to specific instances and lack the ability to produce generalizable or reusable knowledge structures. This limitation highlights the need for methods that blend interpretability with structured and actionable insights. One promising approach is concept induction, which facilitates human reasoning through compact, rule-based outputs that are both comprehensible and widely applicable in operational settings.

2.3 Concept Induction as an Interpretable Approach

We avoid using traditional machine learning methods such as neural networks due to their inherent lack of interpretability. The goal of our approach is not only to detect faults but also to provide explanations that are both understandable and trustworthy to human operators. This requirement rules out most machine learning-based classification techniques, which often act as "black boxes" and require retraining whenever new data or labels become available [2].

We instead adopt concept induction, a transparent method aligned with the **Factors $\implies$ Problem** paradigm. This approach enables the identification of causal relationships between observed physical factors and resulting machine failures, producing transparent rules or explanatory structures that facilitate understanding. These rules not only help associate factors with a problem but also aid in root cause extraction through post-analysis of the discovered knowledge. Unlike root cause classification approaches that prioritize accuracy and rely on opaque models, our approach emphasizes clarity and flexibility, making it particularly suitable for contexts where human understanding and adaptability are crucial.

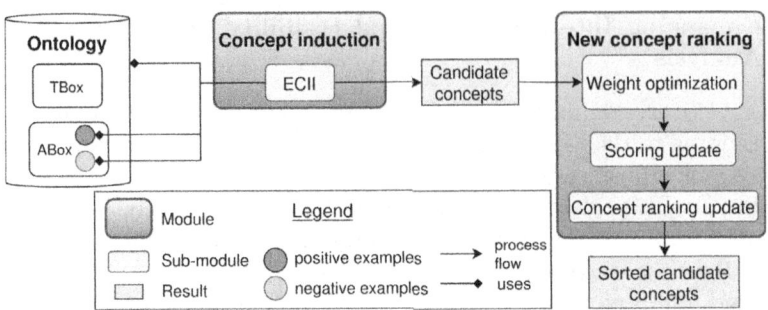

Fig. 1. The RCIQ4.0 framework

3 RCIQ4.0: Root Cause Induction for Quality4.0

In this section, we propose a novel approach for explainable quality issues identification in manufacturing processes. The proposed approach, as shown in Fig. 1 uses concept induction to uncover and explain the root causes of quality issues.

A key component of the approach is an ontology that allows the representation of defective (positive examples) and non-defective products (negative examples), machines data, and machines failures. The ontology is described in Sect. 3.1. The *Concept induction* module uses the ECII algorithm to perform concept induction on the ontology, thereby obtaining a first preliminary list of concept expressions to describe the defective products. Each concept generated by the *Concept induction* module is associated with a set of evaluation criteria defined in Sect. 3.3, which forms the basis of a new scoring function based on a weighted sum. Sorted concepts provide insights into the potential causes of the quality issue and are presented to the operator as explanatory information.

3.1 Ontological Model for Quality Assurance

The proposed approach relies on the *Context Ontology* [11], which provides a formal representation of the manufacturing domain. It represents the elements of a factory, such as machines, products, processes, and sensors, with special emphasis on modeling relevant situations that represent abnormal behaviors.

We introduce here the concepts and relations of the *Context Ontology* that are relevant to our approach. Machine and Product are modeled as sub-concepts of Resource, representing machines and products respectively. Another relevant concept is Situation. A situation represents a particular set of conditions relevant to a given scenario. An abnormal situation denotes atypical manufacturing conditions, formalized as constraints derived from expert knowledge. The Quality_Issue concept is a sub-concept of Situation to describe quality issues detected on products. Finally, the Cause concept represents the possible causes that provoke a situation. A situation is linked to its causes through the hasCauses relation. Regarding the relations, the two most important ones for our approach are `isDefective`, to indicate whether or not a product passed quality control, and `involvedInSituation`, to assert that a resource is involved in one or more particular situation(s).

This ontology provides the basic concepts and relationships that allow the representation of the information to describe a product and the different situations that occur on the machines that perform operations on the products. For example, the `Product ⊓ ∃involvedInSituation.HighTemperature` concept allows to represent all instances that are products and that are concerned by the situation `HighTemperature`. These concepts and relationships are then used to build new concepts to differentiate between products that pass quality control and those that do not.

3.2 Concept Induction Module

We aim to differentiate between products that pass or fail quality control and to identify one or more potential root causes in abnormal machine situations. According to [32], although concept induction is primarily used to generate ontology axioms (TBox) from instance data (ABox), it can also serve as a means of explanation by producing class expressions that help distinguish between correctly and incorrectly classified scenes. These explanations are interpretable and typically expressed using description logic. Consequently, we adopt concept induction to formalize complex class descriptions that characterize products failing to meet quality standards. Among the existing frameworks allowing this type of concept induction, we can cite DL-Learner [4] and ECII [25].

DL-Learner is derived from Inductive Logic Programming and proceeds by concept refinement. A candidate concept expression C_0 is assessed as follows: if $\mathcal{O} \models C(a)$ for all $a \in P$, and $\mathcal{O} \not\models C(b)$ for all $b \in N$, hold, then several candidate refinements (concept expressions more or less general) of C_0 are proposed. The most suitable option is designated as the new candidate concept expression, C_1. The process is then repeated until a perfect solution is found or a termination criterion is met [32]. For each candidate concept, the DL-Learner framework makes many external calls to a description logic reasoner. In the event of substantial expressive ontology and the utilization of extensive example sets, these calls can necessitate a significant amount of calculation [25].

ECII is a concept induction algorithm that selects a finite set $\{C_1,\ldots,C_n\}$ of complex class expressions over $\mathcal{L}$ and additional complex class expressions, resulting in $\mathcal{O}' = \mathcal{O} \cup \{A_k \equiv C_k | k = 1,\ldots,n\}$ where A_i are atomic classes not occurring in $\mathcal{O}$. Then, a reasoner is used to compute the membership of all individuals from the examples in all atomic classes from $\mathcal{O}'$. Finally, candidate class expressions are generated using a combination of constructors, negation, and atomic classes. This strategy minimizes the number of reasoner invocations, although it comes at the cost of narrowing the search space for potential expressions. ECII is selected for its efficiency in generating complex description logic class expressions, particularly in ontologies that are rich with axioms. However, since the method can yield hundreds of candidate concepts, an effective ranking process becomes essential to determine which expressions merit further consideration. As our objective is to explain quality issues in manufacturing processes, the concepts generated by the ECII framework must be both exhaustive and precise. To assess this, we consider the following illustrative example. In the context outlined in Sect. 3.1, concept induction is applied to characterize defective products, treating them as positive examples, while compliant products serve as negative ones. The first concept learned is `Product`, which encompasses all instances regardless of quality. Although this concept has broad coverage, it lacks discriminative power, as it includes both defective and compliant products without distinction. By contrast, a second, more specific concept is `Product ⊓ involvedInSituation.HighTemperature`. This refined concept is more precise, as it targets only those products involved in high-temperature scenarios. However, its coverage is limited, potentially omitting other relevant defective cases directly related to this specific situation.

This point highlights the typical trade-off in concept induction: general concepts offer higher coverage but less precision, while specific ones enhance precision but limit generalizability. Since ECII ranks candidate concepts solely based on coverage, the broader but less informative concept is ranked highest, while more meaningful yet narrower concepts are ranked lower. To truly support explainable quality analysis, it is essential to identify concepts that strike a balance between relevance and generality, capturing the defining characteristics of the target group without overgeneralization. Relying on coverage alone is insufficient for selecting such representative concepts.

3.3 New Concept Ranking Module

The aim is to create the most precise concepts, covering as many defective products as possible. To that end, the original ECII framework is modified to evaluate concepts generated with a reasoner: the generated candidate classes in ECII are introduced into the ontology as subclasses of a common `Candidate` class. Each candidate is defined by its corresponding rule expression, making it logically equivalent to the set of individuals satisfying that expression. This integration enables the formal encoding of rule semantics within the ontology. To rank concepts while balancing coverage and specificity, a new score is introduced, which considers three factors: coverage, precision, and concept hierarchy.

In the original implementation, coverage is defined as the total number of correctly classified individuals across both the positive and negative sets. (Eq. 1).

$$\text{ECII\_coverage} = \frac{\text{TruePositive} + \text{TrueNegative}}{\text{TotalPositive} + \text{TotalNegative}} \quad (1)$$

where TruePositive and TrueNegative denote, respectively, the number of positive instances correctly classified as positive and the number of negative instances correctly classified as negative. Similarly, TotalPositive and TotalNegative represent the total number of positive and negative instances within each dataset.

Specifically, an individual from the positive set is considered identified only if it satisfies all components of the concept (i.e., conjunctive conditions). This classification is performed locally by verifying whether an individual satisfies the conditions defined by the concept using syntactic matching rather than logical inference. In our adaptation, we refine the definition of coverage (Eq. 2) to focus solely on correctly classified positive examples, i.e. products that failed Quality Control (QC) and are correctly described by the concept. Additionally, instead of relying on syntactic checks, we use ontology-based reasoning to determine whether an individual is entailed by a concept, using inferred class memberships. This choice allows for a more semantically grounded and faithful evaluation of the concept's explanatory power.

$$\text{coverage} = \frac{\text{Number of defective products identified by the concept}}{\text{Total number of defective products}} \quad (2)$$

We also introduce two metrics that are not included in ECII. The first one is precision (Eq. 3), meaning the proportion of true positives inferred by the concept. The second one is hierarchy (Eq. 4), meaning the depth of the concept among all candidate class concepts. The objective is to evaluate whether the concept targets the failed products (true positives) and avoids the good ones (false positives), as well as its generalization and specificity ratio, by knowing how deep the generated concept is. For each concept, precision is calculated by dividing the number of defective products inferred by the total number of products identified by the concept.

$$\text{precision} = \frac{\text{Number of defective products identified by the concept}}{\text{Total number of products identified by the concept}} \quad (3)$$

The hierarchy-based score is calculated by measuring the depth of the class in the ontology hierarchy. The maximum depth of all candidate concepts is used to normalize the value. In our scoring system, more specific concepts (those with higher hierarchy-based scores) are preferred over more general ones.

$$\text{hierarchy} = \frac{\text{Concept depth}}{\text{Maximum depth}} \quad (4)$$

Concepts are evaluated using a multiple criteria decision analysis method [3]. The goal is to rank the concepts by combining the three previously defined evaluation criteria. Their complementary nature allows for a more comprehensive and nuanced assessment. Since each criterion is normalized to a range between 0 and 1, they can be effectively aggregated using a weighted sum (Eq. 5) with the associated weights, α, β, and γ.

$$\begin{aligned}\text{score} = \alpha \times \text{coverage} + \beta \times \text{precision} + \gamma \times \text{hierarchy}\\ \text{with } \alpha, \beta, \gamma \in [0, 1] \text{ and } \alpha + \beta + \gamma = 1\end{aligned} \quad (5)$$

To identify the optimal combination of weights α, β, and γ, the scoring function defined in Eq. 5 is optimized under specific constraints. It draws on principles from multi-criteria decision making [17], optimization heuristics [33], and rule learning techniques [10]. An optimization problem is posed (Eq. 6) that aims to minimize the negative average score of the top-k concepts.

$$\min_{\alpha,\beta,\gamma} -\frac{1}{k} \sum_{i \in T_k(\alpha,\beta,\gamma)} s_i \quad \text{with} \quad s_i = \alpha \times c_i + \beta \times p_i + \gamma \times h_i \qquad (6)$$

In Eqs. 5 and 6, α, β and γ are respectively the weights for coverage (noted c_i), precision (p_i) and hierarchy (h_i). $T_k(\alpha, \beta, \gamma)$ is the top-k concepts with the highest scores, where k is the number of top concepts considered (e.g., 3) and i is the considered concept. As constraints, we consider that the sum of the weights must be 1 (Eq. 7), that as we seek to obtain an exhaustive and specific concept, coverage is as important as hierarchy, they must be equal (Eq. 8), that precision is, therefore, less important than the other two and must be inferior or equal to them (Eqs. 9, 10) and as each weight should have an impact on the score, all bounds are between 0.1 and 1 (Eq. 11).

$$\alpha + \beta + \gamma = 1 \qquad \text{(weights sum to 1)} \qquad (7)$$
$$\alpha = \gamma \qquad \text{(coverage = hierarchy weight)} \qquad (8)$$
$$\alpha \geq \beta \qquad \text{(coverage} \geq \text{precision)} \qquad (9)$$
$$\gamma \geq \beta \qquad \text{(hierarchy} \geq \text{precision)} \qquad (10)$$
$$0.1 \leq \alpha, \beta, \gamma \leq 0.45 \qquad \text{(coverage/precision/hierarchy bounds)} \qquad (11)$$

We have presented here an enhanced ranking strategy within an existing Concept Induction framework for explainable quality analysis. Building on the ECII framework, we introduce a new evaluation and scoring mechanism based on quantitative metrics to improve the selection of relevant concepts. The proposed ranking methodology is applied to selected use cases to assess its effectiveness in supporting root cause identification and interpretation.

4 Case Study

To evaluate the RCIQ4.0 approach, we employ a manufacturing use case containing machine sensor values, machine failures, and product quality control. Several datasets were considered, including Explainable AI Drilling Dataset [31], Microsoft Azure Predictive Maintenance [21], and Analog Dataset [15]. Those datasets contain machine sensor values and the possibility to detect abnormal machine situations. However, the first two lack any reference to products or quality control, while the third one simulates quality issues by removing components, focusing more on detecting missing parts than actual quality control. This study uses the Predictive Maintenance dataset [20], which provides product information (ID and type), sensor values, and machine failure data, covering two of the three key criteria required. As quality control observations are absent, we initially use product type as a proxy for quality (Sects. 4.1–4.2). We then extend this approach by generating synthetic quality control labels based on the dataset's values and descriptions (Sects. 4.3 and 4.4). The RCIQ4.0 approach and experimental data and results are available online[1].

Table 1. Feature summary of the AI4I 2020 Predictive Maintenance Dataset

Feature	Description
General	
Product ID	Unique identifier for each product
Type	Product quality: L (low), M (medium), H (high)
Temperature Features	
Air Temperature [K]	Random walk, mean 300 K, $\sigma = 2$ K. Normal range: [294, 306] K
Process Temperature [K]	Air temp + 10 K, $\sigma \approx 2.24$ K, mean 310 K. Normal range: [305, 315] K
Temperature Differential (Process - Air)	Normally ≈ 10 K. Below 8.6 K indicates heat dissipation failure
Machine Features	
Rotational Speed [rpm]	Based on 2860 W power, normal range: 700-750 rpm
Torque [Nm]	Normally distributed, mean 40 Nm, $\sigma = 10$ Nm, range: [10, 70] Nm
Tool Feature	
Tool Wear [min]	Wear increases with type: H=5, M=3, L=2 mins; Failures: 200âÅŞ240 mins
Failure Types	
Tool Wear Failure (TWF)	Triggered between 200âÅŞ240 mins of tool wear
Heat Dissipation Failure (HDF)	Temperature diff. < 8.6 K & Speed < 1380 rpm
Power Failure (PWF)	Power < 3500 W or > 9000 W
Overstrain Failure (OSF)	Torque × Tool Wear > 11000(L), 12000(M), 13000(H)
Random Failure (RNF)	Random chance: 0.1% per data point

4.1 Dataset Overview

As mentioned above, the retained dataset is the Predictive Maintenance Dataset [20] (available online). It contains fourteen features described in Table 1. The sensor value features (temperature, machine, and tool features) are used to create constraints, which are then combined into situations and integrated into the *Context Ontology* [11]. Failure types are considered as machine situations and linked to the constraints.

4.2 Application of the RCIQ4.0 Framework

In line with the principle of concept induction, our objective is to generate complex description logic class expressions from a knowledge base to explain quality issues. A representative part of the dataset used is composed of 1000 elements, where each product type and situation is in the same proportion as in the original dataset. Among products, 602 are type L products, 293 are type M products, and 105 are type H products. A total of 34 products are involved in abnormal machine situations, while 966 products are not. To identify the root causes, it is essential to differentiate products based on the outcomes of quality control

---

[1] https://gitlab.insa-rouen.fr/lcharbonnier/rciq4.0.

assessments. The ECII framework requires two sets of examples: a positive set containing instances representing the concept we aim to describe and a negative set containing instances that do not belong to it. Given the absence of explicit quality control outcomes, the Type attribute is used as a proxy. We thus interpret the product types as follows: products of type H or M are considered to have passed quality control, while products of type L are considered to have failed. Therefore, 602 products are deemed defective, while 398 are compliant.

As ECII requires two sets of examples, this labeling approach enables the characterization of non-conforming products through the concepts it derives. A first evaluation of concepts is conducted with the three best concepts selected based on their coverage rate, i.e., the proportion of positive examples correctly captured by each concept. The quality of the concepts is then assessed using confusion matrices, which illustrate the rates of true positives, false positives, true negatives, and false negatives.

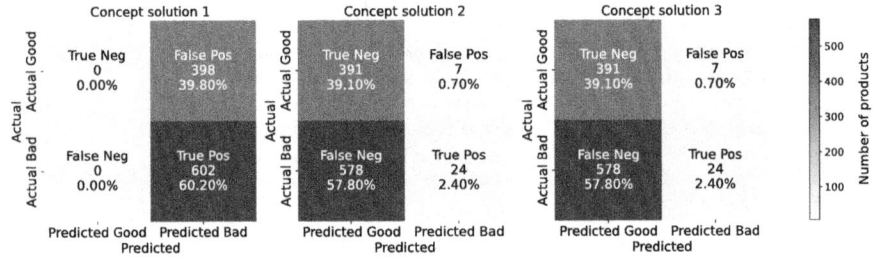

Fig. 2. Confusion matrices for the three concepts with the highest coverage, as determined by the ECII ranking, showing the number/rate of true/false positives and negatives based on predicted vs. actual product types. The color scheme reflects quantity: light blue for fewer products, and dark blue for more. (Color figure online)

As illustrated in Fig. 2, the first concept, Product, is a suitable representation for defective products that failed the quality control, but not for products that passed. Indeed, it cannot distinguish defective products from compliant ones because it represents them all. As we also know that all positive and negative examples are products, there is no interest in considering the concept Product alone. Furthermore, the two other matrices for concepts 2 and 3 are identical. This point arises from the fact that one concept directly represents a machine situation, while the other combines that concept with the Product. Concepts 2 and 3 are respectively:

$$(\text{Product}) \sqcap \exists \text{involvedInSituation}.((\text{Sit-TWF}) \sqcup (\text{Sit-HDF}) \sqcup \qquad (12)$$
$$(\text{Sit-PWF}) \sqcup (\text{Sit-RNF}) \sqcup (\text{Sit-OSF}))$$

$$\exists \text{involvedInSituation}.((\text{Sit-TWF}) \sqcup (\text{Sit-HDF}) \sqcup \qquad (13)$$
$$(\text{Sit-PWF}) \sqcup (\text{Sit-RNF}) \sqcup (\text{Sit-OSF}))$$

Figure 2 also shows that the number of defective products is much higher (602) than the number of products involved in an abnormal machine situation (≈ 20). This yields relatively low coverage of the concepts (around 0.04), making it challenging to draw a reliable interpretation based solely on this metric. To overcome the weakness of coverage, we have introduced new metrics in Sect. 3.3. Each metric is normalized to contribute to a weighted composite score. Since coverage remains an important metric for quantifying the number of products captured by a concept, we normalize it by dividing it by the maximum observed coverage (Eq. 14), ensuring its impact is comparable to the other two metrics. As previously noted, this is feasible because the maximum achievable coverage remains limited, given that only a small proportion of defective products are linked to identifiable abnormal situations relative to the total number of defective products.

$$\text{normalized\_coverage} = \frac{\text{Coverage}}{\text{Maximum coverage}} \qquad (14)$$

where Coverage is defined in Eq. 2, and Maximum coverage refers to the highest coverage observed among all concepts.

The weights α, β, γ are determined through an optimization problem that considers the relative importance of each metric within the domain and an exploratory analysis aimed at maximizing the correlation between the composite score and observed performance. Results of the optimization problem defined in Eq. (6) *for this specific case* are obtained using the *scipy.optimize* module[2], in Eq. (15).

$$\alpha = \beta = \gamma = 0.333 \qquad (15)$$

The weights employed in this case are instance-specific and derived from the characteristics of the underlying data. For other scenarios, the weights must be obtained by solving the corresponding optimization problem using the results from the selected dataset.

The weights obtained are then updated in the weighted sum used as a score in RCIQ4.0, and new results are obtained. We present the final results for the five best concepts selected, ranked according to their weighted score in Table 2. The new metrics put forward more specific concepts. This point is due to taking into account the hierarchy and precision of the concept, as well as adjusting how coverage is calculated. Although the chosen quality control parameter is not an ideal fit, meaningful concepts can still be extracted. The results offer a more balanced performance assessment —combining coverage, precision, and hierarchy— and yield potentially explainable root causes for the quality issue. The object property `involvedInSituation`, which links a product to a situation, provides insight into the abnormal machine conditions associated with defective products. In this case, the system can inform the operator that the quality issue may be related to a fault occurring in `Situation-HDF`.

---

[2] https://docs.scipy.org/doc/scipy/reference/generated/scipy.optimize.minimize.html.

Table 2. Obtained concepts and metrics comparison. The `Original` column shows the framework's original metric (ecii_coverage Eq. 1), while the `New metrics` column includes our proposed metrics: coverage, normalized coverage, hierarchy, precision, and score (Eqs. 2, 14, 4, 3 and 5). The Score metric, defined as the combination of the other metrics according to Eqs. 5, is used to rank the concepts in descending order.

Concepts	Original	New metrics				
	Cov.	Cov.	NCov.	Hier.	Prec.	Score
∃involvedInSit.(Sit-HDF)	0.012	0.020	0.500	**1.00**	0.857	**0.786**
∃involvedInSit.((Sit-OSF) ⊔ (Sit-HDF))	0.017	0.028	**0.708**	0.75	0.850	0.769
∃involvedInSit.((Sit-RNF) ⊔ (Sit-HDF))	0.014	0.023	0.583	0.75	**0.875**	0.736
∃involvedInSit.((Sit-HDF) ⊔ (Sit-TWF))	0.014	0.023	0.583	0.75	**0.875**	0.736
∃involvedInSit.((Sit-PWF) ⊔ (Sit-HDF))	0.017	0.028	**0.708**	0.75	0.739	0.732

The dataset lacks adequate information specific to Quality Assurance. To overcome this limitation, we introduce an additional labeling scheme informed by the following references [9,14,19,28–30,35]. These sources enable us to infer potential quality issues from the available data.

4.3 Dataset Feature Augmentation and Additional Labeling

During an inspection, visible flaws such as heat damage, warping, precision loss, and surface quality are checked. This subsection outlines the motivation for enriching the Predictive Maintenance dataset by introducing a new `Quality Control` label, along with five synthetic observational quality indicators. By using machine sensor readings, these enhancements replicate a post-production quality inspection setup, allowing for the simulation of product defects in conjunction with existing machine failures. The dataset includes the following features that can be used to recreate quality issues:

- **Torque [Nm]**, which is a measure of the rotational force applied during a process (e.g. drilling, milling, turning) [29]. According to [9,19], torque is tightly linked to material resistance, high torque could mean the material is too hard, or the tool is worn out. Misalignment or stress can also happen if the torque is too high or too low. It might indicate a misfit or lack of grip and dimensional inaccuracy as irregular torque often results in uneven cuts, bad finishes, or deviations from tolerances [28]. Therefore, torque can be used to simulate dimensional accuracy (higher torque means poor accuracy) and power instability marks (lower torque means possible power inconsistency).
- **Process Temperature [K]** reflects internal heating from friction, cutting, or electrical components [14,30].
- **Air Temperature [K]** impacts the environment, affecting cooling and thermal expansion. Excessive temperature causes thermal deformation like warping or bending [28], surface defects like burn marks, and material property

Table 3. Evaluation of the impact of each failure type on product quality.

Failure Type	Product impacted?	Description
TWF	Maybe	Only if the tool is not replaced. Should be flagged for *Review*.
HDF	Yes	Heat issues degrade material quality. Mark as *Faulty*.
PWF	Yes	Power instability impacts reliability. Mark as *Faulty*.
OSF	Yes	Overstrain likely causes structural defects. Mark as *Faulty*.
RNF	Probably not	Random and rare. Usually not critical. Mark as *Review*.

Table 4. "Explanation of the Quality Control label values.

Label	Meaning
Good	No failures detected. The product meets all criteria.
Review	Minor or uncertain issue (high surface roughness or `Random Failure`). Needs extra check.
Faulty	Serious defect detected (burn and power instability marks or poor dimensional accuracy). Reject it.

degradation (brittleness or soft spots). Thus, process and air temperature can be used to simulate thermal deformation and burn marks.

- **Tool Wear [min]** measures how long a tool has been in use. A worn tool [35] creates a rougher surface, generates more heat by friction, and reduces precision. Tool wear can be used to simulate surface roughness.

With this knowledge, five synthetic quality-related features are introduced to simulate what might be observed during quality inspection. Parameters and their limits defined in Sect. 4.1 are used to determine the values. Recognizing that not all machine failures result in product defects, we differentiated the failure impacts accordingly; the correspondence is shown in Table 3. Two features are based on heat damage. The first one, *Burn Marks*, is a sign of overheating. A mark is considered if a situation HDF happens during the creation of the product or if `Process temperature` exceeds 320 K. The second, *Thermal Deformation*, is based on excessive temperature. A deformation is considered if `Process temperature` exceeds 315 K or `Air temperature` exceeds 305 K.

Three additional features are defined based on torque measurements, machine fault events, and tool wear data. The first one, *Dimensional Accuracy*, defines three categories for the accuracy. **Poor** if a situation OSF happens during the creation of the product or if `Torque` exceeds 60 Nm, **Acceptable** if it is between 50 and 60 Nm and **Good** if it is under 50 Nm. The second, *Power Instability Marks*, are artifacts resulting from power instability. A mark is considered if a situation PWF happens during the manufacturing process or if `Torque` is under 10 Nm. The third feature, *Surface Roughness*, serves as an indicator of expected surface quality. Three values are based on `Tool wear` : **High** if it exceeds 200 min, **Medium** if it is between 100 and 200 min, and **Low** if it is under 100 min.

Table 5. Obtained concepts and metrics comparison. The `Original` column shows the framework's original metric (ecii_ coverage Eq. 1), while the `New metrics` column includes our proposed metrics: coverage, normalized coverage, hierarchy, precision, and score (Eqs. 2, 4, 3 and 5, 14). The Score metric, defined as the combination of the other metrics according to Eq. 5, is used to rank the concepts in descending order.

Concepts	Original	New metrics				
	Cov.	Cov.	NCov.	Hier.	Prec.	Score
∃involvedInSit.((Sit-PWF) ⊔ (Sit-HDF))	0.023	0.223	0.742	0.75	1.000	**0.831**
∃involvedInSit.(Sit-HDF)	0.014	0.136	0.452	**1.00**	1.000	0.817
∃involvedInSit.((Sit-OSF) ⊔ (Sit-HDF))	0.020	0.194	0.645	0.75	1.000	0.798
∃involvedInSit.((Sit-OSF) ⊔ (Sit-PWF) ⊔ (Sit-HDF))	0.027	0.262	**0.871**	0.50	1.000	0.790
∃involvedInSit.((Sit-RNF) ⊔ (Sit-PWF) ⊔ (Sit-HDF))	0.025	0.243	0.806	0.50	1.000	0.769

A new column, `Quality Control`, is added to the dataset based on failure indicator columns in Table 4, allowing to implement a more realistic quality control for the products. We can then use it to distinguish between failed products and good ones and use these two sets as examples in RCIQ4.0.

4.4 Application of the RCIQ4.0 Framework on the New Dataset

The same portion of the original dataset is used, relabeled with the quality control data defined above. Accordingly, the positive set comprises products marked as *Faulty* or *Review*, whereas the negative set includes those marked as *Good*. This choice results in 103 defective and 897 compliant products.

Table 5 presents the top five concepts ranked by weighted score. `Coverage` is significantly higher than in Table 2 (0.194–0.262 vs. 0.020–0.028), reflecting a larger share of defective products linked to abnormal situations (30 : % vs. 4%). As expected, concepts with higher `Hierarchy` (e.g., 1.00 or 0.75) score better, indicating the ranking favors specificity. `Precision` remains consistently at 1.0, unlike previous values (0.739–0.875), due to the direct link between quality control and machine situations. Overall, the combination of `Coverage` and `Hierarchy` provides a reliable ranking, with the top concept achieving a strong balance of all three metrics.

The proposed metrics effectively highlight precise and interpretable concepts that distinguish between failed and good products. Grounded in observable machine situations, these concepts reveal explainable root causes, providing operators with actionable and trustworthy insights into defect origins.

5 Conclusion and Future Works

We introduce RCIQ4.0, an approach for identifying potential causes of product quality issues on a production line using sensor data from manufacturing equipment. The method differentiates products based on quality control outcomes and leverages a Concept Induction framework to support explainability and root cause analysis. The objective is to extract precise, discriminative concepts that effectively differentiate between compliant and non-compliant products. To improve the selection process, a new evaluation approach is introduced, integrating three key dimensions: instance coverage, classification precision, and hierarchical relevance within the concept space. This composite measure supports a more informed selection of the most meaningful concepts, thereby aiding in the identification of likely causes of quality defects. The approach is validated on the Predictive Maintenance dataset, where an ontology is instantiated with product data, quality control results, and sensor-derived machine failure events. Experimental results demonstrate that the proposed scoring mechanism enhances concept induction performance, enabling more accurate and interpretable identification of factors associated with defective products. The resulting concepts can serve as a comprehensive explanation of the root causes of quality issues.

However, concepts generated using ECII may remain limited in their explanatory power, as the method does not take into account all the information available in the ontology. As a direction for future work, it would be valuable to consider the types and properties of individuals linked to those provided as examples. This could enrich the concepts by incorporating elements related to contextual factors, such as machines and components.

As a further perspective, neuro-symbolic approaches represent a promising direction for addressing more complex use cases that extend beyond the scope of the present work. For example, AutoCL [18] offers a scalable alternative to ECII that can be applied to larger datasets, while methods such as OntoLearn [7] provide robust frameworks for enriched ontology-driven learning and concept extraction. Coupling such approaches with the methodologies presented in this study could open new avenues for scaling, enhancing, and diversifying concept discovery in varied scenarios.

Acknowledgments. This work was supported by the French National Research Agency (grant number ANR-22-CE92-0007).

Disclosure of Interests. The authors have no competing interests to declare that are relevant to the content of this article.

References

1. Abdelrahman, O., Keikhosrokiani, P.: Assembly line anomaly detection and root cause analysis using machine learning. IEEE Access **8**, 189661–189672 (2020). https://doi.org/10.1109/ACCESS.2020.3029826
2. Barredo Arrieta, A., et al.: Explainable Artificial Intelligence (XAI): concepts, taxonomies, opportunities and challenges toward responsible AI. Inform. Fusion **58**, 82–115 (2020). https://doi.org/10.1016/j.inffus.2019.12.012
3. Belton, V., Stewart, T.J.: Multiple criteria decision analysis: an integrated approach. Kluwer (2002)

4. Bühmann, L., Lehmann, J., Westphal, P.: DL-Learner—A framework for inductive learning on the Semantic Web. J. Web Semantics **39**, 15–24 (Aug 2016). https://doi.org/10.1016/j.websem.2016.06.001
5. Charbonnier, L., Giustozzi, F., Saunier, J., Zanni-Merk, C.: Towards a semantic approach to detection of quality issues in manufacturing 4.0. Proc. Comput. Sci. **246**, 2439–2448 (2024). https://doi.org/10.1016/j.procs.2024.09.479
6. Dell'Aglio, D., Della Valle, E., van Harmelen, F., Bernstein, A.: Stream reasoning: a survey and outlook. Data Sci. **1**(1–2), 59–83 (2017)
7. Demir, C., et al.: Ontolearn–a framework for large-scale owl class expression learning in Python. J. Mach. Learn. Res. **26**(63), 1–6 (2025)
8. Detzner, A., Rückschloß, R., Eigner, M.: Root-cause analysis with interactive decision trees. In: 2020 24th International Conference Information Visualisation (IV), pp. 322–327 (Sep 2020). https://doi.org/10.1109/IV51561.2020.00060
9. Dunwoody, K.: Automated identification of cutting force coefficients and tool dynamics on CNC machines. Ph.D. thesis, University of British Columbia (2010). https://doi.org/10.14288/1.0070939, https://open.library.ubc.ca/soa/cIRcle/collections/ubctheses/24/items/1.0070939
10. Fürnkranz, J.: Separate-and-conquer rule learning. Artif. Intell. Rev. **13**(1), 3–54 (1999). https://doi.org/10.1023/A:1006524209794
11. Giustozzi, F., Saunier, J., Zanni-Merk, C.: Context modeling for industry 4.0: an ontology-based proposal. Proc. Comput. Sci. **126**, 675–684 (2018). https://doi.org/10.1016/j.procs.2018.08.001
12. Giustozzi, F., Saunier, J., Zanni-Merk, C.: Abnormal situations interpretation in industry 4.0 using stream reasoning. Proc. Comput. Sci. **159**, 620–629 (2019)
13. Giustozzi, F., Saunier, J., Zanni-Merk, C.: A semantic framework for condition monitoring in Industry 4.0 based on evolving knowledge bases. Semantic Web **15**(2), 583–611 (Apr 2024). https://doi.org/10.3233/SW-233481
14. Haneen H., Abdulaali, Samer M., Abdul Ahleem, A.K.J.K.: The Effect of Machining Parameters on the Temperature Distribution in Metal Cutting Operation | IIETA. https://doi.org/10.18280/ijht.400515
15. Harik, R., et al.: Analog and Multi-modal Manufacturing Datasets Acquired on the Future Factories Platform (Jan 2024). https://doi.org/10.48550/arXiv.2401.15544, arXiv:2401.15544 [cs]
16. Huang, H., Shah, T., Karigiannis, J., Evans, S.: Deep root cause analysis: unveiling anomalies and enhancing fault detection in industrial time series. In: 2024 International Joint Conference on Neural Networks (IJCNN), pp. 1–8 (Jun 2024). https://doi.org/10.1109/IJCNN60899.2024.10650906
17. Keeney, R.L., Raiffa, H.: Decisions with Multiple Objectives: Preferences and Value Trade-Offs. Cambridge University Press, Cambridge (1993). https://doi.org/10.1017/CBO9781139174084
18. Li, J., Satheesh, S., Heindorf, S., Moussallem, D., Speck, R., Ngomo, A.C.N.: AutoCL: AutoML for concept learning. In: Explainable Artificial Intelligence, pp. 117–136 (2024). https://doi.org/10.1007/978-3-031-63787-2_7
19. Matsubara, A., Ibaraki, S.: Monitoring and control of cutting forces in machining processes: a review. Int. J. Autom. Technol. **3**(4), 445–456 (July 2009). https://doi.org/10.20965/ijat.2009.p0445
20. Matzka, S.: Explainable artificial intelligence for predictive maintenance applications. In: 2020 Third International Conference on Artificial Intelligence for Industries (AI4I), pp. 69–74 (2020). https://doi.org/10.1109/AI4I49448.2020.00023
21. Microsoft: Azure/AI-PredictiveMaintenance (May 2018). https://github.com/Azure/AI-PredictiveMaintenance, original-date: 2018-01-11T23:43:24Z

22. e Oliveira, E., Miguéis, V.L., Borges, J.L.: Automatic root cause analysis in manufacturing: an overview & conceptualization. J. Intell. Manufact. **34**(5), 2061–2078 (Jun 2023). https://doi.org/10.1007/s10845-022-01914-3
23. Raisul Islam, M., et al.: Deep learning and computer vision techniques for enhanced quality control in manufacturing processes. IEEE Access **12**, 121449–121479 (2024). https://doi.org/10.1109/ACCESS.2024.3453664
24. Rehak, J., Sommer, A., Becker, M., Pfrommer, J., Beyerer, J.: Counterfactual root cause analysis via anomaly detection and causal graphs. In: 2023 IEEE 21st International Conference on Industrial Informatics (INDIN), pp. 1–7 (Jul 2023). https://doi.org/10.1109/INDIN51400.2023.10218245, iSSN: 2378-363X
25. Sarker, M.K., Hitzler, P.: Efficient concept induction for description logics. In: Proceedings of the Thirty-Third AAAI Conference on Artificial Intelligence and Thirty-First Innovative Applications of Artificial Intelligence Conference and Ninth AAAI Symposium on Educational Advances in Artificial Intelligence, vol. 33, pp. 3036–3043. AAAI Press (Jan 2019). https://doi.org/10.1609/aaai.v33i01.33013036
26. Scholl, C., Spiegler, M., Ludwig, K., Eskofier, B.M., Tobola, A., Zanca, D.: An integrated framework for data quality fusion in embedded sensor systems. Sensors **23**(8), 3798 (2023). https://doi.org/10.3390/s23083798
27. Shabur, M.A.: A comprehensive review on the impact of Industry 4.0 on the development of a sustainable environment. Discover Sustain. **5**(1), 97 (May 2024). https://doi.org/10.1007/s43621-024-00290-7
28. SMART Vietnam: Preventing Warping and Distortion. http://smartsheetmetal.com.vn/en/news/preventing-warping-and-distortion-a-guide-for-sheet-metal-fabricators.html
29. Unipulse: Torque meter that measures rotating force. https://www.unipulse.tokyo/en/mm_log/20210127-torque.html
30. U.S. department of Energy: Process Heat Basics. https://www.energy.gov/eere/iedo/process-heat-basics
31. Wallsberger, R., Knauer, R., Matzka, S.: Explainable artificial intelligence in mechanical engineering: a synthetic dataset for comprehensive failure mode analysis. In: 2023 Fifth International Conference on Transdisciplinary AI (TransAI), pp. 249–252 (Sep 2023). https://doi.org/10.1109/TransAI60598.2023.00032
32. Widmer, C.L., et al.: Towards human-compatible XAI. J. Web Semantics **79**, 100807 (Dec 2023). https://doi.org/10.1016/j.websem.2023.100807
33. Witzgall, C., Fletcher, R.: Practical methods of optimization. In: Mathematics of Computation, vol. 53, p. 768 (Oct 1989). https://doi.org/10.2307/2008742
34. Zhang, C., Hu, D., Yang, T.: Research of artificial intelligence operations for wind turbines considering anomaly detection, root cause analysis, and incremental training. Reliab. Eng. Syst. Safety **241**, 109634 (Jan 2024). https://doi.org/10.1016/j.ress.2023.109634
35. Şahin, O., Karayel, D., Ertürk, M.A., Nart, E., Seçgin, O.: Experimental investigation of the effects of coolant temperature on cutting tool wear in the machining process. Machines **12**(10), 677 (2024). https://doi.org/10.3390/machines12100677

An Optimized Framework for DSPG Synthesis and Trust Network Analysis with Subjective Logic

Koffi Ismael Ouattara[1,2](✉), Ana Petrovska[1], Ioannis Krontiris[1], Theo Dimitrakos[1], and Frank Kargl[2]

[1] Huawei Technologies, Munich, Germany
{koffi.ismael.ouattara,ana.petrovska,ioannis.krontiris,
theo.dimitrakos}@huawei.com
[2] Ulm Universität, Ulm, Germany

Abstract. Subjective Logic-based trust reasoning requires the network to be a Directed Series-Parallel Graph (DSPG). However, most real-world trust graphs do not meet this condition, and existing transformation methods often remove uncertain edges, causing unnecessary information loss. In this paper, we propose a new DSPG synthesis framework that prioritizes structural integrity and information preservation. At its core is the concept of Parallel Non-intersecting Path Subnetworks (PNPS), which refines existing definitions and enables clearer identification of DSPG violations. We also introduce optimized synthesis criteria that admit more edges while maintaining DSPG compliance. In addition to the theoretical contributions from the framework, we also propose an algorithm for DSPG synthesis that ensures correctness, avoids edge removal, and enhances trust inference. Our experiments demonstrate reduced uncertainty in derived opinions and more reliable decision-making in trust-based systems.

Keywords: Subjective Logic · Trust Network Analysis · Directed Series-Parallel Graphs · Uncertainty Reasoning

1 Introduction

Trust Network Analysis with Subjective Logic (TNA-SL) is a framework for reasoning under uncertainty in graphs that model trust relationships. It leverages Subjective Logic operators such as fusion and discounting to derive opinions along trust paths. A key requirement of TNA-SL is that the underlying trust network must be a Directed Series-Parallel Graph (DSPG), which ensures the sound application of these operators. When the network does not satisfy the DSPG property, a DSPG transformation process is applied to modify the graph, often by discarding edges. However, this transformation may result in the removal of relevant trust information, leading to suboptimal derived opinions.

The process of modifying a non-DSPG into a DSPG is called *DSPG Transformation* (also referred to as DSPG Synthesis throughout the paper), whereas the process of deriving a final trust opinion through root-to-leaf propagation in the DSPG graph is called *DSPG analysis*.

Problem. Despite its utility, TNA-SL—as originally proposed by Jøsang [4]—has several limitations. Namely, it introduces complexity both in its logic and in its implementation; and it relies on intricate criteria involving nesting levels of edges, which are difficult to apply. A simple transformation into a DSPG is generally achieved by removing uncertain paths, assuming that reducing uncertainty is the primary goal. Yet, this approach may sacrifice structurally meaningful information that could enrich trust reasoning and reduce overall uncertainty. Park [13] has also shown that the canonical transformation does not always yield the least uncertain opinion, further questioning the method's optimality.

Contribution. In this paper, we introduce an optimized framework for DSPG transformation that enhances trust reasoning while preserving structural integrity. We make three main contributions:

1. As part of our optimized framework for DSPG synthesis, we first define the concept of *Parallel Non-intersecting Path Subnetwork (PNPS)*, which refines the original definition of Parallel Path Subnetwork (PPS) and provides a new foundation for DSPG analysis. This makes the DSPG analysis easier to implement and more optimized. Second, we propose an *Optimized Criteria for DSPG Synthesis*. Our criteria ensure that only edges that truly violate DSPG properties are removed.
2. As a second contribution, we design a *new algorithm for DSPG Synthesis* that guarantees both correctness and maximal information retention. It avoids unnecessary edge removal and improves downstream trust evaluations, as we demonstrate through empirical analysis.
3. Finally, we validate our theoretical framework and algorithmic contributions through empirical evaluation.

To facilitate reproducibility, the complete implementation code, experimental data, and supplementary materials—including detailed algorithmic specifications and proofs, are available in our GitHub repository [9].

Structure. The remainder of the paper is organized as follows. Section 2 provides the necessary background on Subjective Logic and DSPGs. Section 3 formalizes the problem addressed in this work, highlighting the limitations of existing DSPG transformation approaches. In Sect. 4, we introduce the concept of Parallel Non-intersecting Path Subnetworks and present our reformulation of DSPG analysis, including the revised DSPG criteria. Section 5 details the proposed Optimized DSPG Transformation algorithm. Section 6 presents an empirical evaluation of the approach, focusing on uncertainty reduction and information preservation. Section 7 discusses related work on DSPG theory and trust network simplification. We reflect on the broader implications and limitations of our method in Sect. 8, and finally, in Sect. 9 we conclude our paper.

2 Subjective Logic Preliminaries

2.1 Subjective Opinions

Subjective Logic (SL) [4] is a probabilistic logic framework designed to reason under uncertainty by explicitly modeling belief, disbelief, and uncertainty. It is widely used in reputation based system [8] and neural network trust assessment [10,11]. It extends classical and Bayesian logic to support subjective opinions that reflect partial or incomplete knowledge. Subjective Logic introduces uncertainty as a first-class element, permitting random variables to explicitly quantify confidence (or lack thereof) in a given proposition. The notion of *subjective opinion* is one of the main building blocks of the SL theory. A binomial subjective opinion about an event x of binary variable X held by agent A is represented as: $\omega^A_{X=x} = (b, d, u, a)$ where b is the belief mass supporting $X = x$ being true, d is the disbelief mass supporting $X = x$ being false, u is the uncertainty mass (i.e., the lack of evidence), and a is the base rate (the prior probability of $X = x$).

These components satisfy the constraint: $b + d + u = 1$, and the projected probability of $X = x$ being true is defined as: $P(x) = b(x) + a(x) \cdot u(x)$.

Subjective Logic provides a rigorous mathematical framework for reasoning in environments where knowledge is incomplete, conflicting, or uncertain—an essential feature in trust-based systems.

2.2 Subjective Trust Networks

A subjective trust network models the trust relationships among various agents or entities using Subjective Logic opinions. Each node in the network represents an entity, and each directed edge represents the trust of one entity toward another, expressed as a binomial opinion. Formally, a trust network is represented as a directed graph $G = (V, E)$ where each edge $(A, B) \in E$ carries an opinion ω^A_B about the trustworthiness of B according to A. To infer trust from a source node to a target node that are not directly connected, SL employs two key operators:

- **Discounting** ($\otimes$) [2,12]: Used to propagate trust through intermediaries and it captures the concept of trust transitivity. If A trusts B, and B trusts C, then A can derive a discounted opinion about C (cf. Figure 1a).

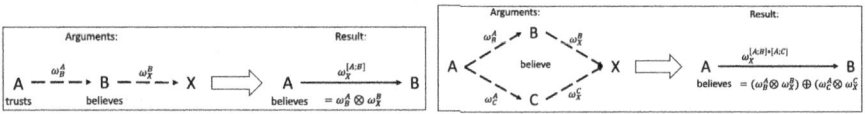

(a) Trust discounting of opinions (b) Fusion of trust-discounted opinions

Fig. 1. Trust operators [4].

- **Fusion** (⊕) [7]: Used to combine multiple trust opinions about the same entity (cf. Figure 1b).

These operations require that the underlying graph structure satisfies certain properties. In particular, trust computation using only these operators is guaranteed to be valid and well-defined when the graph is a Directed Series-Parallel Graph (DSPG). When the network is not a DSPG, transformation is necessary—a core focus of this paper.

2.3 Directed Series-Parallel Graphs (DSPG)

In Trust Network Analysis with Subjective Logic (TNA-SL), Directed Series-Parallel Graphs (DSPGs) serve as the canonical structure for enabling valid trust computation using discounting and fusion operators. These operations are only well-defined when applied to graphs that respect specific structural properties, namely those of a DSPG.

We begin by defining the notion of a Series-Parallel Graph, which forms the basis for DSPGs.

Definition 1 (Series-Parallel Graph). *An SP-graph (Series-Parallel graph) can be recursively reduced to a single edge between the source node s and the sink node t using the following two procedures:*

(i) Replace a pair of edges incident to a node of degree 2 (excluding source and sink) with a single edge.
(ii) Replace a pair of parallel edges with a single edge between their common endpoints.

For clarity, Fig. 2 illustrates a step-by-step graph reduction. The example demonstrates four reductions: *Reduction 1* is obtained by applying procedure (i) four times. *Reduction 2* results from two applications of procedure (ii). *Reduction 3* is obtained by two more applications of procedure (i). Finally, in Reduction 4 a single edge is produced by a single application of procedure (ii). The fact that the graph reduces into a single edge in this way proves that it is an SP-graph.

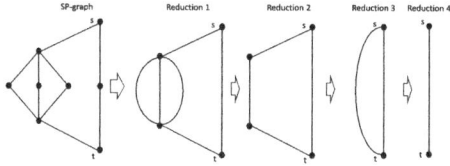

Fig. 2. Procedure for reducing an SP-graph into a single edge, from [4].

An SP-graph that is also directed and acyclic, and that contains a unique source and sink, is referred to as a Directed Series-Parallel Graph (DSPG).

Definition 2. *A DSPG is a directed, acyclic SP-graph composed entirely of paths from a unique source node to a unique sink node.*

These definitions are essential to ensure the proper reduction of DSPGs during trust propagation and to detect potential violations of DSPG structure that require transformation.

Furthermore, in the context of a subjective trust network, DSPG analysis refers to the process of computing the derived opinion of a source on a target using only SL fusion and discounting. This computation is possible only when the trust graph is a DSPG.

To model the structural constraints in DSPG analysis, the following definitions have been introduced in [4]:

Definition 3 (Parallel Path Subnetwork (PPS)). *A Parallel Path Subnetwork (PPS) is a subgraph between two connected nodes A and B where:*

- *the out-degree of node A, denoted outDegree(A) (i.e., the number of outgoing edges from A), is at least 2, and*
- *the in-degree of node B, denoted inDegree(B) (i.e., the number of incoming edges to B), is at least 2.*

Definition 4 (Nesting Level(NL)). *The nesting level of an edge in a DSPG is defined as the number PPSs the edge belongs to.*

Per these definitions, the PPS list in Fig. 3a consists of (A, C), (C, G), and (A, G), yielding an edge nesting level of 2. Furthermore, based on these definitions, Jøsang [4] proposed an algorithm for computing trust over DSPGs. The flowchart of the proposed algorithm can be seen in Fig. 4a. This method replaces each PPS with a single edge during reduction, updating its nesting level accordingly (see Step (f) in Fig. 4a).

3 Problem Statement

In real-world applications, trust networks are often not DSPGs, which prevents direct application of the SL trust operators. Therefore, a transformation step is required to convert a non-DSPG into a DSPG. This step is called *DSPG transformation* or *DSPG synthesis*—terms we use interchangeably throughout this paper.

Several approaches have been proposed in the literature to achieve this transformation. The most common strategy incrementally builds a DSPG by adding one *path* at a time, verifying at each step whether the graph maintains the DSPG property [5,6]. The paths are chosen from the initial non-DSPG graph, that is being transformed during this process. Additionally, the verification process involves assessing the DSPG Synthesis Criteria, which we examine in depth and address its limitations in Sect. 4.3. The primary limitation of this approach lies in its overly restrictive criteria, which can result in the removal of valuable edges and consequent information loss. Furthermore, previously proposed DSPG transformation methods assume that minimizing uncertainty is the primary objective of trust network analysis. This assumption is based on the observation that, during trust fusion, a more uncertain opinion tends to increase the uncertainty of the resulting opinion. Consequently, early solutions such as [5,6] adopted a greedy approach that prioritizes the inclusion of the most certain paths first. However, this reasoning overlooks an important property of cumulative fusion: the fused result is often less uncertain than each of the individual opinions, as we demonstrate in Theorem 1. In such cases, adding additional sources of information—even if they are uncertain—can reduce overall uncertainty.

Theorem 1. *Given two opinions $\omega_X^A = (\mathbf{b}_X^A, u_X^A, \mathbf{a}_X^A)$ and $\omega_X^B = (\mathbf{b}_X^B, u_X^B, \mathbf{a}_X^B)$, the uncertainty of their cumulative fusion $\omega_X^{A \diamond B} = \omega_X^A \oplus \omega_X^B$ is always less than or equal to the minimum of the individual uncertainties: $u_X^{A \diamond B} \leq \min(u_X^A, u_X^B)$*

Proof. From the cumulative fusion formula:

$$u_X^{A \diamond B} = \frac{u_X^A u_X^B}{u_X^A + u_X^B - u_X^A u_X^B}$$

We can show that:

$$\frac{u_X^A}{u_X^{A \diamond B}} = 1 + \frac{u_X^A}{u_X^B} - u_X^A \geq 1 \quad \Rightarrow \quad u_X^A \geq u_X^{A \diamond B}$$

and similarly for u_X^B, which completes the proof.

This insight shifts the transformation objective: rather than prioritizing low-uncertainty paths, the primary goal should be to preserve as much information as possible, ensuring that no valuable trust edge is discarded unnecessarily. As a secondary objective, path inclusion may take into account the relative uncertainty of opinions, possibly prioritizing more informative (even if uncertain) edges over redundant or low-impact ones.

While uncertainty minimization is often desirable, the primary goal of DSPG transformation should be to preserve as much structural trust information as possible without violating the graph constraints required for valid inference. Our method reorients the transformation objective accordingly.

4 Contributions

4.1 New PPS Definition

As a first contribution, we provide an updated definition of the PPS (Definition 3). The updated PPS definition, is necessary for the rest of the contributions that we make as part of the proposed framework.

Definition 5 (Parallel Non-intersecting Path Subnetwork (PNPS)). *A PNPS is a PPS (A, B) for which there exist at least two non-intersecting paths from the source A to the sink B.*

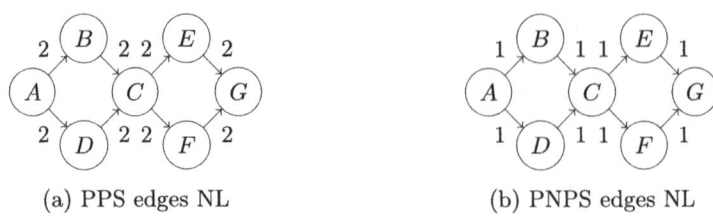

Fig. 3. Comparison of PPS and PNPS structures.

Please note that Nesting Level of a PNPS = $min(NL(edge))$ for all edges inside this PNPS. Figure 3 illustrates the distinction between PPS and PNPS. For example, while (A, G) qualifies as a PPS, it is not a PNPS due to the absence of two non-intersecting paths between A and G.

In the following sections, we introduce a streamlined definition of non-DSPG that enhances both (1) detection efficiency and (2) DSPG synthesis from non-DSPG. Central to this approach is replacing PPS (Parallel Path Subnetworks) with PNPS (Parallel Non-intersecting Path Subnetworks), which provides stronger structural guarantees for DSPG analysis.

4.2 New DSPG Definition

Proposition 1 (DSPG Structural Constraint). *A graph is not a DSPG if and only if there exists a PNPS whose intermediate node has either an outgoing edge to a node outside the PNPS, or an incoming edge from a node outside the PNPS. Equivalently, if it is possible to exit a PNPS from an intermediate node without reaching its target (or, by reversing the graph, to enter before reaching the source), then the graph is not DSPG and violates the DSPG conditions in Definition 1.*

This proposition allows for an optimized detection and reduction strategy: Any PNPS that violates this constraint cannot be reduced to a single edge. Based on this result, we optimized the algorithm proposed by Jøsang by iterating over PNPS structures rather than PPS. Figure 4 compares both algorithms. Below, we formally establish their equivalence by proving the following theorem:

Theorem 2 (PNPS Reduction Preservation and Nesting Update). *Let G be a DSPG, and let $pnps_1$ be a Parallel Non-intersecting Path Subnetwork (PNPS) in G with the maximum Nesting Level. Then:*

1. *(**Isolated Transformation**) Transforming $pnps_1$ into a single edge does not affect the Nesting Level of any other PNPS in the graph.*
2. *(**Nesting Level Update**) The edge that replaces $pnps_1$ has a Nesting Level equal to $NL(pnps_1) - 1$.*

Before proving Theorem 2, we need to introduce several elementary results that characterize the structural relationships between nested PNPSs. These results are necessary to justify both the isolation property and the nesting level update described above.

Theorem 3. *Consider a DSPG and two PNPSs, $pnps_1$ and $pnps_2$, such that $NL(pnps_1) > NL(pnps_2)$. Then:*

1. *If a node s is the common source of both $pnps_1$ and $pnps_2$, then s must have at least one outgoing edge that is in $pnps_2$ but not in $pnps_1$.*
2. *If a node t is the common target of both $pnps_1$ and $pnps_2$, then t must have at least one incoming edge that is in $pnps_2$ but not in $pnps_1$.*

Proof. For part 1 of the theorem. If $NL(pnps_1) > NL(pnps_2)$, then $pnps_1$ and $pnps_2$ don't have the same target (since they already have the same source). Thus:

– either $pnps_1$ is inside $pnps_2$: If s does not have at least one outgoing edge to a node which is inside $pnps_2$ and outside $pnps_1$ it means that all paths from s to target of $pnps_2$ will be through $pnps_1$ since from an intermediate node of $pnps_1$ we cannot go outside $pnps_1$ without reaching the target of $pnps_1$. The consequence is that we will not be able to find two non-intersecting paths therefore the graph is not DSPG;
– or $pnps_1$ is not inside $pnps_2$ and $Nodes(pnps_1) \cap Nodes(pnps_1) \neq \{s\}$: In this case the graph cannot be a DSPG because it means that $pnps_1$ has an intermediate node n_1 inside $pnps_2$ (which are not s) and a node n_2 outside $pnps_2$. n_2 is an intermediate node of $pnps_2$ (otherwise it's the target node of $pnps_2$, and in this case it impossible to have $NL(pnps_1) > NL(pnps_2)$). Therefore, from n_1 (intermediate node of $pnps_2$) we can reach n_2 (outside $pnps_2$) without visiting the target of $pnps_2$
– or $pnps_1$ is not inside $pnps_2$ and $Nodes(pnps_1) \cap Nodes(pnps_1) = \{s\}$: In this case s has at least one outgoing edge to a node which is inside $pnps_2$ and outside $pnps_1$

The part 2 of the theorem is the dual case of item. Reverse the graph and apply the same reasoning.

Corollary 1. *Considering a DSPG, if a PNPS $pnps_1$ is nested in another PNPS $pnps_2$ and $pnps_1 \neq pnps_2$, then $pnps_2$ has at least one edge not in $pnps_1$.*

Proof. If a PNPS $pnps_1$ is nested in another PNPS $pnps_2$, we can distinguish between two cases:

1. $pnps_1$ and $pnps_2$ do not share the same source and also do not share the same target nodes: if they don't have the same source then the path from the source of $pnps_2$ to the source of $pnps_1$ contains edges outside $pnps_1$. Same reasoning if they don't have the same target.
2. $pnps_1$ shares the source or the target (or both) with $pnps_2$: application of Theorems 3 and 3.

We now return to the proof of Theorem 2 stated above.

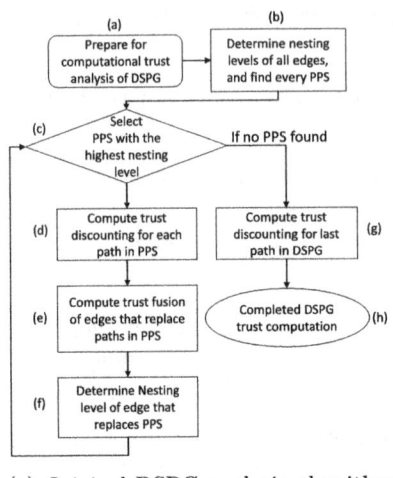
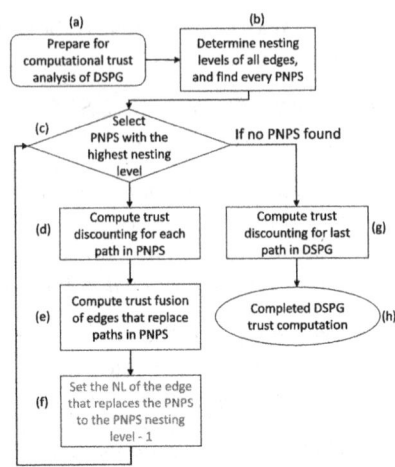

(a) Original DSPG analysis algorithm by Jøsang [4, Ch.15.3]

(b) Our optimized DSPG analysis algorithm

Fig. 4. Comparison of DSPG synthesis algorithms.

Proof. When reducing a PNPS with the maximum Nesting Level (denoted as $pnps_1$), two structural cases arise:

1. $pnps_1$ is a non nested PNPS, or
2. $pnps_1$ is nested within another PNPS (denoted as $pnps_2$).

In case (1), $pnps_1$ has a Nesting Level equal to 1. After its reduction, all other PNPSs remains the same and the resulting edge has a Nesting Level of 0. In the case (2), since at least one edge—denoted as e—in $pnps_2$ is not part of $pnps_1$ (Corrolary 1), $NL(e)$ will remain unchanged and we select it such that its Nesting Level equals that of $pnps_2$ (this follows from Theorems 3 and 3 with $pnps_1$ Nested Level equals $pnps_2$ Nesting Level plus 1. Such a PNPS($pnps_2$) exists, as the Nesting Level increments one by one). As a result, the Nesting Level of $pnps_1$ is preserved, since the new edge has Nesting Level reduced by one which is still greater than or equal to that of $pnps_2$.

4.3 Analysis of DSPG Synthesis Criteria

In Sect. 3, we introduced the DSPG Synthesis Criteria, which determine whether adding a path would violate the DSPG property. These criteria play a key role in DSPG synthesis—the process of transforming a non-DSPG into a DSPG graph. In this section, we first analyze the original criteria proposed by Jøsang and discuss their limitations. Subsequently, in Sect. 4.4, we present our optimized criteria for DSPG synthesis.

The original criteria (Jøsang's criteria) are defined as follows:

1. The target node (of the branch) must be reachable from the source node (of the branch) in the existing graph.
2. The source and target nodes must have equal nesting levels in the existing graph.
3. The nesting level of the source and target nodes must be less than or equal to the nesting level of all intermediate nodes in the existing graph.

Note that we focus on branches rather than root-to-leaf paths, where a branch may consist of a single edge, multiple edges, or an entire path.

In the next step, to enhance clarity and precision, we reformulate the original criteria by formally specifying the conditions under which a branch may be incorporated into a DSPG while ensuring that the resulting graph remains DSPG.

Corollary 2 (DSPG Criteria). *Let A and B be two nodes already existing in the graph. To safely add an edge from A to B without violating the DSPG structure, the following must hold:*

– **Criterion 1:** *There exists at least one path from A to B in the current graph.*
– **Criterion 2:** *If A is an intermediate node in a PNPS p, then B must also be an intermediate node in p; and vice versa.*

These criteria ensure DSPG compliance but are overly conservative— for instance, they may exclude branches that would not compromise the DSPG property. Figure 5a illustrates this limitation: an edge from B to E would be disallowed by Criterion 2 even though it does not break the DSPG condition.

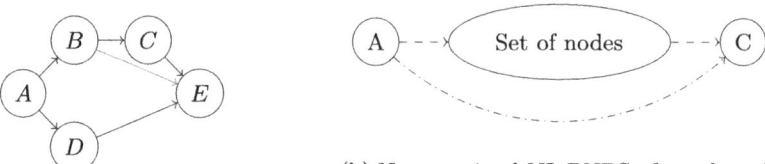

(a) Sub-optimality of Original Criteria

(b) New maximal-NL PNPS after edge addition

Fig. 5. Illustrative example supporting the proof of the DSPG synthesis criteria.

Next, in Theorem 4, we demonstrate the equivalence between the Original Criteria and Corollary 2. To establish this result, we first introduce the concept of Node Nesting Level (NNL). While Jøsang previously defined the Nesting Level (NL) for edges (Definition 4), no formal definition was provided for node nesting levels—despite their implicit use in his criteria as presented above. To address this gap, we define the Node Nesting Level as follows:

Definition 6 (Node Nesting Level (NNL)). *The Nesting Level of a node is equal to the maximum nesting level of all PNPSs in which it is an intermediate node. If the node does not belong to any PNPS as an intermediate node, its nesting level is 0. Note that the Nesting Level of the source and sink of the whole graph will always be equal to 0.*

Contrapositive Reasoning Lemma. We use the following logical lemma in some of our proofs to derive contrapositives of equivalences involving structural criteria.

Lemma 1. *Let H, I, J, and K be logical statements. Suppose we want to prove the equivalence:*
$$(H \wedge I) \Leftrightarrow (J \Leftrightarrow K).$$
We can analyze this equivalence using contrapositive reasoning as follows.
  First, recall that:
$$\neg (H \wedge I) = \neg H \vee \neg I$$
and
$$\neg (J \Leftrightarrow K) = \neg ((J \Rightarrow K) \wedge (K \Rightarrow J)) = (J \wedge \neg K) \vee (K \wedge \neg J).$$

  Therefore, proving the equivalence: $(H \wedge I) \Leftrightarrow (J \Leftrightarrow K)$ is logically equivalent to proving:
$$(J \wedge \neg K) \vee (K \wedge \neg J) \Leftrightarrow \neg H \vee \neg I.$$

  In particular, if we only want to prove a one-way implication: $(H \wedge I) \Rightarrow (J \Rightarrow K)$, we can equivalently prove the contrapositive:
$$(J \wedge \neg K) \Rightarrow (\neg H \vee \neg I).$$

We apply this lemma in the proofs of Theorem 4 and Theorem 5.

Theorem 4 (Equivalence of Criteria). *Jøsang's criteria are logically equivalent to those defined in Corollary 2 when the current graph is DSPG.*

Proof (based on the logical structure outlined in Lemma 1). We want to prove that $NNL(A) = NNL(B)$, and that all intermediate node C between A and B should have $NNL(C) \geq NNL(A) \Leftrightarrow A$ is an intermediate node of a PNPS p if and only if B is an intermediate node of p.

($\Rightarrow$) If A is an intermediate node of a PNPS p and B is not. This means that the sink C of p is before B in a path from A to B. Therefore, $NNL(C) < NNL(A)$. The same logic applies when B is an intermediate node of a PNPS p and A is not.

($\Leftarrow$) If $NNL(A) \neq NNL(B)$ then by definition we can find a PNPS in which one node (A or B) is an intermediate node, but the other not.

4.4 Optimized Criteria for DSPG Synthesis

In this section, we propose optimized criteria for DSPG synthesis, which is a generalization of the original criteria. The optimized criteria are designed to be more inclusive without compromising correctness.

- **Criterion 1:** There exists a path from A to B.
- **Criterion 2:**
   1. If A is an intermediate node in any PNPS p, then B must be inside (either intermediate node or source or target) p.
   2. If B is an intermediate node in any PNPS p, then A must be inside p.

These criteria are an extension of previous ones in the sense that now we allow a branch from source to intermediate node of the same PNPS or from intermediate node to target of the same PNPS—previously disallowed.

Theorem 5 (Soundness and Completeness of Optimized Criteria). *Let $A \to B$ be a branch:*

1. *If it passes the improved criteria above, then the resulting graph is DSPG.*
2. *If the branch does not break the DSPG property, it satisfies the improved criteria.*

Proof (based on the logical structure outlined in Lemma 1). For 1: We know that if A is an intermediate node of a PNPS p then B is an intermediate node of p and if B is an intermediate node of a PNPS p then A is an intermediate node of p implies that the DSPG property not broken. What we need to show in this proof is that adding an edge from the source to an intermediate node or from an intermediate node to the sink inside a PNPS p with maximum Nesting Level does not affect the DSPG property of the graph. We are doing the proof for the maximum NL because it is the same as doing the proof for any PNPS since what we want to know is whether we can still reduce a PNPS to a single edge using the DSPG analysis algorithm depicted in Fig. 4b. During the reduction process, the reduction will be done for this PNPS when the PNPS will be the most nested (the PNPS with maximum Nesting Level).

- add an edge from the source A to an intermediate node C: Assuming that the current PNPS has max NL, adding this branch does not break the DSPG property because after adding this branch the max NL will be increased by one. Then the new PNPS with maximum NL will be the new one created $[A, C]$. This new PNPS will be like Fig. 5b because it is clear that there is only one path from A to C otherwise A and C would have been the source and sink of a PNPS with NL greater than NL of p.
- add an edge from an intermediate node C to the target B: Same logic as before. We can just reverse the graph and use the same proof.

For 2: A to B does not break DPSG property. Assuming that the first criterion of criteria defined in Corollary 2 is fulfilled, then Proposition 1 implies that A to B fulfilled Criterion 2 of the optimized Criteria for DSPG Synthesis.

Theorem 6. *Using nesting levels, these criteria can be restated as:*

- *Criterion 1: A path from A to B exists.*
- *Criterion 2: $|NNL(A) - NNL(B)| \leq 1$ and all intermediate nodes have nesting levels $\geq \min(NNL(A), NNL(B))$.*

The only difference compared to original criteria is that $NNL(A) = NNL(B)$ becomes $|NNL(A) - NNL(B)| \leq 1$ which illustrates the fact that we want to allow edges from source to intermediate nodes or from intermediate nodes to target. Please note that the first criterion prevents adding edges from target to intermediate nodes or from intermediate nodes to source.

Proof. We want to prove that: $|NNL(A) - NNL(B)| \leq 1$ and the nesting level of the source and target nodes must be equal to or less than the nesting level of all intermediate nodes in the existing graph. $\Leftrightarrow$ If Node A is intermediate node of a PNPS p then B is inside (either intermediate node or source or target) p and if Node B is intermediate node of a PNPS p then A is inside (either intermediate node or source or target) p. We reason by contraposition:

$\Rightarrow$) Assume that A is an intermediate node of a PNPS p and B is not inside. This means that the sink C of this PNPS is before B in a path from A to B. Therefore, $NNL(C) < NNL(A) < \max(NNL(A), NNL(B))$. Same logic if B is an intermediate node of a PNPS p and A is not inside.

$\Leftarrow$) Assume that $|NNL(A) - NNL(B)| \geq 2$ then by definition (node nesting level definition) we can find a PNPS p such that one node (A or B) is intermediate node of p but the other is not inside p. Let assume that $NNL(A) > NNL(B)$. Considering the PNPS p that contains A with Nesting Level $= NNL(A)$, it's obvious that B is neither intermediate node of this PNPS (because otherwise his Nesting Level would have been $\geq NNL(A)$, nor a source or sink (because otherwise his NNL would have been $\geq NNL(A) - 1$).

5 Algorithm for DSPG Synthesis

We present a concrete implementation of the DSPG Synthesizer based on the improved criteria defined earlier. Algorithm 1 outlines the proposed synthesis process. Additional details about the algorithm, including implementation, supporting materials, and full correctness proofs, are available in our GitHub repository [9].

In the following, we argue that the algorithm correctly performs DSPG synthesis under the assumption that the variable `nodesToPNPS` is properly maintained. Specifically, we show that correct updates to this mapping ensure both the soundness and efficiency of the synthesis process. Due to space limitations, we omit the full formal proof and detailed behavior of the `UpdatePNPS` function, which can be found in the supplementary material online.

Algorithm 1 Synthesize DSPG from Non-DSPG Graph

Require: DAG $G = (V, E)$
Ensure: DSPG $G' \subseteq G$
1: $paths \leftarrow$ GetAllPaths(G), sorted by uncertainty or length
2: $G' \leftarrow$ paths.pop() ▷ Initialize with most promising path
3: $nodeToPNPS \leftarrow \{\}$ ▷ Track the most nested PNPS membership for each node
4: **while** $paths \neq \emptyset$ **do**
5:     $path \leftarrow$ paths.pop()
6:     $branch \leftarrow$ the first branch of the path not in G
7:     $(src, tgt) \leftarrow$ (source($branch$), target($branch$))
8:     $check \leftarrow$ DSPGChecker($nodeToPNPS, src, tgt$)
9:     **if** $check.bool =$ True **then**
10:         G'.addEdges($branch$)
11:         **for** $n \in$ check.intermediateNodes **do**
12:             UpdatePNPS($nodeToPNPS, n, (src, tgt)$) ▷ Details on github [9]
13:         **end for**
14:     **end if**
15: **end while**

Theorem 7. *Let a and b two nodes, and assume that we have a mapping nodesToPNPS which maps a node to the highest nested PNPS it is part of. Therefore, we have: $nodesToPNPS[a] = \emptyset$ or $b \in nodesToPNPS[a] \Leftrightarrow$ if Node a is intermediate node of a PNPS p then b is inside p*

Proof. $\Rightarrow$) if $nodesToPNPS[a] = \emptyset$ then a is not part of any PNPS. Therefore the second part of the equivalence is True. If $b \in nodesToPNPS[a]$ therefore b is part of the most nested PNPS that contains a. This implies that b is part of any PNPS that contains a because all other PNPSs containing a contain also $nodesToPNPS[a]$.

$\Leftarrow$) if Node a is intermediate node of a PNPS p then b is inside p. It means that b is part of any PNPS a is intermediate node of. Therefore b is part of $nodesToPNPS[a]$ since it is a PNPS for which a is an intermediate node.

6 Evaluation

We assess the practical benefits of our optimized DSPG Synthesis by comparing the final derived trust opinions obtained with and without our criteria, particularly in scenarios where an additional edge could be either retained or discarded.

Considering the trust graph in Fig. 5a. Using our improved criteria, the final opinion expression becomes: $\omega_A^E = \left[\omega_B^A \otimes \left(\left(\omega_C^B \otimes \omega_E^C\right) \oplus \omega_E^B\right)\right] \oplus \left[\omega_D^A \otimes \omega_E^D\right]$ whereas the original criteria produce: $\omega_A^E = \left[\omega_B^A \otimes \left(\omega_C^B \otimes \omega_E^C\right)\right] \oplus \left[\omega_D^A \otimes \omega_E^D\right]$.

This experiment demonstrates the effect of retaining an additional trust edge (ω_E^B) and how it influences the overall uncertainty of the final trust estimate. In Fig. 6 we compare how these two expressions behave in terms of final uncertainty as the uncertainty of ω_E^B increases. We set ω_E^B to (b, b, u) and all others opinion to $\left(\frac{1}{3}, \frac{1}{3}, \frac{1}{3}\right)$.

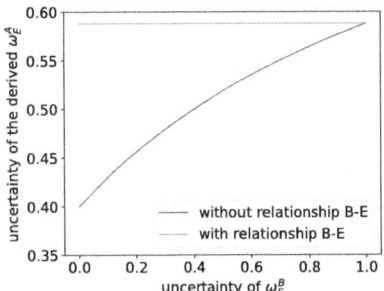
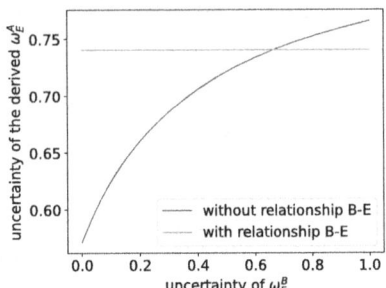

(a) Impact of edge $B \to E$ on the uncertainty of the final derived opinion when using Cumulative Fusion

(b) Impact of edge $B \to E$ on the uncertainty of the final derived opinion when using Averaging Fusion

Fig. 6. Impact of edge $B \to E$ on the uncertainty of the final derived opinion under varying fusion operators.

- **Left plot (Cumulative Fusion):** Including ω_E^B consistently lowers the uncertainty of the final opinion ω_E^A, even when ω_E^B is highly uncertain. This reflects the cumulative fusion property: more opinions—even uncertain ones—can reduce overall uncertainty. Excluding ω_E^B thus removes useful evidence and leads to uniformly higher uncertainty.
- **Right plot (Averaging Fusion):** With averaging fusion, the effect of including ω_E^B depends on its uncertainty. For low $u(\omega_E^B)$, the final opinion is more confident with the edge included. As $u(\omega_E^B)$ nears 1, its impact on the uncertainty becomes negative, eventually exceeding the uncertainty of the case without the edge. This shows averaging fusion is more sensitive to low-quality inputs. Still, removing the edge discards information, which remains undesirable in trust modeling.

7 Related Work

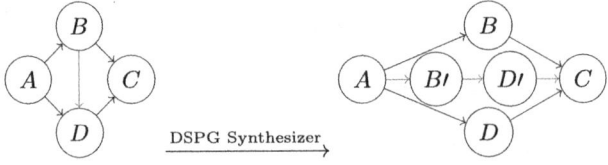

Fig. 7. Park [13] DSPG Transformer.

Trust Network Analysis with Subjective Logic (TNA-SL) was introduced by Jøsang et al. [5,6] and formalized in Jøsang's comprehensive treatment of Subjective Logic [4]. TNA-SL simplifies trust networks into Directed Series-Parallel

Graphs (DSPGs), enabling trust propagation through fusion and discounting operators. To perform this transformation, Jøsang proposed criteria based on node nesting levels and graph topology. However, these criteria are often difficult to implement and may produce altered graphs even when the input graph is already a valid DSPG (as previously shown in Fig. 5a).

Park [13] later analyzed the limitations of these transformation strategies, arguing that they are not optimal in terms of minimizing uncertainty or preserving trust information. Park advocated for alternative interpretations of optimality, emphasizing information preservation during transformation. However Park's work introduces new edges that did not exist before which increases the complexity of the graph, and introduces redundancy (see Fig. 7). Our work extends this direction by redefining the transformation criteria using a novel concept, Parallel Non-intersecting Path Subnetworks (PNPS), that provides more concrete and provable conditions for DSPG validity. This refinement leads to a simplified, loss-minimizing, and implementable DSPG transformer that improves trust inference reliability.

Beyond the SL and trust reasoning literature, recent developments in graph theory provide deeper formal insights into DSPG-like structures. Alur et al. [1] introduced synchronized series-parallel graphs (SSPGs), a robust class of directed acyclic graphs that support ordered and unordered parallelism with synchronization edges. Their work establishes logical expressiveness, determinization, and decision procedures, offering a more compositional and automata-theoretic foundation that could generalize DSPG reasoning. Complementing this, Deligkas et al. [3] proposed a theory of directed graph minors tailored to 2-terminal DAGs (TDAGs), introducing the concept of serial-parallel width. They proved that a TDAG has serial-parallel width one if and only if it is a DSPG, establishing a direct equivalence between graph structure and its routing-theoretic implications. Their complexity results further highlight the limits of efficient DSPG detection and transformation. These theoretical advances support the relevance of our approach, bridging trust network analysis with formal graph theory and enabling principled, rule-based reasoning on uncertain relational structures.

8 Discussion

This work rethinks DSPG transformation strategies in trust networks by shifting the focus from solely minimizing uncertainty to preserving trust structure and evidence. Traditional methods often aggressively remove edges to reduce uncertainty, but this can lead to a loss of valuable information —especially when the original graph is already a valid DSPG. In contrast, our approach introduces more permissive criteria that expand the class of allowable edges (e.g., source-to-intermediate or intermediate-to-sink within a PNPS) without violating DSPG properties. We contribute an optimized algorithm for both DSPG Transformation and DSPG Analysis, grounded in the novel PNPS structure and refined nesting level logic. This algorithm ensures correctness, preserves more edges, and improves trust inference accuracy. By reducing unnecessary edge removal, it supports trust systems that value provenance, redundancy, and robustness. The refined DSPG transformation strategy proposed in this work offers significant advantages for rule-based trust management systems. By preserving a richer set of edges and maintaining the provenance and redundancy inherent in the original trust network, the resulting graphs provide a more faithful substrate for rule evaluation. From a machine learning perspective, the enhanced edge preservation and structural integrity of the transformed DSPGs directly benefit graph-based learning models, such as Graph Neural Networks (GNNs) [14]. Retaining more of the original trust structure allows these models to capture subtle patterns of trust propagation and redundancy, which are crucial for accurate trust inference and anomaly detection.

9 Conclusion

We presented an optimized framework for DSPG synthesis that enhances trust network analysis by preserving structural information and reducing unnecessary edge removal. By introducing the PNPS structure and refining DSPG synthesis criteria, our approach enables more accurate and robust trust inference using Subjective Logic. The proposed algorithm maintains correctness while achieving better information retention and lower uncertainty in derived opinions. This work offers a practical and theoretically grounded improvement over existing methods, paving the way for more trustworthy and explainable reasoning in uncertain graph-based systems.

Acknowledgments. The authors would like to acknowledge Prof. Gabriele Lenzini and Dr. Huseyin Demirci (University of Luxembourg) for their prior work and discussions that led to the formulation of the PNPS definition. The definition adopted in this chapter builds upon concepts developed during earlier collaborative work on the Strunee research activities. We gratefully recognize their intellectual contribution to the conceptual foundations related to PNPS.

References

1. Alur, R., Stanford, C., Watson, C.: A robust theory of series parallel graphs. Proc. ACM Program. Lang. **7**(POPL) (2023). https://doi.org/10.1145/3571230
2. Bhuiyan, T., Jøsang, A., Xu, Y.: An analysis of trust transitivity taking base rate into account. In: 2009 Symposia and Workshops on Ubiquitous, Autonomic and Trusted Computing, pp. 34–39 (2009).https://doi.org/10.1109/UIC-ATC.2009.64
3. Deligkas, A., Meir, R.: Directed graph minors and serial-parallel width (2019). https://arxiv.org/abs/1711.01806
4. Jøsang, A.: Subjective Logic: A Formalism for Reasoning Under Uncertainty, 1st edn. Springer Publishing Company, Incorporated (2016)
5. Jøsang, A., Bhuiyan, T.: Optimal trust network analysis with subjective logic. In: 2008 Second International Conference on Emerging Security Information, Systems and Technologies, pp. 179–184 (2008). https://doi.org/10.1109/SECURWARE.2008.64

6. Jøsang, A., Hayward, R., Pope, S.: Trust network analysis with subjective logic. In: Proceedings of the 29th Australasian Computer Science Conference, CRPIT Volume 48, Hobart, Australia **48** (2006). https://doi.org/10.1145/1151699.1151710
7. Jøsang, A., Wang, D., Zhang, J.: Multi-source fusion in subjective logic. In: 2017 20th International Conference on Information Fusion (Fusion), pp. 1–8 (2017). https://doi.org/10.23919/ICIF.2017.8009820
8. Liu, Y., Li, K., Jin, Y., Zhang, Y., Qu, W.: A novel reputation computation model based on subjective logic for mobile ad hoc networks. Futur. Gener. Comput. Syst. **27**(5), 547–554 (2011). https://doi.org/10.1016/j.future.2010.03.006, https://www.sciencedirect.com/science/article/pii/S0167739X10000518
9. Ouattara, K.I.: Directed series parallel graph synthesis (2025). https://github.com/Ouatt-Isma/Directed-Series-Parallel-Graph-Synthesis. Accessed 16 June 2025
10. Ouattara, K.I., Krontiris, I., Dimitrakos, T., Kargl, F.: Assessing AI training dataset trustworthiness - a use case on bias, accepted at BIAS 2025 Workshop, ECML PKDD 2025
11. Ouattara, K.I., Krontiris, I., Dimitrakos, T., Kargl, F.: Quantifying calibration error in neural networks through evidence-based theory. In: Proceedings of the 28th International Conference on Information Fusion (FUSION) (2025). accepted at Fusion 2025
12. Ouattara, K.I., Petrovska, A., Hermann, A., Trkulja, N., Dimitrakos, T., Kargl, F.: On subjective logic trust discount for referral paths. In: 2024 27th International Conference on Information Fusion (FUSION), pp. 1–8 (2024). https://doi.org/10.23919/FUSION59988.2024.10706345
13. Park, Y.: On the optimality of trust network analysis with subjective logic. Adv. Electr. Comput. Eng. **14**, 49–54 (2014). https://doi.org/10.4316/AECE.2014.03006
14. Zhou, J., et al.: Graph neural networks: a review of methods and applications (2021). https://arxiv.org/abs/1812.08434

When Does Naïve Evaluation Work for Datalog?

Heng Liu[✉] and Eugenia Ternovska

School of Computing Science, Simon Fraser University, Burnaby, Canada
{liuhengl,ter}@sfu.ca

Abstract. Query answering over incomplete data is typically predicated on the notion of certain answers, comprising the set of tuples that appear in the query result across all possible complete databases. Computing certain answers is often computationally expensive, with lower bounds such as coNP-hardness or even undecidability in many cases. One tractable approach is naïve evaluation, which treats nulls as fresh constants and applies standard query evaluation. While naïve evaluation is known to compute certain answers for positive Datalog, its behavior for more expressive extensions of Datalog has remained less understood. This paper identifies syntactic extensions of Datalog for which naïve evaluation computes certain answers.

Keywords: Incomplete data · Datalog · Certain answers · Preservation theorems

1 Introduction

Uncertainty arises naturally in many applications where a database is not fully specified, such as data exchange [11]. Unknown or missing values are typically represented using marked nulls [9]. An incomplete database implicitly defines a set of complete databases, each representing a plausible interpretation of the available data based on how the nulls are instantiated. The standard semantic framework is that of *certain answers*—the set of tuples that appear in the result of a query under all possible completions [16,21]. However, computing certain answers is coNP-complete for conjunctive queries with inequalities [1] and non-recursive Datalog with negation [6]. Indeed, coNP-hardness or even undecidability are common for certain answer computation when considering more expressive query languages [20].

Since precise computation of certain answers is often intractable, applications requiring efficient query evaluation must adopt alternative strategies. One tractable alternative is *naïve evaluation*[1], which treats nulls as distinct constants not occurring in the database and applies a standard query evaluation

---

[1] We follow the terminology of [10,14] for query evaluation over incomplete databases. It should not be confused with the "naive" Datalog evaluation strategy based on computing a fixpoint of the immediate consequence operator, and its "semi-naive" optimization used in Datalog engines.

procedure. Naïve evaluation is known to compute certain answers for unions of conjunctive queries (UCQs) under both open-world (OWA) and closed-world (CWA) assumptions [17]. Subsequent work extends this result to a broader class of first-order queries under the CWA [13].

A key insight in [13] is that naïve evaluation computes certain answers *exactly* when the query is homomorphism-preserving. Our work builds on this insight, further investigating preservation theorems for Datalog extensions and the associated incompleteness semantics under which naïve evaluation computes certain answers exactly.

Our main contributions are the identification of Datalog extensions, namely Datalog($\leq, \neq$), Datalog($\neg^{semi_C}$), and Datalog($\neg^{st_C}$), for which naïve evaluation is guaranteed to compute certain answers under the Weak Closed World Assumption with Unique Name Assumption (WCWA^{UNA}), the Closed World Assumption with Extension (CWA$^+$), and standard CWA semantics, respectively.

Novelty. This is the first systematic characterization of when naïve evaluation computes certain answers for Datalog extensions over incomplete data. We establish preservation theorems that align four incompleteness semantics (OWA, WCWA^{UNA}, CWA$^+$, and CWA) with syntactic extensions of Datalog, including novel constant-guarded variants. Our results extend the applicability of naïve evaluation to practical settings, such as querying incomplete property graphs.

2 Preliminaries

This section defines incomplete databases, standard semantics, and the notion of certain answers, which form the foundation of our study.

2.1 Complete and Incomplete Databases

We model incomplete databases using marked nulls to represent unknown values. Let *Const* and *Null* be disjoint, countably infinite sets representing constants and marked nulls, respectively. In particular, elements of set *Null* are denoted by $\perp_i$ for some identifier $i \in \mathbb{N}$.

A *schema* σ is a finite set of relation symbols $\{R_1, \ldots, R_m\}$, each with a fixed arity. A *database instance* D over a schema σ is a finite set of relations $\{R_1^D, \ldots, R_m^D\}$. The set of all constants and nulls appearing in these relations is called the *active domain* of D, denoted $adom(D)$. Formally, a database instance is a structure $(adom(D), R_1^D, \ldots, R_m^D))$, where for each relation symbol $R_i \in \sigma$ with arity k_i, we have $R_i^D \subseteq ((Const \cup Null)^{k_i}$. For each relation R_i^D, we have $R_i^D \subseteq (Const \cup Null)^{k_i}$, where k_i is the arity of R_i.

We refer to database instances simply as databases, using symbols such as D, D_1, etc. For a tuple $\bar{a} \in R^D$, we write $R(\bar{a})$ to denote this tuple in the relation R, when D is clear from context; we often specify a database by listing all such tuples. We define the sets $Const(D) := Const \cap adom(D)$ and $Null(D) := Null \cap adom(D)$.

A database is *complete* if $adom(D) \subseteq Const$; otherwise, it is *incomplete*. We say that D_2 is a *subdatabase* of D_1, written $D_2 \sqsubseteq D_1$, if they share the same schema σ and have $R_i^{D_2} \subseteq R_i^{D_1}$ for all $R_i \in \sigma$.

2.2 Semantics of Incomplete Databases

We now define three semantics for interpreting incomplete data: the *Closed World Assumption (CWA)* [23], the *Weak Closed World Assumption* [13] *with Unique Name Assumption (WCWA^{UNA})*, and the *Open World Assumption (OWA)* [17]. A fourth semantics, *Closed World Assumption with Extension (CWA$^+$)*, is defined separately in Sect. 5.

A *completion* of an incomplete database D is a complete database, denoted D', that represents a plausible interpretation of the missing data. The set of all possible completions for D is known as its *semantics* and is denoted $[\![D]\!]_X$, where X represents a specific choice of semantics.

The basis for defining these semantics is the *valuation function*, a mapping $f : Null(D) \to Const$. The WCWA^{UNA} semantics is characterized by a valuation function f^{UNA} that satisfies two conditions. First, f^{UNA} must be *injective* (i.e., one-to-one). Second, it must assign each null to a fresh constant not already present in the database. Formally, this means f^{UNA} is a one-to-one mapping $f^{UNA} : Null(D) \to Const \setminus Const(D)$.

Applying a valuation f to D yields a complete database, $f(D)$, by replacing each null with a constant. Depending on the semantics, a final completion D' might be identical to $f(D)$ (as in CWA) or a larger database that contains $f(D)$ (as in WCWA^{UNA} and OWA).

Our notational convention is to use D for incomplete databases and exclusively use primed symbols such as D', D'', etc., to denote their completions. Note that for any given D, different valuation functions can produce different sets of possible completions.

Formally, the semantics are defined as follows:

$$[\![D]\!]_{\text{CWA}} = \{D' \mid D' = f(D) \text{ for some valuation } f\},$$

$$[\![D]\!]_{\text{WCWA}^{\text{UNA}}} = \left\{ D' \;\middle|\; \begin{array}{l} D' \text{ is complete,} \\ f^{UNA}(D) \subseteq D' \text{ for some one-to-one valuation } f^{UNA}, \\ adom(D') = f^{UNA}(Null(D)) \cup Const(D). \end{array} \right\},$$

$$[\![D]\!]_{\text{OWA}} = \{D' \mid D' \text{ is complete, } f(D) \subseteq D' \text{ for some valuation } f\}.$$

The following containment relationships follow directly from the definitions above:

$$[\![D]\!]_{\text{CWA}} \subseteq [\![D]\!]_{\text{OWA}} \quad \text{and} \quad [\![D]\!]_{\text{WCWA}^{\text{UNA}}} \subseteq [\![D]\!]_{\text{OWA}}.$$

These semantics do not form a single containment chain, as WCWA^{UNA} and CWA are not directly comparable.

Example 1. Consider an incomplete database $D = \{Friend(a, \bot_1)\}$ with a valuation $f(\bot_1) = b$. Under CWA, the only completion is $\{Friend(a, b)\}$. Under

WCWA^{UNA}, since additional facts using constants from $f(\mathit{Null}(D)) \cup \mathit{Const}(D)$ are allowed, a valid completion could be $\{\mathit{Friend}(a,b), \mathit{Friend}(b,a)\}$. The OWA allows new domain elements, so a completion such as $\{\mathit{Friend}(a,b), \mathit{Friend}(b,c)\}$ is permitted in $[\![D]\!]_{\text{OWA}}$.

2.3 Query and Certain Answers

A *query* Q of arity n is a mapping that, given a database D, returns a subset of $\mathit{adom}(D)^n$. When $n = 0$, the query is called a *Boolean query*, as it evaluates to a truth value (i.e., *true* or *false*) rather than a set of tuples.

In this work, we focus on *generic queries*, which are invariant under renaming of the domain of constants. This notion reflects a classical principle in database theory known as *data independence* [2], which asserts that query evaluation should not depend on the specific identities of data values, but only on the structure of the data.

Definition 1 (Generic Query [10]). *A query Q is called* generic *if, for every bijection $\pi : \mathit{Const} \to \mathit{Const}$ and every database D over Const, we have:*

$$Q(\pi(D)) = \pi(Q(D)),$$

where π is applied element-wise.

For example, a query that returns *true* if and only if the constant *Alice* appears in the input database is not generic: renaming *Alice* would change the result. All queries considered in this paper are generic.

Let Q be a query of arity n, and let X represent a specific choice of semantics. The *certain answers* to Q over D under X-semantics, denoted $\mathit{cert}_X(D,Q)$, is the set of tuples $t \in \mathit{Const}^n$ such that $t \in Q(D')$ for every $D' \in [\![D]\!]_X$.

Definition 2 (Certain Answers). *Let Q be a query of arity n, D an incomplete database, and $X \in \{OWA, WCWA^{UNA}, CWA^+, CWA\}$ denotes the choice of semantics. Then:*

- *If $n \geq 1$, a tuple $t \in \mathit{Const}^n$ belongs to $\mathit{cert}_X(D,Q)$ iff $t \in Q(D')$ for all $D' \in [\![D]\!]_X$;*
- *If $n = 0$ (i.e., Q is Boolean), then $\mathit{cert}_X(D,Q) = \mathit{true}$ iff $Q(D') = \mathit{true}$ for all $D' \in [\![D]\!]_X$.*

The corresponding decision problem is defined as follows:

Problem: $CERTAIN(X,Q)$
Input: An incomplete database D and a tuple $t \in \mathit{Const}^n$
Question: Is $t \in \mathit{cert}_X(D,Q)$?

We focus on the data complexity [30] of this problem, where the query is considered fixed and the database varies.

2.4 Homomorphisms

Homomorphisms play a central role in formalizing both the semantics of incomplete databases and various query preservation properties. Let D and D' be databases over the same schema. A *database homomorphism* from D to D' is a function $h : adom(D) \to adom(D')$ such that:

1. for all constants $c \in Const(D)$, we have $h(c) = c$; and
2. for every relation symbol R of arity k and every tuple $\bar{a} \in adom(D)^k$, if $\bar{a} \in R^D$, then $h(\bar{a}) \in R^{D'}$.

A homomorphism is called *one-to-one* (resp. *onto*) if it is one-to-one (resp. onto) on the active domain. It is *strong onto* if, in addition to being onto on the active domain, it satisfies the following: for every relation symbol R and every tuple $\bar{b} \in R^{D'}$, there exists a tuple $\bar{a} \in R^D$ such that $h(\bar{a}) = \bar{b}$.

Let $\mathcal{H}$ denote a class of database homomorphisms (e.g., all homomorphisms, onto homomorphisms, or strong onto homomorphisms). A query Q is said to be *preserved under* $\mathcal{H}$ if, for all databases D and D', if there is a homomorphism $h \in \mathcal{H}$ from D to D', then for every tuple $\bar{a} \in Q(D)$ we have $h(\bar{a}) \in Q(D')$. For Boolean queries, this means that $D \models Q$ implies $D' \models Q$.

Finally, a homomorphism that is one-to-one, onto, and strong is called an *isomorphism*. An isomorphism from D to D' indicates that the two databases are structurally identical.

3 Naïve Evaluation and Homomorphism Preservation

This section reviews the connection between naïve evaluation and homomorphism preservation theorems.

The principle of *naïve evaluation* is to treat nulls as fresh, distinct constants and evaluate the query using standard techniques. For example, consider a database $\{R(1, \perp_1), R(\perp_1, 2)\}$. A Boolean query $\exists x R(1, x) \wedge R(x, 2)$ naïvely evaluates to true by, first, replacing $\perp_1$ with a constant c, and then evaluating this query over $\{R(1, c), R(c, 2)\}$.

Definition 3 (Naïve Evaluation [10]). *Let $f : Null(D) \to Const \setminus Const(D)$ be a bijection (i.e., a one-to-one and onto mapping). The naïve evaluation of a query Q over an incomplete database D is defined as:*

$$Q_{naive}(D) = f^{-1}(Q(f(D))).$$

For generic queries, the choice of f does not affect the result. Any two such bijections f_1 and f_2 are related by a permutation $\pi = f_2 \circ f_1^{-1}$ on a subset of Const. This π can be extended to a bijection on Const that is the identity on $Const(D)$. By genericity, we have $Q(f_2(D)) = Q(\pi(f_1(D))) = \pi(Q(f_1(D)))$, and thus $f_2^{-1}(Q(f_2(D))) = f_2^{-1}(\pi(Q(f_1(D)))) = (f_2^{-1} \circ \pi)(Q(f_1(D))) = f_1^{-1}(Q(f_1(D)))$. Therefore, $Q_{naive}(D)$ is independent of the specific choice of f.

Definition 4 (Naïve Evaluation Works). *Let Q be an n-ary generic query. We say naïve evaluation works for $CERTAIN(X,Q)$ if, for every incomplete database D, we have:*

$$Q_{naive}(D) \cap Const(D)^n = cert_X(D,Q).$$

The central question is: *under what conditions does naïve evaluation work?* A classical result provides a foundational answer:

Theorem 1 ([17]). *Let Q be a generic union of conjunctive query of arity n. Then:*
$$Q_{naive}(D) \cap Const(D)^n = cert_{OWA}(D,Q) = cert_{CWA}(D,Q).$$

We aim to generalize this result to several Datalog extensions and additional semantics, using the lens of homomorphism preservation. The key idea is:

> If a class of homomorphisms characterizes a semantics of incomplete databases, and a generic query is preserved under those homomorphisms, then naïve evaluation works.

3.1 Semantics of Incomplete Databases and Homomorphisms

We begin by revisiting the semantics of incomplete databases via database homomorphisms. The authors of [14] established a connection between homomorphisms and relational semantics of incompleteness for OWA, CWA, and WCWA. However, their proof cannot be directly applied to $WCWA^{UNA}$. For clarity and completeness, we present a self-contained proof aligned with our completion-based semantics.

Theorem 2 (Homomorphism for Incomplete Databases). *Let D be an incomplete database and D' a complete database over the same schema σ. Then:*

- *$D' \in [\![D]\!]_{OWA}$ iff there exists a database homomorphism $h : adom(D) \to adom(D')$;*
- *$D' \in [\![D]\!]_{WCWA^{UNA}}$ iff there exists a one-to-one and onto database homomorphism $h : adom(D) \to adom(D')$;*
- *$D' \in [\![D]\!]_{CWA}$ iff there exists a strong onto database homomorphism $h : adom(D) \to adom(D')$.*

Proof. Each case follows by constructing a valuation f from a homomorphism h (and vice versa), in the following manner:
Case of OWA. ($\Rightarrow$) Suppose $D' \in [\![D]\!]_{OWA}$. Then there exists a valuation $f : Null(D) \to Const$ such that $f(D) \subseteq D'$. Define a function $h : adom(D) \to adom(D')$ by:

$$h(x) = \begin{cases} x & \text{if } x \in Const(D), \\ f(x) & \text{if } x \in Null(D). \end{cases} \quad (1)$$

This h satisfies $h(c) = c$ for all $c \in Const(D)$. For any tuple $\bar{a} \in R^D$ (i.e., a tuple in the relation R of database D), we have $h(\bar{a}) \in R^{f(D)}$ by construction. Since

$f(D) \subseteq D'$, it follows that $h(\bar{a}) \in R^{D'}$. Thus, h is a database homomorphism from D to D'.

($\Leftarrow$) Conversely, given a database homomorphism $h : adom(D) \to adom(D')$, we define a valuation function f by restricting h to the nulls in D, denoted as $h|_{Null(D)}$. We first show that $h|_{Null(D)}$ is a valuation function and then that it satisfies the OWA condition.

1. Proof that $h|_{Null(D)}$ is a valuation function: Since D' is complete, h maps all elements to constants. In particular, $h|_{Null(D)}$ maps nulls to constants, so it is a valuation.
2. OWA Condition: Let $f = h|_{Null(D)}$. For any $R(\bar{a}) \in D$, we have $f(\bar{a}) = h(\bar{a})$, and since h is a homomorphism, $h(\bar{a}) \in R^{D'}$. Hence, $f(\bar{a}) \in R^{D'}$, so $f(D) \subseteq D'$.

This satisfies the definition of OWA semantics, completing the proof of this case.

Case of WCWA^{UNA}. ($\Rightarrow$) Assume $D' \in [\![D]\!]_{\text{WCWA}^{\text{UNA}}}$, witnessed by a one-to-one valuation $f^{\text{UNA}} : Null(D) \to Const \setminus Const(D)$ such that (1) $f^{\text{UNA}}(D) \subseteq D'$ and (2) $adom(D') = f^{\text{UNA}}(Null(D)) \cup Const(D)$. Define h from f^{UNA} using Eq. 1.

To show that h is onto, observe: $h(adom(D)) = h(Const(D)) \cup h(Null(D)) = Const(D) \cup f^{\text{UNA}}(Null(D)) = adom(D')$.

To show that h is one-to-one, consider distinct $x, y \in adom(D)$. If both are in $Const(D)$, then $h(x) = x \neq y = h(y)$. If both are in $Null(D)$, then $f^{\text{UNA}}(x) \neq f^{\text{UNA}}(y)$ since f^{UNA} is one-to-one. If one is in $Const(D)$ and the other in $Null(D)$, then $h(x) \neq h(y)$ because $f^{\text{UNA}}(Null(D))$ and $Const(D)$ are disjoint. Hence, h is a one-to-one and onto database homomorphism.

($\Leftarrow$) Suppose $h : adom(D) \to adom(D')$ is a one-to-one and onto database homomorphism. Define $f^{\text{UNA}} = h|_{Null(D)}$. Then f^{UNA} is one-to-one, and since D' is complete, it maps nulls to constants. Suppose for contradiction that $f^{\text{UNA}}(y) = c$ for some $c \in Const(D)$. Then $h(y) = c = h(c)$ with $y \neq c$, contradicting that h is one-to-one. Hence, f^{UNA} maps into $Const \setminus Const(D)$.

Since h is a homomorphism, for any tuple $\bar{a} \in R^D$, we have $h(\bar{a}) \in R^{D'}$. Because $f^{\text{UNA}}(\bar{a}) = h(\bar{a})$, it follows that $f^{\text{UNA}}(D) \subseteq D'$. Moreover, since h is onto,
$$adom(D') = h(adom(D)) = Const(D) \cup f^{\text{UNA}}(Null(D)).$$
Therefore, $D' \in [\![D]\!]_{\text{WCWA}^{\text{UNA}}}$.

Case of CWA. ($\Rightarrow$) Assume $D' \in [\![D]\!]_{\text{CWA}}$. We show there exists a strong onto homomorphism $h : adom(D) \to adom(D')$. By definition of CWA, there is a valuation f such that $D' = f(D)$. We construct h from f using Eq. 1 as before. We must show h is strong onto.

- Onto: Since $D' = f(D)$, we have $adom(D') = adom(f(D)) = f(Null(D)) \cup Const(D)$. As shown in the WCWA^{UNA} case, this condition makes h onto.

- Strong: We must show that for every tuple $\bar{b} \in R^{D'}$, there exists a $\bar{a} \in R^D$ such that $h(\bar{a}) = \bar{b}$. Let $\bar{b} \in R^{D'}$ be any tuple in D'. Since $D' = f(D)$, there must exist a tuple $\bar{a} \in R^D$ such that $f(\bar{a}) = \bar{b}$. By definition, $h(\bar{a}) = f(\bar{a})$, so we have found a $\bar{a} \in R^D$ such that $h(\bar{a}) = \bar{b}$.

Since h is both onto and strong, it is a strong onto database homomorphism.

($\Leftarrow$) Assume there exists a strong onto database homomorphism $h : adom(D) \to adom(D')$. We show $D' \in [\![D]\!]_{\text{CWA}}$. Define $f = h|_{Null(D)}$. We must prove that $D' = f(D)$ by showing containment in both directions.

1. $f(D) \subseteq D'$: This follows directly from h being a homomorphism, as shown in the OWA case.
2. $D' \subseteq f(D)$: This relies on the strong property of h. Let $\bar{b} \in R^{D'}$ be any tuple in D'. Since h is strong, there exists a tuple $\bar{a} \in R^D$ such that $h(\bar{a}) = \bar{b}$. Since $f(\bar{a}) = h(\bar{a})$, we have $\bar{b} = f(\bar{a}) \in R^{f(D)}$. Thus, any tuple in D' is also in $f(D)$.

Since containment holds in both directions, $D' = f(D)$, implying that $D' \in [\![D]\!]_{\text{CWA}}$. □

Our assumption of an infinite supply of constants ensures that, for every incomplete database D, there exists an instance $D' \in [\![D]\!]_X$ such that there is an isomorphism between D and D'. This property is referred to as *strong saturation* [14].

Thus, if a generic query Q of arity n is preserved under a class of homomorphisms $\mathcal{H}$ that corresponds to a semantics $[\![D]\!]_X$, then naïve evaluation computes certain answers: $Q_{naive}(D) \cap Const(D)^n = cert_X(D, Q)$.

Corollary 1 (Homomorphism Preservation and Naïve Evaluation). *Let Q be a n-ary generic query.*

- *If Q is preserved under database homomorphisms, then naïve evaluation works for OWA semantics.*
- *If Q is preserved under one-to-one and onto database homomorphisms, then naïve evaluation works for $WCWA^{UNA}$ semantics.*
- *If Q is preserved under strong onto database homomorphisms, then naïve evaluation works for CWA semantics.*

By Corollary 1, to ensure naïve evaluation computes certain answers exactly, it suffices to identify Datalog variants preserved under specific classes of homomorphisms.

4 Datalog Extensions and Homomorphism Preservation

This section defines Datalog variants and establishes their preservation properties.

4.1 Datalog and Its Extensions

We first review standard Datalog and then define several syntactic extensions primarily by incorporating novel Constant-Guarded predicates.

Datalog Basics. We begin with the core components. An *atom* is an expression of the form $P(\bar{t})$, where P is a predicate symbol and $\bar{t}$ is a tuple of terms. A *term* is either a variable or a value, where a value is an element from the set of constants and marked nulls ($Const \cup Null$). An atom that contains no variables, only values from $Const \cup Null$, is called a ground atom or a *fact*.

A *Datalog rule* has the form $H \leftarrow P_1, \ldots, P_m$, where the head H and the body atoms $\{P_1, \ldots, P_m\}$ are atoms. The atoms that constitute a rule must contain only variables as terms (i.e., no constants appear directly in rules). Rules must be *safe*: any variable appearing in the head H must also appear in an atom in the body.

A *Datalog program* P is a finite set of such rules. Its schema, $sch(P)$, is partitioned into extensional (EDB) predicates, which appear only in rule bodies, and intensional (IDB) predicates, which are defined in rule heads. A *Datalog query* is a program P with a designated IDB predicate Q as its output. The arity of the query, say n, is the arity of this designated predicate Q. Thus, the query defines a mapping from an input database D (containing the EDB facts) to an n-ary relation, which is a subset of $adom(D)^n$.

Datalog with Negation. We consider two extensions, both requiring *safe negation* (variables in a negated atom must also appear in a positive atom within the same body). *Semi-positive Datalog* allows negation only over EDB predicates. *Stratified Datalog* is a more general framework that allows negation over both EDB and IDB predicates, as long as the program is stratified (i.e., there are no recursive calls through negation).

Order-Invariant Datalog and Datalog($\leq, \neq$). We follow the framework in [27], which defines a linear order $\leq$ on $adom(D)$ using EDB predicates: $initial(x)$ (true if x is the least element), $final(x)$ (greatest element), and $succ(x, y)$ (true if y is the immediate successor of x). A program is *order-invariant* if its evaluation is independent of the particular order.

We define Datalog($\leq, \neq$) as Order-Invariant Datalog extended with inequality atoms $x \neq y$, where x and y are variables appearing in the same rule body.

Constant-Guarded Predicates and Extensions. Following [5], We define a unary EDB predicate $C(x)$ that identifies constants in the input incomplete database D: $C(x)$ is true if and only if $x \in Const(D)$.

We then define the novel notion of a *constant-guarded predicate*, P_C, for any predicate P:

- If P is an EDB predicate, $P_C(\bar{x})$ holds if and only if the fact $P(\bar{x})$ is present in the input database D and each variable $x_i \in \bar{x}$ satisfies $C(x_i)$.

- If P is an IDB predicate, its constant-guarded predicate P_C is also an IDB predicate. Its rules are derived from the rules for P: for each rule in the program defining P of the form:

$$P(\bar{x}) \leftarrow P_1(\bar{x}_1), \ldots, P_m(\bar{x}_m)$$

where each $P_i(\bar{x}_i)$ is a body atom, we add the following corresponding rule for P_C:

$$P_C(\bar{x}) \leftarrow P_{1,C}(\bar{x}_1), \ldots, P_{m,C}(\bar{x}_m) \qquad (2)$$

where each $P_{i,C}$ is the constant-guarded predicate of the body predicate P_i.

Constant-Guarded Datalog extensions use C and the P_C to restrict negations to constants:

- **Datalog($\neq^c$):** Permits inequality atoms $x \neq y$ only if both x and y are explicitly guarded by $C(x)$ and $C(y)$ in the same rule body.
- **Datalog($\neg^{semic}$):** In semi-positive Datalog, all negated EDB atoms must appear as $\neg P_C(\bar{x})$. Every variable x_i in $\bar{x}$ must be explicitly guarded by $C(x_i)$ in the rule body where $\neg P_C(\bar{x})$ appears.
- **Datalog($\neg^{stc}$):** In stratified Datalog, all negated atoms must be written as $\neg P_C(\bar{x})$. If P is an IDB predicate, its P_C is an IDB predicate derived via the rule in Eq. 2, and resides in the same stratum as P. Each variable x_i in the negated atom $\neg P_C(\bar{x})$ must also be explicitly guarded by $C(x_i)$ in the rule body.

4.2 Preservation Properties

We are ready to prove that specific Datalog extensions are preserved under various types of homomorphisms.

Theorem 3 (Homomorphism Preservation for Datalog Extensions).

- *Datalog($\neq^c$) is preserved under database homomorphisms.*
- *Datalog($\leq, \neq$) is preserved under one-to-one and onto database homomorphisms.*
- *Datalog($\neg^{stc}$) is preserved under strong onto database homomorphisms.*

Proof. The semantics of a Datalog query Q over a database D can be formalized using derivation trees, also known as proof trees. A fact t belongs to $Q(D)$ if and only if there exists a finite proof tree for t constructed from D and the rules of Q. A *proof tree* of t is a tree such that: (1) each node is labeled with a fact; (2) the root is labeled with t; (3) each leaf is labeled with a fact from D; and (4) each internal node corresponds to a ground instance of a rule from Q, with the node's label being the rule's head and its children labeled by the atoms in the rule's body.

To prove preservation, we assume a fact $t \in Q(D)$ is witnessed by a proof tree T. For an incomplete database D, this evaluation $Q(D)$ corresponds to the naïve evaluation, $Q_{naive}(D)$. We then demonstrate that applying the homomorphism h to every node label in T results in a new tree, $h(T)$, which is a proof tree for $h(t)$ constructed from D' and the rules of Q.

Case of Datalog($\neq^c$). Let Q be a Datalog($\neq^c$) query and let $h : adom(D) \to adom(D')$ be a database homomorphism. Let T be a proof tree for $t \in Q(D)$. We now show, by structural induction on the height of T, that for every subtree T' of T rooted at A, the transformed subtree $h(T')$ is a proof tree deriving $h(A)$ from D' using the rules of Q.

Base case (leaves). Let $A = P(\bar{a})$ be a leaf node in T, so $P(\bar{a}) \in D$. Since h is a database homomorphism, we have $P(h(\bar{a})) \in D'$. Therefore, $h(A)$ is a fact in D', and the leaf in $h(T)$ is justified.

Inductive step (internal nodes). Let $A = H(\bar{a})$ be an internal node in T, with children labeled $P_1(\bar{a}_1), \ldots, P_m(\bar{a}_m)$. We argue that each $h(P_i(\bar{a}_i))$ is derivable from D':

- If $P_i(\bar{a}_i)$ is a positive atom, then by the inductive hypothesis, the subtree rooted at $P_i(\bar{a}_i)$ transforms into a proof tree deriving $h(P_i(\bar{a}_i))$ from D'.
- If $P_i(\bar{a}_i)$ is an inequality atom, then by the Datalog($\neq^c$) restriction, it must be of the form $c_1 \neq c_2$ where c_1, c_2 are constants. Since h is a database homomorphism, it fixes constants, so $h(c_1) \neq h(c_2)$ remains true.

Therefore, all body atoms of the rule instance are satisfied under h, and the rule derives $H(h(\bar{a}))$ from D'. Repeating this construction at each node, we conclude that $h(T)$ is a proof tree deriving $h(t)$ from D' using Q. This proves that Datalog($\neq^c$) queries are preserved under database homomorphisms.

Case of Datalog($\leq, \neq$). It has been shown in [27] that Datalog($\leq$) queries are preserved under bijective (i.e., one-to-one and onto) homomorphisms, and that Datalog with inequality is preserved under one-to-one homomorphisms [19]. We sketch a proof for our case as follows. Since generic queries are invariant under bijection, we may, without loss of generality, assume that the domains of D and D' coincide, and hence $D \subseteq D'$. Then, by construction, $h(T)$ is a proof tree that derives $h(t)$ from D'.

Case of Datalog($\neg^{st_C}$). Let Q be a Datalog($\neg^{st_C}$) query, and let $h : adom(D) \to adom(D')$ be a strong onto database homomorphism. We show that $h(T)$ is a proof tree deriving $h(t)$ from D' using the rules of Q.

The reasoning for positive atoms is analogous to that in the Datalog($\neq^c$) case. We focus on negated atoms. The proof proceeds by induction on the number of strata.

- Base Case (Datalog($\neg^{semi_C}$)): Negation is allowed only over C-guarded EDB atoms of the form $\neg P_C(\bar{c})$. Due to the presence of C-guards, $\bar{c}$ must consist of constants. Since h is strong and fixes constants, $\neg P_C(h(\bar{c})) = \neg P_C(\bar{c})$ remains true in D'. As h also preserves positive atoms, all body atoms are preserved, and $h(T)$ is a proof tree of $h(t)$.

– Inductive Step (Datalog($\neg^{st_C}$)): Negated atoms may now refer to constant-guarded IDB predicates from lower strata. For any such predicate P_C, its rules are defined solely in terms of constant-guarded predicates. Because the derivation rules and constant facts remain identical across D and D', the set of facts derivable for P_C is unchanged. Therefore, if $\neg P_C(\bar{x})$ is true in D, it remains true in D'.

By the inductive hypothesis, the preservation of negated atoms from lower strata holds, and $h(T)$ is a proof tree for $h(t)$.

□

Example 2. Consider the query $Q(x) \leftarrow P(x,y), C(x), x \neq y$. This is a query where y is not C-guarded. Let $D = \{P(a, \bot_1), P(b, \bot_2)\}$. Naïvely evaluating Q on D yields $Q_{naive}(D) = \{a, b\}$. However, consider the valuation f_1 where $f_1(\bot_1) = a$ and $f_1(\bot_2) = b$. This yields the complete database $D_1 = f_1(D) = \{P(a, a), P(b, b)\}$, for which $Q(D_1) = \emptyset$.

Remark 1. This counterexample also illustrates that, beyond constant-guarding variables in negations, requiring the P_C form for negated EDB predicates (as in Datalog($\neg^{semi_C}$)) is essential. For instance, the semi-positive Datalog query $Q(x) \leftarrow P(x, y), C(x), \neg P(x, x)$. Using the same D and D_1, we would find $Q_{naive}(D) = \{a, b\}$ but $Q(D_1) = \emptyset$.

4.3 Application of Datalog($\neg^{st_C}$)

In this section, we demonstrate that Datalog($\neg^{st_C}$) can be utilized for querying property graphs that contain incomplete data.

Graph databases are emerging as essential tools for managing richly interconnected data [28]. A key challenge is that incomplete data are ubiquitous across high-impact domains such as fraud detection [29] and social network analytics [22].

A *property graph* is a data model commonly used in graph databases, where data is represented as a graph consisting of nodes (or vertices) and relationships (or edges). Both nodes and relationships can have an arbitrary number of key-value pairs, referred to as *attributes* or *properties*. The incompleteness of a property graph arises from the presence of *null values* in these properties, indicating missing or unknown information.

We adopt a partial schema from the Linked Data Benchmark Council's (LDBC) Social Network Benchmark (SNB) [4] as a representative example. The SNB defines a standard schema for modeling social networks as property graphs, including entity types such as *Person* and *Organisation*, and relationship types such as *workAt*. Each entity or relationship may have associated attributes, some of which may be incomplete. For instance, a *Person*'s *locationIP* or *email* may be unknown and represented by a null.

We encode the property graph using EDB predicates:

– *Person(id, firstName, lastName, gender, birthday, email, speaks, browserUsed, locationIP, creationDate)*,

- $workAt(personId, orgId)$,
- $TrustedOrganisation(orgId)$, and
- $BlacklistedIP(ipAddress)$.

Attributes serving as identifiers (e.g., id, $personId$, $orgId$) are constants and never null; nulls may occur only in property attributes such as $locationIP$.

Example: Identifying At-Risk Accounts from Blacklisted IPs. A critical task in platform security is to identify user accounts created from suspicious or untrusted network locations. The following query identifies individuals who registered using a blacklisted IP address and who have not been otherwise "cleared" (for instance, by being an employee of a trusted organization). The query returns each such person's name and email address. We model this query in Datalog($\neg^{st_C}$) as follows:

- **Stratum 1:** Identify the set of cleared person IDs. Although we write the rule using constant-guarded EDB predicates such as $workAt_C$, both predicates involve only non-nullable identifier attributes in the schema (e.g., $personId$ and $orgId$). As a result, the constant-guarded versions coincide with the original predicates, and can be used directly.

    $ClearedPerson_C(personId) \leftarrow$
    $\qquad workAt_C(personId, orgId), TrustedOrganisation_C(orgId)$

- **Stratum 2**: Define the main query. This rule finds all people who registered from an IP address on a known blacklist, but who have not been otherwise cleared.

    $AtRiskAccount(firstName, lastName, email) \leftarrow$
    $\qquad Person(id, firstName, lastName, ip, \ldots, email, \ldots),$
    $\qquad BlacklistedIP(ip),$
    $\qquad C(id), \neg ClearedPerson_C(id)$

This example illustrates that Datalog($\neg^{st_C}$) can compute certain answers over incomplete property graphs. In this setting, the need for explicitly constant-guarded predicates is obviated by the schema itself: identifiers for nodes and edges (e.g., person IDs, organization IDs) are not allowed to be null.

5 Other Preservation Theorems

We now investigate a semantics not captured directly by homomorphisms: the *Closed World Assumption with Extension* (CWA$^+$). This semantics generalizes the standard CWA by permitting additional facts over an extended active domain.

A database D_2 is an *extension* of a database D_1 (over the same schema) if $adom(D_1) \subseteq adom(D_2)$ and for every relation symbol R, the restriction of R^{D_2}

to $adom(D_1)$ equals R^{D_1}. That is, D_2 preserves all facts of D_1 over $adom(D_1)$, and may add new facts in D_2 that involve at least one new domain element from $adom(D_2) \setminus adom(D_1)$.

Example 3. Let $D_1 = \{Friend(a,a)\}$ and $D_2 = \{Friend(a,a), Friend(b,a)\}$. Then D_2 is an extension of D_1. In contrast, $D_3 = \{Friend(a,a), Friend(b,a), Friend(a,b)\}$ is not an extension of D_2, since it introduces a new fact $Friend(a,b)$ over existing domain elements.

The semantics of CWA^+ are defined as:

$$[\![D]\!]_{\text{CWA}^+} = \{D'' \mid D'' \text{ is an extension of some } D' \in [\![D]\!]_{\text{CWA}}\}.$$

A query Q is said to be *preserved under extensions* if for any databases D_1 and D_2, with D_2 an extension of D_1, it holds that:

$$\bar{a} \in Q(D_1) \Rightarrow \bar{a} \in Q(D_2).$$

In the case of Boolean queries, preservation under extensions means that if $Q(D_1) = true$, then $Q(D_2) = true$ for any extension D_2 of D_1.

Proposition 1 ([25]). *Semi-positive Datalog queries are preserved under extensions.*

Datalog($\neg^{semic}$) queries, being a subclass of Datalog($\neg^{stc}$), are preserved under strong onto database homomorphisms. Furthermore, since Datalog($\neg^{semic}$) queries are also a subclass of semi-positive Datalog, they are preserved under extensions. Combining these properties, we arrive at the following proposition:

Proposition 2. *If Q is a generic Datalog($\neg^{semic}$) query, then naïve evaluation works for CWA^+ semantics.*

6 Related Work

Incomplete data in the form of marked nulls was introduced to model missing values in relational databases [9]. Query evaluation over such data is naturally defined via certain answers [16,21], which are answers true under every possible valuation of the nulls. However, computing certain answers is generally intractable, with coNP-complete complexity [3].

A tractable alternative to this complexity is naïve evaluation, which involves evaluating queries as if nulls were regular values. A central insight is that naïve evaluation computes certain answers exactly when the query is preserved under appropriate classes of homomorphisms [14]. For first-order logic, this connection is well-understood. Specifically, existential-positive queries are preserved under homomorphisms [26], positive queries under onto homomorphisms [24], and positive queries with universal guards under strong onto homomorphisms [14].

Datalog programs may have recursion and thus require a separate preservation analysis. While positive Datalog is known to be preserved under general homomorphisms, Datalog with inequality is only preserved under one-to-one homomorphisms [19]. Furthermore, Datalog with constant-guarded inequality is preserved under database homomorphisms [5].

The landscape becomes more complex for semi-positive Datalog, where negation is allowed in limited forms. Although the homomorphism-closed fragment of semi-positive Datalog has the same expressive power as positive Datalog [12], this equivalence does not extend to the property of *monotonicity*, where $Q(D_1) \subseteq Q(D_2)$ if $D_1 \subseteq D_2$. The monotone fragment of semi-positive Datalog is strictly more expressive than positive Datalog when inequalities are permitted; this gap closes only when inequalities are disallowed [18].

The preservation properties and expressive power of other Datalog extensions have also been studied in recent years, notably [27]. For example, order-invariant Datalog queries are preserved under one-to-one and onto homomorphisms [27]. However, preservation theorems for other classes of homomorphisms—and their implications for the correctness of naïve evaluation—remain less understood, and are studied in this paper.

Another line of research addresses incomplete information using languages from the Datalog$^\pm$ family, also known as *existential rules* or *tuple-generating dependencies (TGDs)* [8,15]. In this framework, incompleteness is introduced intensionally: TGDs are Datalog-like rules with existentially quantified variables in their heads, which can generate new, unknown values that did not exist in the EDB. Reasoning is performed via the *chase* procedure, which systematically applies the TGDs to materialize a universal model with marked nulls of the database [7]. A conjunctive query is then evaluated naïvely against this universal model to find certain answers. Our approach is complementary: we focus on identifying when naïve evaluation works over marked nulls.

7 Conclusion and Future Work

We have identified cases where naïve evaluation works over incomplete databases under four different interpretations of incompleteness. These results are summarized in the table below. The result in the first line was established in the context of data exchange by [5]; all remaining results are proven in this paper, following a methodology inspired by [14]. Our work enables efficient certain answer computation using naïve evaluation on broader extensions of Datalog. Several directions for future work can be developed based on this study. First, while we illustrate the expressive power of our Datalog extensions on a property graph example, a practical implementation of C-guarded enforcement has yet to be explored. Integrating static or runtime checks into systems like LogicBlox is a natural next step. Second, a deeper expressivity analysis is needed to identify which real-world queries fall within Datalog($\neg^{st_C}$).

Completion Semantics	Naïve evaluation works if query Q is
Open World Assumption (OWA)	Datalog($\neq^c$) [5]
Weak Closed World Assumption with Unique Name Assumption (WCWA^{UNA})	Datalog($\leq, \neq$)
Closed World Assumption with Extension (CWA$^+$)	Datalog($\neg^{semi_C}$)
Closed World Assumption (CWA)	Datalog($\neg^{st_C}$)

Acknowledgements. This research is funded by the Natural Sciences and Engineering Research Council of Canada (NSERC). The authors thank the reviewers for their helpful feedback.

References

1. Abiteboul, S., Duschka, O.M.: Complexity of answering queries using materialized views. In: Proceedings of the Seventeenth ACM SIGACT-SIGMOD-SIGART Symposium on Principles of Database Systems, pp. 254–263. PODS '98, Association for Computing Machinery, New York, NY, USA (1998). https://doi.org/10.1145/275487.275516
2. Abiteboul, S., Hull, R., Vianu, V.: Foundations of Databases (1995)
3. Abiteboul, S., Kanellakis, P., Grahne, G.: On the representation and querying of sets of possible worlds. Theor. Comput. Sci. **78**(1), 159–187 (1991). https://doi.org/10.1016/0304-3975(51)90007-2
4. Angles, R., et al.: The LDBC social network benchmark. CoRR abs/2001.02299 (2020)
5. Arenas, M., Barceló, P., Reutter, J.: Query languages for data exchange: beyond unions of conjunctive queries. In: Proceedings of the 12th International Conference on Database Theory, pp. 73–83. ICDT '09, ACM, New York, NY, USA (2009). https://doi.org/10.1145/1514894.1514904
6. Bruijn, J., Heymans, S.: Complexity of the stable model semantics for queries on incomplete databases. In: Proceedings of the 10th International Conference on Logic Programming and Nonmonotonic Reasoning, pp. 101–114. LPNMR '09, Springer-Verlag, Berlin, Heidelberg (2009). https://doi.org/10.1007/978-3-642-04238-6_11
7. Calì, A., Gottlob, G., Kifer, M.: Taming the infinite chase: query answering under expressive relational constraints. J. Artif. Int. Res. **48**(1), 115–174 (2013)
8. Calì, A., Gottlob, G., Lukasiewicz, T.: A general datalog-based framework for tractable query answering over ontologies. J. Web Semant. **14**, 57–83 (2012). https://doi.org/10.1016/j.websem.2012.03.001, special Issue on Dealing with the Messiness of the Web of Data
9. Codd, E.F.: Extending the database relational model to capture more meaning. ACM Trans. Database Syst. **4**(4), 397–434 (1979). https://doi.org/10.1145/320107.320109

10. Console, M., Guagliardo, P., Libkin, L., Toussaint, E.: Coping with incomplete data: recent advances. In: Proceedings of the 39th ACM SIGMOD-SIGACT-SIGAI Symposium on Principles of Database Systems, pp. 33–47. PODS'20, Association for Computing Machinery, New York, NY, USA (2020). https://doi.org/10.1145/3375395.3387970
11. Fagin, R., Kolaitis, P.G., Miller, R.J., Popa, L.: Data exchange: semantics and query answering. Theoret. Comput. Sci. **336**(1), 89–124 (2005). https://doi.org/10.1016/j.tcs.2004.10.033, database Theory
12. Feder, T., Vardi, M.: Homomorphism closed vs. existential positive. In: 18th Annual IEEE Symposium of Logic in Computer Science, 2003. Proceedings, pp. 311–320 (2003). https://doi.org/10.1109/LICS.2003.1210071
13. Gheerbrant, A., Libkin, L., Sirangelo, C.: When is naive evaluation possible? In: Proceedings of the 32Nd ACM SIGMOD-SIGACT-SIGAI Symposium on Principles of Database Systems, pp. 75–86. PODS '13, ACM, New York, NY, USA (2013). https://doi.org/10.1145/2463664.2463674
14. Gheerbrant, A., Libkin, L., Sirangelo, C.: Naïve evaluation of queries over incomplete databases. ACM Trans. Database Syst. **39**(4) (2015). https://doi.org/10.1145/2691190.2691194
15. Gottlob, G., Lukasiewicz, T., Pieris, A.: Datalog+/-: questions and answers. In: Proceedings of the Fourteenth International Conference on Principles of Knowledge Representation and Reasoning, pp. 682–685. KR'14, AAAI Press (2014)
16. Grant, J.: Null values in a relational data base. Inf. Process. Lett. **6**(5), 156–157 (1977). https://doi.org/10.1016/0020-0190(77)90013-8
17. Imieliński, T., Lipski, W.: Incomplete information in relational databases. J. ACM **31**(4), 761–791 (1984). https://doi.org/10.1145/1634.1886
18. Ketsman, B., Koch, C.: Datalog with negation and monotonicity. International Conference on Database Theory (ICDT) (2020). https://doi.org/10.5446/46837
19. Kolaitis, P.G.: On the Expressive Power of Logics on Finite Models, pp. 27–123. Springer Berlin Heidelberg, Berlin, Heidelberg (2007). https://doi.org/10.1007/3-540-68804-8_2
20. Libkin, L.: How to define certain answers. In: Proceedings of the 24th International Conference on Artificial Intelligence, pp. 4282–4288. IJCAI'15, AAAI Press (2015)
21. Lipski, W.: On semantic issues connected with incomplete information databases. ACM Trans. Database Syst. **4**(3), 262–296 (1979). https://doi.org/10.1145/320083.320088
22. Mercorio, F., Mezzanzanica, M., Moscato, V., Picariello, A., Sperlí, G.: DICO: a graph-DB framework for community detection on big scholarly data. IEEE Trans. Emerg. Top. Comput. **9**(4), 1987–2003 (2021). https://doi.org/10.1109/TETC.2019.2952765
23. Reiter, R.: On closed world databases. In: Webber, B.L., Nilsson, N.J. (eds.) Readings in Artificial Intelligence, pp. 119–140. Morgan Kaufmann (1981). https://doi.org/10.1016/B978-0-934613-03-3.50014-3
24. Rosen, E.: Some aspects of model theory and finite structures. Bull. Symbolic Logic **8**(3), 380–403 (2002). https://doi.org/10.2178/bsl/1182353894
25. Rosen, E., Weinstein, S.: Preservation theorems in finite model theory. In: Leivant, D. (ed.) Logic and Computational Complexity, pp. 480–502. Springer Berlin Heidelberg, Berlin, Heidelberg (1995). https://doi.org/10.1007/3-540-60178-3_99
26. Rossman, B.: Homomorphism preservation theorems. J. ACM **55**(3) (2008). https://doi.org/10.1145/1379759.1379763

27. Rudolph, S., Thomazo, M.: Expressivity of datalog variants – completing the picture. In: Proceedings of the 25th International Joint Conference on Artificial Intelligence. New-York, United States (2016)
28. Sakr, S., et al.: The future is big graphs: a community view on graph processing systems. Commun. ACM **64**(9), 62–71 (2021). https://doi.org/10.1145/3434642
29. Srivastava, S., Singh, A.K.: Fraud detection in the distributed graph database. Cluster Comput. **26**(1), 515–537 (2022). https://doi.org/10.1007/s10586-022-03540-3
30. Vardi, M.Y.: The complexity of relational query languages (extended abstract). In: Proceedings of the Fourteenth Annual ACM Symposium on Theory of Computing, pp. 137–146. STOC '82, Association for Computing Machinery, New York, NY, USA (1982). https://doi.org/10.1145/800070.802186

Scalable Evaluation of Rule-Based Recommender Systems: Algorithms and Benchmarks

Len Feremans[(✉)] and Bart Goethals

Department of Computer Science, University of Antwerp, Antwerp, Belgium
{len.feremans,bart.goethals}@uantwerpen.be

Abstract. Recommender systems help users to identify the most relevant items from a huge collection of items. Rule-based recommenders offer efficient, interpretable, accurate, and trustworthy recommendations, addressing key challenges in recommender design. Using association rules having a single or multiple conditions, we build transparent white-box models, especially for long-tail items. Moreover, recent studies challenge the trade-off between interpretability and accuracy. However, aspects beyond accuracy and efficiency—such as popularity bias, coverage, diversity, and comprehensibility—have largely been overlooked in prior evaluations. Additionally, well-known higher-order rule-based recommender methods lack scalability. Finally, many methods have been proposed that vary in rule form, scoring measures, aggregation and inference strategies. We introduce RuleRec, a scalable toolkit offering six seminal rule-based recommenders. We extend Apriori, MSApriori and adaptive-support rule mining, thereby presenting novel algorithms based on the generalization of pairwise rule-mining using an inverted index. We find that the proposed algorithms are an order of magnitude more efficient. Finally, we empirically evaluate six rule-based recommender algorithms on six benchmark datasets, comparing their accuracy, efficiency, diversity, popularity bias, and comprehensibility. To our knowledge, this is the first work to provide an efficient open-source implementation and comparative evaluation over multiple rule-based recommenders.

1 Introduction

Recommender systems (RS) are important in the current age where end-users are overwhelmed with information from news websites, social media, e-commerce, music and video services and emerging applications such as health care. Challenges for RS are limited user preference information and implicit feedback, where there is a high amount of uncertainty attached to interpreting observed user behaviour [11]. Another challenge is the cold start scenario, where user-item interactions are unavailable because the user or item is new.

A perceived disadvantage of traditional rule-based models such as decision trees and association rules is their relatively low accuracy compared to state-of-the-art deep learning methods. In the seminal paper [22], Rudin argues that it is a myth that there is a trade-off between accuracy and interpretability. Goethals et al. conclude that the trade-off exists but that for the majority of datasets the difference is rather small [9]. Ludewig et al. find that a simple rule-based method (SR) outperforms recent deep learning-based RS in 4 out of 8 sequential recommendation datasets [16]. More recent approaches leveraging attention mechanisms and large language models could achieve superior accuracy, but this comes at the cost of increased training time and reduced trustworthiness. Deep learningbased RS are only post hoc explainable, where post hoc explanations are uncertain and not always faithful to the black-box model [20].

Most authors who develop new RS methods focus on accuracy, but the increase in accuracy is often marginal, whereas computational resource requirements have increased substantially. More recently, different authors recognize RS quality requirements beyond accuracy, such as fairness, trustworthiness, and diversity. The trustworthiness of an RS is enhanced by: (i) providing explanations for recommendations; (ii) taking the causability of a decision into account; (iii) ensuring recommendations are robust against noise in the data and adversarial attacks; (iv) managing popularity bias; (v) increasing diversity; (vi) ensuring calibration and fair exposure; (vii) and comprehension of the model [2,9,25,28].

In addition, in emerging and high-stakes domains, such as healthcare, education, or the legal domain, precise and interpretable recommendations are a requirement. Rule-based RS have several interesting properties, namely: (i) intrinsic interpretability; (ii) the ability to identify accurate patterns and rules locally; (iii) the capability to learn from both user interactions and content/context features; (iv) the potential for rule list optimization and ensembles to increase accuracy; (v) high efficiency; (vi) capture higher-order interactions; (vii) capture short-term and dynamic user preferences; (viii) and learn online directly from user feedback. In this paper, we compare different RS, and measure the diversity, popularity bias, and comprehensibility of rule-based RS, which is often not reported in original work. Finally, we tackle scalability issues that are common in traditional higher-order rule mining methods. We make the following contributions:

- We analyze the literature and categorize and compare a wide variety of rule-based recommendation algorithms proposed in the past decades.
- We introduce RuleRec, a new toolkit that contains efficient algorithms of a wide variety of rule-based recommenders. Technically, we extend Apriori-based rule mining algorithms to efficiently scale to large datasets.
- We perform an independent evaluation study using six publicly available benchmark datasets from different domains, including e-commerce, news, and music. We extend prior work by comparing precision, recall, coverage, popularity bias, diversity, comprehensibility, and runtime.

2 Background and Definitions

First, we introduce some background terminology for recommender systems and rule mining.

2.1 Collaborative-Filtering Based Recommender Systems

Recommender systems learn models from historical user interactions. Let U be the set of users and I the set of items. Each user (or session) $p \in U$ has a set of implicit interactions $p = \{s_1, s_2, \ldots, s_k\}$, where $s_i \in I$ denotes a positive action (e.g., a click). Interactions are typically logged online as tuples of user, item, and optionally time. All interactions can be represented as a sparse useritem matrix $R \in \mathbb{R}^{|U| \times |I|}$, since most users interact with only a few items in a large catalog. Depending on the dataset, interactions may represent product purchases, clicks on movies or songs, or news article views.

The goal of a recommender system is to suggest the most relevant items for each user. Content-based methods rely on user and item metadata (e.g., recommending other thrillers by John Grisham if the user liked one), while collaborative filtering leverages useritem interactions (e.g., users who liked "The Firm" also like X). In this work, we focus on collaborative filtering, although rule-mining methods can exploit metadata, interaction data, or both.

To compare approaches, we evaluate systems offline. A model $\mathcal{M}$ is trained on historical interactions and, during inference, produces top-n recommendations for each user. Users are split into training and test sets. For each test user $p \in U_{\text{test}}$, interactions are partitioned into observed p^{obs} and held-out p^{held} sets. The model generates a ranked list $\hat{p} = \hat{s}_1, \ldots, \hat{s}_n$ from p^{obs}, which is then compared with p^{held}. Evaluation uses recall@k, rank-aware measures such as NDCG@k, and secondary metrics addressing popularity bias and diversity.

2.2 Apriori

Agrawal et al. introduced Apriori, the first method for mining patterns and association rules in large databases [3]. Apriori uses breadth-first search to generate singletons, pairs, triples, etc., and discovers itemsets X that exceed a minimum support threshold θ, often set low (e.g., covering 1% of instances). Crucial to the efficiency of Apriori is the anti-monotonicity of support, i.e. for each set of items X the support, or the number of occurrences in a database, is smaller for any superset Z of X. Next, Apriori outputs association rules for each frequent itemset thereby partitioning the itemset into an antecedent and consequent. Given an itemset $X = \{A, B\}$, we generate a rule $A \to B$ where:

$$\mathit{conf}(A \to B) = P(B \mid A) = \frac{\mathit{support}(A \wedge B)}{\mathit{support}(A)} \text{ and } \mathit{support}(X) = \sum_{p \in U} 1_{EQ}(X \subseteq p).$$

Here, $1_{EQ}(\mathit{predicate})$ is an indicator function that returns 1 if the predicate is true, and 0 otherwise. Apriori also prunes rules with confidence below a minimum threshold, denoted as γ. In RS, the consequent typically is a single item. If the rule matches with the user history, the consequent of the rule is recommended to the user. We review RS that mine itemsets with different support thresholds [15], or mine the top-k confident rules directly [14,17]. In Sect. 4, we discuss how to scale Apriori to large, sparse datasets.

3 Review of Existing Rule-Based RS Methods

In this section we review seminal rule-based recommender methods. Existing work mainly differs in the following aspects:

- Many RS restrict conditions to a single item, yielding "because you like X, we recommend Y" rules. Others RS adapt Apriori to enumerate higher-order conditions, yielding "because you like X_1 and X_2 and we recommend Y".
- Items are ranked using scores such as confidence, cosine similarity, or adjusted confidence. Rules may be chosen by their maximum score or by aggregating similarities across rules with the same consequent.
- Recommendation (or reasoning) strategies vary: some incorporate sequential patterns or history filtering, crucial in domains where time matters (e.g., news or music).
- Mining approaches differ, with various constraints and pruning strategies to limit the combinatorial search space.

An overview of the seminal rule-based recommender systems compared in this work is shown in Table 1. An example is shown in Fig. 1.

3.1 Recommendations Based on Pairwise Association Rules

Ludewig et al. propose Simple Association Rules (AR), which is based on pairwise association rules [16]. Let U denote the set of all users and p contains a time-ordered list of items $p = (s_1, \ldots, s_k)$. We compute the confidence for each item pair s_i, s_j using

$$conf(s_i \to s_j) = \frac{support(s_i \wedge s_j)}{support_{LEN}(s_i)} \text{where}$$

	Inception	Titanic	The Matrix	Avatar
User 1		✓	✓	
User 2	✓		✓	✓
User 3		✓		✓
User 4	✓	✓	✓	
User 5	✓	✓	?	?

Fig. 1. Example of the user-item interaction matrix. For **User 5** different rule-based recommender systems yield the following Top-1 recommendation: a) Pairwise rules: We find *Inception* $\to$ *The Matrix* ($conf = \frac{2}{2}$) and *Titanic* $\to$ *Avatar* ($conf = \frac{1}{3}$). So recommend *The Matrix*. b) Higher-order rules: We find $\{Inception, Titanic\} \to$ *The Matrix* ($conf = \frac{1}{1}$), so recommend *The Matrix*. c) Similarity-based: Both *Inception* and *Titanic* have higher cosine similarity with *The Matrix* ($cos = \frac{2}{3} + \frac{2}{3}$) than *Avatar* ($cos = \frac{1}{2} + \frac{1}{\sqrt{3}\sqrt{2}}$), so recommend *The Matrix*.

$$support_{LEN}(s_i) = \sum_{p \in U} 1_{EQ}(s_i \in p) \cdot (|p| - 1).$$

Our definition of AR is equivalent to that of Ludewig et al. under the assumption that every item s_i occurs once in each session. The denominator is different from the traditional confidence definition which Ludewig motivates as a normalisation against the number of rules. However, we argue this formulation mainly imposes a severe penalty for longer user sessions. For top-n recommendations we compute:

$$score_{AR}(p, s_i) = conf(s_k \to s_i)$$

That is, we compute recommendations based on s_k, the last clicked item in the observed user session. We store the top-n rules with the highest confidence for each antecedent. Since we generate rules with rare items in the antecedent, this method yields high recall and coverage; however, low confidence and support values may reduce precision.

3.2 Recommendations Based on Pairwise Sequential Rules

The second pairwise method uses sequential rules (SR) and was proposed by Kamehkhosh et al. [12] and found to be competitive with deep learning methods in [16]. We consider the probability of a transition from an item A to B where A occurs before B. In contrast, Markov Chains model the transition from items occurring consecutively. The authors propose a weighting for sequential rule confidence, where the weight decays based on the number of items separating the interaction between A and B in a session. We compute the confidence for each sequential pair s_i, s_j using:

$$conf(s_i \to s_j) = \frac{support_{DUR}(s_i, s_j)}{support(s_i)} \quad \text{where}$$

$$support_{DUR}(s_i, s_j) = \sum_{p \in S} \frac{1_{EQ}(\langle s_i, s_j \rangle \prec p)}{duration(s_i, s_j)}$$

We use the notation $\langle s_i, s_j \rangle \prec p$ to denote that item s_i occurs before s_j in session p. The duration of two items s_i and s_j is defined by the number of items between s_i and $s_j + 1$. Intuitively, if s_i is always just before s_j, the denominator will be 1. During inference, they rank top-n recommendations for items based on the pairwise confidence with the last interacted item.

3.3 Item-Based Collaborative Filtering

Deshpande et al. introduced item-based collaborative filtering (IBCF) that makes predictions based on the k items with the highest similarity, defined using cosine similarity [5]. The cosine similarity between two item vectors **x** and **y** is given by the following formula:

$$cos(\mathbf{x},\mathbf{y}) = \frac{\sum_{i=1}^{n} x_i y_i}{\sqrt{\sum_{i=1}^{n} x_i^2} \cdot \sqrt{\sum_{i=1}^{n} y_i^2}}$$

where x_i and y_i are the components of the vectors **x** and **y**, and n is the number of dimensions (in this case, users who have rated both items). Assuming binary implicit feedback, we rewrite the previous equation as [4]:

$$cos(s_i, s_j) = \frac{support(s_i \wedge s_j)}{\sqrt{support(s_i)} \cdot \sqrt{support(s_j)}} = \mathit{conf}(s_i \rightarrow s_j)^{\frac{1}{2}} \cdot \mathit{conf}(s_j \rightarrow s_i)^{\frac{1}{2}}. \tag{1}$$

To generate the top-n recommendations for a given user based on IBCF, we compute:

$$score_{IBCF}(p, s_j) = \sum_{s_i \in p} cos\_top\_k(s_i, s_j) \text{ where}$$

$$cos\_top\_k(s_i, s_j) = \begin{cases} cos(s_i, s_j) & \text{if } cos(s_i, s_j) \text{ ranked in top-}k \text{ for } s_i \\ 0 & \text{otherwise} \end{cases}.$$

The parameter k is introduced to increase efficiency, since we only need to store $k \cdot |I|$ rules. If k is sufficiently large (default set to 100), an increase in k will typically not change the order of the top-n items recommendations assuming $n \ll k$. We note that Deshpande also studied using confidence, scaling the support of s_j, and normalization based on the length of each session. IBCF is closely related to AR, because predictions are based on the association between item pairs. A key difference with AR is that for computing the score we aggregate the similarities for each consequent, and typically use the full user history.

3.4 Higher-Order Association Rules Using Multiple Support Thresholds and Window-Based Recommendations by Mobasher

Mobasher et al. leverages Apriori to discover higher-order itemsets that are frequent [18]. A potential advantage of higher-order association mining is the discovery of highly confident rules that have larger antecedents. A problem with Apriori, is that if we set the minimal support threshold too low, we generate too many patterns. On the other hand, if we set the threshold too high, we miss "nuggets", i.e., rare but strong rules. Hence, Mobasher adopts MSApriori thereby using multiple minimum support levels [15]. A pattern X is frequent subject to multiple support levels if:

$$support(X) \geq \min_{i \in X}(MIS(i)) \quad \text{where}$$

$$MIS(i) = \begin{cases} support(i) \cdot \beta & \text{if } support(i) \geq \theta \\ \theta & \text{otherwise} \end{cases}. \tag{2}$$

Here θ is the global minimal support threshold and β controls the relative support. The intuition is that we want to limit ourselves to enumerating many higher-order patterns consisting of frequent (or popular) items. Additionally, we constrain the maximal size d of each itemset, usually set to 3 or 4. After mining frequent itemsets X, we generate all rules $X \setminus \{y\} \rightarrow \{y\}$ and discard rules below the minimal confidence threshold γ. For generating recommendations, the authors propose an *all-kth-order* approach inspired by Markov chain models and makes prediction by matching rules of size $d, d-1, \ldots, 2$ until a recommendation is generated. Additionally, they only consider the last $d-1$ items in the user's history. The rationale behind this process is that higher-order rules, by taking a larger fraction of the (most recent) user's history into account, increase precision. Finally, the authors propose to index rules using a Frequent Itemset Graph before generating recommendations [18]. However, we find this does not scale to larger datasets with millions of users and items, and present a more efficient solution in Sect. 4.

3.5 Adaptive-Support Higher-Order Association Rules by Lin

A second method that mines higher-order rules for recommendations was proposed by Lin [14,17]. Again, the motivation is to discover "nuggets", i.e. rare but strong rules. A crucial difference with the previous method, is that we do not define a minimal support threshold, do not filter the user history, and do not prioritize longer rules. Instead, Lin proposes to discover between $[k_{min}, k_{max}]$ confident rules local to each possible consequent item. The algorithm directly finds confident rules for each consequent item instead of the common two-phase approach where we first mine frequent itemsets and then extract confident rules [15,17]. The authors report that mining more than k_{max} (e.g. 100) rules for each item does not improve recommendation accuracy and avoids an unnecessarily large runtime. For making rule-based recommendations, we compute the top-n eligible rules with the highest confidence.

3.6 Higher-Order Rule-Based Recommendations Using Adjusted Confidence and Default Rules by Rudin

More recently, Rudin proposed a rule-based recommender thereby combining ideas from statistical learning with association rule mining. The main novelty is that items are ranked on the adjusted confidence measure, which provides an improved estimate of the true conditional probability [23]. For mining association rules they propose to use an existing algorithm, such as Apriori or FP-Growth. For recommendations, all rules are ranked on adjusted confidence for each user, and as such, there is no threshold on the minimal confidence. Additionally, if fewer than n matching rules are found we fall back on rules with empty antecedents, effectively providing popularity-based recommendations. The adjusted confidence is defined as:

$$conf_{ADJ}(X \rightarrow s_j) = \begin{cases} \frac{support(X \wedge s_j)}{support(X)+K} & \text{if } X \neq \emptyset \\ \frac{support(s_j)}{|S|+K} & \text{otherwise} \end{cases}. \qquad (3)$$

Table 1. An overview of seminal rule-based recommender systems in RuleRec.

Method	Rule form	Scoring	Mining strategy	Reasoning step
Simple association rules [16]	$x \to y$	Confidence weighted by session length	Enumerate all item pairs	History filtering and use rule with maximal confidence
Sequential rules [12]	$x \to y$	Confidence weighted by duration	Enumerate all sequential pairs	History filtering and use rule with maximal confidence
Item-based CF [5]	$x \to y$	Cosine similarity	Enumerate all similar pairs	Aggregate the similarity using all items in the history
Association rules with multiple support thresholds [18]	$x_1, \ldots x_d \to y$	Confidence priorizing longer rules	Apriori with multiple minimum support levels	Window-based history filtering and use rule with maximal confidence
Adaptive-support association rules [14]	$x_1, \ldots x_d \to y$	Confidence	Apriori local to each consequent with adaptive support levels	Full history and use rule with maximal confidence
Sequential Event Prediction [23]	$x_1, \ldots x_d \to y \, \{\} \to y$	Adjusted confidence	Apriori	Full history and use rule with maximal confidence or default rule

where K is a hyper-parameter. The intuition is that K bounds the support of both the left and right-hand side of the rule. They find that, if the confidence of two rules is similar, support should be used to break ties, which is what adjusted confidence does. Experimentally, they report that accuracy is maximized for small values of K and the effect is higher than tuning the minimal support and confidence thresholds.

4 RuleRec: An Efficient Rule-Based Recommender Library

We propose RuleRec, a lightweight library for pre-processing, rule mining, rule-based recommendation, and evaluation. A disadvantage of the original methods for higher-order rule mining is that they do not scale to sparse datasets with millions of users, items and interactions. We want to ensure higher-order mining is not dramatically less efficient than pairwise rule mining, when generating rules that are more precise by having multiple conditions in the antecedent. Hence, we developed scalable algorithms for rule mining in large, sparse datasets, leveraging techniques such as projection-based support counting, and reverse indexing. Additionally, we separate rule mining from inference, allowing for configurable strategies for selecting, ranking, and explaining recommendations.

4.1 Pairwise Methods

To compute the similarity-matrix, or the confidence between all item pairs, the naïve algorithm has a complexity of $O(|I|^2)$. We propose a generic method for the implementation of AR, SR and IBCF. Where we compute and rank pairwise rules on confidence or similarity scores, using Eq. 1 for the latter [4]. Crucial for efficiency is that we depend on the number of entries in the user-item interaction matrix $R \in \mathbb{R}^{|U| \times |I|}$, typically having less than 1% non-zero entries. We leverage an inverted index, where items and users are indexed. By iterating over the inverted indices, we compute only nonzero co-occurrence counts. This approach is embarrassingly parallel and highly effective for sparse datasets. This process is illustrated in the first three steps of Fig. 2. Finally, for generating recommendations and explanations, we propose a reusable module, RFER, which is discussed later.

4.2 Efficiently Mining Higher-Order Association Rules in Sparse Datasets

In this section, we propose new algorithms to improve the efficiency of Apriori [3], MSApriori [15] and adaptive support mining [14,17]. The key idea of our method is to compute all co-occurrences using an inverted index similar to pairwise recommenders, but generalized for higher-order itemsets. That is, we consider each frequent itemset of size k as a new virtual item, and maintain a list of all users who interacted with the itemset. The use of *projection*-based indexing has two advantages: candidate-free generation and fast support computation for higher-order itemsets. We remark that candidate-free enumeration is also used in FP-Growth [10,26].

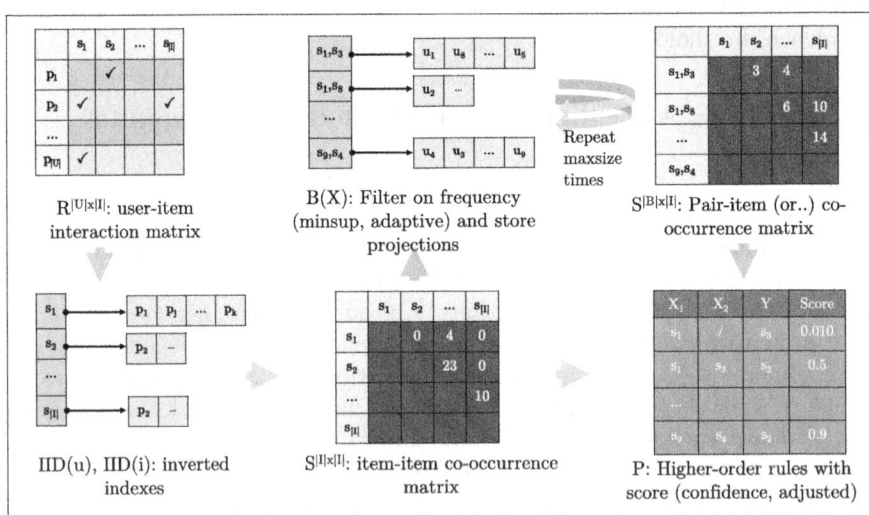

Fig. 2. Proposed algorithm for efficient pairwise and Apriori-based rule mining and recommendations.

Extending Apriori. Similar to Apriori, we search for frequent itemsets using breadth-first search. That is, at each level we generate patterns of size k, and prune patterns that are not frequent. The proposed algorithm, Apriori++, is illustrated in Fig. 2. First, we compute an inverted index for pairs, and compute co-occurrences. For higher-order itemsets we generalize the process. Formally, given a pattern $X_k = \{s_i, \ldots, s_j\}$, we define a projection $B(X_k)$, as the set of users that interacted with all items in X_k. For any candidate superset $X_{k+1} = X_k \cup \{s_k\}$, we need to locate all users interacting with X_k and s_k. Instead of computing the support as

$$support(X_{k+1}) = |\bigcap_{s_i \in X_{k+1}} IID(s_i)|.$$

We compute:
$$support(X_{k+1}) = |B(X_k) \cap IID(s_i)|.$$

Hence, amortized, only a single intersection is necessary. Moreover, the size of the projection significantly decreases as pattern length increases. In addition, we probe the projection and the inverted index. That is, for any candidate superset $X_{k+1} = X_k \cup \{s_k\}$, it holds that:

$$s_k \in \bigcup_{u_i \in B(X_k)} IID(u_i).$$

The consequence is that any candidate superset X_{k+1} occurs at least once in a user session. We repeat the creation of projections for pattern of size k, computing co-occurrences for patterns of size $k+1$, and prune patterns of size $k+1$ on frequency. Finally, we collect all varying-length frequent itemsets and compute rules and their confidence, which is a trivial step. The worst-case complexity is similar to Apriori, but the use of projections significantly reduces the practical runtime. We make a list of all frequent patterns of size $1, 2, \ldots d$ level-wise. Assuming $d = 4$, this results in at most $|I|^4$ candidates. However, if we prune infrequent patterns at each level k, using the threshold θ, the number of candidates is much lower. In Sect. 5, we compare the effectiveness of the proposed method against prior work [7].

Extending MSApriori. The rationale behind MSApriori, is we discover "nuggets", i.e. infrequent, but strong association rules. Extending MSApriori is trivial, since crucial steps such as computing projections, and the co-occurrence matrix level-wise are independent of the differences in any level-wise pruning strategy. Hence, we adopt the aforementioned algorithm, but prune itemsets of size k using Eq. 2 instead of using a single threshold θ.

Extending Adaptive mining. The miner proposed by Lin is different in design, since the goal is to find the top-k rules with the highest confidence for each consequent item. The first key difference, is that the threshold on minimal support is adaptive, and we run Apriori with varying minimal support threshold, until the number of rules of the form $X \to s_t$ is in the configurable range $[k_{min}, k_{max}]$ [14]. However, in each iteration, we have to enumerate patterns and rules local to each item $s_t \in I$. Hence, the described optimisations are applicable, such as the use of an inverted index, co-occurrence matrices, projections and generalization to higher-order itemsets. For brevity, we discuss a novel algorithm for adaptive-support mining in the Supplementary material, where we adapt co-occurrence and projection-based computation from Apriori++ but constrained to itemsets of the form $X \cup \{s_t\}$.

4.3 RFER: An Efficient and General Approach for Generating Recommendations

Several authors do not discuss any strategies to efficiently calculate rule-based recommendations [5,14] or propose complex and inefficient solutions [18]. We propose a general component to Retrieve, Filter, Explain and Rank rules (RFER). RFER assumes a large catalog of rules as input, and the history of selected users. We perform the following steps:

- First, the user history is preprocessed by selecting the full history or the last item(s)
- Next, eligible rules are retrieved from a potentially large rule catalog using a two-step process.
- Next, we create recommendations by ranking rules with the highest confidence measure, size, or aggregating rules have the same consequent.
- Finally, we link each recommendation, with the rule(s) causing the recommendation to enable explanations and analysis of the comprehensibility.

By logically separating rule mining and rule-based reasoning, we enable more variation than originally proposed. That is, history filtering, default rules, and various ranking and aggregation strategy for inference in rule-based recommendations, can be combined independently from any rule mining method. We observe that even if the number of rules is large, the number of eligible rules for a single user u is likely very small. Hence, we construct a simple rule index by mapping antecedents to rules using a hash map. For retrieval, we simply probe the hash map and filter eligible rules in a second phase. Previous work, suggested using a Frequent Itemset Graph [18]. However, storing and traversing the complete graph, i.e. keeping all pairwise and higher-order rules and relations between sub- and supersets is memory-intensive and computationally inefficient.

4.4 Higher-Order Methods

We now discuss the implementation of the three higher-order rule-based recommender from Table 1. For MOB, we use MSApriori++ and RFER for making recommendations. During inference, we perform history filtering using a sliding window, and prioritize longer rule, by ranking on size, and only secondary on confidence. For LIN, we use the novel, efficient algorithm of Adaptive mining for mining rules and RFER for inference, where we rank rules on confidence and use rule support to break ties. Finally, for RUDIN we use Apriori++ to mine rules.

After mining, we compute the adjusted confidence for each rule using Eq. 3. We generate recommendations using RFER, prioritize rules on adjusted confidence, and use default, popularity-based recommendations if fewer than top-n recommendations are generated.

5 Experiments

In this section, we aim to answer the following research questions: **RQ1**: How do the rule-based RS compare on accuracy? **RQ2**: How do the rule-based RS compare on runtime? What is the runtime of Apriori++ compared to Apriori? **RQ3**: How do the rule-based RS compare on diversity and popularity bias? **RQ4**: How do the rule-based RS compare on comprehensibility?

5.1 Experimental Setup

In our experiments, we evaluated rule-based RS on six real-world datasets from the e-commerce, news, and music domains. All datasets and the RuleRec library are publicly available[1].

Datasets. We evaluated six implicit-feedback datasets from music (30Music, AOTM), e-commerce (Retailrocket, RCS15), and news (CLEF, EBNeRD). Metadata was not used. We applied standard preprocessing: removing reconsumed items and filtering users/items with fewer than five interactions. On average, the datasets contain 610k users, 47k items, and 4.8M interactions. The news datasets have smaller item catalogs upto 5k, while the largest dataset, RCS15, includes 1.2M users, 34k items, and 10M interactions.

Evaluation Protocol. We created a random split of disjoint users using 80% for training and 20% for evaluation following the strong generalization principle. For evaluation, we hide the last 20% of interactions of test users, and generate the top-20 recommendations.

Evaluation Metrics. We report NDCG, recall, F1, and precision. We also report user coverage, i.e. the percentage of users with at least one recommendation. We measure the following secondary measures: intra-list list diversity [28], item coverage [2], and the average percentage of long-tail item recommendations (APLT) [1]. For comprehensibility, we report the number of rules. Additionally, we propose to report crucial statistics related to rule form and popularity bias, including the percentage of rules with 2 conditions, the percentage of rules with a popular item as consequent, and the percentage of rules between long-tail items. Here, popular items are defined as those items cumulatively covering 80% of all user-item interactions. A summary of well-known evaluation measures is presented in Table 3.

---

[1] RuleRec is implemented in Java and Python, open-source and available at https://bitbucket.org/len_feremans/rule-based-recommenders/.

Parameter Selection. We selected parameters after exploring the effect using grid search. Similar to [14,18], we also report a precision-recall trade-off, having maximal recall with lower confidence and support thresholds, and maximal precision (and F1) using a higher confidence thresholds. In Table 2 we present the parameter setting used in our experiments, tuned for recall (and diversity), and for prediction (and F1). We set *normalize* to True for IBCF, and the adjusted confidence parameter K to 0.001 for RUDIN resulting in optimal recall for both methods. For higher-order methods we set d to 3, resulting in rules consisting of 1 or 2 conditions.

5.2 RQ1: How Do the Rule-Based RS Compare on Accuracy?

First, we compare all methods on NDCG and recall. For brevity, we report average results in Table 4. Detailed results are available in the supplementary material. Our first observation is that SR, on average, is the most accurate method, performing best on 3 out of 6 datasets for recall and 4 out of 6 for NDCG. This aligns with its known strong performance in sequential recommendation [16]. Second, since AR and SR base predictions on only the last interaction, this confirms that history filtering is a simple yet effective strategy for improving

Table 2. Parameter settings for optimal recall (and NDCG, diversity and coverage) and F1 (and precision and comprehensibility) after grid search.

	AR	SR	IBCF	MOB	LIN	RUDIN
Optimal recall	$k = 20$	$k = 20$	$k = 200$	$\theta = 2, \beta = 0.1$	$k_{min} = 20, k_{max} = 200$	$\theta = 10$
	$\gamma = 0.0$	$\gamma = 0.0$	$\gamma = 0.0$	$\gamma = 0.001$	$\gamma = 0.001$	$\gamma = 0.001$
Optimal F1	$k = 20$	$k = 20$	$k = 50$	$\theta = 5, \beta = 0.1$	$k_{min} = 5, k_{max} = 50$	$\theta = 10$
	$\gamma = 0.25$	$\gamma = 0.25$	$\gamma = 0.25$	$\gamma = 0.25$	$\gamma = 0.25$	$\gamma = 0.25$

Table 3. Overview of evaluation metrics

Metric	Description
Hitrate, NDCG, MRR [21]	Measure the relevance, rank-aware or otherwise, of top-n recommendations.
Precision, recall, F1, AUROC [21]	Measure the precision, recall, and the precision-recall trade-off when generating recommendations while varying the confidence threshold.
Item coverage [2]	Number of distinct items appearing in any top-k recommendation, also referred to as aggregate diversity.
Popularity bias [1]	Average popularity of recommended items and percentage of long-tail item recommendations.
Diversity [28]	Average dissimilarity of all pairs of items in recommendation lists.
Calibration, fairness [25]	Difference in distribution of an attribute between training and recommended items. More recently studied as a fairness constraint.
Model comprehension [9]	Number of rules, length of antecedent, rule structure etc. important towards comprehension.

ranking. Third, there is no universal best method: IBCF (cosine similarity) performs best on AOTM, while LIN achieves the highest recall on two datasets. Among higher-order methods, LIN outperforms RUDIN and especially MOB, which has the lowest recall. We attribute this to LIN's pruning strategy, which ensures at least k_{min} rules per item, yielding more pairwise rules. Finally, in terms of precision and F1, AR is the clear winner, while RUDIN performs worst. MOB achieves a relatively high F1 score despite its lower recall.

5.3 RQ2: How Do the Rule-Based RS Compare on Runtime?

In Table 4, we also report the average runtime of each method. Our implementation of pairwise methods, as well as higher-order methods MOB and LIN, completes rule mining and recommendation within 10 min. Given that the largest dataset, RCS15, contains over 1 million users and 10 million interactions, and that we generate recommendations for 250k users, training and inference require less than 2 ms per user. For RUDIN, which uses Apriori, we set θ to 10 to reduce runtime, yet it still exceeded one hour on three datasets. In contrast, MOB and LIN gain efficiency from multiple or adaptive support thresholds.

We also compared Apriori++ with Apriori from the SPMF Library [7]. With a high support threshold $\theta = 93$ and $d = 3$, SPMF took over 300s to find 867 itemsets on the 30Music dataset. At $\theta = 5$, it ran out of memory. Apriori++, in contrast, completed in under 1s for $\theta = 93$ (300× faster), and within 12s for $\theta = 5$, discovering 1.9 million itemsets. Since a large number of rules is often required for high recall and coverage, we conclude that classic implementations of Apriori (and related methods like MSApriori and FPGrowth) do not scale well on sparse recommender datasets with millions of users and items.

Table 4. Average results of rule-based RS on NDCG, recall, precision, F1 and runtime on six datasets.

		AR	SR	IBCF	MOB	LIN	RUDIN
NDCG@20	Average	0.220	**0.246**	0.167	0.146	0.189	0.157
	Wins	1	**4**	1	0	0	0
Recall@20	Average	0.408	**0.427**	0.366	0.266	0.391	0.328
	Wins	0	**3**	1	0	2	0
Precision@20	Average	**0.059**	0.044	0.029	0.040	0.041	0.018
	Wins	**4**	1	1	0	0	0
F1@20	Average	**0.188**	0.088	0.109	0.163	0.108	0.067
	Wins	**4**	1	0	0	1	0
Runtime	Average	20.1 s	**19.2 s**	55.5 s	35.7 s	183.0 s	3151.7 s
	Wins	1	**3**	0	0	0	2

5.4 RQ3: How Do the Rule-Based RS Compare on Diversity and Popularity Bias?

In Table 5 we report the results for diversity, coverage and popularity bias. Concerning diversity, IBCF and RUDIN perform best both scoring 0.88 on average, and MOB performs poorly, which is possibly caused by the window-based inference strategy. Concerning item coverage and average percentage of long-tail recommendation, we find that LIN and SR outperform other methods, where IBCF, MOB, and RUDIN exhibit greater popularity bias, as they recommend more popular items. For user coverage, most methods, generate recommendations for all users on most datasets, except MOB. Since MOB decreases diversity, increases popularity bias, and has low item and user coverage, this method performs poorly. We conclude that, only AR, SR and LIN perform well on all secondary evaluation measures.

5.5 RQ4: How Do the Rule-Based RS Compare on Comprehensibility?

In Table 6, we report statistics on model comprehension and popularity bias. Pairwise methods AR and SR yield the fewest rules, typically $k \cdot |I|$. For IBCF, k is fixed at 200, producing a much larger rule set, reduced comprehensibility, and more complex explanations. Higher-order methods generate fewer rules than IBCF. MOB and RUDIN vary greatly, as their rule counts are highly sensitive to pruning thresholds; for instance, RUDIN has the largest rule set on three datasets and the smallest on three others. For news datasets with smaller $|I|$, all methods yield fewer rules—except RUDIN. From Table 6, we also observe that LIN discovers more pairwise rules than MOB and RUDIN. RUDIN mainly produces rules with popular consequents, whereas MOB and LIN generate more with long-tail antecedents and consequents. These findings suggest that postprocessing and rule-set optimization may be promising directions for future work. Although the total number of rules is high, domain experts can still filter and review those relevant to specific items. To better capture model complexity, we recommend Sankey plots [24]. These visualize the flow between user recommendations, eligible rules, and relevant items, offering insight into model behavior—something which is not possible with black-box models. Further examples are provided in the supplementary material.

6 Related Work

Wu et al. developed a framework based on FP-Growth and distributed processing for scalable rule-based recommendations [26]. Their work complements ours but differs from our work in two key aspects: they focus on distributed processing with load-balancing and partitioning for parallel speed-up, and they propose a single rule-mining algorithm with alternative confidence measures. Several authors have empirically studied higher-order rule-based recommenders.

Deshpande et al. examined similarity measures, normalization strategies, and parameter effects such as k [5]. They report IBCF often outperforms Apriori; however, we find Lin's adaptive-support method surpasses IBCF. More recent work extends the above methods: Osadchiy et al. [19] use pairwise association rules with aggregated confidence and support; Forsati et al. [6] mine higher-order rules ranked by frequency and dwell time; Yap and Gedikli personalize rule selection based on similar sessions [8,27]; and Rudin [23] learns weights for all pairwise associations to optimize a target objective. Finally, SR has been extended with higher-order sequential rules weighted by duration for news recommendation [13]. Most studies still evaluate mainly accuracy on datasets from a single domain.

Table 5. Average results of rule-based RS on diversity, item coverage, average percentage long-tail item recommendation, and user coverage on six datasets.

		AR	SR	IBCF	MOB	LIN	RUDIN
Diversity	Average	0.845	0.862	0.881	0.579	0.869	**0.883**
	Wins	0	0	4	0	0	2
Item coverage	Average	69.2%	77.9%	52.5%	47.8%	**81.1%**	33.1%
	Wins	0	1	1	0	4	0
APLT	Average	14.4%	**18.6%**	7.9%	13.9%	17.2%	8.1%
	Wins	0	4	1	1	0	0
User coverage	Average	99.0%	98.6%	99.9%	80.6%	99.9%	**100%**

Table 6. Average results of rule-based RS on comprehensibility, rule size, and rule popularity bias on six datasets.

		AR	SR	IBCF	MOB	LIN	RUDIN
Number of rules	Average	843.4k	**757.6k**	3067.9k	1990.4k	2841.7k	1920.3k
Rules of size 3	Average	0%	0%	0%	49%	8%	**67%**
Rules pop. cons.	Average	64%	61%	68%	53%	37%	**89%**
Long-tail rules	Average	31%	32%	27%	**39%**	39%	7%

7 Conclusion

We analyzed the literature to categorize and compare a broad range of rule-based recommendation algorithms. Our study revealed substantial differences in rule structure, confidence measures, pruning strategies, mining constraints, and inference. Notably, existing higher-order rule mining methods often fail to scale on large, sparse datasets. Moreover, prior research has focused primarily on accuracy, neglecting critical factors like efficiency, diversity, popularity bias, and comprehension. To address these gaps, we implemented and evaluated a diverse set of representative algorithms in RuleRec—an open-source, lightweight, and scalable library featuring modules for preprocessing, evaluation, visualization, and various rule-based recommenders. We evaluated all methods on six benchmark datasets, yielding insights into trade-offs in accuracy, comprehensibility, diversity, and popularity bias. Pairwise and sequential association rule methods with history filtering show strong NDCG performance. Higher-order approaches, such as Lin's adaptive-support technique, provide clear benefits in recall and item coverage. Our proposed Apriori-based rule mining algorithms achieve up to 300× speed-up over a well-known baseline. All recommender systems complete within minutes on large, sparse datasets. We extend rule mining through level-wise generation, adaptive or multiple threshold pruning, and projection-based data structures. Our modular design further decouples rule mining from inference, offering greater flexibility and efficiency than prior systems. In domains demanding transparency, fairness, and efficiency—such as healthcare, education, or public services—rule-based recommenders provide a compelling alternative. A limitation of our study is the lack of detailed analysis on how hyper-parameters and dataset characteristics (e.g., sparsity and popularity bias) affect effectiveness. For future work, we recommend advancing rule mining, exploring multi-objective optimization, and conducting independent evaluation studies.

Acknowledgements. L.F. is funded on Research Fund Flanders grant 12B0V24N.

References

1. Abdollahpouri, H., Burke, R., Mobasher, B.: Managing popularity bias in recommender systems with personalized re-ranking. In: The Thirty-Second International FLAIRS Conference (2019)
2. Adomavicius, G., Kwon, Y.: Improving aggregate recommendation diversity using ranking-based techniques. IEEE Trans. Knowl. Data Eng. **24**(5), 896–911 (2011)
3. Agrawal, R., Srikant, R.: Fast algorithms for mining association rules. In: Proceedings of the 20th International Conference on Very Large Data Bases (VLDB), vol. 1215, pp. 487–499. Santiago, Chile (1994)
4. Aiolli, F.: Efficient top-n recommendation for very large scale binary rated datasets. In: Proceedings of the 7th ACM Conference on Recommender Systems, pp. 273–280 (2013)
5. Deshpande, M., Karypis, G.: Item-based top-n recommendation algorithms. ACM Trans. Inform. Syst. **22**(1), 143–177 (2004)
6. Forsati, R., Meybodi, M.R., Neiat, A.G.: Web page personalization based on weighted association rules. In: 2009 International Conference on Electronic Computer Technology, pp. 130–135 (2009)
7. Fournier-Viger, P., et al.: The spmf open-source data mining library version 2. In: Joint European Conference on Machine Learning and Knowledge Discovery in Databases, pp. 36–40 (2016)
8. Gedikli, F., Jannach, D.: Neighborhood-restricted mining and weighted application of association rules for recommenders. In: International Conference on Web Information Systems Engineering, pp. 157–165 (2010)
9. Goethals, S., Martens, D., Evgeniou, T.: The non-linear nature of the cost of comprehensibility. J. Big Data **9**(1), 30 (2022)

10. Han, J., Pei, J., Yin, Y., Mao, R.: Mining frequent patterns without candidate generation: a frequent-pattern tree approach. Data Min. Knowl. Disc. **8**(1), 53–87 (2004)
11. Jannach, D., Quadrana, M., Cremonesi, P.: Session-based recommender systems. In: Recommender Systems Handbook, pp. 301–334. Springer (2022)
12. Kamehkhosh, I., Jannach, D., Ludewig, M.: A comparison of frequent pattern techniques and a deep learning method for session-based recommendation. In: RecTemp@RecSys, pp. 50–56 (2017)
13. Karimi, M., Feremans, L., Cule, B., Goethals, B.: Session-based news recommendation using cohesive patterns. In: 2024 IEEE International Conference on Big Data (BigData), pp. 440–447 (2024)
14. Lin, W., Alvarez, S.A., Ruiz, C.: Efficient adaptive-support association rule mining for recommender systems. Data Min. Knowl. Disc. **6**, 83–105 (2002)
15. Liu, B., Hsu, W., Ma, Y.: Mining association rules with multiple minimum supports. In: Proceedings of the Fifth ACM SIGKDD International Conference on Knowledge Discovery and Data Mining, pp. 337–341 (1999)
16. Ludewig, M., Jannach, D.: Evaluation of session-based recommendation algorithms. User Model. User-Adap. Interact. **28**(4), 331–390 (2018)
17. Ma, B., Liu, B., Hsu, Y.: Integrating classification and association rule mining. In: Proceedings of the Fourth International Conference on Knowledge Discovery and Data Mining (1998)
18. Mobasher, B., Dai, H., Luo, T., Nakagawa, M.: Effective personalization based on association rule discovery from web usage data. In: Proceedings of the 3rd International Workshop on Web Information and Data Management, pp. 9–15 (2001)
19. Osadchiy, T., Poliakov, I., Olivier, P., Rowland, M., Foster, E.: Recommender system based on pairwise association rules. Expert Syst. Appl. **115**, 535–542 (2019)
20. Ribeiro, M.T., Singh, S., Guestrin, C.: Why should i trust you?: Explaining the predictions of any classifier. In: Proceedings of the 22nd ACM SIGKDD International Conference on Knowledge Discovery and Data Mining, pp. 1135–1144 (2016)
21. Ricci, F., Rokach, L., Shapira, B.: Introduction to recommender systems handbook. In: Recommender systems Handbook, pp. 1–35. Springer (2010)
22. Rudin, C.: Stop explaining black box machine learning models for high stakes decisions and use interpretable models instead. Nature Mach. Intell. **1**(5), 206–215 (2019)
23. Rudin, C., Letham, B., Salleb-Aouissi, A., Kogan, E., Madigan, D.: Sequential event prediction with association rules. In: Proceedings of the 24th Annual Conference on Learning Theory, pp. 615–634 (2011)
24. Schmidt, M.: The sankey diagram in energy and material flow management: Part ii: Methodology and current applications. J. Ind. Ecol. **12**(2), 173–185 (2008)
25. Steck, H.: Calibrated recommendations. In: Proceedings of the 12th ACM Conference on Recommender Systems, pp. 154–162 (2018)
26. Wu, Z., Li, C., Cao, J., Ge, Y.: On scalability of association-rule-based recommendation: a unified distributed-computing framework. ACM Trans. Web **14**(3), 1–21 (2020)
27. Yap, G.E., Li, X.L., Yu, P.S.: Effective next-items recommendation via personalized sequential pattern mining. In: International Conference on Database Systems for Advanced Applications, pp. 48–64 (2012)
28. Zhang, M., Hurley, N.: Avoiding monotony: Improving the diversity of recommendation lists. In: Proceedings of the 2008 ACM Conference on Recommender Systems, pp. 123–130 (2008)

Rule2Text: Natural Language Explanation of Logical Rules in Knowledge Graphs

Nasim Shirvani-Mahdavi[✉][iD], Devin Wingfield, Amin Ghasemi, and Chengkai Li[✉][iD]

University of Texas at Arlington, 701 S Nedderman Dr, Arlington, TX 76019, USA
{nasim.shirvanimahdavi2,dtw8917,mxg6185}@mavs.uta.edu, cli@uta.edu

Abstract. Knowledge graphs (KGs) often contain sufficient information to support the inference of new facts. Identifying logical rules not only improves the completeness of a knowledge graph but also enables the detection of potential errors, reveals subtle data patterns, and enhances the overall capacity for reasoning and interpretation. However, the complexity of such rules, combined with the unique labeling conventions of each KG, can make them difficult for humans to understand. In this paper, we explore the potential of large language models to generate natural language explanations for logical rules. Specifically, we extract logical rules using the AMIE 3.5.1 rule discovery algorithm from the benchmark dataset FB15k-237 and two large-scale datasets, FB-CVT-REV and FB+CVT-REV. We examine various prompting strategies, including zero- and few-shot prompting, including variable entity types, and chain-of-thought reasoning. We conduct a comprehensive human evaluation of the generated explanations based on correctness, clarity, and hallucination, and also assess the use of large language models as automatic judges. Our results demonstrate promising performance in terms of explanation correctness and clarity, although several challenges remain for future research. All scripts and data used in this study are publicly available at https://github.com/idirlab/KGRule2NL.

Keywords: Knowledge graphs · Logical rules · Natural language explanation · Large language models · Interpretability

1 Introduction

Knowledge graphs (KGs) encode factual information as triples of the form (subject s, predicate p, object o). They are integral to a wide range of artificial intelligence tasks and applications [9,12]. Although large-scale KGs (e.g., Freebase [3] and Wikidata [21]) contain a vast number of triples, they are often incomplete, which adversely affects their usefulness in downstream applications. However, KGs often hold sufficient information to infer new facts [7,19]. For example, if a KG indicates that a certain woman is the mother of a child, it is quite likely that her husband is the child's father. Identifying such rules can help infer highly probable missing facts which can be further verified by human data workers or experts. In addition to enhancing the completeness of KGs, such rules can also aid in detecting potential errors, deepening our understanding of the data's inherent patterns, and facilitating reasoning and interpretability [7,14]. Rule learning systems, such as AMIE [2,8] and AnyBURL [13], derive Horn rules for symbolic reasoning and link prediction in KGs. These rules can serve as explanations for specific predictions; for instance, such rules can assist domain scientists in uncovering underlying missing relationships within their data.

However, rules are often challenging to comprehend for humans, especially for non-experts. The difficulty arises from the abstract logical structure and the complexity of the rules; the number of logical components, referred to as atoms, as well as the nuanced nature of entity and relation labels within each KG. For instance, as explained in [20], label of predicates in the Freebase dataset follow the format /[domain]/[type]/[label] (e.g., /american_football/player_rushing_statistics/team). Without proper background knowledge about such differences in KG labels, evaluating logical rules can become cumbersome.

One way to address this challenge is by providing natural language explanations for logical rules, which enhance accessibility and usability, aid KG management in cross-disciplinary contexts, and improve transparency for researchers and practitioners. Pre-defined templates can generate such explanations, but this approach is not scalable, as it is impractical to manually extract all logical rules from a large KG and define templates for each. To handle unseen rules, solutions leveraging large language models (LLMs) are promising due to LLMs' generative abilities and generalization capabilities. To the best of our knowledge, this is the first work to examine the effectiveness of LLMs in generating natural language explanations for logical rules; related work is presented in Sect. 2.

We mined the rules by the AMIE 3.5.1 algorithm, the latest version released in 2024, using the widely used cross-domain benchmark dataset FB15k-237 [4] and two properly preprocessed large-scale variants of the Freebase dataset, FB-CVT-REV and FB+CVT-REV [20] (Sect. 3). We investigated a range of prompting strategies, such as zero and few-shot prompting [11], incorporating an instance of the rule, including variable entity types and Chain-of-Thought (CoT) reasoning [22] (Sect. 4). To evaluate the quality of the generated explanations, we conducted detailed human evaluations based on criteria such as correctness, clarity, and hallucination. Additionally, we explored the potential of LLM-as-a-judge [24] for this task (Sect. 5). Our findings indicate that combining CoT prompting with variable type information yields the most accurate and readable explanations. Overall, our findings highlight a promising direction for this task. We conclude the work and outline potential avenues for future research in Sect. 6. All the scripts and data produced from this work are available from our GitHub repository at https://github.com/idirlab/KGRule2NL.

2 Related Work

Prior work in natural language generation from logical forms, such as Logic2Text [5] and SLEtoNL [23], generates high-fidelity text from structured tables and sequential logic. While effective for their specific domains, these models are limited in explaining knowledge graph rules. They rely on input structures that are fundamentally different from the Horn clauses we use. Furthermore, they prioritize fluent summaries over pedagogical explanations and neglect the crucial semantic roles of entities, types, and relations within knowledge graphs. Another relevant area is the encoding and translation of natural rules [1,6], which converts natural language rule expressions into a formal logical format. This work aims to acquire rules from human expertise, whereas our approach focuses on interpreting and explaining existing rules. Similarly, Chain of Logic [17] improves how large language models apply compositional rules to factual scenarios. However, this approach also assumes the rules are already available and ready for reasoning, which differs from our goal of providing explanations for them. In the broader context of KG-to-text generation, Shi et al. [18] tackle the challenge of generating natural language descriptions from KG triples while mitigating hallucinations in large-scale, open-domain settings. While their work shares the goal of converting structured knowledge into natural language, it focuses on factual triple descriptions rather than rule explanations.

3 Rule Selection from Knowledge Graphs

3.1 Rule Mining Algorithm

We employed AMIE 3.5.1, a well-established rule learning system in its latest version, due to its comprehensive metrics for rule evaluation as well as its proven compatibility with our chosen benchmark datasets. In AMIE, a rule has a body (antecedent) and a head (consequent), represented as $B_1 \land B_2 \land \ldots \land B_n \Rightarrow H$, or in simplified form $\vec{B} \Rightarrow H$. The body consists of multiple *atoms* B_1, ..., B_n and the head H itself is also an atom. In an atom $r(\mathbf{h},\mathbf{t})$, which is another representation of a triple $(\mathbf{h}, r, \mathbf{t})$, the subject and/or the object are variables to be instantiated. The prediction of the head can be carried out when all the body atoms can be instantiated in the KG. In AMIE, the concept of *support* quantifies the amount of evidence (i.e., correct predictions) for each rule in the data. It is defined as the number of distinct (subject, object) pairs in the head of all valid instantiations of the rule in the KG. The concept of *head coverage*, a proportional version of *support*, is the fraction of *support* over the number of facts in relation r, where r is the relation in the head atom. The *standard confidence* of a rule is the fraction of *support* over the number of instantiations of the rule body. To mine the rules, we used the default settings of AMIE for optimized performance, with minimum thresholds of 0.1 for *head coverage* and *standard confidence*, and a maximum threshold of 3 for the number of atoms.

3.2 Datasets

For our experiments, we leveraged three datasets. FB15k-237, a small subset of the Freebase dataset, was selected as it is a widely used benchmark for KG completion, recognized for avoiding the data leakage issues of FB15k [4]. Its multi-domain coverage makes it well-suited for extracting logical rules with diverse relations. FB-CVT-REV and FB+CVT-REV [20] datasets (Statistics shown in Table 1) are large-scale variants of the Freebase dataset designed to eliminate the data leakage issue previously identified in FB15k. FB+CVT-REV includes mediator entities (i.e., Compound Value Type nodes) originally present in Freebase to represent n-ary relations. In contrast, FB-CVT-REV converts n-ary relationships centered on a CVT node into binary relations by concatenating the edges that connect entities through the CVT node, a method also used in FB15k-237. As shown in Table 1, the conversion process has resulted in a higher number of rules in these two datasets compared to those in FB+CVT-REV. Including these datasets facilitates the analysis of large-scale data and the effects of mediator nodes and concatenated relationships on the derived rules and generated explanations.

The label of a concatenated relation is formed by merging the labels of two underlying relations. As a result, the label becomes lengthy, taking the format of *domain1/type1/label1./domain2/type2/label2*. Notably, the domains and even types can sometimes be identical in concatenated labels, but label1 and label2 are always distinct. This format differs from the simpler structure of standard relations, which follow the format of *domain/type/label*. Thus, this added complexity can pose a greater challenge for LLMs in generating natural language explanations. For instance, consider the triple (Dallas Cowboys, /american_football/game_passing_statistics/team./american_football/game_passing_statistics/player, Tony Romo). Following the aforementioned format, this relation indicates that Dallas Cowboys and Tony Romo participated in an n-ary relationship involving additional entities, with this property representing the result of converting the n-ary relationship to the binary format.

4 Methodology

4.1 Prompting Strategies

To generate natural language explanations for logical rules, we conducted our experiments in three phases. All scripts and prompts, rules, generated explanations, and annotated data are available at our GitHub repository. In all prompts used in our experiments, we provided background knowledge to the models to enhance their understanding of the syntax and labels of the datasets. This content includes the format of predicates in the datasets as mentioned in Sect. 3. This background knowledge is particularly important because, in rules that involve concatenated relations, the resulting lengthy labels with multiple components can easily confuse the model.

Phase 1: Zero-Shot vs. Few-Shot Prompting. In the first phase, we compared zero-shot and few-shot prompting strategies using rules from a small subset of the Freebase dataset, specifically FB15k-237. The objective was to assess the impact of in-context examples on explanation quality and establish a baseline. The few-shot prompt includes two (rule, explanation) pairs as examples. In this phase and phase 2, we employed OpenAI's GPT-3.5 Turbo model for its balance of performance, efficiency, and cost-effectiveness. A total of 100 rules with the highest head coverage were selected for human evaluation, covering a broad range of domains, from music and media to medicine and space. To ensure the quality of the annotations and mitigate potential subjectivity, we tasked three individuals with annotating the data. For each rule, annotators were shown both the rule and a concrete instantiation to aid understanding, along with two generated explanations, one from zero-shot prompting and one from few-shot. Their task was to identify which explanation better captured the semantics of the rule. In cases of comparable semantic accuracy, the more naturally worded explanation was preferred. After selecting the better explanation, annotators rated it using the evaluation metrics described in Sect. 4.2. As discussed in Sect. 5, the few-shot prompting strategy did not yield significant improvements over the zero-shot baseline.

Phase 2: Utilizing Variable Entity Types in The Prompt. This phase initially incorporated rule instantiations into the prompt design. However, analysis of the generated explanations revealed persistent limitations in the model's ability to identify variable entity types, leading us to adopt integration of these types in the prompt. For instance, in the rule ?b /time/event/instance_of_recurring_event World Series => World Series /sports/sports_championship/events ?b, World Series is a constant entity and ?b is a variable entity. In Freebase datasets, entities can belong to multiple types. Consequently, each variable entity is associated with a list of types. Given an edge type and its edge instances, there is *almost* a function that maps from the edge type to a type that all subjects in the edge instances belong to, and similarly, *almost* such a function for objects [20]. For the example above, the variable ?b's types are either /time/event or /sports/sports_championship_event. For this phase, three annotators annotated 100 rules, rules with the highest head coverage, 50 top rules from FB-CVT-REV, and 50 from FB+CVT-REV. Unlike the previous phase, the annotators were asked to complete metric evaluations for explanations from both prompts, the zero-shot prompt as our baseline, and the prompt incorporating variable type. As discussed in Sect. 5, our findings show that providing variable type information significantly improved the model's performance in generating accurate explanations.

Phase 3: Comparing Models and Chain-of-Thought Prompting. Building on the strong impact of incorporating variable entity types into the prompts, we further leveraged the reasoning capabilities enabled by CoT prompting. This prompt guides the model through five reasoning steps. First, it parses the rule and identifies its components, including constant entities, variable entities, and relations. Second, for each variable entity, it determines the most contextually relevant type. Third, it interprets each atom in the rule using the selected types. Fourth, it synthesizes the information to infer the rule's overall implication. Finally, it generates a concise natural language explanation. The prompt also includes two illustrative examples with CoT reasoning to support the model's understanding. In this phase, we expanded our evaluation to include two additional models, GPT-4o Mini and Gemini 2.0 Flash, alongside GPT-3.5 Turbo. These models were selected to provide a balanced comparison in terms of performance, efficiency, and cost-effectiveness. Three annotators evaluated new explanations, generated via CoT prompting by the three models, for the same set of rules used in phase 2. As discussed in Sect. 5, GPT-3.5 Turbo shows improved performance compared to phase 2, while Gemini 2.0 Flash achieves the highest overall performance, followed by GPT-4o Mini.

4.2 Evaluation Metrics for Generated Explanations

To evaluate the generated explanations, we used the following metrics for human and automatic evaluation.

Correctness: Evaluation of the explanation's accuracy on a scale from 1 (completely incorrect) to 5 (fully correct). Correctness refers to the explanation's inclusion of all components of the rule, presented in the exact logical order specified by the rule.

Clarity: Evaluation of the explanation on a scale from 1 (very unclear) to 5 (very clear). Clarity refers to the ease with which the explanation can be understood and how naturally it reads. This metric exclusively assesses the explanation, independent of the correctness of the underlying rule.

# of missed entities: The number of entities present in the rule but not stated in the explanation.

# of missed relations: The number of relations (i.e., predicates) present in the rule but not stated in the explanation.

# of hallucinated entities: The number of entities absent from the rule but incorrectly stated in the explanation.

# of hallucinated relations: The number of relations absent from the rule but incorrectly stated in the explanation.

Rule logicalness: Although the meaningfulness of a rule is not directly related to the generation of explanations, we asked the annotators to rate the rules on a scale from 1 (not logically sound) to 2 (moderately logical), and 3 (logically sound). This metric exclusively evaluates the rule itself, without considering the explanation.

Perplexity: Given the absence of reference sentences for comparison with the explanations, as our automatic evaluation metric, we computed perplexity [10] using GPT-2 [16]. Perplexity measures how well a language model predicts a sequence of words, with lower values indicating more predictable and naturally flowing text. While it is a useful measure of the model's fluency and coherence, it is not an indication of the correctness of the explanations.

5 Experiments and Results

Phase 1. The annotated data, available on our GitHub repository, represents an aggregation of input from three annotators. For each rule, we select the explanation receiving the majority vote and calculate the average of the measures for that chosen explanation only. For instance, if annotators 1 and 2 selected the explanation generated from the zero-shot prompt for a particular rule, while the third annotator chose the explanation from the few-shot prompt, we only averaged the measures provided by annotators 1 and 2 for that rule.

Table 2 presents the average of all measures for all annotated rules (denoted as all), as well as for explanations generated from zero and few-shot prompts separately (denoted as prompt 1 and prompt 2, respectively). Specifically, for rules where the explanation generated from prompt 1 was favored by the majority of annotators, the table reports the average measures for those explanations. The same approach is applied to rules where explanations from prompt 2 were preferred. Additionally, we provide these measures for the subset of rules where annotators unanimously selected the same explanation (denoted as unanimous), comparing them to the remaining rules with majority voting (denoted as majority). The measures # missed entities, # missed relations, # hallucinated entities, # hallucinated relations, correctness, clarity, logicalness, and perplexity are denoted as m ent, m rel, h ent, h rel, correctness, clarity, logical, and perplexity in Table 2 (and 3) respectively.

These results demonstrate the model, overall, generates relatively accurate and clear explanations with low perplexity. Among the 100 sentences selected for human annotation, 49 were assigned to explanation 2, derived from the few-shot prompt, while the remaining sentences were assigned to explanation 1. Notably, annotators reached unanimous agreement on 48% of the rules. Furthermore, the number of missed or hallucinated elements is negligible. Our observations indicate that most hallucinations stem from the labels of relations, particularly concatenated relations. The model tends to generate additional entities or relations to explain the complex labels associated with concatenated relations.

Table 1. Statistics of the datasets

dataset	# of triples	# of rules
FB15k-237	310,116	6,320
FB-CVT-REV	125,124,274	14,355
FB+CVT-REV	134,213,735	2,965

Table 2. Evaluation results on the annotated data in phase 1

	m ent↓	m rel↓	h ent↓	h rel↓	correctness↑	clarity↑	logical↑	perplexity↓
all	0.10	0.04	0.29	0.10	4.36	4.67	2.36	36.14
prompt 1	0.14	0.05	0.25	0.07	4.40	4.69	2.29	37.85
prompt 2	0.06	0.03	0.34	0.12	4.32	4.64	2.44	34.36
unanimous	0.13	0.03	0.35	0.12	4.34	4.68	2.29	33.80
majority	0.08	0.05	0.24	0.07	4.37	4.66	2.43	38.30

Phase 2. Table 3 presents the results for this phase, averaged across all annotators. Explanation 2, generated using the variable type prompt, consistently shows higher correctness and clarity across all categories, highlighting the importance of type information for model comprehension. Both explanation types have minimal missing entities and relations. However, Explanation 2 also shows slightly higher

hallucination rates and increased perplexity. Rules with three atoms and those involving concatenated relations generally receive lower correctness and clarity scores, likely due to their increased complexity. Interestingly, despite these lower scores, annotators rated the rules from these two categories as more logically coherent.

Table 3. Evaluation results on the annotated data in phase 2

	explanation from zero-shot prompt							explanation from variable type prompt						
	logical↑	m ent↓	m rel↓	h ent↓	h rel↓	correct↑	clarity↑	perplexity↓	m ent↓	m rel↓	h ent↓	h rel↓	correct↑	clarity↑	perplexity↓
all	2.58	0.06	0.10	0.22	0.09	3.94	4.12	29.05	0.05	0.07	0.21	0.13	4.21	4.19	33.07
2 atoms	2.50	0.03	0.04	0.08	0.05	4.22	4.35	34.10	0.31	0.41	0.15	0.16	4.25	4.30	38.59
3 atoms	2.62	0.08	0.13	0.31	0.12	3.78	3.99	26.21	0.07	0.08	0.24	0.11	4.18	4.12	29.97
binary	2.59	0.08	0.10	0.18	0.08	4.04	4.22	31.02	0.06	0.03	0.20	0.11	4.32	4.28	34.11
mediator	2.51	0.08	0.13	0.16	0.06	4.15	4.13	24.22	0.01	0.11	0.16	0.06	4.36	4.2	28.65
concatenated	2.60	0.02	0.08	0.35	0.15	3.63	3.91	27.63	0.05	0.11	0.25	0.20	3.88	3.99	33.33

Phase 3. Given the negligible number of hallucinated and missing entities and relations, we evaluated the explanations in phase 3 using only correctness, clarity, and perplexity. Table 4 presents the results. Overall, the models exhibit trends similar to those observed in Phase 2. For example, all models perform better on shorter rules, particularly those with only two atoms, and achieve higher performance on rules involving only binary relations compared to those with concatenated ones. GPT-3.5 Turbo shows improved performance with CoT prompting compared to its performance using only variable entities. This improvement is consistent across all categories except for rules that include mediator nodes. GPT-4o Mini is the second-best performing model and demonstrates relatively strong performance on rules containing at least one concatenated relation. Gemini 2.0 Flash demonstrates the best overall performance. Its explanations are the most concise, though in rare instances, it includes remarks such as, "Note: This rule is likely flawed." Notably, the lowest clarity scores across all models are observed for rules involving mediator nodes. Additionally, most models exhibit their highest perplexity on rules with only two atoms, which is somewhat unexpected given the simplicity of these rules.

Table 4. Evaluation results on the annotated data in phase 3

	GPT-3.5 Turbo			GPT-4o mini			Gemini 2.0 Flash		
	correct↑	clarity↑	perplexity↓	correct↑	clarity↑	perplexity↓	correct↑	clarity↑	perplexity↓
all	4.28	4.26	32.40	4.45	4.53	31.57	4.67	4.70	27.19
2 atoms	4.38	4.43	34.08	4.52	4.62	40.96	4.80	4.76	29.98
3 atoms	4.22	4.17	31.46	4.42	4.51	26.26	4.61	4.68	25.62
binary	4.40	4.42	34.58	4.50	4.58	33.52	4.70	4.71	27.77
mediator	4.13	4.07	26.26	4.24	4.49	26.82	4.69	4.63	26.92
concatenated	4.10	4.07	31.57	4.50	4.51	30.38	4.63	4.75	26.19

LLM-as-a-Judge. One of the limitations of this work is the absence of ground truth data, which restricts our ability to fine-tune models effectively. A potential solution lies in leveraging the LLM-as-a-judge approach. If a reliably fair and consistent judge model can be designed, it becomes possible to use a strong model, such as Gemini 2.0 Flash, to generate (rule, explanation) pairs. The judge can then evaluate these pairs, and those receiving high scores can be treated as pseudo-ground truth for fine-tuning smaller open-source models. Additionally, low-scoring examples can be analyzed to identify patterns and better understand the types of explanations or rules that pose challenges for the model.

To explore this direction, we developed an LLM-as-a-judge prompt. LLM-based judges often exhibit bias toward models from their family [15], for example, GPT models tend to favor responses generated by other GPT models. To account for this potential bias, we evaluated the performance of the two best models, GPT-4o Mini and Gemini 2.0 Flash, using both GPT-4o Mini and Gemini 2.0 Flash as judges. This resulted in a total of four evaluation settings for a more balanced comparison. Since clarity can be a highly subjective metric, we focused our analysis on correctness. The information provided to the LLM judges was identical to that given to human annotators: the rule, an instance of the rule, the list of variable types, and the explanation. Table 5 presents the correlation between LLM judges and human annotators. Because annotator scores are averaged across multiple individuals, they are represented as floating-point numbers, whereas LLM judge scores are integers. To ensure a fair comparison, we rounded the annotator scores to the nearest whole number before computing correlation coefficients. We used Spearman correlation to measure rank-order agreement, assessing how similarly the judges and annotators rank the explanations. Pearson correlation was used to evaluate the strength of the linear relationship between their actual scores. Both LLM judges show moderate agreement with annotators on the correctness of explanations generated by GPT-4o Mini. Gemini 2.0 Flash also aligned reasonably well with annotators when evaluating its own outputs, whereas GPT-4o Mini showed weak agreement in that setting. Although these results are not ideal, they point to a promising direction for future work in leveraging LLMs for scalable evaluation and dataset generation.

Table 5. Correlation between LLM judges and annotators for correctness

Judge	Explanation generated by	Spearman	Pearson
GPT-4o mini	GPT-4o mini	0.528	0.595
Gemini 2.0 Flash	GPT-4o mini	0.498	0.603
GPT-4o mini	Gemini 2.0 Flash	0.221	0.208
Gemini 2.0 Flash	Gemini 2.0 Flash	0.429	0.527

6 Conclusion and Future Work

We employed three LLMs with multiple prompting strategies to generate natural language explanations for logical rules extracted by the AMIE algorithm from three datasets at varying scales. Human evaluation indicated encouraging results regarding accuracy and clarity, although rule complexity presents challenges for future research. Our findings indicate that the combination of Chain-of-Thought prompting and variable type information yields the most accurate and readable explanations. Future research can extend this work by evaluating LLM performance on more complex rules beyond AMIE's extraction capabilities, exploring additional knowledge bases such as Wikidata, which encode facts differently, and constructing reference explanations to fine-tune LLMs for improved generation quality.

Acknowledgments. This material is based upon work supported by the National Science Foundation under Grants TIP-2333834. We also extend our gratitude to the Texas Advanced Computing Center (TACC) for providing computing resources for this work's experimentation.

References

1. Æsøy, K., Ozaki, A.: Rule learning as machine translation using the atomic knowledge bank. arXiv:2311.02765 (2023)
2. Betz, P., Galárraga, L., Ott, S., Meilicke, C., Suchanek, F., Stuckenschmidt, H.: PyClause-simple and efficient rule handling for knowledge graphs. In: IJCAI, pp. 8610–8613 (2023)
3. Bollacker, K., Evans, C., Paritosh, P., Sturge, T., Taylor, J.: Freebase: a collaboratively created graph database for structuring human knowledge. In: SIGMOD, pp. 1247–1250 (2008)
4. Bordes, A., Usunier, N., Garcia-Durán, A., Weston, J., Yakhnenko, O.: Translating embeddings for modeling multi-relational data. In: NeurIPS, pp. 2787–2795 (2013)
5. Chen, Z., et al.: Logic2Text: high-fidelity natural language generation from logical forms. arXiv:2004.14579 (2020)
6. Clark, P., Tafjord, O., Richardson, K.: Transformers as soft reasoners over language. arXiv preprint arXiv:2002.05867 (2020)
7. Galárraga, L., Teflioudi, C., Hose, K., Suchanek, F.M.: Fast rule mining in ontological knowledge bases with AMIE++. VLDB **24**(6), 707–730 (2015)
8. Galárraga, L.A., Teflioudi, C., Hose, K., Suchanek, F.: AMIE: association rule mining under incomplete evidence in ontological knowledge bases. In: WWW, pp. 413–422 (2013)
9. Ji, S., Pan, S., Cambria, E., Marttinen, P., Philip, S.Y.: A survey on KGs: representation, acquisition, and applications. TNNLS **33**(2), 494–514 (2021)
10. Jurafsky, D., Martin, J.H.: Speech and Language Processing. Prentice Hall (2009)
11. Kermani, A., Perez-Rosas, V., Metsis, V.: A systematic evaluation of LLM strategies for mental health text analysis: fine-tuning vs. prompt engineering vs. RAG. In: The 10th Workshop on CLPsych, p. 172 (2025)
12. Kiafar, B., Ravva, P.U., Joy, A.A., Daher, S., Barmaki, R.L.: Mena: Multimodal epistemic network analysis for visualizing competencies and emotions. arXiv preprint arXiv:2504.02794 (2025)
13. Meilicke, C., Chekol, M.W., Betz, P., Fink, M., Stuckeschmidt, H.: Anytime bottom-up rule learning for large-scale KGC. VLDB **33**(1), 131–161 (2024)

14. Nakashole, N., Sozio, M., Suchanek, F.M., Theobald, M.: Query-time reasoning in uncertain RDF KBs with soft and hard rules. VLDS **884**(6), 15–20 (2012)
15. Panickssery, A., Bowman, S., Feng, S.: LLM evaluators recognize and favor their own generations. NeurIPs **37**, 68772–68802 (2024)
16. Radford, A., Wu, J., Child, R., Luan, D., Amodei, D., Sutskever, I.: Language models are unsupervised multitask learners. OpenAI Blog **1**(8) (2019)
17. Servantez, S., Barrow, J., Hammond, K., Jain, R.: Chain of logic: rule-based reasoning with large language models. arXiv:2402.10400 (2024)
18. Shi, X., Zhu, Z., Zhang, Z., Li, C.: Hallucination mitigation in natural language generation from large-scale open-domain knowledge graphs. In: EMNLP, pp. 12506–12521 (2023)
19. Shirvani-Mahdavi, N., Akrami, F., Li, C.: On large-scale evaluation of embedding models for knowledge graph completion. arXiv:2504.08970 (2025)
20. Shirvani-Mahdavi, N., Akrami, F., Saeef, M.S., Shi, X., Li, C.: Comprehensive analysis of Freebase and dataset creation for robust evaluation of knowledge graph link prediction models. In: Payne, T.R., et al. (eds.) ISWC, pp. 113–133. Springer (2023). https://doi.org/10.1007/978-3-031-47243-5_7
21. Vrandečić, D., Krötzsch, M.: Wikidata: a free collaborative knowledge base. CACM **57**(10), 78–85 (2014)
22. Wei, J., et al.: Chain-of-thought prompting elicits reasoning in large language models. NeurIPS **35**, 24824–24837 (2022)
23. Wu, X., Cai, Y., Lian, Z., Leung, H.f., Wang, T.: Generating natural language from logic expressions with structural representation. TASLP **31**, 1499–1510 (2023)
24. Zheng, L., et al.: Judging LLM-as-a-judge with MT-bench and chatbot arena. NeurIPS **36**, 46595–46623 (2023)

Minimizing Side-Effects in Virtual Knowledge Graph Updates

Romuald Esdras Wandji[1](✉) and Diego Calvanese[2]

[1] Department of Computing Science, Umeå Universitet, Umeå, Sweden
romuald.esdras.wandji@umu.se
[2] Faculty of Engineering, Free University of Bozen-Bolzano, Bolzano, Italy
diego.calvanese@unibz.it

Abstract. In Virtual Knowledge Graphs (VKGs), access to a relational data source is provided through an ontology that is linked to the data source via declarative mappings. While the problem of query answering in VKGs has been studied extensively over the past years, much less attention has been devoted to the problem of instance-level updates over the VKG, realized by updating the underlying data source. Due to the form of VKG mappings, translating VKG updates into a source updates might lead to side-effects in the VKG, i.e., unwanted insertions or deletions. In this paper, we build on a recent proposal for translating VKG updates into source updates, and extend it by introducing the notion of compensation, which are additional updates that aim at reverting side-effects. We provide a novel algorithm relying on multiple levels of compensation and show that it computes source updates with minimal side-effects in the VKG.

1 Introduction

The Virtual Knowledge Graph (VKG) approach (formerly known as ontology-based data Access – OBDA) [5, 16, 19, 20] is a well-established paradigm for data access and integration, which has been investigated extensively, especially in the context where the data sources to be accessed or integrated are relational. In VKGs, an ontology encapsulates essential domain knowledge and is linked to the data source via declarative mappings, exposing to users a virtual knowledge graph. Users can issue high-level ontological queries over such VKG, and these are automatically translated, using both the ontology axioms and the mappings, into equivalent low-level queries (like SQL in a relational setting) that the underlying database engine can execute. The ontology is usually specified in a lightweight language, and in this paper we consider as ontology language $DL\text{-}Lite_R$, which can capture conceptual modeling formalisms and enjoys efficient reasoning. Most importantly, $DL\text{-}Lite_R$ based VKG systems enjoy *first-order rewritability*, i.e., any (union of) conjunctive queries issued over the ontology can be rewritten considering both the ontology's axioms and the declarative mappings into a SQL query that, when executed over the underlying relational data sources, computes the entailed answers [5,6].

The primary reasoning service offered by VKG systems is *query answering*, which is carried out through *query rewriting* and *query unfolding* [5, 16]. However, little attention has been paid to the issue of updating VKGs, which allows one to take advantage of the knowledge graph's capacity to handle incomplete information and provide support for update operations over the source data through the lens of the ontology. More specifically, we are interested in instance-level (or ABox) updates in VKGs, where updates are applied over the extensional level of the system (the VKG), and need to be translated into equivalent updates over the source. Such a feature will allow content owners to fully manage all information at the level of the ontology, and hence detach from low-level details of the underlying source structure and organization.

Several challenges need to be taken into account when updating a VKG through the ontology. One has to deal first with potential inconsistencies between the ontology and the provided update, and second, with the translation of the update to the underlying data source using the schema mappings. The first problem has been studied in the literature in the context of knowledge base update and belief revision [9,12,13,18], which also consider ontologies specified in DLs [22]. The second one is connected to the well-known and well-studied *view update* problem [3,8,11]. Hence, the typical steps in the VKG update framework are: *(1)* the user poses an instance-level update request $\mathcal{U}_A$ over the knowledge base (KB) $\mathcal{K} = \langle \mathcal{T}, \mathcal{M}(D) \rangle$ of a VKG instance. *(2)* The instance level (i.e., virtual ABox) $\mathcal{M}(D)$ of $\mathcal{K}$ is updated and possibly repaired w.r.t. the ontology $\mathcal{T}$ (according to a chosen repair semantics, see, e.g., [22]), which produces the actual update $\mathcal{U}'_A$ to be executed over $\mathcal{K}$. *(3)* A process called *translation* takes $\mathcal{U}'_A$ and $\mathcal{K}$ to produce a set $\mathbf{U}_D = \{\mathcal{U}_D^1, \ldots, \mathcal{U}_D^n\}$ of possible updates over the source database. *(4)* Finally, a translation $\mathcal{U}_D^i$ in $\mathbf{U}_D$ is chosen, for which the knowledge base $\mathcal{K}' = \langle \mathcal{T}, \mathcal{M}(D_i) \rangle$ is as close as possible to $\mathcal{K}$, where D_i is the source database obtained by applying $\mathcal{U}_D^i$ to D.

Considering that there is already a vast literature on ontology update and corresponding semantics to handle possible inconsistencies, in this paper, we abstract from repair at the ontology level (Step 2), and concentrate instead on the translation of the ABox update into source updates (Step 3), and on the selection of the actual translation to adopt (Step 4). Therefore, we assume that the actual update that gets executed over the VKG instance already includes the update operations realizing the repair (hence, coincides with $\mathcal{U}'_A$). Then, the distance between $\mathcal{K}'$ and $\mathcal{K}$ is the *side-effect* that represents insertions or deletions in the VKG that are due to the way the mapping $\mathcal{M}$ propagates the source update to the ontology level. Recently, two methods have been proposed to translate ABox deletions and insertions into source deletions and insertions, respectively [17]. However, the assumption of considering translations that are of the same type as the corresponding ABox updates might lead to side-effects that are not minimal.

Example 1. As a motivating example, consider a data source with two relations: $RS(res, sup)$ that relates researchers to their supervisor(s), and $SG(sup, gr)$ that relates supervisors to the grants they have access to. The information in this source has to be integrated into a VKG whose ontology contains a role *access*, relating researchers to grants, and a class *supervises* relating supervisors with their students. We consider a mapping $\mathcal{M}$ between this source schema and the ontology consisting of the following assertions:

$$\exists y. RS(x,y) \wedge SG(y,z) \rightsquigarrow access(x,z);$$
$$RS(x,y) \rightsquigarrow supervises(y,x).$$

Let us assume that we have a database with a single tuple $D = \{SG(\text{sup1}, \text{grant1})\}$, and an update that consists of inserting the ABox fact $supervises(\text{sup1}, \text{john})$. Based on the mapping $\mathcal{M}$, the only translation of such update is the insertion of $RS(\text{john}, \text{sup1})$ in D, which will lead to an extra insertion of $access(\text{john}, \text{grant1})$. However, the translation that consists of updating the database by inserting $RS(\text{john}, \text{sup1})$ and deleting $SG(\text{sup1}, \text{grant1})$, is an exact translation in D of the ABox update. We observe that combining both insertions and deletions in the source data has lead to an exact translation of a given ABox insertion. Notice also that deleting a database fact concerning grants to reflect an ABox insertion concerning supervision might seem counterintuitive. However, in the situation represented by our (admittedly very simple) example, where the only mapping assertions are the ones provided above, the specified database update, consisting of both a deletion of a tuple and an insertion of a tuple, exactly captures the intention of the user to only insert the ABox fact $supervises(\text{sup1}, \text{john})$. ◁

In this paper, we propose to translate each ABox update operation (consisting of insertions or deletions only) in general through a combination of both database insertions and deletions. The additional update operations are meant to compensate possible side-effects caused by database updates, and we formalize the notion of minimal side-effect in our enriched setting. We then propose methods to recursively compute maximal compensations so as to find translations with minimal side-effects, and in particular translations that are side-effect-free (*exact translation*) whenever an exact translation exists.

The rest of the paper is structured as follows. In Sect. 2, we provide the necessary technical preliminaries. In Sect. 3 we provide an algorithm for minimal (both in the source and the ABox) direct translations of ABox updates. In Sect. 4 we introduce the notion of maximal compensation, and in Sect. 5 we use it to compute updates with minimal side-effects. Finally, Sect. 6 concludes the paper.

2 Preliminaries

We now introduce the notions about description logics (DLs), databases, and VKGs necessary to understand the technical development in the paper, assuming familiarity with the syntax and semantics of first-order logic (FOL). In general, when convenient, we will view a tuple of elements (constants, variables, etc.) as equivalent to the set of such elements. E.g., if c is a tuple of constants and D is a set, we might write $c \subseteq D$ to mean that every element of c is in D. We consider countably infinite and pairwise disjoint alphabets $\mathbf{N}_C$ of *concept names*, $\mathbf{N}_P$ of *role names*, and $\mathbf{N}_I$ of constants.

Description Logic Knowledge Bases. A DL *knowledge base* (KB) $\mathcal{K} = \langle \mathcal{T}, \mathcal{A} \rangle$ consists of a *TBox* $\mathcal{T}$ (also called *ontology*), capturing intensional information, and an *ABox* $\mathcal{A}$, providing extensional information. We consider DLs of the *DL-Lite* family [6,16], and specifically *DL-Lite$_R$*, which is the formal counterpart of the tractable OWL 2 QL profile of the Web Ontology Language (OWL 2) [15]. A *DL-Lite$_R$* TBox is a finite set of assertions of the form $B_1 \sqsubseteq B_2$ (*concept inclusion*), $B_1 \sqsubseteq \neg B_2$ (*concept disjointness*),

$R_1 \sqsubseteq R_2$ (*role inclusion*), or $R_1 \sqsubseteq \neg R_2$ (*role disjointness*). Here, R (possibly subscripted) denotes an atomic role $P \in \mathbf{N}_P$ or its inverse P^-, while B (possibly subscripted) denotes a *basic concept*, which is either an atomic concept $A \in \mathbf{N}_C$, or a concept of the form $\exists R$. For a TBox $\mathcal{T}$, we use $\mathcal{T}^+$ to denote the set of concept and role inclusions in $\mathcal{T}$, and $\mathcal{T}^-$ to denote the set of concept and role disjointness assertions in $\mathcal{T}$, hence $\mathcal{T} = \mathcal{T}^+ \cup \mathcal{T}^-$. A DL-Lite$_R$ ABox is a finite set of assertions of the form $A(c)$ or $P(c,c')$, with $A \in \mathbf{N}_C$, $P \in \mathbf{N}_P$, and $c, c' \in \mathbf{N}_I$.

The semantics of a DL KB is given, as usual, in terms of first-order interpretations [2]. We make use of the standard notions of *model*, *consistency*, and *logical implication*.

Instance Level Updates in DL KBs. We consider updates to a DL KB $\langle \mathcal{T}, \mathcal{A} \rangle$ consisting of a pair $\mathcal{U}_A = \langle \mathcal{U}_A^-, \mathcal{U}_A^+ \rangle$, where $\mathcal{U}_A^-$ and $\mathcal{U}_A^+$ are sets of ABox facts, respectively to be deleted and inserted from the KB, such that $\mathcal{U}_A^- \subseteq \mathcal{A}$ and $\mathcal{U}_A^+ \cap \mathcal{A} = \emptyset$. In this paper, we are concerned with how VKG mappings affect updates, not how the TBox affects the consistency of the updates. Therefore, we follow [17] and consider that inserting $\mathcal{U}_A^+$ amounts to inserting $cl_\mathcal{T}(\mathcal{U}_A^+)$, which represents the *closure* of $\mathcal{U}_A^+$ w.r.t. $\mathcal{T}$, that is, the set of ABox assertions over individuals in $\mathcal{U}_A^+$ that are logically implied by $\langle \mathcal{T}, \mathcal{U}_A^+ \rangle$. Similarly, deleting $\mathcal{U}_A^-$ amounts to deleting $invcl_\mathcal{T}(\mathcal{U}_A^-)$, which represent the *inverse closure* of $\mathcal{U}_A^-$ [22]. Both $cl_\mathcal{T}(\mathcal{U}_A^+)$ and $invcl_\mathcal{T}(\mathcal{U}_A^-)$ can be computed in polynomial time in the size of $\mathcal{U}_A^+, \mathcal{U}_A^-$, and $\mathcal{T}$ [6,22]. We also assume that the update does not request to both insert and delete the same ABox fact, and since we prioritize data consistency, this means that $cl_\mathcal{T}(\mathcal{U}_A^+) \cap invcl_\mathcal{T}(\mathcal{U}_A^-) = \emptyset$.

Relational Databases and Queries. A *database schema* is a finite set $\mathcal{S} = \{r_1/n_1, \ldots, r_k/n_k\}$ of relation schemas, where each r_i is a predicate name of arity n_i. A database instance D over $\mathcal{S}$ maps each predicate r/n in $\mathcal{S}$ to an n-ary relation, denoted r^D. An *atom* for r/n has the form $r(t_1, \ldots, t_n)$, or simply $r(\mathbf{t})$, where each t_j is a term, which can be a constant from $\mathbf{N}_I$ or a variable. If all t_j's are constants, the atom is called ground, or simply a *tuple*.

A FOL formula over a relational schema $\mathcal{S}$ is constructed over the relation names in $\mathcal{S}$, the equality predicate $=$, and the constants in $\mathbf{N}_I$. A formula φ with free variables $\mathbf{x}$ is denoted $\varphi(\mathbf{x})$, and is also called a (relational) *query* with *answer variables* $\mathbf{x}$. The formula is *closed* when $\mathbf{x}$ is empty. The closed formula obtained from $\varphi(\mathbf{x})$ by replacing the variables in $\mathbf{x}$ by the corresponding constants in $\mathbf{c}$ is denoted $\varphi(\mathbf{c})$.

A *conjunctive query* (CQ) $Q(\mathbf{x})$ over the schema $\mathcal{S}$ is a query defined by a formula of the form $\exists \mathbf{y}. \varphi(\mathbf{x}, \mathbf{y})$, where $\varphi = r_1(\mathbf{t}_1) \wedge \cdots \wedge r_n(\mathbf{t}_n)$ is a conjunction of atomic formulae whose variables belong to $\mathbf{x} \cup \mathbf{y}$. The variables $\mathbf{y}$ are called *existential variables*. We also express such CQ as a logical rule of the form $Q(\mathbf{x}) \leftarrow r_1(\mathbf{t}_1), \ldots, r_n(\mathbf{t}_n)$, where $Q(\mathbf{x})$ is called the *head* and $r_1(\mathbf{t}_1), \ldots, r_n(\mathbf{t}_n)$ the *body* of the rule. A *union of conjunctive queries* (UCQ) is a finite disjunction of CQs with the same answer variables, also represented as a finite set of rules with the same head.

2.1 Virtual Knowledge Graphs

We recall the main elements of the VKG framework, also known as *Ontology-based Data Access* (OBDA) [16, 19], where declarative mappings are used to connect a TBox $\mathcal{T}$ to a relational data source with schema $\mathcal{S}$.

A *VKG mapping* $\mathcal{M}$ from $\mathcal{S}$ to $\mathcal{T}$ consists of a set of *mapping assertions* of the form $Q(\boldsymbol{x}) \rightsquigarrow E(\boldsymbol{t}(\boldsymbol{x}))$, where $Q(\boldsymbol{x})$ is a CQ (called *source query*) over $\mathcal{S}$ of arity $n > 0$, and $E(\boldsymbol{t}(\boldsymbol{x}))$ is an atom (called *target atom*) over $\mathcal{T}$ with variables in $\boldsymbol{x}$. Such atom has the form $A(t_1(\boldsymbol{x}_1))$, with $A \in \mathbf{N}_C$, or $P(t_1(\boldsymbol{x}_1), t_2(\boldsymbol{x}_2))$, with $P \in \mathbf{N}_P$, where the terms $t_1(\boldsymbol{x}_1)$ and $t_2(\boldsymbol{x}_2)$ denote so-called *IRI-templates*, obtained by applying (skolem) functions to the answer variables of the source query. Such IRI-templates[1] are used to generate strings representing object *IRIs* (Internationalized Resource Identifiers) or (RDF) literals, starting from database values retrieved by the source query in the mapping. In practice, it is desired that each IRI can be constructed by at most one IRI template, and we make such an assumption here; formally, the union of all the IRI templates is an *injective* function, i.e., there is a unique way to reconstruct from a string s, the actual IRI-template $t(\boldsymbol{x})$ and the constituent values $\boldsymbol{v}$ used to generate $s = t(\boldsymbol{v})$. Moreover we assume that for each IRI-template $f(x_1, \ldots, x_n)$, we have also n *inverse templates*[2] $f^1, \ldots, f^n$ such that $f^i(f(v_1, \ldots, v_n)) = v_i$, for each $i \in [1..n]$ and for all possible values $v_1, \ldots, v_n$ instantiating the variables $x_1, \ldots, x_n$.

A VKG mapping $\mathcal{M}$ from $\mathcal{S}$ to $\mathcal{T}$, which we also call a *source-to-ontology mapping* (*so-mapping*), maps a database instance D of $\mathcal{S}$ to the (*unique*) ABox

$$\mathcal{M}(D) = \{\mathsf{as}(E(\boldsymbol{t}(\boldsymbol{x})), \boldsymbol{x} \mapsto \boldsymbol{o}) \mid (\boldsymbol{x} \mapsto \boldsymbol{o}) \in Q(\boldsymbol{x})^D, (Q(\boldsymbol{x}) \rightsquigarrow E(\boldsymbol{t}(\boldsymbol{x}))) \in \mathcal{M}\}$$

where $\boldsymbol{x} \mapsto \boldsymbol{o}$ represents a solution mapping from the evaluation $Q(\boldsymbol{x})^D$ of the source query $Q(\boldsymbol{x})$ over the database instance D, and the term $\mathsf{as}(E(\boldsymbol{t}(\boldsymbol{x})), \boldsymbol{x} \mapsto \boldsymbol{o}))$ denotes the ABox assertion obtained by applying the solution mapping $\boldsymbol{x} \mapsto \boldsymbol{o}$ to $E(\boldsymbol{t}(\boldsymbol{x}))$. This application typically involves replacing $\boldsymbol{x}$ with $\boldsymbol{o}$ in the templates in $\boldsymbol{t}(\boldsymbol{x})$ (using appropriate string concatenation operations). It is also convenient to consider a so-mapping $\mathcal{M}$ as the set of pairs $\{(D, \mathcal{M}(D)) \mid D \text{ is a database instance of } \mathcal{S}\}$, so that $(D, \mathcal{A}) \in \mathcal{M}$ is an alternative notation for $\mathcal{A} = \mathcal{M}(D)$. Notice that, since a concept name A (or role name P) might appear as target atom of multiple mapping assertions, the source query that generates the instances of A (or P) is in general a UCQ.

We are now ready to formalize the VKG setting. A *VKG specification* is a tuple $\mathcal{P} = \langle \mathcal{T}, \mathcal{M}, \mathcal{S} \rangle$, where $\mathcal{T}$ is a *DL-Lite$_R$* TBox (typically expressed in OWL 2 QL), $\mathcal{S}$ is a data source schema, and $\mathcal{M}$ is a set of so-mappings from $\mathcal{S}$ to $\mathcal{T}$. A *VKG instance* is a pair $\langle \mathcal{P}, D \rangle$ where D is a source instance of $\mathcal{S}$. Its semantics is defined in terms of FO interpretations over $\mathcal{T}$. An interpretation $\mathcal{I}$ is a *model* of $\langle \mathcal{P}, D \rangle$ if it is a model of the DL KB $\langle \mathcal{T}, \mathcal{M}(D) \rangle$.

We recall also the notion of *mapping saturation* [14], which allows one to compile into the mapping $\mathcal{M}$ the inclusion assertions of $\mathcal{T}$ that do *not* involve an existential quantification $\exists R$ in the right-hand side. Specifically, to compute the *mapping saturation* $\mathsf{sat}_{\mathcal{T}}(\mathcal{M})$ *of* $\mathcal{M}$ w.r.t. $\mathcal{T}$, we start from $\mathcal{M}$, and repeatedly add implied mapping

---
[1] IRI-templates correspond to the R2RML *string templates*.
[2] These correspond to the rr:inverseExpression of R2RML.

assertions. E.g., if $Q(x) \rightsquigarrow A_1(t(x))$ is in $sat_T(\mathcal{M})$ and $A_1 \sqsubseteq A_2$ is in T, we add to $sat_T(\mathcal{M})$ also $Q(x) \rightsquigarrow A_2(t(x))$; similarly for inclusions $\exists R \sqsubseteq A$ and $R_1 \sqsubseteq R_2$.

As shown in [17], when dealing with ABox updates and their side-effects in the VKG setting, we can assume w.l.o.g. that $\langle \mathcal{P}, D \rangle$ is a VKG instance, where $\mathcal{P} = \langle T^-, \mathcal{M}, \mathcal{S} \rangle$ is a VKG specification whose mapping $\mathcal{M}$ has been saturated w.r.t. an original TBox T, and where T^- consists of the disjointness assertions of T. In the following, we make such an assumption.

2.2 Lineage and Schema Mapping Recovery

We adopt some definitions by [17]. For a given assertion in the ABox, its lineage (also called *provenance*) consists of the minimal set of source tuples that generate the assertion through the VKG mapping. Formally:

Definition 1 (Lineage). *Let $\mathcal{P} = \langle T, \mathcal{M}, \mathcal{S} \rangle$ be a VKG specification, $\langle \mathcal{P}, D \rangle$ a VKG instance, and $f \in \mathcal{M}(D)$ an ABox assertion. A subset $B \subseteq D$ is a* lineage branch *of f if $f \in \mathcal{M}(B)$, and for every $B' \subsetneq B$, $f \notin \mathcal{M}(B')$. The* lineage *of f, denoted* lineage$(f, \mathcal{P}, D)$, *is the set of all lineage branches of f.* ◁

For an so-mapping $\mathcal{M}$, a *reverse mapping* describes a novel mapping now going from T back to $\mathcal{S}$, called *ontology-to-source mapping (os-mapping)*. We consider such a mapping $\widehat{\mathcal{M}}$ as a set of pairs $(\mathcal{A}, D)$, with $\mathcal{A}$ an ABox for T and D a database instance of $\mathcal{S}$, called *solution* of $\mathcal{A}$ under $\widehat{\mathcal{M}}$. Moreover, we define $\widehat{\mathcal{M}}(\mathcal{A}) = \{D \mid (\mathcal{A}, D) \in \widehat{\mathcal{M}}\}$. We are interested in os-mappings that maintain semantic consistency with the relationship established by $\mathcal{M}$, and which intuitively represent the inverse of such relationship, in line with the notion of *inverse mapping* for the relational setting [10].

Notice that an so-mapping $\mathcal{M}$ is a function, since it generates from a database instance D a unique ABox $\mathcal{M}(D)$. Instead, due to the non-injectiveness of so-mappings, its reverse $\widehat{\mathcal{M}}$ in general is not a function, but a relation that maps an ABox to a set of database instances. In order to construct the reverse of an so-mapping $\mathcal{M}$, we rely on the notion of *MR-os-mapping* as introduced by [17], which is based on the *maximum recovery* for schema mappings introduced in the database exchange setting [1], but adapt it in Sect. 3 to the more general case we consider here.

3 Update Translation in VKGs

In VKGs, the central challenge in dealing with ABox updates, lies in translating them into appropriate source updates. In [17], two algorithms are proposed that respectively handle translations of only ABox deletions and only ABox insertions. Also in the solution proposed there, the fundamental assumption is made that ABox deletions are translated into a set of source deletions only, and similarly for ABox insertions. As discussed in the introduction, such kinds of translations might not produce translations of ABox updates with minimal side-effects.

In this paper, we overcome the limitations of the previous work and extend our former translation framework along two directions: *(i)* We lift the restriction on the form of ABox translation: A set of ABox deletions (or of ABox insertions) could now be translated to a combination of both source deletions and source insertions, with the aim of obtaining the minimum side-effects. *(ii)* We consider also update operations that consist of a combination of deletions and insertions. *(iii)* We allow the use of different IRI-templates for the same predicate in the targets of mappings.

We now extend the notion of update translation in VKGs as introduced in [17]. Moreover, we introduce the notion of direct translation, which refers to translations that are of the same nature as the original ABox update, i.e., ABox insertions translate to source insertions, and ABox deletions translate to source deletions.

Definition 2 (Direct deletion translation). *Let $\mathcal{U}_A^-$ be a set of ABox deletions. A set $\mathcal{U}_D^-$ of source deletions is a* direct translation *of $\mathcal{U}_A^-$ in $\mathcal{J}$ if $\mathcal{U}_A^- \cap \mathcal{M}(D \setminus \mathcal{U}_D^-) = \emptyset$. We say that $\mathcal{U}_D^-$ is an* exact direct translation *of $\mathcal{U}_A^-$ in $\mathcal{J}$ if $\mathcal{M}(D \setminus \mathcal{U}_D^-) = \mathcal{M}(D) \setminus \mathcal{U}_A^-$.* ◁

An exact direct translation of the ABox deletion $\mathcal{U}_A^-$ ensures that requested deletions are perfectly reflected in the final (virtual) ABox generated from the data source via the mapping $\mathcal{M}$. A non-exact translation may inadvertently delete additional ABox facts not initially specified in $\mathcal{U}_A^-$. Following, we call the set of these facts that are unintendedly deleted from the ABox a *side-effect*. We can proceed in a symmetric way for ABox insertions.

Definition 3 (Direct insertion translation). *Let $\mathcal{U}_A^+$ be a set of ABox insertions. A set $\mathcal{U}_D^+$ of source insertions is a* direct translation *of $\mathcal{U}_A^+$ in $\mathcal{J}$ if $\mathcal{U}_A^+ \subseteq \mathcal{M}(\mathcal{U}_D^+)$ and $\langle \mathcal{T}^-, \mathcal{M}(D \cup \mathcal{U}_D^+) \rangle$ is consistent. $\mathcal{U}_D^+$ is an* exact direct translation *of $\mathcal{U}_A^+$ in $\mathcal{J}$ if $\mathcal{M}(D \cup \mathcal{U}_D^+) = \mathcal{M}(D) \cup \mathcal{U}_A^+$.* ◁

In the definition, we require that $\mathcal{U}_A^+ \subseteq \mathcal{M}(\mathcal{U}_D^+)$ to ensure that the translation $\mathcal{U}_D^+$ alone is enough to generate $\mathcal{U}_A^+$ through $\mathcal{M}$. However, notice that, by complying with the minimal change principle, $\mathcal{U}_D^+$ might contain tuples already present in D and therefore will result in fewer tuples inserted over D when $\mathcal{U}_D^+$ is added to D.

Hence, an exact translation of the ABox insertion $\mathcal{U}_A^+$ will insert only the requested facts into the (virtual) ABox. In contrast, a non-exact translation could lead to the insertion of additional facts beyond $\mathcal{U}_A^+$. The side-effect is the set of these facts that are unintendedly inserted into the ABox. If the side-effect causes an inconsistency with the disjointness assertions in $\mathcal{T}^-$, then the (non-exact) translation $\mathcal{U}_D^+$ is ruled out to maintain data integrity in the VKG instance. Notice also that a (direct) insertion translation might not exist, either because some facts in $\mathcal{U}_A^+$ cannot be obtained via the mapping (because the set of lineage branches is empty), or because the side-effects would necessarily violate the disjointness assertions in $\mathcal{T}^-$.

To comply with the minimal change principle in update translation, it is essential to ensure that a change in the ABox results in a minimal change in the source data. Building on this principle, we propose extending the definition of translation for ABox updates so as to ensure that the translation of ABox updates remains minimal in the source data, characterized by the following definition.

Definition 4 (Minimal direct translation). *Let $\mathcal{U}_A^-$ be a set of ABox deletions. A direct translation $\mathcal{U}_D^-$ of $\mathcal{U}_A^-$ in $\mathcal{J}$ is* minimal *if every proper subset of $\mathcal{U}_D^-$ is not a translation of $\mathcal{U}_A^-$ in $\mathcal{J}$. Similarly, let $\mathcal{U}_A^+$ be a set of ABox insertions. A direct translation $\mathcal{U}_D^+$ of $\mathcal{U}_A^+$ in $\mathcal{J}$ is* minimal *if every proper subset of $\mathcal{U}_D^+$ is not a translation of $\mathcal{U}_A^+$ in $\mathcal{J}$.* ◁

Algorithm 1: MINTRANSDEL $(\mathcal{J}, \mathcal{U}_A^-)$

input : A VKG instance $\mathcal{J} = \langle \mathcal{P}, D \rangle$. A set $\mathcal{U}_A^-$ of ABox deletions.
output: A set of source direct translations of $\mathcal{U}_A^-$.
1 $\mathbf{B} = \{B_1, \ldots, B_n\} \leftarrow \bigcup_{f \in \mathcal{U}_A^-} \text{lineage}(f, \mathcal{P}, D);$ // Compute lineage branches in D
2 $\mathbf{S} \leftarrow \{\{t_1, \ldots, t_n\} \mid t_i \in B_i, \text{for } i \in [1..n]\};$
3 $\mathbf{U}_D^- \leftarrow \{\};$
4 **for each** translation $T \in \mathbf{S}$ **do**
5      $add \leftarrow true;$
6   **for each** translation $T^* \in \mathbf{U}_D^-$ **do**
7   **if** $T^* \subsetneq T$ **or** COMPARE$_\mathcal{J}^-(T^*, T) = $ '<' **then** $add \leftarrow false;$
8   **else if** $T \subsetneq T^*$ **or** COMPARE$_\mathcal{J}^-(T, T^*) = $ '<' **then** $\mathbf{U}_D^- \leftarrow \mathbf{U}_D^- \setminus \{T^*\};$
9   **if** add **then** $\mathbf{U}_D^- \leftarrow \mathbf{U}_D^- \cup \{T\}$
10 **return** $\mathbf{U}_D^-$

Algorithm 2: FILTERBRANCHES $(\mathbf{S})$

input: A set $\mathbf{S}$ of branches, each of the form $\bigcup_{i=1}^{n} \{\exists \mathbf{w}_i . \varphi_i(\mathbf{a}_i, \mathbf{w}_i)\}$.
output: A set $\mathbf{B}^*$ of CQs, each representing a minimal update.
1 $\mathbf{B} \leftarrow \{\bigwedge_{i=1}^{n} \exists \mathbf{w}_i . \varphi_i(\mathbf{a}_i, \mathbf{w}_i) \mid \bigcup_{i=1}^{n} \{\exists \mathbf{w}_i . \varphi_i(\mathbf{a}_i, \mathbf{w}_i)\} \in \mathbf{S}\}$
2 $\mathbf{B}^* \leftarrow \{\}$
3 **for each** branch $B \in \mathbf{B}$ **do**
4      $add \leftarrow true;$
5   **for each** branch $B^* \in \mathbf{B}^*$ **do**
6   **if** $B \sqsubseteq B^*$ **then** $add \leftarrow false;$
7   **else if** $B^* \sqsubseteq B$ **then** $\mathbf{B}^* \leftarrow \mathbf{B}^* \setminus \{B\};$
8   **if** add **then** $\mathbf{B}^* \leftarrow \mathbf{B} \cup \{B\};$
9 **return** $\mathbf{B}^*$

Algorithm 1 (MINTRANSDEL) extends the algorithm presented in [17] so that it returns all minimal direct translations of a set of ABox deletions. It makes use of the function lineage$(f, \mathcal{P}, D)$, defined in [17], which computes the set of lineage branches in database D for an ABox assertion f. It also exploits an abstract function COMPARE$_\mathcal{J}^-$ that compares two translations T_1 and T_2 of ABox deletions in terms of their side-effect and returns '<', if T_1 has less side-effect than T_2 based on the considered metric.

Theorem 5. *Let $\mathcal{U}_A^-$ be a set of ABox deletions. Then* MINTRANSDEL$(\mathcal{J}, \mathcal{U}_A^-)$ *returns every minimal source direct translation of $\mathcal{U}_A^-$ in $\mathcal{J}$.*

For the minimal direct translation of ABox insertions, we make use of some notation and definitions taken from [17], but adjust them to the more general setting adopted here. First, we assume w.l.o.g. that mapping assertions are *normalized* in the following sense: the head of a mapping assertion contains only variables of the form x_i for $i \in \mathbb{N}$, no variable appears more than once, and the indexes i of variables x_i increase from left to right. Hence, in any n-ary tuple $\mathbf{t}(\mathbf{x}) = (t_1(\mathbf{x}_1), \ldots, t_n(\mathbf{x}_n))$, where $\mathbf{x}_i \subseteq \mathbf{x}$,

Algorithm 3: MINTRANSINS $(\mathcal{J}, \mathcal{U}_A^+)$

input: A VKG instance $\mathcal{J} = \langle \langle \mathcal{T}, \mathcal{M}, \mathcal{S} \rangle, D \rangle$.
 A set $\mathcal{U}_A^+$ of ABox insertions.
output: A set of source direct translations of $\mathcal{U}_A^+$.

1 Compute the MR-os-mapping $\widehat{\mathcal{M}}^{mr}$ of $\mathcal{M}$;
2 Compute the insertion tree $\mathbf{B}$ of $\mathcal{U}_A^+$ w.r.t. $\widehat{\mathcal{M}}^{mr}$;
3 $\mathbf{U}_D^+ \leftarrow \{\}$;
4 **for each** branch $B \in$ FILTERBRANCHES($\mathbf{B}$) of the form $\exists w.\varphi(\boldsymbol{a}, \boldsymbol{w})$ **do**
5    $\quad \Delta_w \leftarrow \{b_1, \ldots, b_{|w|}\} \cup \Delta_A \cup \Delta_D$, where Δ_A and Δ_D are the constants in $\mathcal{U}_A^+$ and D respectively, and each b_i is a fresh value from $\mathbf{N}_I$ not in $\Delta_A \cup \Delta_D$;
6    $\quad$ **for each** assignment $\eta(\boldsymbol{w}) \subseteq \Delta_w$ **do**
7      $\quad\quad T \leftarrow \gamma(\varphi(\boldsymbol{a}, \eta(\boldsymbol{w})))$;
8      $\quad\quad add \leftarrow true$;
9      $\quad\quad$ **for each** translation $T^* \in \mathbf{U}_D^+$ **do**
10     $\quad\quad\quad$ **if** $(T^* \setminus D) \subsetneq (T \setminus D)$ **or** COMPARE$_{\mathcal{J}}^+(T^*, T) = $ '<' **then** $add \leftarrow false$;
11     $\quad\quad\quad$ **else if** $(T \setminus D) \subsetneq (T^* \setminus D)$ **or** COMPARE$_{\mathcal{J}}^+(T, T^*) = $ '<' **then**
         $\quad\quad\quad\quad \mathbf{U}_D^+ \leftarrow \mathbf{U}_D^+ \setminus \{T^*\}$;
12     $\quad\quad$ **if** add **then** $\mathbf{U}_D^+ \leftarrow \mathbf{U}_D^+ \cup \{T\}$
13 **return** $\mathbf{U}_D^+$

---

of IRI-templates appearing in the head of a mapping assertion, $t_i(\boldsymbol{x}_i) \neq t_j(\boldsymbol{x}_j)$ when $i \neq j$, and we define $\boldsymbol{u}_{t(\boldsymbol{x})}$ as an n-tuple $(u_1, \ldots, u_n)$ of pairwise distinct variables. We then define $V_{t(\boldsymbol{x})} = V^1 \wedge \cdots \wedge V^n$, where each V^i is obtained as follows: *(a)* if $t_i(\boldsymbol{x}_i)$ is a variable y in $\boldsymbol{x}$, then V^i is the equality $y = u_i$, *(b)* otherwise, if $t_i(\boldsymbol{x}_i)$ is an IRI-template $f(y_1, \ldots, y_k)$, where each y_j is a variable in $\boldsymbol{x}$, then V^i is $(y_1 = f^1(u_i)) \wedge \cdots \wedge (y_k = f^k(u_i))$, where each f^j is the j-th inverse template of f. Finally, for a concept or role F in the target of a mapping $\mathcal{M}$, let $\mathbf{IRI}_{\mathcal{M}}(F) = \{t(\boldsymbol{x}) \mid F(t(\boldsymbol{x}))$ is the target of some mapping assertion in $\mathcal{M}\}$.

Definition 6 (MR-os-mapping). *For a concept or role F in the target of $\mathcal{M}$, Let $\mathcal{M}_{F(t(\boldsymbol{x}))} = \bigcup_{\ell=1}^{k} \{\exists \boldsymbol{w}_\ell.\varphi_\ell(\boldsymbol{x}, \boldsymbol{w}_\ell) \leadsto F(t(\boldsymbol{x}))\}$ be the set of all mapping assertions of $\mathcal{M}$ with $F(t(\boldsymbol{x}))$ in the target. Then, we define the so-mapping $\widehat{\mathcal{M}}^{mr}_{F(t(\boldsymbol{x}))} = \bigcup_{\ell=1}^{k} \{F(\boldsymbol{u}_{t(\boldsymbol{x})}) \leadsto \exists \boldsymbol{w}_\ell.\varphi_\ell(\boldsymbol{x}, \boldsymbol{w}_\ell) \wedge V_{t(\boldsymbol{x})}\}$. Finally, we call $\widehat{\mathcal{M}}^{mr} = \bigcup_{F \in \mathcal{T}} \bigcup_{t(\boldsymbol{x}) \in \mathbf{IRI}_{\mathcal{M}}(F)} \widehat{\mathcal{M}}^{mr}_{F(t(\boldsymbol{x}))}$ the MR-os-mapping of $\mathcal{M}$.* ◁

The *insertion tree* of $\mathcal{U}_A^+$ is defined as the set of all *insertion branches* of $\mathcal{U}_A^+$, where each insertion branch represents a possible rewriting of $\mathcal{U}_A^+$ in the source schema. For convenience, we also make use of γ, defined as $\gamma(\bigwedge_{i=1}^{n} r_i(\boldsymbol{a}_i)) = \bigcup_{i=1}^{n} \{r_i(\boldsymbol{a}_i)\}$, to transform a conjunction of facts into a set of tuples.

As an extension to the method proposed in [17], the insertion algorithm MINTRANSINS (Algorithm 3) consists of two stages. In the first stage, it first computes (at Line 2) the insertion tree with respect to the MR-os-mapping $\widehat{\mathcal{M}}^{mr}$, and then filters out redundant branches from the insertion tree using FILTERBRANCHES (Algorithm 2). Since each branch is a CQ, the latter algorithm removes a branch B if (as a

CQ) it is contained in another branch B^*. Indeed, if $B \sqsubseteq B^*$, every atom of B^* can be homomorphically mapped to an atom of B [7], hence B^* will result in fewer facts that need to be inserted in the database, if chosen instead of B as a branch for the insertion. Hence, branch B can be removed. The second stage is analogous to the one of [17], but uses the branches returned by FILTERBRANCHES to find the translations to insert in the database that give rise to minimal side-effects. Notice that, when comparing translations for containment (Lines 10 and 11), we do so considering only the tuples that are not already in D.

Theorem 7. *Let $\mathcal{U}_A^+$ be a set of ABox insertions. Then* MINTRANSINS$(\mathcal{J}, \mathcal{U}_A^+)$ *returns every minimal source direct translation of $\mathcal{U}_A^+$ in $\mathcal{J}$.*

4 Compensations and Their Maxima

As noticed, given a VKG instance and an ABox update $\mathcal{U}_A$, if there is no exact direct translation $\mathcal{U}_D$ (with no side-effect) of $\mathcal{U}_A$, we can attempt to find an extra update operation that can be carried out in the data source to minimize the side-effect in the ABox caused by the update in the data. We call such an extra operation a *compensation of the side-effect*. In the rest of the paper, we assume that an ABox update has the form $\mathcal{U}_A = \langle \mathcal{U}_A^-, \mathcal{U}_A^+ \rangle$, such that $\mathcal{U}_A^- \cap \mathcal{U}_A^+ = \emptyset$[3], and similarly we consider as corresponding source updates $\mathcal{U}_D = \langle \mathcal{U}_D^-, \mathcal{U}_D^+ \rangle$ where $\mathcal{U}_D^- \cap \mathcal{U}_D^+ = \emptyset$. Coherently, we extend the notion of side-effect to handle such combined updates. In what follows, we denote $D \cup \mathcal{U}_D^+ \setminus \mathcal{U}_D^-$ by $D \bullet \mathcal{U}_D$. Similarly, for $\mathcal{A} \bullet \mathcal{U}_A$.

Definition 8 (Combined side-effect). *Let $\mathcal{U}_A = \langle \mathcal{U}_A^-, \mathcal{U}_A^+ \rangle$ be an ABox update, and $\mathcal{U}_D = \langle \mathcal{U}_D^-, \mathcal{U}_D^+ \rangle$ a source update. The* combined side-effect $E_\mathcal{J}(\mathcal{U}_A, \mathcal{U}_D)$ *caused by $\mathcal{U}_D$ for $\mathcal{U}_A$ is $\langle E^-, E^+ \rangle$, where $E^- = (\mathcal{M}(D) \bullet \mathcal{U}_A) \setminus \mathcal{M}(D \bullet \mathcal{U}_D)$ is called the* deletion side-effect *and $E^+ = \mathcal{M}(D \bullet \mathcal{U}_D) \setminus (\mathcal{M}(D) \bullet \mathcal{U}_A)$ is called the* insertion side-effect. ◁

Intuitively, the deletion side-effect E^- represents tuples that should remain in the ABox but have been deleted and therefore should be added back. Symmetrically, the insertion side-effect E^+ represents unwanted tuples that have been inserted and that therefore should be removed. Note that none, one, or both of E^- and E^+ in the combined side-effect might be empty.

For a given ABox update $\mathcal{U}_A$ and its corresponding source update $\mathcal{U}_D$ with deletion side-effect E^-, we would now like to find extra source insertions that minimize E^-.

Definition 9 (Compensation by insertion). *A non-empty set Θ^+ is a* compensation by insertion *of $E_\mathcal{J}(\mathcal{U}_A, \mathcal{U}_D)$ if there are two disjoint sets E_Δ^- and E_Δ^+ of ABox assertions such that $\mathcal{U}_A^- \cap E_\Delta^+ = \emptyset$, $E_\Delta^- \neq \emptyset$, $E_\Delta^- \subseteq E^-$, and $E_\mathcal{J}(\mathcal{U}_A, \langle \mathcal{U}_D^-, \mathcal{U}_D^+ \cup \Theta^+ \rangle) = \langle E^- \setminus E_\Delta^-, E^+ \cup E_\Delta^+ \rangle$.* ◁

In the compensation by insertion, the aim is to minimize the deletion side-effect E^- caused by the deletion of $\mathcal{U}_D^-$ in the data source. And this is achieved when a non-empty subset E_Δ^- of E^- is re-inserted when the compensation is applied in the source.

---

[3] Since it suffices to consider TBoxes that consists of disjointness assertions only, we have that $\mathcal{U}_A^- = invcl(\mathcal{U}_A^-)$, and $\mathcal{U}_A^+ = cl(\mathcal{U}_A^+)$.

However, attempting to minimize E^- might also lead to extra insertions E_Δ^+ in the ABox. To maintain the initially requested deletion $\mathcal{U}_A^-$ unaffected by the compensation, we require that $\mathcal{U}_A^- \cap E_\Delta^+ = \emptyset$.

Similar to compensating deletion side-effects by extra source insertions, we can compensate insertion side-effects by extra source deletions.

Definition 10 (Compensation by deletion). *A non-empty set $\Theta^- \subseteq D$ is a compensation by deletion of $E_\mathcal{J}(\mathcal{U}_A, \mathcal{U}_D)$ if there are two disjoint sets E_Δ^- and E_Δ^+ of ABox assertions such that $\mathcal{U}_A^+ \cap E_\Delta^- = \emptyset$, $E_\Delta^+ \neq \emptyset$, $E_\Delta^+ \subseteq E^+$, and $E_\mathcal{J}(\mathcal{U}_A, \langle \mathcal{U}_D^- \cup \Theta^-, \mathcal{U}_D^+ \rangle) = \langle E^- \cup E_\Delta^-, E^+ \setminus E_\Delta^+ \rangle$.* ◁

The aim of compensating by deletion is to minimize the insertion side-effect E^+ caused by the insertion of $\mathcal{U}_D^+$ in the data source. And this is achieved when a non-empty subset E_Δ^+ is removed from E^+ when the compensation is applied in the source. However, attempting to minimize E^+ might lead to deletions E_Δ^- in the ABox in addition to E_Δ^+. Similarly to the case of compensation by insertion, to maintain the initially requested insertion $\mathcal{U}_A^+$ unaffected by the compensation, we require that $\mathcal{U}_A^+ \cap E_\Delta^- = \emptyset$.

Example 2. Consider the VKG instance $\mathcal{J} = \langle \mathcal{P}_1, D \rangle$ of our motivating example, where $\mathcal{P}_1 = \langle \emptyset, \mathcal{M}_1, \mathcal{S}_1 \rangle$, and D in this case consists of the following tuples $D = \{SG(\text{sup1}, \text{grant1}); SG(\text{sup1}, \text{grant2})\}$. Then, given $\mathcal{M}_1$, the ABox insertion $\mathcal{U}_A^+ = \{supervises(\text{sup1}, \text{john})\}$ and a corresponding source insertion $\mathcal{U}_D^+ = \{RS(\text{john}, \text{sup1})\}$, we obtain the side-effect $E_\mathcal{J}(\langle \emptyset, \mathcal{U}_A^+ \rangle, \mathcal{U}_D) = \langle \emptyset, \{access(\text{john}, \text{grant1}); access(\text{john}, \text{grant2})\} \rangle$. A possible compensation by deletion might consists of an extra source deletion $\Theta_1^- = \{SG(\text{sup1}, \text{grant1})\}$. Therefore, we obtain $E_\mathcal{J}(\langle \emptyset, \mathcal{U}_A^+ \rangle, \langle \Theta_1^-, \mathcal{U}_D^+ \rangle) = \langle \emptyset, \{access(\text{john}, \text{grant2})\} \rangle\}$. ◁

Our formalization of compensation in VKGs relates to any possible operation that can be carried out in the source to bring the resulting ABox closer to what the end user expects after a given ABox update operation. Given the nature of VKG mappings, different compensations can be applied for a given ABox update and its source translation, which leads to the need of comparing compensations.

In Example 2, if there is another compensation by deletion Θ_2^- such that $E_\mathcal{J}(\langle \emptyset, \mathcal{U}_A^+ \rangle, \langle \mathcal{U}_D^- \cup \Theta_2^-, \mathcal{U}_D^+ \rangle) = \langle \emptyset, \emptyset \rangle$, then one would prefer Θ_2^- over Θ_1^-. In general, if Θ^- is a compensation by deletion of $E_\mathcal{J}(\mathcal{U}_A, \mathcal{U}_D)$, then the smaller the side-effect in $E_\mathcal{J}(\mathcal{U}_A, \langle \mathcal{U}_D^- \cup \Theta^-, \mathcal{U}_D^+ \rangle)$ due to undesired insertions, the better Θ^- is. When the insertion side-effects are equal, we also consider the deletion side-effects.

Definition 11. *Let Θ_1^-, Θ_2^- be compensations by deletion of $E_\mathcal{J}(\mathcal{U}_A, \mathcal{U}_D)$ s.t. $E_\mathcal{J}(\mathcal{U}_A, \langle \mathcal{U}_D^- \cup \Theta_1^-, \mathcal{U}_D^+ \rangle) = \langle E^- \cup E_1^-, E^+ \setminus E_1^+ \rangle$ and $E_\mathcal{J}(\mathcal{U}_A, \langle \mathcal{U}_D^- \cup \Theta_2^-, \mathcal{U}_D^+ \rangle) = \langle E^- \cup E_2^-, E^+ \setminus E_2^+ \rangle$. We say that Θ_1^- is better than Θ_2^- for $E_\mathcal{J}$, and write $\Theta_2^- \prec_\mathcal{J} \Theta_1^-$, if $E_2^+ \subsetneq E_1^+$ or we have that both $E_2^+ = E_1^+$ and $E_1^- \subsetneq E_2^-$.*

◁

Similarly, we can define an order between compensations by insertion. This means that if Θ^+ is a compensation by insertion of $E_\mathcal{J}(\mathcal{U}_A, \mathcal{U}_D)$, then the smaller the side-effect in $E_\mathcal{J}(\mathcal{U}_A, \langle \mathcal{U}_D^-, \mathcal{U}_D^+ \cup \Theta^+ \rangle)$ due to undesired deletions, the better Θ^+ is. And if the deletion side-effects are equal, we also consider the insertion side-effects.

Definition 12. Let Θ_1^+, Θ_2^+ be compensations by insertion of $E_{\mathcal{J}}(\mathcal{U}_A, \mathcal{U}_D)$ s.t. $E_{\mathcal{J}}(\mathcal{U}_A, \langle \mathcal{U}_D^-, \mathcal{U}_D^+ \cup \Theta_1^+ \rangle) = \langle E^- \setminus E_1^-, E^+ \cup E_1^+ \rangle$ and $E_{\mathcal{J}}(\mathcal{U}_A, \langle \mathcal{U}_D^-, \mathcal{U}_D^+ \cup \Theta_2^+ \rangle) = \langle E^- \setminus E_2^-, E^+ \cup E_2^+ \rangle$. We say that Θ_1^+ is better than Θ_2^+ for $E_{\mathcal{J}}$, and write $\Theta_2^+ \prec_{\mathcal{J}} \Theta_1^+$ if $E_2^- \subsetneq E_1^-$ or we have that both $E_2^- = E_1^-$ and $E_1^+ \subsetneq E_2^+$. ◁

If, for a given ABox update $\mathcal{U}_A$ and its source translation $\mathcal{U}_D$, there exists a compensation by deletion Θ^- such that there is no other compensation of $E_{\mathcal{J}}(\mathcal{U}_A, \mathcal{U}_D)$ that is better, then we say that Θ^- is a *maximal compensation by deletion* that can be executed over the source data to minimize the insertion side-effects. Analogously, we can define a *maximal compensation by insertion* Θ^+ that can be executed over the source data to minimize the deletion side-effects.

Definition 13. A set Θ_1^- is a maximal compensation by deletion of $E_{\mathcal{J}}(\mathcal{U}_A, \mathcal{U}_D)$ if there is no compensation by deletion Θ_2^- of $E_{\mathcal{J}}(\mathcal{U}_A, \mathcal{U}_D)$, such that $\Theta_1^- \prec_{\mathcal{J}} \Theta_2^-$. ◁

Example 3 (Continued from Example 2). The set Θ_2^- that consists of the extra source deletion $\Theta_2^- = \{SG(\mathtt{sup1}, \mathtt{grant1}); SG(\mathtt{sup1}, \mathtt{grant2})\}$ is a maximal compensation by deletion, and we have that $E_{\mathcal{J}}(\langle \emptyset, \mathcal{U}_A^+ \rangle, \langle \mathcal{U}_D^- \cup \Theta_2^-, \mathcal{U}_D^+ \rangle) = \langle \emptyset, \emptyset \rangle$. ◁

Definition 14. A set Θ_1^+ is a maximal compensation by insertion of $E_{\mathcal{J}}(\mathcal{U}_A, \mathcal{U}_D)$ if there is no compensation by insertion Θ_2^+ of $E_{\mathcal{J}}(\mathcal{U}_A, \mathcal{U}_D)$, such that $\Theta_1^+ \prec_{\mathcal{J}} \Theta_2^+$. ◁

4.1 Characterizing Maximal Compensations

From the definition of maximal compensation for both deletion and insertion given in the previous section, we notice that, in principle, it can be difficult to verify whether a compensation Θ^- is maximal or not. This is mainly due to the fact that it will require comparing Θ^- with all other compensations. In other words, it will require comparing the source deletion implied by Θ^- with every other possible source deletion, leading to minimizing the corresponding insertion side-effects. In this section, we focus on the problem of characterizing maximal compensations by deletion or insertion for a given ABox insertion or deletion, respectively.

For ABox insertions, a maximal compensation by deletion should ensure that no further tuples can be deleted from the data source to minimize the insertion side-effect further. This is the case when all ABox assertions in the insertion side-effect have at least one branch in the database that contributes to the initial ABox update.

Proposition 15. Let $E_{\mathcal{J}}(\mathcal{U}_A, \mathcal{U}_D) = \langle E^-, E^+ \rangle$ and let Θ^- be a compensation by deletion such that $E_{\mathcal{J}}(\mathcal{U}_A, \langle \mathcal{U}_D^- \cup \Theta^-, \mathcal{U}_D^+ \rangle) = \langle E^- \cup E_\Delta^-, E^+ \setminus E_\Delta^+ \rangle$. Then, Θ^- is a maximal compensation by deletion if and only if for every $f \in E^+ \setminus E_\Delta^+$ there exists a branch $B \in \mathsf{lineage}(f, \mathcal{P}, D \bullet \langle \mathcal{U}_D^- \cup \Theta^-, \mathcal{U}_D^+ \rangle)$ such that $B \subseteq \mathcal{U}_D^+$.

For ABox deletions, one needs to ensure that no extra tuples can be inserted in the data source to minimize the deletion side-effect. Based on that, an intuitive way to characterize a maximal compensation by insertion is to check whether the assertions in the deletion side-effect cannot be inserted back without affecting the initially requested ABox deletion.

Proposition 16. *Let* $E_{\mathcal{J}}(\mathcal{U}_A,\mathcal{U}_D) = \langle E^-, E^+ \rangle$ *and let* Θ^+ *be a compensation by insertion such that* $E_{\mathcal{J}}(\mathcal{U}_A, \langle \mathcal{U}_D^-, \mathcal{U}_D^+ \cup \Theta^+ \rangle) = \langle E^- \setminus E_\Delta^-, E^+ \cup E_\Delta^+ \rangle$. *Then,* Θ^+ *is a maximal compensation by insertion if and only if for every* $f \in E^- \setminus E_\Delta^-$, *we have that* $\mathcal{U}_A^- \cap \mathcal{M}(D \bullet \langle \mathcal{U}_D^-, \mathcal{U}_D^+ \cup \Theta^+ \rangle \cup T) \neq \emptyset$ *for every minimal translation by insertion* T *of* $\{f\}$.

5 Side-Effect Minimization in VKG Updates

We discuss now how to effectively minimize side-effects in VKG updates through an approach that recursively applies compensations for previously carried out data source insertions or deletions. We deal first with the case where we start with the insertion operation and with the corresponding compensation by deletion.

5.1 Computing Maximal Compensations by Deletion

For an ABox insertion $\mathcal{U}_A^+$, the goal of the compensation by deletion is to reduce the insertion side-effect E^+, while ensuring that the initial insertion $\mathcal{U}_A^+$ remains unaffected. However, we observe that while attempting to reduce E^+, we might inadvertently increase the deletion side-effect E^-. Due to the nature of VKG mappings, it might not always be possible to eliminate the insertion side-effects without affecting the initial ABox insertion. E.g., in Example 2, if $\mathcal{M}$ includes the assertion $RS(x,y) \rightsquigarrow Researcher(x)$, then the translation $RS(\texttt{john},\texttt{sup1})$ of the ABox insertion $supervise(\texttt{sup1},\texttt{john})$ will lead to the insertion side-effect $E^+ = \{Researcher(\texttt{john}), access(\texttt{john},\texttt{grant1})\}$. In this case, it is impossible to delete the assertion $Researcher(\texttt{john})$ without affecting the original insertion.

When the insertion side-effect E^+ cannot be completely removed, we try to find its maximal subset that can be removed without affecting the original ABox insertion. In other words, we try to find a subset of the data source whose deletion will lead to a maximal compensation by deletion. Algorithm CompByDel (Algorithm 4) takes as input a VKG instance $\mathcal{J}$, an ABox update $\mathcal{U}_A$, and its translation $\mathcal{U}_D = \langle \mathcal{U}_D^-, \mathcal{U}_D^+ \rangle$, and computes the set of direct translations by deletion (computed by MinTransDel) of the insertion side-effect (i.e., the second component of $E_{\mathcal{J}}(\mathcal{U}_A,\mathcal{U}_D)$) for the updated database $D \bullet \mathcal{U}_D$. It then eliminates (at Line 3) the tuples in $\mathcal{U}_D^+$ from each such translation, to ensure that tuples that are to be inserted are not part of the compensation by deletion. This is why we require that in the translation $\mathcal{U}_D$ given as input, $\mathcal{U}_D^+$ is minimal. We also observe that $\mathcal{U}_D^+$ might include tuples that originally were in D, and that therefore are actually *not* inserted (again) as part of the database update. However, since they are part of $\mathcal{U}_D^+$, Line 3 ensures that all tuples of $\mathcal{U}_A^+$ are kept in the ABox update.

Theorem 17. *Every set in* CompByDel$(\mathcal{J},\mathcal{U}_A,\mathcal{U}_D)$ *is a maximal compensation by deletion of* $E_{\mathcal{J}}(\mathcal{U}_A,\mathcal{U}_D)$.

5.2 Computing Maximal Compensations by Insertion

Similarly to how we address compensation by deletion for ABox insertions, the goal of compensation by insertion for ABox deletions is to reduce the deletion side-effect E^-,

Algorithm 4: COMPBYDEL $(\mathcal{J}, \mathcal{U}_A, \mathcal{U}_D)$

input : A VKG instance $\mathcal{J} = \langle \mathcal{P}, D \rangle$. An ABox update $\mathcal{U}_A$.
  A translation $\mathcal{U}_D = \langle \mathcal{U}_D^-, \mathcal{U}_D^+ \rangle$ of $\mathcal{U}_A$, where $\mathcal{U}_D^+$ is minimal.
output: A set of source deletions.

1 $\langle E^-, E^+ \rangle \leftarrow E_{\mathcal{J}}(\mathcal{U}_A, \mathcal{U}_D)$;
2 $\mathbf{T} = \{T_1, \ldots, T_n\} \leftarrow \text{MINTRANSDEL}(\langle \mathcal{P}, D \bullet \mathcal{U}_D \rangle, E^+)$;
3 $\mathbf{U}_D^- \leftarrow \{T \setminus \mathcal{U}_D^+ \mid T \in \mathbf{T}\}$;
4 **return** $\mathbf{U}_D^- \setminus \{\emptyset\}$;

Algorithm 5: COMPBYINS $(\mathcal{J}, \mathcal{U}_A, \mathcal{U}_D)$

input : A VKG instance $\mathcal{J} = \langle \mathcal{P}, D \rangle$. An ABox update $\mathcal{U}_A = \langle \mathcal{U}_A^-, \mathcal{U}_A^+ \rangle$.
  A translation $\mathcal{U}_D = \langle \mathcal{U}_D^-, \mathcal{U}_D^+ \rangle$ of $\mathcal{U}_A$, where $\mathcal{U}_D^-$ is minimal.
output: A set of source insertions.

1 $\langle E^-, E^+ \rangle \leftarrow E_{\mathcal{J}}(\mathcal{U}_A, \mathcal{U}_D)$;
2 $\mathbf{T} = \{T_1, \ldots, T_n\} \leftarrow \text{MINTRANSINS}(\langle \mathcal{P}, D \bullet \mathcal{U}_D \rangle, E^-)$;
3 $\mathbf{S} \leftarrow \{T \setminus \mathcal{U}_D^- \mid T \in \mathbf{T}\}$;
4 $\mathbf{U}_D^+ \leftarrow \emptyset$;
5 **for each** translation $\Theta^+ \in \mathbf{S}$ such that $\Theta^+ \neq \emptyset$ **do**
6 $\quad \langle E_1^-, E_1^+ \rangle \leftarrow E_{\mathcal{J}}(\mathcal{U}_A, \langle \mathcal{U}_D^-, \mathcal{U}_D^+ \cup \Theta^+ \rangle)$;
7 $\quad$ **if** $E_1^+ \cap \mathcal{U}_A^- = \emptyset$ **then** $\mathbf{U}_D^+ \leftarrow \mathbf{U}_D^+ \cup \{\Theta^+\}$;
8 **return** $\mathbf{U}_D^+$;

---

while ensuring that the initial deletion $\mathcal{U}_A^-$ remains unaffected. Also, note that while attempting to reduce E^-, we might unintendedly increase the insertion side-effect E^+.

Algorithm COMPBYINS (Algorithm 5) takes as input a VKG instance $\mathcal{J}$, an ABox update $\mathcal{U}_A$, and its source translation $\mathcal{U}_D$, and computes the set of direct translations by insertion (computed by MINTRANSINS) of the deletion side-effect (i.e., the first component of $E_{\mathcal{J}}(\mathcal{U}_A, \mathcal{U}_D)$) for the updated database $D \bullet \mathcal{U}_D$. It then eliminates (at Line 3) the tuples in $\mathcal{U}_D^-$ from each translation to ensure disjointness between the final insertion and deletion translations. Finally, for each translation, it computes the insertion side-effect E_1^+ (Line 6) and rejects the translation if it contains some tuple from $\mathcal{U}_A^-$ (Line 7).

Theorem 18. *Every set $\Theta^+ \in \text{COMPBYINS}(\mathcal{J}, \mathcal{U}_A, \mathcal{U}_D)$ is a maximal compensation by insertion of $E_{\mathcal{J}}(\mathcal{U}_A, \mathcal{U}_D)$.*

5.3 Computing Source Translations with Minimal Side-Effects

We now leverage the notion of compensation to minimize side-effects for translating a given ABox update. Since insertions and deletions are managed separately, our compensation mechanism will consist of a recursive sequence of insertions and deletions to minimize side-effects in the ABox. This means that, for a given ABox insertion $\mathcal{U}_A^+$ (resp., deletion $\mathcal{U}_A^-$) in $\mathcal{J}$, our algorithm returns a set of possible translations $\mathcal{U}_D = \langle \mathcal{U}_D^-, \mathcal{U}_D^+ \rangle$ over the source with minimum side-effects.

Algorithm 6: POSTINSERTION $(\mathcal{J}, \mathcal{U}_A^+, \mathbf{T})$

input : A VKG instance $\mathcal{J} = \langle \mathcal{P}, D \rangle$. A set $\mathcal{U}_A^+$ of ABox insertions.
A set $\mathbf{T}$ of source translations of $\mathcal{U}_A^+$.
output: A set of source translations of $\mathcal{U}_A^+$.

1 $\mathbf{U}_D \leftarrow \emptyset$;
2 **for each** translation $\langle \mathcal{U}_D^-, \mathcal{U}_D^+ \rangle \in \mathbf{T}$ **do**
3     $\Theta^- = \{\Theta_1^-, \ldots, \Theta_n^-\} \leftarrow$ COMPBYDEL$(\mathcal{J}, \mathcal{U}_A, \langle \mathcal{U}_D^-, \mathcal{U}_D^+ \rangle)$;
4   **if** $\Theta^- = \emptyset$ **then** $\mathbf{U}_D \leftarrow \mathbf{U}_D \cup \{\langle \mathcal{U}_D^-, \mathcal{U}_D^+ \rangle\}$;
5   **else**
6   **for each** compensation $\Theta^- \in \Theta^-$ **do**
7          $\Theta^+ = \{\Theta_1^+, \ldots, \Theta_m^+\} \leftarrow$ COMPBYINS$(\mathcal{J}, \mathcal{U}_A, \langle \mathcal{U}_D^- \cup \Theta^-, \mathcal{U}_D^+ \rangle)$;
8   **if** $\Theta^+ = \emptyset$ **then** $\mathbf{U}_D \leftarrow \mathbf{U}_D \cup \{\langle \mathcal{U}_D^- \cup \Theta^-, \mathcal{U}_D^+ \rangle\}$;
9   **else**
10             $\mathbf{S} = \{\langle \mathcal{U}_D^- \cup \Theta^-, \mathcal{U}_D^+ \cup \Theta^+ \rangle \mid \Theta^+ \in \Theta^+\}$;
11             $\mathbf{U}_D \leftarrow \mathbf{U}_D \cup$ POSTINSERTION$(\mathcal{J}, \mathcal{U}_A^+, \mathbf{S})$;

12 **return** $\mathbf{U}_D$;

For the case of insertion, Algorithm POSTINSERTION (Algorithm 6) takes as input an ABox insertion $\mathcal{U}_A^+$ and a set $\mathbf{T}$ of possible source translations. For each translation $\mathcal{U}_D = \langle \mathcal{U}_D^-, \mathcal{U}_D^+ \rangle \in \mathbf{T}$, it tries to minimize the insertion side-effect by applying COMPBYDEL (Algorithm 4) (at Line 3), which will lead to compensations by deletion of the initial insertion $\mathcal{U}_D^+$. For each compensation by deletion Θ^-, it tries to minimize the deletion side-effect by applying COMPBYINS (Algorithm 5) (at Line 7), which will lead to compensations by insertion Θ^+. At Line 11, it adds to the solution $\mathbf{U}_D$ a recursive call of POSTINSERTION over $\mathcal{U}_A^+$ and the set $\mathbf{S}$ of all possible pairs of compensations by deletion Θ^- and by insertion Θ^+. Note that, if the set of compensations is empty, the algorithm keeps the solution without compensation (see Lines 4 and 8).

Theorem 19. *Let $\mathcal{J} = \langle \mathcal{P}, D \rangle$ be a VKG instance where $\mathcal{P} = \langle \emptyset, \mathcal{M}, \mathcal{S} \rangle$, $\mathcal{U}_A^+$ an ABox insertion, and $\mathbf{T}$ a set of translations of $\mathcal{U}_A^+$ over $\mathcal{J}$. Then, Algorithm* POSTINSERTION$(\mathcal{J}, \mathcal{U}_A^+, \mathbf{T})$ *always terminates.*

Finally, we propose Algorithm INSERTION (Algorithm 7) for an ABox insertion $\mathcal{U}_A^+$ over a VKG instance. It first computes the set of direct translations of $\mathcal{U}_A^+$ (Line 1) and applies the POSTINSERTION (Algorithm 6) mechanism on each direct translation (Line 2). It then compares the obtained translations and filters out the ones that lead to larger side-effects according to the abstract comparison function COMPARE$_\mathcal{J}$ (Lines 5 to 10). Notice that COMPARE$_\mathcal{J}$ compares two translations Θ_1 and Θ_2 in terms of their side-effect, and similar to COMPARE$_\mathcal{J}^-$ and COMPARE$_\mathcal{J}^+$, returns '<' if Θ_1 has less side-effects that Θ_2.

Theorem 20. *Let $\mathcal{J} = \langle \mathcal{P}, D \rangle$ be a VKG instance where $\mathcal{P} = \langle \emptyset, \mathcal{M}, \mathcal{S} \rangle$ and $\mathcal{U}_A^+$ an ABox insertion. Then, Algorithm* INSERTION$(\mathcal{J}, \mathcal{U}_A^+)$ *computes a set of source translations of $\mathcal{U}_A^+$ with minimal side-effect.*

Algorithm 7: INSERTION $(\mathcal{J}, \mathcal{U}_A^+)$

input : A VKG instance $\mathcal{J} = \langle \mathcal{P}, D \rangle$. A set $\mathcal{U}_A^+$ of ABox insertions.
output: A set of source translations of $\mathcal{U}_A^+$ with minimal side-effect.

1 $\mathbf{T} = \{T_1, \ldots, T_n\} \leftarrow \text{MINTRANSINS}(\mathcal{J}, \mathcal{U}_A^+)$;
2 $\Theta \leftarrow \text{POSTINSERTION}(\mathcal{J}, \mathcal{U}_A^+, \{\langle \emptyset, T \rangle \mid T \in \mathbf{T}\})$;
3 $\mathbf{U}_D \leftarrow \{\}$;
4 **for each** translation $\Theta \in \Theta$ **do**
5   **if** $\langle \mathcal{T}, \mathcal{M}(D \bullet \Theta) \rangle$ is consistent **then**
6      $add \leftarrow true$;
7   **for each** translation $\Theta^* \in \mathbf{U}_D$ **do**
8   **if** $\text{COMPARE}_{\mathcal{J}}(\Theta^*, \Theta) =$ '<' **then** $add \leftarrow false$;
9   **else if** $\text{COMPARE}_{\mathcal{J}}(\Theta, \Theta^*) =$ '<' **then** $\mathbf{U}_D \leftarrow \mathbf{U}_D \setminus \{\Theta^*\}$;
10   **if** add **then** $\mathbf{U}_D \leftarrow \mathbf{U}_D \cup \{\Theta\}$;
11 **return** $\mathbf{U}_D$;

The deletion procedure is symmetric to the insertion procedure. Algorithm POST-DELETION takes as input an ABox deletion $\mathcal{U}_A^-$ and a set $\mathbf{T}$ of possible source translations, and recursively applies compensations by insertion and deletion until no further compensation is possible. Algorithm DELETION takes as input an ABox deletion $\mathcal{U}_A^-$, computes a set $\mathbf{T}$ of possible direct translations, and also applies Algorithm POST-DELETION to minimize the side-effects of the deletions caused by the translations in $\mathbf{T}$.

6 Conclusions

This paper builds upon recent work on instance-level updates in VKGs [17]. Specifically, we propose a compensation procedure to address side-effects caused by ABox deletions and insertions, aiming to minimize unintended deletions and insertions, respectively. We introduce the concept of order among compensations for given ABox updates, leading to the notion of maximum compensation, and we explore its properties and justify its role in minimizing side-effects. Based on that, we proposed two methods, DELETION and INSERTION, that respectively take ABox deletions and ABox insertions, and recursively apply a sequence of maximum compensations by insertion and deletion in order to converge towards an update with minimum side-effect in the ABox. The computation of the maximum recovery and the lineage of ABox assertions that are essential parts of our proposed methods can be done at compile time, and the translation of ABox deletions can be done at run-time and is exponential in the size of its lineage branches. However, the translation of ABox insertions remains challenging due to the non-injective nature of VKG mappings. The complexity of finding the right combination is exponential in the size of the data source and the provided ABox insertion. In a practical setting, constraints over the source data or various techniques can be used to derive the right assignments.

We are currently working on implementing our algorithms by exploiting the query reformulation techniques of state-of-the-art tools for VKGs, specifically the open source system Ontop [4, 21].

Acknowledgments. This research has been partially supported by the Wallenberg AI, Autonomous Systems and Software Program (WASP), funded by the Knut and Alice Wallenberg Foundation, by the HEU project CyclOps (GA n. 101135513), by the Province of Bolzano and FWF through project OnTeGra (DOI 10.55776/PIN8884924), by the Province of Bolzano and EU through projects ERDF-FESR 1078 CRIMA, and ERDF-FESR 1047 AI-Lab, by MUR through the PRIN project 2022XERWK9 S-PIC4CHU, and by the EU and MUR through the PNRR project PE0000013-FAIR.

References

1. Arenas, M., Pérez, J., Reutter, J., Riveros, C.: The language of plain SO-tgds: composition, inversion and structural properties. J. Comput. Syst. Sci. **79**(6), 763–784 (2013). https://doi.org/10.1016/j.jcss.2013.01.002
2. Baader, F., Calvanese, D., McGuinness, D., Nardi, D., Patel-Schneider, P.F. (eds.): The Description Logic Handbook: Theory, Implementation and Applications. Cambridge University Press (2003). https://doi.org/10.1017/CBO9780511711787
3. Bancilhon, F., Spyratos, N.: Update semantics of relational views. ACM Trans. Database Syst. **6**(4), 557–575 (1981). https://doi.org/10.1145/319628.319634
4. Calvanese, D., Cogrel, B., Komla-Ebri, S., Kontchakov, R., Lanti, D., Rezk, M., Rodriguez-Muro, M., Xiao, G.: Ontop: answering SPARQL queries over relational databases. Semantic Web J. **8**(3), 471–487 (2017). https://doi.org/10.3233/SW-160217
5. Calvanese, D., et al.: Ontologies and databases: the *DL-lite* approach. In: Tessaris, S., et al. (eds.) Reasoning Web 2009. LNCS, vol. 5689, pp. 255–356. Springer, Heidelberg (2009). https://doi.org/10.1007/978-3-642-03754-2_7
6. Calvanese, D., De Giacomo, G., Lembo, D., Lenzerini, M., Rosati, R.: Tractable reasoning and efficient query answering in description logics: the DL-lite family. J. Automated Reason. **39**, 385–429 (2007). https://doi.org/10.1007/s10817-007-9078-x
7. Chandra, A.K., Merlin, P.M.: Optimal implementation of conjunctive queries in relational data bases. In: Proceedings of the 9th ACM Symposium on Theory of Computing (STOC), pp. 77–90 (1977)
8. Dayal, U., Bernstein, P.A.: On the correct translation of update operations on relational views. ACM Trans. Database Syst. **7**(3), 381–416 (1982). https://doi.org/10.1145/319732.319740
9. De Giacomo, G., Oriol, X., Rosati, R., Savo, D.F.: Instance-level update in DL-Lite ontologies through first-order rewriting. J. Artif. Intell. Res. (2021). https://doi.org/10.1613/jair.1.12414
10. Fagin, R.: Inverting schema mappings. ACM Trans. Database Syst. **32**(4), 25:2–25:53 (2007). https://doi.org/10.1145/1292609.1292615
11. Fagin, R., Ullman, J.D., Vardi, M.Y.: On the semantics of updates in databases. In: Proceedings of the 2nd ACM Symposium on Principles of Database Systems (PODS), pp. 352–365 (1983). https://doi.org/10.1145/588058.588100
12. Flouris, G.: On belief change in ontology evolution. AI Commun. **19**(4), 395–397 (2006)
13. Katsuno, H., Mendelzon, A.: On the difference between updating a knowledge base and revising it. In: Proceedings of the 2nd International Conference on Principles of Knowledge Representation and Reasoning (KR), pp. 387–394 (1991)
14. Kontchakov, R., Rezk, M., Rodríguez-Muro, M., Xiao, G., Zakharyaschev, M.: Answering SPARQL queries over databases under OWL 2 QL entailment regime. In: Mika, P., et al. (eds.) ISWC 2014. LNCS, vol. 8796, pp. 552–567. Springer, Cham (2014). https://doi.org/10.1007/978-3-319-11964-9_35

15. Motik, B., Cuenca Grau, B., Horrocks, I., Wu, Z., Fokoue, A., Lutz, C.: OWL 2 Web Ontology Language Profiles (second edition). W3C Recommendation, World Wide Web Consortium (2012). http://www.w3.org/TR/owl2-profiles/
16. Poggi, A., Lembo, D., Calvanese, D., De Giacomo, G., Lenzerini, M., Rosati, R.: Linking data to ontologies. J. Data Semant. **10**, 133–173 (2008). https://doi.org/10.1007/978-3-540-77688-8_5
17. Wandji, R.E., Calvanese, D.: Ontology-based update in virtual knowledge graphs via schema mapping recovery. In: Proceedings of the 8th International Joint Conferenvce on Rules and Reasoning (RuleML+RR), pp. 59–74 (2024). https://doi.org/10.1007/978-3-031-72407-7_6
18. Winslett, M.: Updating Logical Databases. Cambridge University Press (1990)
19. Xiao, G., et al.: Ontology-based data access: a survey. In: Proceedings of the 27th International Joint Conference on Artificial Intelligence (IJCAI), pp. 5511–5519. IJCAI Org. (2018). https://doi.org/10.24963/ijcai.2018/777
20. Xiao, G., Ding, L., Cogrel, B., Calvanese, D.: Virtual knowledge graphs: an overview of systems and use cases. Data Intell. (2019). https://doi.org/10.1162/dint_a_00011
21. Xiao, G., et al.: The virtual knowledge graph system Ontop. In: JZ, J.Z., et al. (eds.) ISWC 2020. LNCS, vol. 12507, pp. 259–277. Springer, Cham (2020). https://doi.org/10.1007/978-3-030-62466-8_17
22. Zheleznyakov, D., Kharlamov, E., Nutt, W., Calvanese, D.: On expansion and contraction of DL-Lite knowledge bases. J. Web Semant. **57**, 100484 (2019). https://doi.org/10.1016/j.websem.2018.12.002

Rule Extraction and Interaction-Aware Explainability for AI-Driven Malware Detection

Peter Anthony[1](✉)[🆔], Kefas Rimamnuskeb Galadima[2][🆔], Zekeri Adams[1][🆔], Monday Onoja[1][🆔], Daniel Arp[3][🆔], Martin Homola[1][🆔], and Štefan Balogh[2][🆔]

[1] Comenius University in Bratislava, Mlynská dolina, 84248 Bratislava, Slovakia
{peter.anthony,zekeri.adams,monday.onoja,martin.homola}@fmph.uniba.sk
[2] Slovak University of Technology in Bratislava, Ilkovičova 3,
84104 Bratislava, Slovakia
{rimamnuskeb.kefas,stefan.balogh}@stuba.sk
[3] Technische Universität Wien, Vienna, Austria
daniel.arp@tuwien.ac.at

Abstract. As machine learning becomes integral to malware detection, the demand for interpretability has become critical, not only to understand model decisions, but also to support actionable insights for analysts. While post-hoc techniques like SHAP, LIME, and Anchor offer feature attributions or instance-level rules, they fail to capture generalized semantic patterns across malware samples. To address this, we propose a unified and extensible explainability framework for binarized malware features, offering three levels of interpretability: (1) first-order explanations (individual feature effects), (2) second-order explanations (pairwise interactions revealing nonlinear dependencies), and (3) higher-order, rule-based explanations that formalize joint feature contributions for deeper analytical insight. Our framework builds on an MLP-based detector trained on the EMBER dataset. It first uses SHAP to assess global feature relevance and then introduces two key extensions: (i) a SHAP-based interaction formalism that reveals synergistic and antagonistic effects among features, and (ii) a generalized Anchor algorithm that extracts symbolic, reusable rules to illuminate model behavior and malware patterns. Our global rules achieve an F1 score of 83% on EMBER and perfectly reconstruct nonlinear decision boundaries in synthetic benchmarks (100% F1 on the XoR dataset). Analysis of EMBER's extracted rules reveals that the black-box model's logic often relies on structural anomalies, prioritizing statistical patterns rather than capturing meaningful behavioral patterns indicative of known malware tactics.

Keywords: Explainable Malware Detection · XAI · SHAP · Anchor Explainer · EMBER Dataset

1 Introduction

The rapid evolution of malware has transformed the cybersecurity landscape, with adversaries employing increasingly sophisticated techniques to evade detection and exploit vulnerabilities [1,2]. As organizations and individuals face unprecedented threats, the need for robust and interpretable malware detection systems has never been more critical [3]. Machine learning (ML), particularly deep learning, has emerged as a powerful tool to identify malicious software, offering the ability to analyze vast datasets and detect patterns that traditional signature-based methods may miss [4]. However, the opacity of many ML models, especially deep neural networks, poses a significant challenge without understanding *why* that a model classifies a file as malicious, and security analysts struggle to trust, validate, or act on its predictions [5].

Explainability in malware detection is not just a theoretical concern; it is a practical necessity. Security operations centers (SOCs) rely on actionable insights to respond to threats, and regulatory frameworks increasingly demand transparency in automated decision-making systems [6]. Post-hoc explainability techniques such as SHAP (SHapley Additive exPlanations) [7], LIME (Local Interpretable Model-agnostic Explanations) [8], and Anchor [9] have gained traction as a solution to the opacity of black-box models. Although these tools have become standard in the explainable AI toolkit, their application to malware detection exposes several critical limitations, especially when used in isolation.

First, techniques such as SHAP and LIME are primarily designed to provide attribution of features under the assumption of independent additive feature effects [10]. This assumption breaks down in domains like malware detection, where binary features often interact in linear, logic-like ways. For example, a particular *API* call might only be suspicious if executed in conjunction with another behavioral indicator, such as writing to a registry. Traditional additive models fail to capture such contextual dependencies, resulting in explanations that may be incomplete or even misleading, leaving analysts with an incomplete picture of the behavior of the model [11].

Second, while SHAP offers global insight by aggregating local attributions across samples, it does not expose interaction effects unless explicitly extended. Similarly, LIME focuses on local fidelity around a single instance, providing valuable but narrow-scope explanations. Neither technique provides a structured way to surface interpretable logic-based rules that hold across multiple samples.

Third, Anchor provides a promising approach by generating human-readable decision rules with precision guarantees. However, it is inherently instance-specific. Each explanation applies only to a single input, limiting its generalizability and reusability across the dataset. Analysts are thus left without a principled way to extract general behavioral signatures or reusable detection logic.

Together, these limitations highlight the need for a more comprehensive approach to explainable malware detection, where a holistic understanding of malware behavior is essential. Hence, this work introduces a unified, multi-perspective framework for explainable malware detection that explicitly targets the diverse interpretability needs of cybersecurity analysts. We consider a multilayer perceptron (MLP)-based malware detection model trained on binarised features extracted from the EMBER dataset [12]. We then apply our framework, which is grounded in three complementary dimensions of explanation.

Using SHAP, we identify which binary features, representing discrete behavioral indicators, are the most influential in the model's decision across the entire dataset (global relevance). This helps analysts prioritize features based on their statistical impact. Secondly, we introduce a novel extension of SHAP to move beyond additive attribution to second-order extraction (direction-aware pairwise feature interaction analysis). This extension reveals conditional relationships between features. It uncovers whether a feature's effect is amplified, diminished, or reversed depending on the state of another. This is particularly vital in malware analysis, where combinations of behaviors or characteristics (e.g. `is_dll = 1` and `has_signature = 0`) often signal threats more clearly than individual attributes. Finally, to bridge the gap between model behavior and human reasoning, we extend the Anchor algorithm to extract generalized symbolic rules from the trained model. Unlike traditional Anchor, which only provides instance-specific rules, our extension aggregates rules across multiple representative samples - selected using a clustering-based strategy to produce global human-interpretable logic that reflects the model's inner decision patterns. These rules are actionable: they can be validated, reused, or even deployed independently to discriminate malware. In summary, our contributions are as follows:

1. A unified three-level interpretable approach for malware detection spanning: (i) first-order (feature attribution), (ii) second-order (nonlinear feature interactions) and (iii) higher-order (rule-based) explanations, enabling granular analysis from local decisions to global semantic patterns.
2. We formalize a novel extension of SHAP that enables second-order abstraction, offering deeper and more nuanced insights into model behavior by analyzing interactions between features and their compound impact on classification outcomes. This quantifies synergistic/antagonistic feature pairs, exposing latent model dependencies missed by additive explanation methods.
3. We extend the use of Anchor beyond localized instance-level explanations by proposing a method to derive rule-based global explanations. These generalized rules can be used effectively to interpret model behavior between samples and to support rule-based classification of unseen instances. Achieving an F1 score of 83% on a real-world Windows malware dataset (EMBER), proving that these rules retain discriminative power without the original model.

The remainder of this paper is organized as follows. In Sect. 2, we discuss the background and related work. Sections 3 and 4 detail our proposed framework for extending SHAP, explaining how pairwise feature interactions are modeled to uncover hidden dependencies in malware classification, and our extended Anchor method for generalized rule extraction to derive interpretable global rules from model predictions. Section 5 outlines the experimental design, including dataset preparation, model training, and explanation generation. Section 6 presents our multi-level explainability results, and Sect. 7 concludes the study.

2 Background and Related Work

The fields of malware detection and explainable AI (XAI) have seen significant advancements in recent years. In this section, we review the relevant literature in three key areas: (1) malware detection using machine learning, (2) explainability techniques in machine learning, and (3) the application of explainability in cybersecurity operations.

2.1 Malware Detection Using Machine Learning

Traditional malware detection methods, such as signature-based approaches, have been shown to be ineffective against modern polymorphic malware [2,13]. However, ML-based approaches, particularly deep learning models like CNNs and RNNs, have shown superior ability to detect unseen threats by automatically learning representations from raw data [2,4,14]. The application of machine learning (ML) in malware detection has proven to be more effective, enabling the detection of previously unseen malware by learning patterns from large datasets [14]. Previous efforts focused on static features like API calls, byte sequences, and Portable Executable (PE) headers, with recent works shifting focus to dynamic and hybrid features to improve robustness.

Despite this progress, these models are often opaque, limiting their trustworthiness and operational deployment in real-world cybersecurity contexts [5,14,15].

2.2 Explainability Techniques in Machine Learning

Post-hoc explainability methods such as SHAP (SHapley Additive exPlanations) [7], LIME (Local Interpretable Model-Agnostic Explanations) [8] and Anchor [9] have gained popularity as a way to deal with the opacity of complicated models. SHAP, which is based on cooperative game theory, quantifies feature contributions across datasets to offer both local and global explanations. In contrast, LIME employs simpler models to approximate the decision boundary and perturbs individual instances in order to focus on local interpretability. SHAP and LIME have been investigated in a number of papers for malware classification tasks [16–19]. For example, LIME has provided localized explanations that explain why particular samples are flagged [17,20], whereas SHAP has been used to uncover important discriminative traits such as entropy and API calls [16,21]. To increase efficiency and sparsity, some have extended LIME, such as in Hierarchical LIME (H-LIME) [17]. Notwithstanding their efficacy, these methods are frequently limited to first-order (individual feature) explanations, and their insights do not have the contextual depth required for a sophisticated understanding of malware behaviour.

Some studies have explored the combined use of SHAP and LIME, leveraging their complementary strengths for malware detection. For instance, Gulmez et al. [22] proposed a hybrid approach that used SHAP for the global features importance and LIME for local explanations in the detection of ransomware. Similarly,

Kumar et al. [18] experimented with SHAP and LIME in a malware dataset containing malicious and benign Windows executable files, extracting features using a hybrid approach that combines binary hexadecimal calls and DLLs from Windows PE. In another study, Mane and Rao [23] proposed a deep neural network for intrusion detection, using SHAP, LIME, and Boolean Decision Rules via Column Generation(BRCG) frameworks to interpret the predictions made by black-box model to extract global and instance-wise explanations, and to also help experts understand and fine-tune AI models. Similarly, Baghirov [19] employed LIME and SHAP to evaluate experiments in a multiclass CICMaldroid data set. Although these studies combine local and global approaches, which are comprehensive in gaining deep knowledge of the model decision-making process, they also revealed that the combined approach was computationally expensive, particularly for large-scale datasets. In addition, the explanations provided by SHAP and LIME were not always aligned, leading to potential confusion for analysts.

Sharma et al. [24] propose an interpretable Decision Tree approach to verify the effectiveness of a malware detection that is extensible and explicable by exploiting tactics, techniques, and procedures (TTP) from the MITRE ATTACK framework. The study used a RADAR system, a system that processes network traffic into a knowledge graph. It then makes use of a TTP Detection Engine to identify matching TTPs based on feature-based and heuristic-based rules applied to the network flow data. The TTP-based classification system uses classifiers (decision trees) for each TTP to determine if flows exhibit malicious behavior and aggregates their findings using defined policies (P1, P2, P3) to classify malicious samples. The study evaluates RADAR on a large dataset of more than 2.2 million samples and demonstrates that its malware detection capability is comparable to other state-of-the-art non-interpretable systems, achieving an AUC score of 0.868 with Policy P2. However, a study by Mojžiš and Kenyeres [25] opined that while decision trees are interpretable, complex trees with many branches can be difficult for users to understand.

Prity et al. [26], propose a hybrid approach using LIME, SHAP, and PDPs (Partial Dependence Plots) to examine the performance of machine learning (ML) algorithms in malware classification. The study integrated interaction-aware techniques, such as partial dependency plots, into the surrogate model to improve the understanding of feature interactions and their collective influence on model predictions within the LIME analysis. Similarly, Galli et al. [15], use a hybrid approach, experimenting with LIME, SHAP, LRP, and Attention mechanisms with a focus on behavioral malware detection (BMD). This proposed BMD framework aims to evaluate the effectiveness, strengths, and weaknesses of four XAI methods (LIME, SHAP, LRP, and Attention mechanisms) used in explaining deep learning models. However, their explanations are typically limited to the first-order explanation, and lacks clearer explanations for non-experts on the interactions between features in malware detection.

Research Gaps: As shown in Table 1, and related studies, most studies have provided a wide level of transparency to black-box models using different

Table 1. Comparison of Explanation Capabilities in Malware Detection Research

Study	Used Methods	First-order (Single Feature)	Second-order (Interactions)	Higher-order (Global Rules)
[20]	LIME	Local	✗	✗
[19]	SHAP, LIME	Local+Global	✗	✗
[27]	SHAP	Local+Global	✗	✗
[18]	SHAP, LIME	Local+Global	✗	✗
[21]	SHAP	Local+Global	✗	✗
[17]	H-LIME, LIME	Local	✓	✗
[24]	Decision Tree	Local+Global	✗	✓
[28]	Tree-LIME	Local	✗	✗
[26]	LIME, SHAP, PDPs	Local+Global	✗	✗
[15]	LIME, SHAP, LRP, Attn.	Local+Global	✗	✗
[23]	LIME, SHAP, BRCG	Local+Global	✗	✓
Ours	SHAP, Anchor	Local+Global	✓	✓

explainable AI (XAI) methods in malware detection, with significant achievements. However, their explanations are mostly limited to first-order (individual feature) or second-order (multiple features) or local rules, which may not capture complex feature interactions for a detailed global model understanding.

Our framework directly addresses these gaps by: (1) introducing a multilevel explanation hierarchy that bridges local feature attributions with global behavioral patterns, (2) formalizing second-order feature interactions to expose the implicit logic of complex detectors, and (3) deriving reusable symbolic rules that maintain detection fidelity without the original black box enabling both interpretation and standalone deployment.

3 Extended SHAP Framework: Direction-Aware Pairwise Feature Interaction Analysis

3.1 Motivation and Background

We consider a binary classifier $f : \mathbb{B}^n \to [0, 1]$, such as an MLP-based malware detector, operating with boolean input features $\mathbf{x} \in \mathbb{B}^n$. SHAP (SHapley Additive exPlanations) [7] provides a principled way to decompose the model output into additive contributions.

$$f(\mathbf{x}) = \phi_0 + \sum_{i=1}^{n} \phi_i(\mathbf{x}), \qquad (1)$$

where $\phi_0 = \mathbb{E}[f(\mathbf{x})]$ is the expected model output (the baseline), and $\phi_i(\mathbf{x})$ captures the marginal impact of the feature x_i. While [29] proposed an extension of SHAP that has interaction effects and defines SHAP interaction values. This extension demonstrates strong agreement with human intuition, improvements in run-time, improved clustering performance, and better identification of influential features, but it inherently assumes that feature effects are additive and shows interactions between features; but, these interactions are not relative to the combined impacts made by the features. This limits its ability to capture conditional logic and joint effects between features, which are particularly common in binary, logic-driven domains, such as malware detection.

3.2 Pairwise SHAP Interaction Formulation

To capture joint behavior between features, we define the interaction term $\psi_{ij}(x)$ for a feature pair (x_i, x_j) at input instance x as

$$\psi_{ij}(x) = \mathbb{E}[f(x) \mid x_i, x_j] - \phi_0 - \phi_i(x) - \phi_j(x). \quad (2)$$

This measures the residual effect of the pair (x_i, x_j) that is not explained by their individual SHAP contributions. For Boolean features where $x_i, x_j \in \{0, 1\}$, this formulation becomes computationally efficient, since only the four joint configurations of (x_i, x_j) must be evaluated.

To incorporate these pairwise effects into the additive SHAP framework of Equation (1), we extend the decomposition as

$$f(x) \approx \phi_0 + \sum_{i=1}^{n} \phi_i(x) + \sum_{i<j} \psi_{ij}(x), \quad (3)$$

where the second summation runs over all unordered feature pairs. This extension makes explicit how pairwise interaction terms complement the standard additive SHAP values, allowing the model explanation to account for conditional logic and joint dependencies between features, quantifying the pairwise effect on model output.

3.3 Algorithmic Realization

We first compute SHAP values $\phi_i(\mathbf{x})$ using the DeepExplainer (or KernelSHAP if model agnosticism is required). To reduce computational overhead, we approximate the background distribution by applying k-means clustering to the training data. Typically, $k = \min(1000, n/20)$ provides a good balance between representativeness and efficiency. Representative explanation instances are selected through stratified sampling, anchored around cluster centroids to ensure diversity in the input space.

To estimate pairwise effects, we evaluated each feature pair (i, j) in the four binary combinations. For each pair and value configuration (a, b), we isolate the subset of data $S_{ab}^{ij} = \{\mathbf{x} \mid x_i = a, x_j = b\}$. The corresponding pairwise effect is then estimated as Equation (4). Here, x denotes an input instance drawn from the reference dataset used for SHAP computation, rather than an arbitrary element of the full Boolean space $\{0,1\}^n$. Thus, S_{ab}^{ij} consists only of those data points in the sampled background set for which $x_i = a$ and $x_j = b$. In practice, this avoids exponential growth, since the set is drawn from a manageable sample of the training distribution (cluster centroids) rather than the complete combinatorial input space.

$$\psi_{ij}(a,b) = \frac{1}{|S_{ab}^{ij}|} \sum_{\mathbf{x} \in S_{ab}^{ij}} [\phi_i(\mathbf{x}) + \phi_j(\mathbf{x})] - \phi_0. \tag{4}$$

To ensure statistical robustness, we eliminate configurations where $|S_{ab}^{ij}|$ is below a threshold τ_{samples} (typically 5). We also ignore weak interactions where $|\psi_{ij}(a,b)|$ falls below a small threshold (e.g., 0.005). These filters allow us to focus only on strong, well-supported interactions while significantly reducing computational cost.

Visualization and Interpretation: We visualize interactions using an interactive query system. Possible queries include queries for (i) top k interactions, (ii) top k interaction with specific (selected) features, and (iii) query for specific feature pairs. For any selected pair of characteristics (i, j), we report the interaction values for the four possible pair combinations $\psi_{ij}(a,b)$ together with their corresponding sample counts.

Values are color-coded by directionality: orange for positive effects (malware), blue for negative effects (benign), and gray for data insufficient. This visual encoding intuitively highlights antagonistic versus synergistic feature interactions.

4 Extended Anchor Framework: Global Rule Extraction

This section details our framework, which extends the Anchor algorithm beyond its traditional local, instance-level usage. The outcome is a set of symbolic logic rules that generalize across multiple malware samples, yielding an interpretable and class-discriminative model.

4.1 Background: Anchor Explanations

The Anchor algorithm [9] explains the model predictions through local high-precision rules called *anchors*. For a classifier f and instance $\mathbf{x}$, an anchor A satisfies:

$$\mathbb{P}_{\mathbf{z} \sim \mathcal{D}(\cdot|A)} [f(\mathbf{z}) = f(\mathbf{x})] \geq \tau \tag{5}$$

where $\mathbf{z} \sim \mathcal{D}(\cdot \mid A)$ denotes sampling perturbed instances $\mathbf{z}$ from a distribution that fixes features in A to their values in $\mathbf{x}$ while randomly varying others. The precision threshold $\tau \in [0,1]$ (typically 0.95) ensures the prediction $f(\mathbf{x})$ remains stable under these perturbations. These anchors are inherently local and tailored to specific instances.

4.2 From Local to Global Explanations

Local anchors provide valuable information for individual samples but do not characterize class-level behavior. In malware detection, we require global rules that are symbolic, generalizable, and interpretable. Our goal is to extract such rules by aggregating, filtering, and simplifying anchors across multiple samples.

The proposed framework progresses in several stages. We begin by selecting malware samples that are true positives. For each sample, a local anchor is generated using the standard Anchor algorithm with a high precision threshold ($\tau \geq 0.95$). These anchors are then transformed into symbolic clauses and aggregated into a single disjunctive normal form (DNF) formula. Redundant clauses are pruned using ablation-based simplification [30], yielding a concise and interpretable global rule.

4.3 Formal Methodology

Sample Selection. Let $\mathcal{D} = \{(\mathbf{x}_i, y_i)\}_{i=1}^{N}$ denote the dataset, and let f be a binary classifier. We extract the subset of samples that are true positives ($\mathcal{X}_{TP}$):

$$\mathcal{X}_{TP} = \{\mathbf{x}_i \mid f(\mathbf{x}_i) = y_i = 1\} \quad (6)$$

This ensures that anchors are generated only for malware samples correctly identified by the model.

Anchor Extraction. For each $\mathbf{x} \in \mathcal{X}_{TP}$, we apply the Anchor algorithm to generate a local rule $A(\mathbf{x})$, represented as a conjunction of literals $A(\mathbf{x}) = l_1 \wedge l_2 \wedge \cdots \wedge l_k$. Each literal l_j corresponds to a feature condition, e.g., feature$_j$ or ¬feature$_j$. During generation, only anchors that satisfy $\tau \geq 0.95$ are returned.

Symbolic Rule Construction. Each anchor $A(\mathbf{x})$ is converted into a symbolic logic clause ψ_i. Aggregating all such clauses yields a raw global rule in disjunctive normal form:

$$\varphi_{\text{raw}} = \bigvee_{i=1}^{M} \psi_i \quad (7)$$

This formula captures a general pattern via a disjunction of conjunctions.

Simplification via Ablation. To reduce redundancy, we apply an ablation-based simplification. For each clause $\psi_i \in \varphi_{\text{raw}}$, we temporarily remove it and evaluate the resulting formula $\varphi'' = \varphi_{\text{raw}} \setminus \{\psi_i\}$. If Accuracy($\varphi''$) $\geq$ Accuracy(φ_{raw}) then ψ_i is permanently removed. This process is repeated iteratively until no further simplifications are possible.

Final Rule. The resulting symbolic formula is the final global rule:

$$\varphi_{\text{final}} = \bigvee_{i=1}^{K} \psi_i \quad (8)$$

This interpretable rule can be used for both classification and explanation purposes. It encodes generalized behavior and is easily represented in propositional logic or human-readable form.

5 Experimental Design

In this section, we present our *holistic approach to explainability in malware detection*, integrating SHAP and Anchor to provide global and local explanations, together with actionable insights into model predictions (Code repository:https://github.com/pointers1/RuleXAI_Malware). The overall workflow is summarized in Fig. 1.

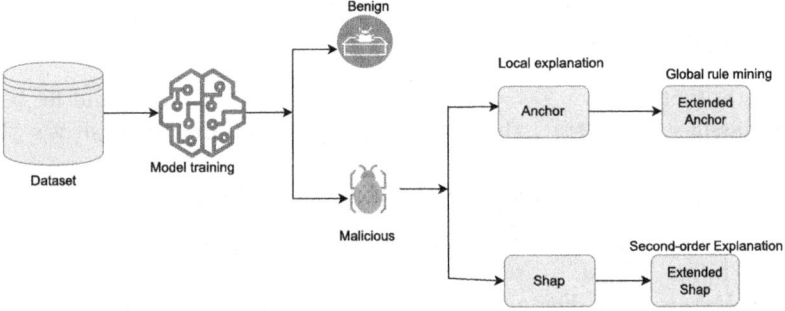

Fig. 1. Overview of our workflow.

5.1 Dataset and Preprocessing

The primary dataset used for our experiment is the popular EMBER (Endgame Malware BEnchmark for Research) dataset developed by Anderson and Roth [12], comprising 1.1 million samples: 400,000 malicious, 400,000 benign and 300,000 unlabeled executable binaries. For our experiments, we used a Decision Tree algorithm to perform feature selection, extracting the top 50 most informative features from the data set. We divide the extracted samples further into 60% for training, 20% for validation, and 20% for testing.

To further validate the generalization capability of our rule extraction pipeline, we use the synthetically controlled XoR dataset from Kaggle which contains 1,000 samples. Its logical structure provides an ideal testbed to validate our rule extraction algorithm's ability to capture non-linear decision boundaries.

5.2 Model Training

We developed an MLP-based malware classifier, which processes statically extracted malware features through a feedforward architecture.

Our classifier processes 50-dimensional preprocessed input feature vectors through a hierarchical architecture with two dense layers (512 and 256 with ReLU-activated units, respectively), each followed by dropout regularization (0.4 and 0.2 rates). The model culminates in a sigmoid output layer for estimating the probability of malware. We trained the network using Adam optimizer, learning rate(lr=0.001) with binary cross-entropy loss in a stratified 60-20-20 train-validation-test split, implementing early stopping (patience=3) and full random seed control (seed=42) for reproducibility.

5.3 Evaluation Metrics

To evaluate the MLP model and the extracted rules, we employed standard metrics commonly used in malware detection, including precision, recall, false positive rate and F1-score. Additionally, we evaluate complexity, defined as the total number of literals in the rules when expressed in disjunctive normal form.

5.4 Explanation Generation

Our methodology focuses on building a unified explanation framework for the classification of binary malware. Given a black-box classifier $f : \mathbb{B}^n \rightarrow [0,1]$, trained in binary feature vectors **x**, we aim to understand and communicate the behavior of the model from three orthogonal perspectives.

1. Global feature relevance.
2. Second-order abstraction (pairwise interaction).
3. Rule-based symbolic explanation.

To this end, our approach consists of three components:

Feature Attribution (Global Feature Relevance): We leverage SHAP to assess how individual features contribute to predictions. provides a global understanding by computing the Shapley value ϕ_i for each characteristic x_i, capturing its average marginal contribution across all samples.

Interaction-Aware Explanation With Extended SHAP: To capture complex inter-feature dependencies often found in binary logic-driven domains, we apply our extension of SHAP to quantify `pairwise` interactions.

- These interactions are computed in the four binary configurations $\{0,1\}^2$, allowing directional insight into the synergistic or antagonistic behavior of the characteristics.
- We apply statistical filtering to retain only interactions above a significance threshold and to eliminate poorly supported configurations.

Symbolic Rule Extraction With Extended Anchor Framework: Lastly, we apply the extended anchor (see Sect. 4) to the global symbolic rule using only the training and validation set. We set n representative samples to 200 samples for the extraction of global rules. We evaluated the extracted rule on the test set (unseen during training and rule extraction).

6 Results and Discussion

This section presents the results and discussion of our experiments. Table 2 compares the performance of the original MLP model with our global rules derived from both datasets. The black box MLP achieves strong detection capability with an F1 score of 91.30% and even perfect performance (F1 = 1.0) in the XoR dataset. These results establish a performance baseline for evaluating our interpretability framework's ability to explain the model's decisions.

Table 2. Performance on the EMBER and XoR Dataset

Dataset	Classifier	Accuracy	Precision	Recall	FPR	F1
EMBER	MLP	91.41	92.43	90.20	7.38	91.30
	Derived Rule	83.04	81.32	0.85	19.71	83.50
XoR	MLP	1.00	1.00	1.00	0.00	1.00
	Derived Rule	1.00	1.00	1.00	0.00	1.00

6.1 First-Order Abstraction with SHAP

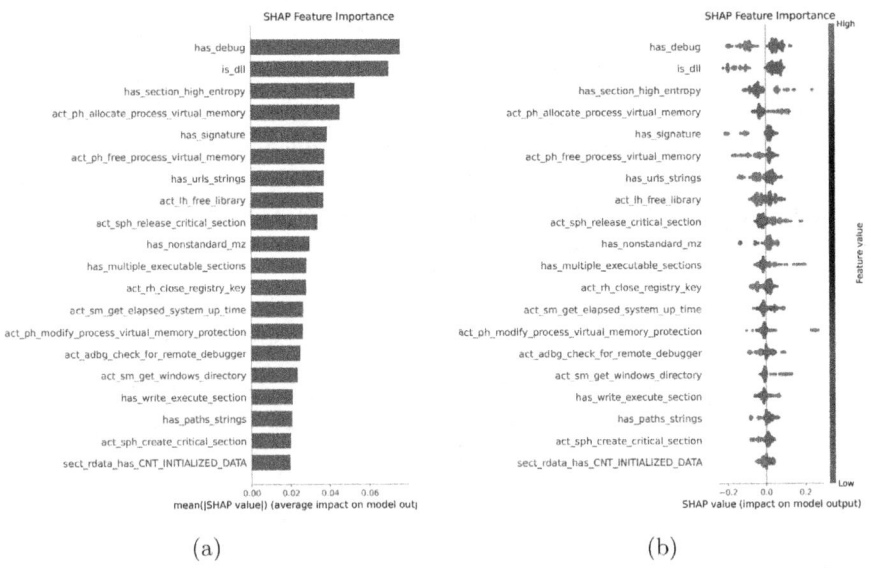

Fig. 2. SHAP explanation visualizations: (a) Summary plot, (b) Beeswarm Plot.

The SHAP analysis reveals three key insights about our model's decision patterns. As shown in Fig. 2a, the three main influential features are has_debug, is_dll, and has_section_high_entropy, indicating these static characteristics disproportionately impact predictions. Figure 2b shows that these features exhibit directional effects: when has_debug=1 (red points), SHAP values are predominantly negative (pushing predictions toward benign), while has_debug=0 (blue) shows positive impact (malware indication). The wide spread of SHAP values for is_dll suggests its effect depends on other feature combinations, a dependency that this first-order analysis cannot disentangle. Similarly, while has_section_high_entropy shows consistent positive influence, the magnitude varies substantially, implying interactions with unobserved features. These patterns confirm that our model relies heavily on structural file attributes, but instance-specific variations highlight the need for higher-order analysis to uncover the latent decision logic.

6.2 Second-Order Abstraction: Pairwise Feature Interactions

Our interaction analysis (second-order level of abstraction) reveals critical non-linear dependencies between features that the baseline SHAP could not capture. Figure 3 shows the strongest pairwise interaction and their effects on the model's prediction. Figure 4 shows the interaction effects of two specific features (has_section_high_entropy and is_dll for all the four possible combinations. Figure 5 highlights how specific features, particularly the topmost feature (has_debug) highlighted by the baseline SHAP modulate predictions when combined with other features. Notably, structural-behavioral synergies (e.g., DLLs performing memory operations) and conditional effects (e.g., debug-section interactions) dominate the top interactions. All interaction plots show the average change in the predicted probability for the feature combinations. Positive values (orange) shift predictions toward malware and negative values (blue) toward benign. Corresponding sample sizes (n) are annotated.

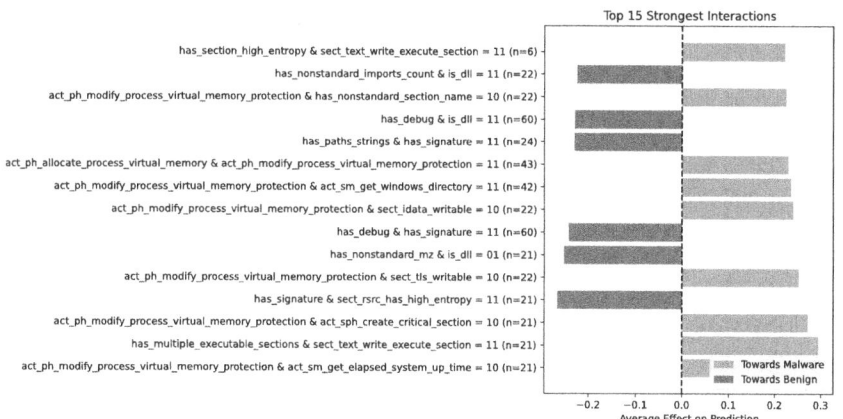

Fig. 3. Top 15 strongest pairwise interaction effects on the model's prediction.

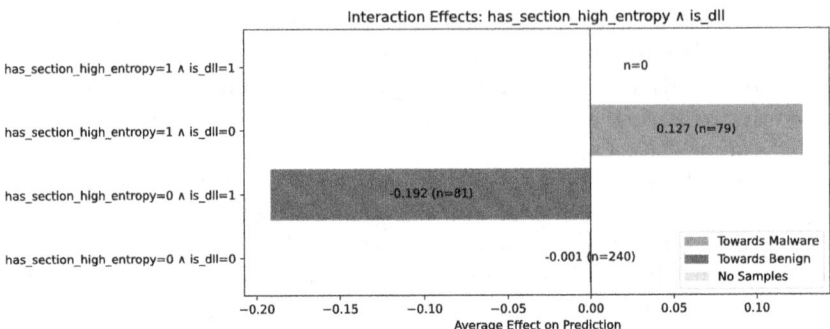

Fig. 4. Interaction effects between has_section_high_entropy and is_dll.

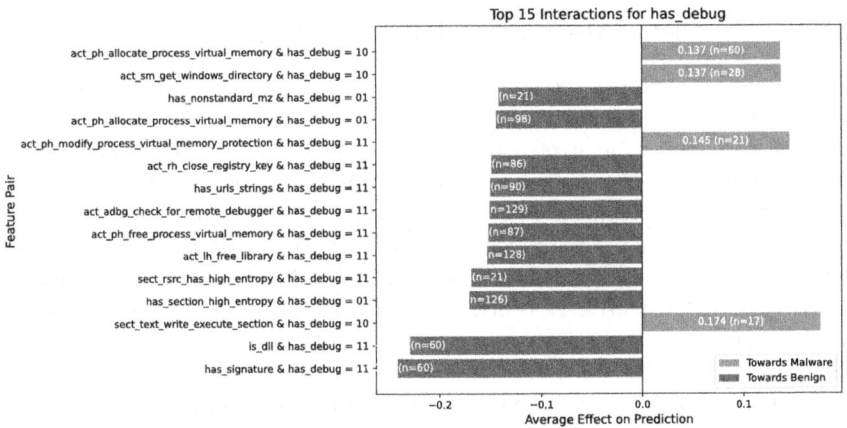

Fig. 5. Top 15 strongest pairwise interactions involving has_debug.

Three key patterns emerge from Fig. 3:

1. **Structural-Behavioral Synergies**: Interactions such as the occurrence of act_sph_create_critical_section and act_ph_modify_process_virtual_memory_protection show that processes which create critical sections while modifying virtual memory protections are more likely to be associated with malicious behavior.

2. **Conditional Effects**: While has_debug=0 alone is indicative for malware (baseline SHAP), its combination with has_signature = 1 (Fig. 5) reverses the effect, revealing that unsigned, debug-less files shift the prediction toward benign.

3. **Entropy Dependencies**: The indication of malware in multiple executable sections strengthens when combined with writable sections (Fig. 3), explaining the variance observed in the first-order analysis. (Figure 4) quantifies these nonlinearities: has_section_high_entropy ∧ is_dll has opposing effects depending on state combinations. This explains why first-order SHAP showed wide value spreads in which the same feature can have opposite impacts based

on co-occurring attributes. In particular, 68% of the top interactions involve pairs of cross categories (structural + behavior), demonstrating that our pairwise interaction analysis reveals patterns that the single-feature analysis would miss.

These results argue compellingly for interaction-aware explainability in malware research. Where baseline SHAP offered isolated feature rankings, the second-order analysis exposes the model's *reasoning chains*: how it combines structural anomalies with runtime behaviors to flag threats. This does not just improve transparency, it surfaces deeper insights (e.g. "Prioritize DLLs performing memory protection changes") that could enhance manual analysis.

6.3 Higher Order Abstraction (Global Rule Extraction)

Table 3 presents the top 5 conjunctions of the global rule extracted from the EMBER ranked according to their F1 score with malware expert review.

Table 3. Sample explanations from extended anchor rules

S/N	Rule
1	¬is_dll ∧ has_write_execute_section ∧ ¬has_relocations ∧ ¬sect_upx1_has_high_entropy (0.91 precision, 0.25 recall)
2	has_nonstandard_mz ∧ ¬sect_reloc_readable ∧ ¬act_lh_get_function_address ∧ ¬is_dll ∧ ¬sect_upx1_has_high_entropy (0.90 precision, 0.24 recall)
3	has_section_high_entropy ∧ ¬sect_reloc_readable ∧ ¬has_debug ∧ ¬act_rh_close_registry_key ∧ ¬has_signature ∧ ¬act_ph_free_process_virtual_memory (0.90 prec., 0.24 recall)
4	has_section_high_entropy ∧ ¬sect_reloc_readable ∧ ¬has_urls_strings ∧ ¬is_dll ∧ ¬act_lh_get_function_address (0.92 precision, 0.23 recall)
5	has_section_high_entropy ∧ has_write_execute_section ∧ ¬has_debug ∧ ¬has_urls_strings (0.91 precision, 0.23 recall)

Expert Comment: Rules like 1 and 2 reflect traits that are commonly associated with malware, such as non-standard file headers or suspicious memory permissions. These indicate potential packing or injection techniques and may be useful as weak indicators. While the rules demonstrate high precisions, most of the rules are too general and do not point to specific malware behaviors. They rely heavily on structural absence (e.g., missing debug info or relocation sections) rather than capturing meaningful behavioral patterns.

The derived rules achieve high precision by combining structural and behavioral features in nuanced ways, reflecting malware analysis heuristics. For example, the top rule (¬is_dll ∧ has_write_execute_section ∧ ¬has_relocations

∧ ¬sect_upx1_has_high_entropy) identifies non-DLL executables with suspicious memory permissions but lacking common packer signatures, a pattern that aligns with known evasion tactics. However, as the expert noted, such rules often rely on structural anomalies (e.g., missing relocations or debug info) rather than explicit malicious behaviors (e.g., API call sequences). While these correlations yield strong precision (0.91), they may not fully capture semantically meaningful threat indicators, suggesting the model prioritizes statistical patterns over grounded malware logic.

Similarly, rules like has_section_high_entropy ∧ ¬sect_reloc_readable ∧ ¬has_debug ∧ ¬act_rh_close_registry_key demonstrate the model's reliance on the absence of benign traits (e.g., debug info, registry operations) as proxies for malice. This aligns with the expert's observation that the rules are "too general" and lean on negative conditions rather than behavioral signatures.

The rules fill key gaps in earlier methods but expose trade-offs:

- First-order SHAP identified important features (e.g., has_write_execute_section) but missed contextual dependencies. The rules resolve this by specifying co-occurrence conditions (e.g., requiring ¬is_dll).
- Second-order interactions exposed pairwise relationships (e.g., entropy + writable sections), but the rules combine multiple literals into actionable logic and precise model decision rationale.

Expert Critique: The rules' reliance on structural negatives (e.g., ¬has_relocations) highlights a potential disconnect between the model's statistical efficacy and malware-specific domain knowledge. Future work could refine rule extraction to prioritize behaviorally meaningful features or consider them.

Moreover, the extended Anchor algorithm successfully extracted the ground-truth logical formula $(Y \land \neg X) \lor (\neg Y \land X)$, achieving perfect performance (F1 = 1.0) on the XoR dataset, demonstrating the method's capability to precisely capture non-linear decision boundaries.

7 Conclusion

This study advances interpretable malware detection through a hierarchical explainability framework that bridges local feature attributions with global behavioral patterns. We present an efficient extension of SHAP that quantifies pairwise, context-aware feature interactions analysis capturing non-linear dependencies, and exposes implicit logic used by complex models; We extend the use of Anchor beyond localized instance-level explanations by proposing a method to derive rule-based global explanation that reflects the model's inner decision patterns, and can independently discriminate malware. Our three-level analysis reveals: (1) First-order SHAP identifies has_debug and memory operations as primary indicators, (2) Second-order interactions expose critical nonlinear dependencies, notably DLLs performing memory protection changes, and (3) Higher-order rules achieve 83% F1-score while maintaining interpretability. The framework successfully addresses key limitations of post-hoc methods by: Resolving directional ambiguities (e.g., has_debug=0 indicates malware alone but benign when co-occurring with signatures); Quantifying contextual effects (e.g. stronger entropy impact with writable sections); Higher-order rules achieve 83% F1-score on EMBER, with perfect performance (100% F1) on the XoR benchmark, demonstrating cross-domain generalization. Analysis of the extracted rules shows that the black box model often relies on structural anomalies, prioritizing statistical patterns rather than meaningful behavioral patterns indicative of known malware tactics. Our results demonstrate that model interpretability need not compromise detection efficacy; instead, such a structured hierarchical explanation can complement black box surfacing actionable malware signatures.

Acknowledgments. Z. Adams, P. Anthony, Š. Balogh, K. R. Galadima, M. Homola, and M. Onoja are funded by the EU NextGenerationEU through the Recovery and Resilience Plan for Slovakia under the project No. 09I05-03-V02-00064. D. Arp is funded by the Vienna Science and Technology Fund (WWTF) through the BREADS project (10.47379/VRG23011).

References

1. Durgaraju, S., Vel, D.V.T., Madathala, H.: The evolution of cyber threats and defenses: a review of innovations and challenges. In: 2025 6th International Conference on Mobile Computing and Sustainable Informatics (ICMCSI) (2025). https://doi.org/10.1109/ICMCSI64620.2025.10883230
2. Szor, P.: The Art of Computer Virus Research and Defense. Addison-Wesley Professional (2005). https://dl.acm.org/doi/abs/10.5555/1050957
3. Anderson, R.J., et al.: Measuring the cost of cybercrime. Econ. Inf. Secur. Priva. (2013). https://doi.org/10.1007/978-3-642-39498-0_12
4. Vinayakumar, R., Alazab, M., Soman, K.P., Poornachandran, P., Venkatraman, S.: Robust intelligent malware detection using deep learning. IEEE Access **7**, 46717–46738 (2019). https://doi.org/10.1109/ACCESS.2019.2906934
5. Arrieta, A.B., et al.: Explainable artificial intelligence (XAI): concepts, taxonomies, opportunities and challenges toward responsible AI. Inf. Fus. **58** (2020). https://doi.org/10.1016/j.inffus.2019.12.012
6. de Magalhães, S.T.: The European Union's General Data Protection Regulation (GDPR). 1st Edition, World Scientific, Singapore, Ch. 15, pp. 529–558 (2020). https://worldscientific.com/doi/abs/10.1142/9789811204463_0015
7. Lundberg, S.M., Lee, S.-I.: A unified approach to interpreting model predictions. In: Advances in Neural Information Processing Systems, vol. 30 (NeurIPS 2017), Curran Associates, Inc., pp. 4765–4774 (2017). https://doi.org/10.48550/arXiv.1705.07874
8. Ribeiro, M.T., Singh, S., Guestrin, C.: why should I trust you?: explaining the predictions of any classifier. In: Proceedings of the Interenational Conference on Knowledge Discovery (KDD) (2016). https://doi.org/10.1145/2939672.2939778
9. Ribeiro, M.T., Singh, S., Guestrin, C.: Anchors: High-precision model-agnostic explanations. In: Proceedings of the AAAI Conference on Artificial Intelligence (2018). https://doi.org/10.1609/AAAI.V32I1.11491

10. Schnake, T., et al.: Towards symbolic XAI — explanation through human understandable logical relationships between features. Inf. Fus. **118**, 102923 (2025). https://doi.org/10.1016/j.inffus.2024.102923
11. Warnecke, A., Arp, D., Wressnegger, C., Rieck, K.: Evaluating explanation methods for deep learning in security (2020). https://doi.org/10.1109/EuroSP48549.2020.00018
12. Anderson, H.S., Roth, P.: EMBER: an open dataset for training static PE malware machine learning models. arXiv preprint arXiv:1804.04637 (2018)
13. Svec, P., Balogh, S., Homola, M.: Experimental evaluation of description logic concept learning algorithm for static malware detection. In: ICISSP, pp. 792–799 (2021)
14. Manthena, H., Shajarian, S., Kimmell, J.C., Abdelsalam, M., Khorsandroo, S., Gupta, M.: Explainable artificial intelligence (XAI) for malware analysis: a survey of techniques, applications, and open challenges. IEEE Access **13** (2025). https://doi.org/10.1109/ACCESS.2025.3555926
15. Galli, A., La Gatta, V., Moscato, V., Postiglione, M., Sperlì, G.: Explainability in AI-based behavioral malware detection systems. Comput. Secur. **141**, 103842 (2024). https://doi.org/10.1016/j.cose.2024.103842
16. Adhikari, D., Thapaliya, S.: Explainable AI for cyber security: interpretable models for malware analysis and network intrusion detection. NPRC J. Multidiscip. Res. **1**(9), 170–179 (2024). https://doi.org/10.3126/nprcjmr.v1i9.74177
17. Mitchell, J., McLaughlin, N., del Rincon, J.M.: Generating sparse explanations for malicious android opcode sequences using hierarchical lime. Comput. Secur. **137**, 103637 (2024). https://doi.org/10.1016/j.cose.2023.103637
18. Basheer, N., Pranggono, B., Islam, S., Papastergiou, S., Mouratidis, H.: Enhancing malware detection through machine learning using XAI with SHAP framework. In: AIAI, pp. 316–329 (2024). https://doi.org/10.1007/978-3-031-63211-2_24
19. Baghirov, E.: A comprehensive investigation into robust malware detection with explainable AI. Cyber Secur. Appl. **3** (2025). https://doi.org/10.1016/j.csa.2024.100072
20. Hafiz, M.F.B., Khan, N.A., Kamal, Z., Hossain, S., Barman, S.: A robust malware classification approach leveraging explainable AI. In: International Conference on Intelligence System for Cybersecurity (ISCS), pp. 1–6 (2024). https://doi.org/10.1109/ISCS61804.2024.10581382
21. Alenezi, R., Ludwig, S.A.: Explainability of cybersecurity threats data using shap. In: IEEE Symposium Series on Computational Intelligence (SSCI), 01–10 (2021). https://doi.org/10.1109/SSCI50451.2021.9659888
22. Gulmez, S., Gorgulu Kakisim, A., Sogukpinar, I.: XRAN: explainable deep learning-based ransomware detection using dynamic analysis. Comput. Secur. **139** 103703 (2024). https://doi.org/10.1016/j.cose.2024.103703
23. Mane, S., Rao, D.: Explaining network intrusion detection system using explainable AI framework, pp. 1–10. arXiv preprint arXiv:2103.07110 (2021)
24. Sharma, Y., Birnbach, S., Martinovic, I.: Exploiting TTPS to design an extensible and explainable malware detection system, vol. 30
25. Mojžiš, J., Kenyeres, M.: Interpretable rules with a simplified data representation - a case study with the ember dataset. In: Silhavy, R., Silhavy, P. (eds.), Data Analytics in System Engineering, Springer International Publishing, pp. 1–10 (2024). https://doi.org/10.1007/978-3-031-53552-9_1
26. Prity, F.S., et al.: Machine learning-based cyber threat detection: an approach to malware detection and security with explainable AI insights. Hum. Intell. Syst. Integr. **6**(1), 61–90 (2024). https://doi.org/10.1007/s42454-024-00055-7

27. Manthena, H., Kimmel, J.C., Abdelsalam, M., Gupta, M.: Analyzing and explaining black-box models for online malware detection. IEEE Access **11**, 25237–25252 (2023). https://doi.org/10.1109/ACCESS.2023.3255176
28. Nwakanma, C.I., Ahakonye, L.A.C., Jun, T., Lee, J.M., Kim, D.S.: Explainable scada-edge network intrusion detection system: tree-lime approach. https://doi.org/10.1109/SmartGridComm57358.2023.10333968
29. Lundberg, S.M., Erion, G.G., Lee, S.-I.: Consistent individualized feature attribution for tree ensembles (2019). arXiv:1802.03888
30. Lakkaraju, H., Bach, S.H., Leskovec, J.: Interpretable decision sets: a joint framework for description and prediction. In: Proceedings of the ACM SIGKDD International Conference on Knowledge Discovery and Data Mining (KDD) (2016). https://doi.org/10.1145/2939672.2939874

Probabilistic Answer Set Programming Driven Ranking of Dynamic Space-Time Belief Models

Julius Monsen[1,3](✉), Jakob Suchan[2,3], and Mehul Bhatt[1,3]

[1] Örebro University, Örebro, Sweden
julius.monsen@oru.se ,
cognitive.vision@codesign-lab.org
[2] Constructor University, Bremen, Germany
[3] CoDesign Lab EU., Örebro, Sweden
https://codesign-lab.org/cognitive-vision

Abstract. A key challenge in embodied, inter(active) vision is reasoning over alternative hypotheses about the dynamics of perceived objects and events, be it for real-time or even offline interpretation. Towards this, we address the problem of generating and ranking grounded visuospatial hypotheses based on a semantically encoded notion of hypothesis preference. Driven by probabilistic Answer Set Programming (ASP), we propose a general framework for modeling and reasoning about diverse preference types tailored to visuospatial interpretation tasks. The effectiveness of our probabilistic visuospatial hypotheses ranking method is demonstrated and evaluated with a community benchmark of Multi-Object Tracking (MOT17), where modeling uncertainty and preference is critical for robust scene interpretation. Furthermore, practical examples also showcase how semantically driven reasoning with preferences can be effectively used in real-world visual sensemaking tasks.

Keywords: Probabilistic Answer Set Programming · Preferential Ranking · Visual Intelligence · Deep Semantics · Cognitive Vision

1 Introduction

The high-level, explainable interpretation of dynamic visual scenes—such as those encountered in autonomous driving, human-robot interaction etc.— remains a fundamental challenge in AI and ML. While contemporary deep learning-driven visual computing excels at processing raw sensory input, it lacks mechanisms for abstract, context-aware, explainable reasoning and learning in a robust and formally verifiable manner. Likewise, relational AI and its practical declarative manifestations offer robust tools for structured / logic-based commonsense representation and reasoning, but typically struggle in their ability to handle large-scale, noisy, incomplete (dynamic) quantitative sensory data.

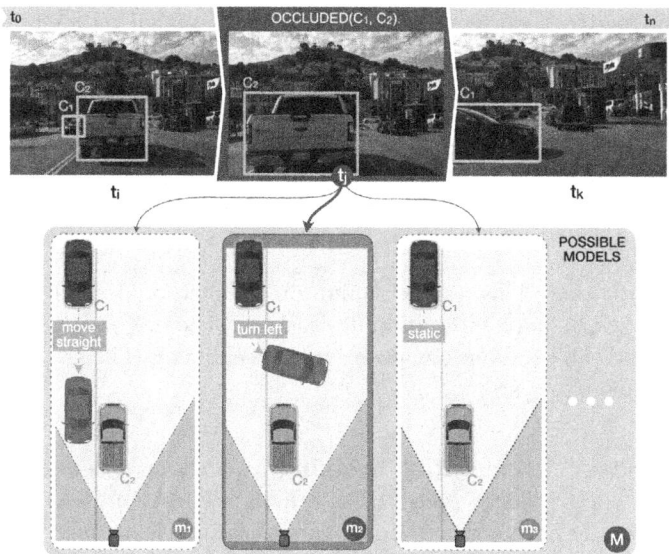

Fig. 1. Dynamic Space-Time Belief Models. An example illustrating the challenge of visual sensemaking. In this traffic scenario, a vehicle is occluded, creating ambiguity about the vehicle's possible trajectory. There are multiple plausible semantically distinct hypotheses—such as the car continuing straight (M1), turning left (M2), or remaining static (M3)—that may be derived and ranked according to, for instance, human safety preferences.

Embodied Visual Intelligence. In recent years, the integration of semantically rooted or knowledge-centric declarative AI methods for commonsense reasoning with deep learning-based visual computing techniques has emerged as a promising research direction aimed at achieving embodied (artificial) visual intelligence [5,23]. Here, visual intelligence corresponds to computational sensemaking under ecologically valid "*in-the-wild*" naturalistic settings where the crucial challenge is that of integrated explainable reasoning and learning about dynamic (inter)active multimodality [5]. To this end, neurosymbolic visual commonsense mechanisms for reasoning about spatio-temporal dynamics integrating semantically driven AI methods for commonsense knowledge representation and reasoning with quantitative visual computing techniques have emerged in particular [24,25]. The general position guiding these neurosymbolic mechanisms is that real-world sensemaking of visual stimuli (such as video) requires the ontological and computational interfacing of diverse multi-faceted methods in AI and ML. This position resonates directly with long-established, but often overlooked, convictions concerning realizing computational models of human-like cognitive vision; to quote Marr [20]:

» "The study of vision must [...] include not only the study of how to extract from images the various aspects of the world that are useful to us, but also an inquiry into the nature of the internal representations by which we capture this information and thus make it available as a basis for decisions about our thoughts and actions."

This perspective underscores the necessity for *internal representations* that are not only *semantically descriptive* but are also *actionable*, i.e., capable of supporting inference, prediction, and semantic preference-driven selection (amongst other things). As an example, consider the example in Fig. 1, aimed at highlighting the need and value for high-level reasoning about space-time dynamics under tight real-time visual sensemaking and control requirements in real-world conditions.

Key Contributions. This research builds on and methodologically advances an ongoing line of work on (computational) *cognitive vision* [4] aimed at integrating symbolic AI and sub-symbolic computer vision techniques. The key contributions presented in this paper are:

C1. Probabilistic Preferential Ranking: A systematic and general characterization of probabilistic preferential ranking of dynamic space-time belief models (temporally evolving, hypotheses about visual elements in a scene) that serves as the computational foundation enabling (re)ordering of neurosymbolically grounded perceptual beliefs emanating from low-level quantitative stimuli. Indeed, probabilistic preferential ranking naturally serves as a tool to not only encode semantic selection of preferences, but also to handle uncertainty that is inherent in quantitative data, thereby accounting for noisy or completely missing data, as well as errors in low-level visual processing methods.

C2. Declarative Neurosymbolic Model: Dynamic space-time preferential ranking is declaratively implemented as a general, neurosymbolic method driven by an integration of probabilistic Answer Set Programming (ASP) [8,14] and low-level visual computing mechanisms (e.g., for object detection). The implemented method is primarily, but not exclusively, driven by supporting the formalization of *policies* that encode both domain-independent and dependent factors such as: **(a)** Constraints relevant to generally applicable commonsense laws pertaining to spatio-temporal dynamics as encountered in everyday "in-the-wild" embodied interaction settings; **(b)** Heuristics representing high-level cognitive preferences characterizing human/cognitive mental model selection mechanisms as part of abductively computing alternate or counterfactual hypotheses computation; and **(c)** Contextual knowledge and other considerations/requirements resulting from the specifics of an application domain/use-case.

Our overall goal is to develop systematically formalized and implemented modular, extensible foundational mechanisms that enable robust neurosymbolic visual sensemaking in real-world problem settings. Therefore, we also showcase and evaluate the practical utility of our proposed probabilistic visuospatial hypotheses ranking methodology with MOT17[1], a computer vision, community established, benchmark focussing on Multi-Object Tracking (MOT) [21].

---

[1] MOT17 Challenge: https://motchallenge.net/data/MOT17/.

2 Background: Declarative Visuospatial Commonsense

An established line of research on computational commonsense representation of space and time is that qualitative representations of spatial, temporal, and spatio-temporal relations (e.g. *front_right, touching, during, approaching*) can effectively map between high-level semantic categories and low-level quantitative data. For instance, abstracting from metric details of the physical world, such relational knowledge can capture 4D space-time regions with both spatial and temporal components [9] for modeling object interactions [26]. The influence of (spatio-linguistic) "path & motion predicates" for grounding complex quantitative data is also well-recognized [19]. Such commonsense characterizations are a promising abstraction mechanism for semantic grounding and automated reasoning about embodied multimodal interaction encompassing space, actions, events, change and motion [3].

Commonsense representations of space, time, and motion naturally align and integrate with knowledge representation (KR) frameworks that support expressive, high-level modeling and reasoning. In this context, ASP [6,7,16] has emerged as a particularly suitable paradigm for formalizing and operationalizing such dynamic, relational knowledge about space, time, and motion [22,24,26]. This is by virtue of the fact that ASP is also one of the most scalable and actively researched methods for non-monotonic reasoning (e.g., required for belief revision), an aspect critical to the technical agenda of this research. Several extensions to the core ASP framework have accrued recently, e.g., functional ASP for modeling specialized continuous domains by satisfiability modulo theory (SMT) integration [1,13], probabilistic ASP [8,15], inductive learning [12], spatial reasoning [26], neurosymbolic integration [25,28].

To reason about uncertainty, which is inherent in visual interpretation tasks, we employ ASP, realized through Plingo [8], a probabilistic extension of Clingo [7]. Plingo is based on the $Lpmln\pm$ formalism—a variant of the probabilistic language $Lpmln$ [14]—that merges declarative logic programming with probabilistic reasoning. This framework is particularly well-suited for our purposes as it provides a well-integrated method for combining hard constraints with probabilistic preferences enabled by soft constraints, i.e. rules that do not strictly eliminate candidate solutions, but instead weight them probabilistically. This allows for representing and reasoning about uncertain knowledge in a declarative manner. Specifically, a Plingo program consists of two parts: (**1**) A hard part, written as normal ASP rules and weak constraints at priority levels greater than 0; and (**2**) A soft part, written as ASP weak constraints on the form $:\sim F[w,l]$ (where F is a formula, w is a real number weight, and l is a nonnegative integer) at priority level 0, that assigns weights to the model, and thereby induces a probability distribution over all stable models.

More formally, we can express the semantics of $Lpmln\pm$ (and in extension Plingo) in terms of a logic program $\Pi = \Pi^{hard} \cup \Pi^{soft}$ where Π^{hard} is the hard part and Π^{soft} is the soft part. Let $SSM(\Pi)$ denote the set of soft stable models of Π. An interpretation (a set of atoms) X is included in this set if it is a stable model of the program formed by the rules in Π that X satisfies (viewed as unweighted rules). To define the probability of such a model, we first define its weight. Let Π_X be the set of weighted rules from Π satisfied by X. The weight of the interpretation, $W_\Pi(X)$, is then the total weight of this subprogram $TW(\Pi_X) = exp(\sum_{w:\ F \in \Pi_X} w)$, as seen in Eq. 1. Finally, the probability $P_\Pi(X)$ of a model $X \in SSM(\Pi)$ is determined by normalizing the weights over all such optimal stable models $W_\Pi(Y)$, as shown in Eq. 2. Here, the limit $\alpha \to \infty$ in the probability formula enforces the infinite weight of hard rules, ensuring that any model violating them receives zero probability. X is then a probabilistic stable model of Π if $P_\Pi(X) \neq 0$.

$$W_\Pi(X) = \begin{cases} TW(\Pi_X) & X \in SSM(\Pi) \\ 0 & \text{otherwise} \end{cases} \quad (1)$$

$$P_\Pi(A) = \lim_{\alpha \to \infty} \frac{W_\Pi(X)}{\sum_{Y \in SSM(\Pi)} W_\Pi(Y)} \quad (2)$$

When comparing two stable models X and Y of Π^{hard}, X is preferred over Y (with respect to the weak constraints Π^{soft}) if there is a level l where X has a lower cost than Y, and at every higher level $l' > l$, their costs are the same [8]. An optimal stable model of Π is a stable model X for which there is no stable model Y of Π^{hard} such that Y is preferred over X with respect to Π^{soft}. In Sect. 3, we will show how such preferences can be specified in a declarative manner within Plingo, and how they can be used to rank different interpretations of a visual scene.

3 Preferential Ranking of Dynamic Space-Time Belief Models

Within the context of this work, we focus on the problem of ranking dynamic space-time belief models, i.e. stable models of a logic program that represent the possible interpretations of the scene and the objects in it over time. To rank these models effectively, it is necessary to define preferences related to key aspects of the visual domain.

3.1 Space and Motion Preliminaries

Our framework adopts a formalization of space, motion, objects, and events inspired by prior work, particularly the approach by [24,25]. At the core of this formalization are two key domains: the spatio-temporal domain Σ_{st}, representing the geometric and temporal aspects of visual objects, and the dynamic domain Σ_{dyn}, capturing higher-level event-based descriptions of change over time.

In the spatio-temporal domain Σ_{st}, we consider a set of domain objects $\mathcal{O} = o_1, \ldots, o_n$, which correspond to entities in the visual scene, e.g. cars and pedestrians. Each object o_i is represented as a spatial entity $\varepsilon_i \in \mathcal{E}$, where $\mathcal{E}$ may include geometric forms like points, lines, or polygons in 2D or 3D space. Temporal dynamics are encoded via a set of discrete time points $\mathcal{T} = \{t_1, \ldots, t_m\}$, and object motion is captured through trajectories $\mathcal{MT}_{o_i} = (\varepsilon_{t_s}, \ldots, \varepsilon_{t_e})$, which describe how spatial entities evolve from start time t_s to end time t_e. Additionally, spatio-temporal relations $\mathcal{R}$ define the qualitative relationships between objects across space and time.

The dynamic domain Σ_{dyn} enriches this structural representation with semantic content in the form of fluents $\Phi = \phi_1, \ldots, \phi_n$ and events $\Theta = \theta_1, \ldots, \theta_n$, which respectively represent the state-dependent properties of the world and the occurrences that alter those states. We say that an event $\theta_i \in \Theta$ is considered possible only if a set of necessary conditions c_j are satisfied. We express this as: $Poss(\theta_i) \leftrightarrow \bigwedge_j c_j$. To reason about these dynamics, we use an ASP-based formalization [18] of the event calculus [10], wherein axioms such as `occurs_at(θ,t)` assert that an event θ occurs at time t, and `holds_at(ϕ,v,t)` asserts that a fluent ϕ takes on a value v at time t.

3.2 Preferences in Dynamic Space-Time Belief Models

We define Σ_{prf} as the domain preferences that can be used to rank dynamic space-time belief models. Σ_{prf} consist of preferences $\mathcal{P}$ that are defined over the events Θ in the dynamic domain Σ_{dyn} where each event $\theta_i \in \Theta$ may involve one or more objects $(\mathcal{O}_{\theta_i})$.

Our notion of preference is defined as a tuple consisting of a set of preference functions (PF_{θ_i}), and a corresponding set of weights $(w_{\theta_i 1})$. The preference function for an event $\theta_i \in \Theta$ is defined over a finite number of objects involved in the event $\{o_1, \ldots, o_n\} \in \mathcal{O}_{\theta_i}$ as follows:

$$PF_{\theta_i} : \mathcal{O}_{\theta_i} \times \ldots \times \mathcal{O}_{\theta_i} \to \mathbb{R} \qquad (3)$$

This results in a set of *preference features* $\mathcal{F}_{\theta_i} = \{f_{\theta_i 1}, \ldots, f_{\theta_i m}\}$ associated with θ_i. These preferences can then be used to guide the ranking of competing space-time belief models by quantifying the desirability of including the event θ_i under the given domain preferences. The preferences may belong to any of the following categories, where they differ in terms of the feature set the preference function is defined over:

- $\mathcal{P}_{\text{geom}}$ denotes preferences based on the geometric properties of the objects in the scene and their dynamics over time. This mostly concerns the spatial entities $\mathcal{E}$ and the motion trajectories $\mathcal{MT}_{o_i}$ of the objects o_i in the scene. For example, we can define preferences involving distances between objects, the size of the objects, the speed of the objects within a certain time interval, the direction of motion, or generally how geometric objects should behave by the laws of physics.
- $\mathcal{P}_{vis}$ denotes preferences based on features extracted from visual data with neural networks. In principle, there is no limitation to what this kind of features can be used to define these preferences. For example, we can define

preferences based on visual appearance features (e.g. re-identification features that compute an embedding similarity between objects), object type classification, the 3D depth of the objects, object pose and orientation as well as aspects in the general context of the scene.
- $\mathcal{P}_{sem}$ denotes preferences based on semantic properties at the object, scene, and conceptual levels. At the object level, these include type, color, affordances, and relationships (e.g., interactions, and hierarchies). Scene-level preferences depend on context, such as layout (indoor, outdoor, traffic) and associated knowledge (e.g., traffic rules). Conceptual-level preferences reflect higher-order aspects like regulations, safety, and norms—for example, obeying traffic signals, maintaining safe distances, or adjusting behavior in school zones. These preferences guide actions toward, for instance, legal and safety-compliant outcomes.
- $\mathcal{P}_{event}$ denotes preferences that are based on the events that can occur in the scene and the causal relationships between them. This is dependent on the dynamic domain Σ_{dyn}. For example, we can define preferences stating that if an object (e.g. a vase) is hit by another object (e.g. a ball), it likely affects the state of one or both objects (e.g. the vase is broken) depending on the the type of objects involved in the event and the motion of the objects.

3.3 Weighting Preference Features

We pair the preference features with weights that quantify the importance of each feature for an event. We define a set of weights as $\mathcal{W}_{\theta_i} = \{w_{\theta_i 1}, \ldots, w_{\theta_i m}\}$ for each event $\theta_i \in \Theta$ and include it in the preference domain Σ_{prf}. The selected events with their associated features and their weights then influence the likelihood of models where particular event patterns occur and ultimately decide if an event θ_i should be preferred or not in the final model X of the logic program Π. In our ASP framework for ranking dynamic spatio-temporal belief models, preferences are encoded using the special theory atom &weight(W) in Plingo. This atom is a special construct that directly associates a numerical weight with the head of the rule it appears in. When the body of a rule is satisfied, its associated &weight(W) value is included in the sum of weights used to calculate the total model weight, $W_\Pi(X)$, as described in Sect. 2. In this context, a higher weight signifies a stronger preference, contributing positively to the model's overall likelihood. For example, we can write:

```
occurs_at(turn_left(car1), curr_time) :- &weight("0.6").
```

to indicate that the event turn_left(car1) is preferred with a weight of 0.6. Then if we have another possibility turn_right(car1) with a weight of 0.2, and only one action can occur at each timestep, the model with the first event turn_left(car1) will be preferred. As an example, a preference may be encoded as follows (note that the @ symbol denotes a call to an external function outside of the answer set solver):

```
w(preference(turn_left(car1)), W) :- possible(turn_left(car1)),
    F = @compute_pref_feature(turn_left(car1)), W = @weight((F), (w)).
```

The expression `W = @weight((F), (w)).` computes the weighted feature value $f_{turn\_left(car1),1} \cdot w_{turn\_left(car1),1}$, where $w_{turn\_left(car1),1} \in [0,1]$. This allows us to express both soft constraints and graded preferences in a fine-grained and interpretable manner. However, Plingo does not natively support computing weights from dynamic expressions within a stable model without modifying the encoding itself at every solver call. To address this, we introduce a preprocessing step that transforms rules (as exemplified in the code snippet above) into explicit weight declarations using Plingo's theory atom by first grounding the `w(Preference, W)` predicates (during which external functions are called) and then re-writing the resulting rules into the following form such that the Plingo solver can process them:

```
preference(turn_left(car1), f) :- &weight("0.6").
```

Additionally, we ensure that the preference weights associated with an event are only considered if that event is selected in a given stable model. If an event is not part of the selected model, then its associated feature weights are excluded from the model's cost computation. This selective inclusion guarantees that the total cost reflects only the features and preferences relevant to the actual interpretation represented by the model. The cost of a dynamic space-time belief model X is calculated as in Eq. 4 by summing the contributions of all features f—over all preference categories— associated with each selected event θ_i in the model, weighted by their corresponding weights.

$$\text{Score}(X) = \sum_{\theta_i \in \Theta_X} \sum_{f_{\theta_{i,j}} \in \mathcal{F}_{\theta_i}} w_{\theta_{i,j}} \cdot f_{\theta_{i,j}}(\mathcal{O}_{\theta_i}) \tag{4}$$

Overall, this weighting mechanism provides a flexible and adaptive way of integrating low-level heterogeneous signals and high-level domain-specific knowledge into the model ranking process, enabling robust interpretation in dynamic visual environments. Taken together, the representational ontology can be summarised as a unified domain Σ defined in (5):

$$\Sigma \equiv_{def} \Sigma_{dyn} <\Phi, \Theta> \cup\ \Sigma_{st} <\mathcal{O}, \mathcal{E}, \mathcal{T}, \mathcal{MT}, \mathcal{R}> \cup\ \Sigma_{prf} <\mathcal{P}, \mathcal{W}> \tag{5}$$

Learning Weights for Preferences: The preference weights roughly assert how important each rule is in deriving a stable model [15]. For simple programs, the weights can be manually specified. However, systematically assigning weights in complex and dynamic domains such as visual sensemaking can be challenging. Above all, the interdependencies between rules can make it difficult to determine the relative importance of individual weights.

In [15], the authors proposed a method for learning the weights of the rules from the observed data. Following similar principles as those used for Maximum Likelihood Estimation (MLE) in the practice of machine learning, they used Markov Chain Monte Carlo (MCMC) sampling, adapted to use ASP solvers for performing the sampling to learn the weights of the rules in a logic program. In line with this approach, we adopt a simpler yet effective strategy for weight selection based on gradient-free random search in the space of possible weights.

While more sophisticated optimization techniques exist and can be implemented in the future, we find that random search is sufficient and robust for exploring the weight space in our case study without making strong assumptions about the continuity or smoothness of the underlying cost landscape.

4 Visual Interpretation with Moving Objects

To demonstrate applicability and to evaluate practical performance of our framework, we present a case study in Multi-Object Tracking (MOT) [21]. We adopt the widely used Tracking-by-Detection paradigm, where the goal is to associate visual observations (detections) with objects tracks over time, maintaining object identities and capturing their dynamic interactions. The association task can be framed as a combinatorial optimization problem, where the objective is to assign detections to object tracks in a way that minimizes a cost function. This cost is typically informed by distance to predicted object locations and feature similarities such as appearance or motion. Algorithms such as the Hungarian algorithm [11] are commonly used to solve this. A well-known approach based on this technique is SORT [2], which uses a Kalman filter to predict object positions and applies the Hungarian algorithm to associate observations with these predictions. However, low-level matching is typically insufficient. High-level reasoning about scene dynamics can help disambiguate uncertain associations and lead to a more coherent understanding of the scene. Preliminary work has shown promise in this direction. For example, a method that jointly addresses observation-object association and explains scene dynamics through high-level events has been proposed in [24]. In this context, the association task can be reframed as a probabilistic reasoning problem. The objective becomes generating and evaluating multiple plausible hypotheses about the scene and object dynamics, and then ranking these hypotheses based on weighted preferences. This is where our framework for ranking dynamic space-time belief models becomes relevant.

4.1 Use-Case: Preferences in Multi-object Tracking

Figure 2 presents an example of the key aspects of the proposed framework. It shows how preferences give rise to multiple models, each representing a different hypothesis about the underlying events involving the objects and observations in the scene. Through the application of preferences and their weighted features, the framework computes a ranking over these models and selects the most plausible interpretation based on the cost. To systematically evaluate the contributions of different preference types, we evaluate three tracker variants. These build incrementally on each other: PRF-SORT, which uses purely geometric preferences akin to SORT; PRF-DeepSORT, which adds appearance-based features; and finally PRF-Track, which further integrates high-level, event-based abductive reasoning. The following subsections will detail the implementation of PRF-Track, as it showcases all facets of our framework, while the other two variants will serve as crucial baselines in the empirical evaluation. Algorithm 1 provides a high-level

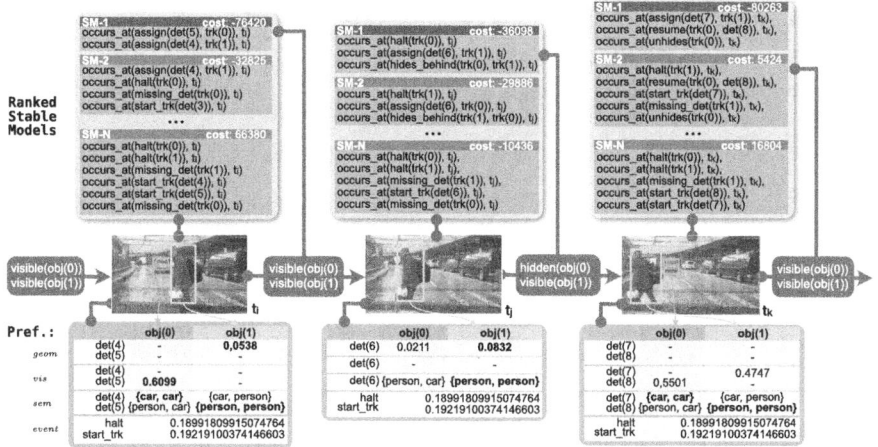

Fig. 2. An example of the ranking process. The figure illustrates how the preferential ranking process creates a set of alternative belief models with different costs (top). Each model represents the scene dynamics, including object interactions and events. In this case a person is walking in front of a car, then the car is occluded and then reappears once the person has passed. At the bottom, we can observe the preferences and their weighted features which are considered in the solving process and ultimately reflected in the costs.

overview of our approach for ranking dynamic space-time belief models in the context of MOT.

I. Domain Predicates and Facts: In line with the formalism presented in Sect. 3.1, the inputs at each timepoint t are a set of visual observations (detections) $\mathcal{VO}_t = \{\varepsilon_{obs_1}, \ldots, \varepsilon_{obs_n}\}$ represented as 2D bounding boxes $\mathcal{E}$, and a set of existing object tracks $\mathcal{MT}_{t-1} = \{\mathcal{MT}_{o_1}, \ldots, \mathcal{MT}_{o_n}\}$. Each detection is characterized by its class (e.g., pedestrian) and a confidence score in the range $[0, 100]$ indicating the likelihood of the object's presence and its classification. In our ASP encoding, these inputs are represented as a set of facts: `det(ID, Type, Conf)` for detections and `trk(ID, Type)` for tracks. The overall task is to find the most plausible model X consisting of a set of tracking events from Θ that explain new detections in light of currently tracked objects.

II. Generating Event Possibilities: In MOT, we have the relevant events $\Theta = \{assign, halt, start, resume\}$. Each event represents a hypothesis about the state transition of an object or observation in the scene: *start* indicates that an observation should initiate a new object track; *assign* denotes an association between an observation and an existing object track; *halt* signals that an object is temporarily not visible (due to occlusion or missing detections); *resume* suggests that an observation is linked to an object previously halted. The next step is to define the conditions under which these events can occur. We use `possible(Event)` to encode the preconditions for event feasibility.

Algorithm 1: Preferential Ranking of Space-Time Belief Models ($\mathcal{V}, \Sigma$)

Data: Visual imagery ($\mathcal{V}$) and background knowledge $\Sigma \equiv_{def} \Sigma_{dyn} \cup \Sigma_{st} \cup \Sigma_{prf}$
Result: Visual Explanations ($\mathcal{EXP}$)

1 $\mathcal{MT} \leftarrow \emptyset, \mathcal{H}^{events} \leftarrow \emptyset$
2 **foreach** $t \in T$ **do**
3   $\quad \mathcal{VO}_t \leftarrow$ observe($\mathcal{V}_t$);
4   $\quad$ **foreach** $trk \in \mathcal{MT}$ **do**
5   $\quad\quad trk_{pred} \leftarrow$ kalman_predict(trk);
6   $\quad \mathcal{ST}_t \leftarrow \mathcal{VO}_t \cup \mathcal{MT} \cup trk_{pred}$
    $\quad$ // Preference extraction
7   $\quad \mathcal{PRFS} \leftarrow \emptyset$;
8   $\quad$ **foreach** $\theta_i \in \Theta$ **do**
9   $\quad\quad$ **foreach** $PF_{\theta_i} \in \mathcal{P}$ **do**
10 $\quad\quad\quad f \leftarrow PF_{\theta_i}(\mathcal{O}_{\theta_i}, ..., \mathcal{O}_{\theta_i})$;
11 $\quad\quad\quad$ **if** possible(θ_i, f) **then**
    $\quad\quad\quad\quad$ // Apply weights to features
12 $\quad\quad\quad\quad \mathcal{PRF}' \leftarrow f \times \mathcal{W}_{\theta_i j}$;
13 $\quad\quad\quad\quad \mathcal{PRFS} \leftarrow \mathcal{PRFS} \cup \mathcal{PRF}'$;
    $\quad$ // ASP solving and ranking
14 $\quad Models \leftarrow$ plingo_solve($\mathcal{PRFS}, \mathcal{V}, \mathcal{ST}, \Sigma$) where $Models = \{(X_1, Cost_1), ...\}$;
15 $\quad \mathcal{H}_t^{events} \leftarrow$ preferred_model($Models$);
16 $\quad \mathcal{H}^{events} \leftarrow \mathcal{H}^{events} \cup \mathcal{H}_t^{events}$
17 $\quad \mathcal{MT} \leftarrow$ update($\mathcal{MT}, \mathcal{VO}_t, \mathcal{H}^{events}$)
18 **return** $\mathcal{EXP} \leftarrow <\mathcal{H}^{events}, \mathcal{MT}>$

For example, an *assign* event is defined by the following rules which check for either a high Re-identification (ReID) similarity or, failing that, a sufficient Intersection over Union (IoU) overlap:

```
possible(assign_reid(Det, Trk)) :- det(Det, Det_Type, Conf), Conf > 50, trk(Trk, Trk_Type),
    not holds_at(hidden(Trk), curr_time), not holds_at(clipped(Trk), curr_time),
    @reid_similarity(Trk, Det) >= reid_threshold.

possible(assign_iou(Det, Trk)) :- det(Det, Det_Type, Conf), Conf > 50, trk(Trk, Trk_Type),
    not holds_at(hidden(Trk), curr_time), not holds_at(clipped(Trk), curr_time),
    @reid_similarity(Trk, Det) < reid_threshold, @iou(Trk, Det) >= iou_threshold.
```

These rules state that a detection is a possible match for a track if (**1**) the detection has a confidence score greater than 50, (**2**) the track is neither hidden nor clipped due to another track occluding it or missing detections, and (**3**) the re-identification (ReID) cosine similarity between the detection and the track is above a defined threshold. We set the ReID and the IoU thresholds to 0.3 and 0.5, respectively.

Similar logic applies to other events. A *resume* event requires the track to have been previously hidden or clipped in addition to similar matching criteria as *assign*, and a *start* event is possible for any new detection with sufficiently high confidence. To prevent spurious tracks from noisy detections we follow common practice and introduce a constraint that a new object is only confirmed after being associated with a detection for three consecutive frames. Finally, any active track is allowed to *halt*, and will be removed from the scene if it remains halted beyond a maximum age threshold. We use a maximum age threshold of 1 frame for PRF-SORT and 30 frames for PRF-DeepSORT and PRF-Track.

III. Forming Plausible Hypotheses: Once the space of possible events is defined, we use choice rules and integrity constraints to generate concrete hypotheses about the events in the scene at timepoint t. Crucially, for each detection and track, exactly one event from the set of possibilities must be chosen. This forms the basis for generating candidate tracking models, where each stable model corresponds to a different combination of plausible events that explains the current state of the scene.

Furthermore, we incorporate abductive reasoning to infer plausible causes behind *halt* and *resume* events. If an active track becomes halted, it must explained by either (i) the object being occluded by another object, identified via spatial overlap (using @overlapping_top(Trk)); or (ii) the object not being overlapped by any detection, suggesting missing observations. Similarly, if a previously halted object reappears, the model must account for this either by determining that it has become visible again after being occluded, or by identifying it as recovering from a clipping scenario.

```
{occurs_at(hides_behind(Trk, Trk2), curr_time):
    Trk2 = @overlapping_top(Trk);
 occurs_at(missing_detections(Trk), curr_time):
    @not_overlapping_top(Trk)
} = 1 :- occurs_at(halt(Trk), curr_time), trk_state(Trk, active).

{occurs_at(unhides_from_behind(Trk, Trk2), curr_time):
    holds_at(hidden_by(Trk, Trk2), curr_time), not holds_at(hidden(Trk2), curr_time),
    @predicted_pos_within_distance(Trk, Det);
 occurs_at(recover(Trk), curr_time):
    holds_at(clipped(Trk), curr_time)
} = 1 :- occurs_at(resume(Trk, Det), curr_time).
```

This abductive layer serves two complementary purposes: (i) enhancing interpretability by offering human-readable explanations for events such as occlusion or reappearance, and (ii) acting as a semantic filter that prunes inconsistent or unsupported event hypotheses.

IV. Ranking Hypotheses with Preferences: To rank the competing hypotheses (stable models), we encode preferences as soft constraints. For MOT, these preferences are based on established features from the literature, such as ReID similarity and IoU overlap. For instance, in the case of the *assign* event, we can use ReID similarity and IoU to quantify how well a detection aligns with an existing object track. We first define ASP rules that link possible events to a weighted feature value.

```
preference(assign_iou(Det, Trk), W) :- possible(assign_iou(Det, Trk)),
    I = @iou(Trk, Det), W = @weight((I), (w1)).

preference(assign_reid(Det, Trk), W) :- possible(assign_reid(Det, Trk)),
    R = @reid_cosine_similarity(Trk, Det), W = @weight((R), (w2)).
```

As described in Sect. 3.3, our preprocessing step transforms these into grounded weighted rules that Plingo use for solving. For example, given a computed ReID similarity of 0.85, it is multiplied by a learned importance weight for the corresponding ReID feature, say $w_{\text{reid}} = 0.4$, yielding the following rule:

```
preference(assign(Det, Trk), reid) :- &weight("0.34").
```

This weight is then used directly by the Plingo solver to bias the selection of one assignment over another and ultimately rank the models. For the events *halt* and *start*, we do not compute feature scores, as these events typically serve as fallback options when other, more informative associations are not possible. Nevertheless, we still assign them preference weights to ensure they are incorporated into the ranking process. These static preferences help balance model selection by penalizing overuse of fallback events while still allowing them when necessary to preserve continuity or recover from uncertainty. However, for the *start* event, we associate slightly different weights depending on whether the concerned detection can be associated with an existing object track, through *assign* or *resume* events. This completes the ranking procedure for dynamic space-time belief models in the context of MOT, enabling interpretable and flexible integration of data-driven signals and high-level reasoning.

V. Learning Preference Weights for Tracking: The final step is to determine the importance weights (e.g., w1, w2 above). Effective weight selection in MOT requires a balance between competing objectives: associating observations accurately, avoiding identity switches, handling occlusions, and maintaining continuity in object trajectories. As discussed in Sect. 3.3, we use a random search strategy to explore the weight space for the preferences. We do this by sampling random weight values for each preference feature, within the defined range $[0, 1]$, and evaluating the tracking performance (for n-sized chunks of frames with n increasing over time to balancing local consistency and long-term identity preservation), optimizing for HOTA score [17] on the MOT17 training split. Once learned, we use these fixed preference weights during the final evaluation on the validation split of MOT17 as described in the following section.

4.2 Empirical Evaluation

We empirically evaluate our declarative tracking framework in terms of both tracking performance and computational efficiency.

I. Tracking Performance: We evaluate the proposed framework for preferential ranking on the validation split of MOT17 [21], a widely used benchmark for MOT. Table 1 summarizes performance across standard tracking metrics: HOTA [17], IDF1, MOTA, association accuracy (AssA), detection accuracy (DetA), and the total number of identity switches (IDs). Here, HOTA serves as the main performance indicator, as it holistically balances detection quality (DetA) with association consistency (AssA). IDF1 is particularly sensitive to long-term trajectory correctness, and the traditional MOTA score aggregates false positives, false negatives, and identity switches.

Table 1. Tracking performance on the MOT17 validation split. Compared are original SORT & DeepSORT with our approach, PRF-SORT, PRF-DeepSORT, PRF-Track.

Method	HOTA	IDF1	MOTA	AssA	DetA	IDs
SORT [2]	59.6	60.4	58.0	59.8	59.5	398
DeepSORT [27]	67.6	70.0	**62.7**	70.6	**64.7**	**250**
PRF-SORT	59.9	60.4	58.7	59.6	60.3	423
PRF-DeepSORT	67.8	**70.5**	62.0	72.2	63.8	298
PRF-Track	**68.0**	70.4	62.0	**72.6**	63.8	268

We compare the original SORT and DeepSORT [27] methods with our declarative counterparts—PRF-SORT, PRF-DeepSORT—and our full implementation PRF-Track, which integrates abductive reasoning and event-driven preferences:

- **PRF-SORT**: Our declarative SORT-inspired implementation in the developed ASP-driven framework. While it mirrors the original SORT in terms of features used for matching, it replaces the Hungarian algorithm with an abductive and declarative ranking approach. Its performance closely matches that of the original SORT, demonstrating that ASP can effectively capture the same geometric matching logic.
- **PRF-DeepSORT**: Our declarative DeepSORT-inspired implementation.
  It leverages the same appearance-based features as DeepSORT but within the preference ranking framework. It slightly improves over DeepSORT in terms of HOTA and AssA, showing the benefit of structured preference-guided reasoning. However, it incurs a minor increase in ID switches.
- **PRF-Track**: This is our complete system, integrating abductive reasoning, as done in the above two methods, with the addition of high-level event-based preferences. It achieves the highest HOTA (68.0) and AssA (72.6), with competitive MOTA and IDF1 scores, and relatively few identity switches. These results illustrate the benefit of preference-guided model selection grounded in interpretable features and event structures.

These results demonstrate that our declarative and logic-based approach is competitive with conventional trackers while offering added benefits in terms of interpretability, modularity, and the ability to embed domain knowledge and preference trade-offs directly into the tracking logic. Moreover, by explicitly modeling events such as occlusion and recovery, our system yields more coherent and explainable tracking behavior in complex scenes.

II. Efficiency and Scalability: Beyond tracking accuracy, we evaluate the computational efficiency and scalability of our declarative trackers. We do not directly compare runtimes with the original implementations of SORT and Deep-SORT. For context, trackers like SORT can often process several hundred frames per second. However, a direct comparison is challenging due to fundamental differences in implementation, and our goal is not to compete on this metric. Instead, our analysis aims to demonstrate that our declarative approach remains computationally feasible for real-world scenarios while offering gains in transparency and explainability. We analyze runtime performance for the three tracker variants by measuring: (1) average preprocessing time (initial grounding) per sequence, (2) average Plingo runtime (grounding + solving) per sequence and per frame, (3) number of event possibilities per frame[2], (4) the size of the grounded logic program (atoms), and (5) models enumerated.

Table 2 reports these averages over sequences and frames respectively. As expected, expressiveness correlates with slight computational overhead. PRF-SORT remains the most lightweight, with an average solve time of 0.0070 s per frame, owing to its simple geometric matching logic. PRF-DeepSORT, which integrates ReID features, shows a slight increase in average grounding + solving time (0.0092 s), reflecting the additional reasoning over visual similarity metrics. PRF-Track, which further incorporates preference-guided abductive reasoning over events, introduces a marginally higher logical complexity (indicated by the average number of atoms per frame). However, with an average of 0.0164 s per frame, it still operates within real-time constraints for most practical applications.

Table 2. Runtime statistics. Average runtime and logical complexity for each tracker variant. Sequence-level times are shown separately from per-frame averages.

Tracker	/Sequence (s)		/Frame				
	Preproc.	Plingo	Plingo (s)	Poss.	Atoms	Solving (ms)	Enum.
PRF-SORT	1.47	3.00	0.0070	42.4	457.2	0.039	2.25
PRF-DeepSORT	6.77	3.86	0.0092	48.8	1065.6	0.088	6.04
PRF-Track	7.95	6.74	0.0164	48.9	1499.2	0.093	5.81

---

[2] At a minimum, equal to the number of objects and detections per frame.

To better understand how runtime scales with input complexity, Fig. 3 show Plingo time plotted against the number of ground atoms and the number of event possibilities, respectively. Across all methods, solving time exhibits an early exponential growth trend as the number of atoms increases. This reflects the greater grounding burden and increased model enumeration under more expressive reasoning conditions. We observe that the number of possible events correlates with a modest increase in Plingo time, and that PRF-Track separates from PRF-SORT and PRF-DeepSORT, being slightly slower due to the additional complexity induced by event-based preferences.

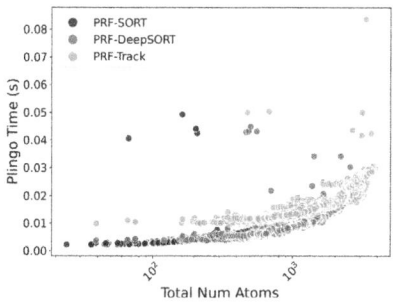
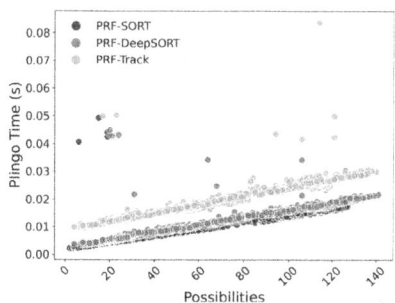

Fig. 3. Comparison of Plingo execution time under different metrics. On the y-axis, we show the Plingo time in seconds for each frame, while the x-axis shows the number of atoms in the logic program (left) and the number of event possibilities (right).

Finally, we note that PRF-DeepSORT and PRF-Track, both using appearance features, exhibit higher variance in solve time per frame with standard deviations of 0.105 ms and 0.097 ms, respectively. In contrast, the simpler PRF-SORT shows a more stable performance with a standard deviation of 0.015ms. Additionally, the results suggest that most of the computational overhead stems from the grounding stage, offering future optimization opportunities.

5 Summary and Outlook

Building on recent developments in neurosymbolic computational cognitive vision using Answer Set Programming (ASP) [23], we develop a declarative system for probabilistically ranking dynamic space-time belief models. Driven by probabilistic extensions of ASP as realized in Plingo, our developed method is conceptually expressive, modular, and enables integration of visual, geometric, semantic, and event-based preference reasoning in a unified declaratively implemented formalism. At its core, our system generates and ranks dynamic scene interpretations, materialized as *stable models*, based on relational, feature-weighted preferences reflecting human-interpretable statistical features. This declarative approach enables seamless integration of diverse preference types aimed at handling ambiguity, partial observability, domain knowledge, or other types of semantic constraints (e.g., those emanating from system design requirements).

Using Multi-Object Tracking (MOT) as a case study, we demonstrate how to express domain knowledge, abductively infer domain-specific events and define interpretable ranking criteria through preference-weighted features such as Intersection over Union (IoU) and re-identification (ReID) similarity. Our results confirm that by treating explanation and selection as a competition between plausible models, and guided by preference structures, one can achieve strong empirical performance while offering gains in transparency, modularity, elaboration tolerance, domain adaptation, and flexibility compared to conventional end-to-end pipelines. In other words, we particularly emphasize that our work is not about development of object tracking per se, i.e., neurosymbolically grounded explainable inference may be performed about any high-level visual or spatial feature of interest. Naturally, challenges for this neurosymbolic framework remain. The performance is inherently bounded by the quality of the sub-symbolic perception modules, and while the reasoning is efficient for complex real-world scenarios as demonstrated in our evaluation, the computational overhead from grounding and solving may limit practical scalability in extreme edge cases with a vast number of interacting objects.

Looking outward, opportunities for future work include extending the framework to more complex visual tasks such as event recognition and intent inference, where the interplay between visual perception and symbolic reasoning can be further explored. Scaling to real-time inference, incorporating richer event ontologies, and enabling tighter integration with neural perceptual modules are key steps toward broader applicability. Ultimately, this work contributes to bridging the gap between symbolic reasoning and modern machine perception, offering a declarative and interpretable path forward for dynamic visual understanding.

Dissemination. Relevant materials pertaining to the developed framework (e.g., code, data) as well as future extensions may be obtained via:
Cognitive Vision. codesign-lab.org/cognitive-vision.

Acknowledgments. We acknowledge funding by the Swedish Research Council (Vetenskapsrådet – VR) through the project *Counterfactual Commonsense* (Project ID: 2022-02960_VR), as well as funding from the Swedish Foundation for Strategic Research (Stiftelsens för Strategisk Forskning – SSF).

Disclosure of Interests. The authors have no competing interests to declare that are relevant to the content of this article.

References

1. Bartholomew, M., Lee, J.: Functional stable model semantics and answer set programming modulo theories. In: IJCAI 2013, Proceedings of 23rd International Joint Conference on Artificial Intelligence, pp. 718–724. IJCAI/AAAI (2013)
2. Bewley, A., Ge, Z., Ott, L., Ramos, F., Upcroft, B.: Simple online and realtime tracking. In: 2016 IEEE International Conference on Image Processing (ICIP). IEEE (2016). https://doi.org/10.1109/icip.2016.7533003
3. Bhatt, M.: Reasoning about space, actions and change: a paradigm for applications of spatial reasoning. In: Qualitative Spatial Representation and Reasoning: Trends and Future Directions. IGI Global (2012)
4. Bhatt, M., Suchan, J.: Cognitive vision and perception: deep semantics integrating AI and vision for reasoning about space, motion, and interaction. In: Proceedings of the 24th European Conference on Artificial Intelligence (ECAI 2020), Including PAIS 2020. Frontiers in Artificial Intelligence and Applications, vol. 325, pp. 2881–2882. IOS Press (2020). https://doi.org/10.3233/FAIA200434
5. Bhatt, M., Suchan, J.: Artificial visual intelligence: perceptual commonsense for human-centred cognitive technologies, pp. 216–242. Springer, Heidelberg (2023). https://doi.org/10.1007/978-3-031-24349-3_12
6. Brewka, G., Eiter, T., Truszczyński, M.: Answer set programming at a glance. Commun. ACM **54**(12), 92–103 (2011). https://doi.org/10.1145/2043174.2043195
7. Gebser, M., Kaminski, R., Kaufmann, B., Schaub, T.: Multi-shot ASP solving with clingo. Theory Pract. Logic Program. **19**(1), 27–82 (2019). https://doi.org/10.1017/S1471068418000054
8. Hahn, S., Janhunen, T., Kaminski, R., Romero, J., Rühling, N., Schaub, T.: Plingo: a system for probabilistic reasoning in clingo based on LP^{mln}. In: Rules and Reasoning - 6th International Joint Conference on Rules and Reasoning, RuleML+RR 2022, Berlin, Germany, 26–28 September 2022, Proceedings. Lecture Notes in Computer Science, vol. 13752, pp. 54–62. Springer, Heidelberg (2022). https://doi.org/10.1007/978-3-031-21541-4_4
9. Hazarika, S.M.: Qualitative spatial change: space-time histories and continuity (2005). https://etheses.whiterose.ac.uk/id/eprint/1325/
10. Kowalski, R., Sergot, M.: A Logic-Based Calculus of Events, pp. 23–55. Springer, Heidelberg (1989). https://doi.org/10.1007/978-3-642-83397-7_2
11. Kuhn, H.W.: The Hungarian method for the assignment problem. Naval Res. Logist. Q. **2**(1–2), 83–97 (1955). https://doi.org/10.1002/nav.3800020109
12. Law, M., Russo, A., Broda, K.: The complexity and generality of learning answer set programs. Artif. Intell. **259**, 110–146 (2018). https://doi.org/10.1016/j.artint.2018.03.005

13. Lee, J., Meng, Y.: Answer set programming modulo theories and reasoning about continuous changes. In: IJCAI 2013, Proceedings of 23rd International Joint Conference on Artificial Intelligence, pp. 990–996. IJCAI/AAAI (2013). http://www.aaai.org/ocs/index.php/IJCAI/IJCAI13/paper/view/6895
14. Lee, J., Talsania, S., Wang, Y.: Computing LPMLN using ASP and MLN solvers. Theory Pract. Log. Program. **17**(5–6), 942–960 (2017). https://doi.org/10.1017/S1471068417000400
15. Lee, J., Wang, Y.: Weight learning in a probabilistic extension of answer set programs. In: Principles of Knowledge Representation and Reasoning: 16th International Conference, KR 2018, pp. 22–31. AAAI Press (2018). https://aaai.org/ocs/index.php/KR/KR18/paper/view/18057
16. Lifschitz, V.: Achievements in answer set programming. Theory Pract. Log. Program. **17**(5–6), 961–973 (2017). https://doi.org/10.1017/S1471068417000345
17. Luiten, J., Osep, A., Dendorfer, P., Torr, P., Geiger, A., Leal-Taixé, L., Leibe, B.: Hota: a higher order metric for evaluating multi-object tracking (2020)
18. Ma, J., Miller, R., Morgenstern, L., Patkos, T.: An epistemic event calculus for asp-based reasoning about knowledge of the past, present and future. In: LPAR-19. 19th International Conference on Logic for Programming, Artificial Intelligence and Reasoning. EPiC Series in Computing, vol. 26, pp. 75–87. EasyChair (2014). https://doi.org/10.29007/zswj
19. Mani, I., Pustejovsky, J.: Interpreting Motion - Grounded Representations for Spatial Language, Explorations in language and space, vol. 5. Oxford University Press (2012). http://ukcatalogue.oup.com/product/9780199601240.do
20. Marr, D.: Vision: A Computational Investigation into the Human Representation and Processing of Visual Information. Henry Holt and Co., Inc., New York (1982)
21. Milan, A., Leal-Taixé, L., Reid, I., Roth, S., Schindler, K.: MOT16: a benchmark for multi-object tracking (2016). http://arxiv.org/abs/1603.00831
22. Schultz, C., Bhatt, M., Suchan, J., Walęga, P.A.: Answer set programming modulo 'Space-Time'. In: Benzmüller, C., Ricca, F., Parent, X., Roman, D. (eds.) RuleML+RR 2018. LNCS, vol. 11092, pp. 318–326. Springer, Cham (2018). https://doi.org/10.1007/978-3-319-99906-7_24
23. Suchan, J., Bhatt, M., Monsen, J.: ASP-driven visual commonsense: a general framework for reasoning about embodied interaction in the wild. In: Principles of Knowledge Representation and Reasoning: Proceedings of the 22nd International Conference, KR 2025, Melbourne, Australia, November 2025. AAAI Press (2025)
24. Suchan, J., Bhatt, M., Varadarajan, S.: Out of sight but not out of mind: an answer set programming based online abduction framework for visual sensemaking in autonomous driving. In: Proceedings of the Twenty-Eighth International Joint Conference on Artificial Intelligence, IJCAI 2019, Macao, China, 10–16 August 2019, pp. 1879–1885. ijcai.org (2019). https://doi.org/10.24963/ijcai.2019/260
25. Suchan, J., Bhatt, M., Varadarajan, S.: Commonsense visual sensemaking for autonomous driving - on generalised neurosymbolic online abduction integrating vision and semantics. Artif. Intell. **299**, 103522 (2021). https://doi.org/10.1016/j.artint.2021.103522
26. Walęga, P.A., Bhatt, M., Schultz, C.: ASPMT(QS): non-monotonic spatial reasoning with answer set programming modulo theories. In: Calimeri, F., Ianni, G., Truszczynski, M. (eds.) LPNMR 2015. LNCS (LNAI), vol. 9345, pp. 488–501. Springer, Cham (2015). https://doi.org/10.1007/978-3-319-23264-5_41

27. Wojke, N., Bewley, A., Paulus, D.: Simple online and realtime tracking with a deep association metric. In: 2017 IEEE International Conference on Image Processing (ICIP), pp. 3645–3649. IEEE (2017). https://doi.org/10.1109/ICIP.2017.8296962
28. Yang, Z., Ishay, A., Lee, J.: Neurasp: embracing neural networks into answer set programming. In: 29th International Joint Conference on Artificial Intelligence, IJCAI-20, pp. 1755–1762. International Joint Conferences on Artificial Intelligence Organization (2020). https://doi.org/10.24963/ijcai.2020/243

Learning Interpretable Probabilistic Models and Schema Axioms for Knowledge Graphs

Ivan Diliso(✉), Nicola Fanizzi, and Claudia d'Amato

ARA/LACAM – Dipartimento di Informatica – University of Bari Aldo Moro, Bari, Italy
i.diliso1@phd.uniba.it, {nicola.fanizzi,claudia.damato}@uniba.it

Abstract. In the context of knowledge graphs expressed in *Description Logics*, we address the problem of learning simple classifiers as probabilistic graphical models from incomplete data. Specifically, we start with a binary encoding of individuals and target Naive Bayes classifiers based on multivariate Bernoullis. Then, we extend these classifiers to two-tier networks that connect classification models to a lower layer consisting of a mixture of Bernoullis. We demonstrate how (probabilistic) axioms or rules can be extracted from these models, thereby improving interpretability. In addition, these models can be initialized leveraging expert knowledge. We present and discuss the results of an empirical evaluation testing the effectiveness of the models on random classification problems across several ontologies.

Keywords: knowledge graph · probabilistic graphical model · interpretability

1 Introduction

In the context of *Knowledge Graphs* (KGs) [8], classifying individual entities is a fundamental problem that enables more complex applications. Even in an approximate form, classification is a nontrivial task when overly simplifying assumptions are not allowed so that the original semantics of the knowledge graphs is preserved.

Current research on graph-structured data focuses on *representation learning* methods [17] that map entities and relations to embedding spaces, where tasks such as classification and link prediction are defined in terms of linear algebra operations. The main downsides of these methods are related to the difficulty of incorporating implicit knowledge that can be extracted precisely from the KG through deductive reasoning and the poor interpretability of complex classification models. The embedding spaces turn out to be difficult to relate to the original features, so these models are treated as black boxes whose decisions are hardly explainable.

As an alternative, to improve the interpretability of models and their decisions, simpler yet effective probabilistic models can be used. These models are inferred from data and ultimately defined in terms of Boolean variables. They leverage basic logic features extracted from primitive classes and properties in the ontology [5,14]. Based on neural learning approaches (e.g. [16]), simple graphical models can be fitted and converted into probabilistic rules or simplified to generate axioms [5,12], ensuring a direct interpretation in terms of the original representation in *Description Logics* (DL) [1].

Building on our previous work [14], we focus on the problem of fitting *multivariate Bernoulli* models. Importantly, unlike previous studies, we adopt a standard binary setting in which the negative case corresponds to an indeterminate membership. The common simplifying assumption for these models is the conditional independence of the input features given the target feature, which characterizes *Naive Bayes* classifiers. This simplifies the model without compromising its effectiveness [4]. We also consider two-tier hierarchical models in which *mixtures of Bernoullis* [7] are used to cluster the individuals into groups before applying the classifier. Along with the standard fitting method based on an EM procedure, we consider a method based on a Bayesian treatment of the number of mixture components, as well as an online model-fitting procedure based on gradient descent. This procedure allows for incremental training of the model as examples become available over time.

Generative models are especially suitable for cases where the available data for fitting is incomplete, a likely situation when reasoning with an open-world assumption, as is typical with large, distributed KGs expressed in a logic representation. Furthermore, they can be used for various applications, including KG completion and refinement, axiom discovery (e.g., disjointness), clustering, and anomaly detection. Unlike more complex models, these classifiers are suitable for easier interpretation, verification and integration by domain experts or any agent that shares the intended semantics of the terminology. For example, existing background knowledge in the form of probabilistic rules or axioms could be integrated into these models.

An experiment aimed at testing the feasibility and effectiveness of such models on a number of random classification problems with different Web ontologies is described. As a baseline, we compared our approach against other simple models: logistic regression classifiers and decision trees [2]. These models are suitable for producing human-understandable decision rules and supporting structured reasoning; therefore, they are appropriate benchmarks in terms of both performance and interpretability.

In this paper, we introduce a Boolean encoding for the individuals in terms of basic features/concepts (Sect. 2). Then, in Sect. 3, a simple model based on multivariate Bernoullis is described, together with details on the probabilistic rules/axioms that can be derived, and its fitting. The model is extended by considering a simple two-tier hierarchy as shown in Sect. 4. An empirical evaluation is described in Sect. 5 with a comparison of some instances of these models on a number of classification tasks on real ontologies and a qualitative assessment of extracted axioms. Finally, Sect. 6 concludes the paper discussing some limitations and possible extensions.

2 Basics

We assume familiarity with the basic notions and the standard notation of Description Logics, as in the following we will focus on knowledge graphs represented through axioms and ultimately as OWL-DL ontologies.

Formally, let $\mathcal{K}$ be a DL *knowledge base* $\mathcal{K} = \langle \mathcal{T}, \mathcal{A} \rangle$, where the *TBox* $\mathcal{T}$ is a set of terminological axioms that regard concepts and roles (i.e. classes and properties) of the domain of interest, and the *ABox* $\mathcal{A}$ contains assertions, i.e. facts[1] regarding the individuals whose collection will be indicated with $\mathsf{Ind}(\mathcal{A})$.

In line with previous works on distances or kernels for these representations [3,6,14], we aim to build models upon a simple encoding of the individuals in a feature space.

However, our approach diverges from previous studies in the way we handle negative membership, especially given the open-world semantics (OWA) of most KGs. Unlike closed-world settings, where the absence of information is interpreted as false, the OWA assumes that information may be missing or incomplete. Therefore, we employ a standard encoding for negative membership, treating the absence of information as indeterminate, rather than as definitively negative. This adjustment is crucial in KGs, where the lack of explicit negative information is common, in addition it plays a key role in guiding the extraction of rule axioms later in the process.

Given an ordered set $\mathcal{F} = \{F_i\}_{i=1}^D$ of basic features, i.e. concepts in the signature of $\mathcal{K}$ or defined in terms of other concepts and roles (classes and properties) therein,[2] we will consider each individual $\mathsf{a} \in \mathsf{Ind}(\mathcal{A})$ as represented by the Boolean vector $\boldsymbol{a} \in \mathbb{B}^D$ ($\mathbb{B} = \{0,1\}$) with each component, $i \in [1:D]$: $a_i = \mathbb{I}(\mathcal{K} \models F_i(\mathsf{a}))$, where $\mathbb{I}(\cdot)$ denotes the indicator function that yields 1 iff the argument holds true. Basically the bit a_i indicates the definite *membership* of a in F_i.

3 A Multivariate Bernoulli Naive Bayes Model

Given individuals x represented as binary vectors $\boldsymbol{x} = [x_1, x_2, \ldots, x_D]^T$, and using a binary output variable y for indicating their membership to the target class C, a *Multivariate Bernoulli Naive Bayes* (MBNB) model, depicted as a probabilistic graph in Fig. 1, defines the joint distribution $P_{\boldsymbol{\Pi}}(\boldsymbol{x}, y)$, where $\boldsymbol{\Pi} = \{\pi, \boldsymbol{p}\}$ specifies the parameters of the output *prior* $P(y)$, with $P(y=1) = \pi$, and of the conditional distribution $P(\boldsymbol{x}|y) = \mathrm{Ber}(\boldsymbol{x}|y; \boldsymbol{p})$ defined as the product of mutually independent Bernoullis for the features:

---

[1] E.g. $C(a)$, $R(b,c)$, easily represented as triples in the context of the KGs.
[2] A set of primitive classes, also including those obtained as restrictions on roles, such as $\exists R.\top$ or $\exists R.C$.

$$P(\boldsymbol{x}|y=1;\boldsymbol{\Pi}) = \text{Ber}(\boldsymbol{x}|y=1;\boldsymbol{p}) = \prod_{i=1}^{D} \text{Ber}(x_i|y=1;p_i) \qquad (1)$$

with $\text{Ber}(x_i = 1|y; p_i) = (p_i)^{x_i}(1-p_i)^{1-x_i}$.

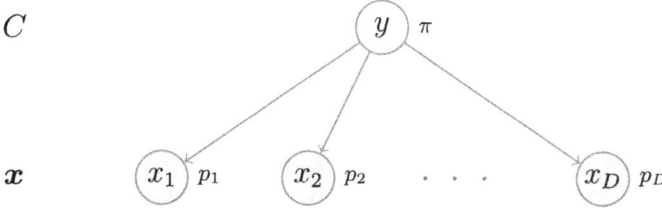

Fig. 1. Multivariate Bernoulli Naive Bayes Model as a belief network.

IF $C(\mathbf{x})$ (with prior π) THEN $\forall i \in [1:D]\ P(x_i|y=1) = \text{Ber}(p_i)$
AND $F_1(\mathbf{x})$ with probability p_1
AND $F_2(\mathbf{x})$ with probability p_2
$\vdots$
AND $F_D(\mathbf{x})$ with probability p_D

Fig. 2. Rule for class C from the model.

3.1 Classification with Multivariate Bernoulli Naive Bayes Model

A classification problem amounts to estimating the state of the output y for an input individual x represented by the Boolean vector $\boldsymbol{x}$. Given the model with $\boldsymbol{\Pi}$, the posterior can be computed using Bayes' rule and Eq. (1):

$$P(y=1|\boldsymbol{x}) = \frac{P(\boldsymbol{x}|y=1)P(y=1)}{P(\boldsymbol{x})} = \frac{\pi \prod_{i=1}^{D}(p_i)^{x_i}(1-p_i)^{1-x_i}}{P(\boldsymbol{x})} \qquad (2)$$

which yields the probabilistic prediction. A 0/1 prediction depends on the more probable case $\hat{y} = \text{argmax}_{b \in \mathbb{B}} P(y=b|\boldsymbol{x})$ which is equivalent to the decision:

IF $P(y=1|\boldsymbol{x}) > 1/2$ THEN $\hat{y} = 1$ ELSE $\hat{y} = 0$

More complex decision procedures can be devised, taking into account the case of *rejection* when the probability is too close to the midpoint value. This can be defined in terms of a cost-sensitive decision made using a different threshold.

3.2 Rules and Conjunctive Class Definitions

In line with similar approaches for models based on features with continuous distributions (e.g. see [16]), a probabilistic *conjunctive rule* for C may be defined as shown in Fig. 2, which can be simplified considering for each $i \in [1:D]$ the conjunct with higher probability. Due to the OWA underlying our setting, the model only extracts and leverages positively thresholded information.

Note that this generative form of rule allows for a way to sample new individuals (*causal* direction). For classification an inference in the opposite (*abductive*) direction is performed.

Given a minimal membership threshold θ_p, an approximate logic definition of the target class C can be extracted from the model by considering the set $\mathcal{F} = \{i \in [1:D] \mid p_i > \theta_p\}$ indicating features positively correlated with the membership to C. Then it is possible to define the approximate axiom:

$$C_{\text{MB}} \sqsubseteq \bigsqcap_{i \in \mathcal{F}} F_i$$

which can be proposed to a domain expert for its validation and possible inclusion in the definition of the target class C.

Note that only some of the basic features are considered, namely those strongly positively correlated with the membership, with a strength quantified by θ_p, reflecting a principled handling of the OWA and the inherent uncertainty in knowledge graphs.

3.3 Fitting the Model

We assume the availability of a complete *training set* $\mathbf{T} = \langle \mathbf{X}, \mathbf{y} \rangle = \{(\boldsymbol{x}^t, y^t)\}_{t=1}^N$ where $\boldsymbol{x}^t$ is the encoding of an individual $\mathbf{x}^t \in \text{Ind}(\mathcal{A})$ and $y^t \in \mathbb{B}$ indicates the actual membership to C.

The naive Bayes classifier can be trained by finding the maximum likelihood (or even the maximum a posteriori) estimate for the parameters $\boldsymbol{\Pi} = \{\boldsymbol{\pi}, \boldsymbol{p}\}$. To make the notation more compact, we set $\boldsymbol{p}_1 = \boldsymbol{p}$ and $\boldsymbol{p}_0 = \mathbf{1}_D - \boldsymbol{p}$. As the probability for a single example is given by

$$P(\boldsymbol{x}^t, y^t \mid \boldsymbol{\Pi}) = P(y^t \mid \pi_{y^t}) P(\boldsymbol{x}^t \mid y^t, \boldsymbol{p}_{y^t}) = \pi_{y^t} \text{Ber}(\boldsymbol{x}^t \mid \boldsymbol{p}_{y^t})$$

then the *log-likelihood* $\mathcal{L}(\boldsymbol{\Pi}) = \log P(\mathbf{T} \mid \boldsymbol{\Pi})$ can be written as:

$$\mathcal{L}(\mathbf{T} \mid \boldsymbol{\Pi}) = \log \prod_{t=1}^N P(\boldsymbol{x}^t, y^t \mid \boldsymbol{\Pi}) = \sum_{b \in \mathbb{B}} N_b \log \pi_b + \sum_{b \in \mathbb{B}} \sum_{t:y^t=b} \sum_{i=1}^D \log \text{Ber}(x_i^t \mid p_{bi})$$

where $N_b = \sum_t \mathbb{I}(y^t = b)$ are the counts of training examples for either membership case ($b \in \mathbb{B}$).

The maximum likelihood estimator (MLE) for the prior proportions $P(y = b)$ is $\hat{\pi}_b = N_b / N$. Since all input features are Bernoulli distributed conditioned on y, i.e. $x_i \mid y \sim \mathrm{Ber}(p_{yi})$, the MLE for the parameters are $\hat{p}_{bi} = N_{bi}/N_b$, $i \in [1:D]$ with $N_{bi} = \sum_t \mathbb{I}(x_i^t = 1 \wedge y^t = b)$.

Actually, one does not expect the features to be independent (conditionally on y) unless they are properly selected (e.g. among the primitive concepts). However, as discussed in [4], a *naive bayes* model can still be quite effective, even when this assumption does not hold true. This is because the model has a limited number of parameters, making it less prone to overfitting. To better avoid this problem, one may resort to a Bayesian approach considering Beta conjugate priors for the parameters [13].

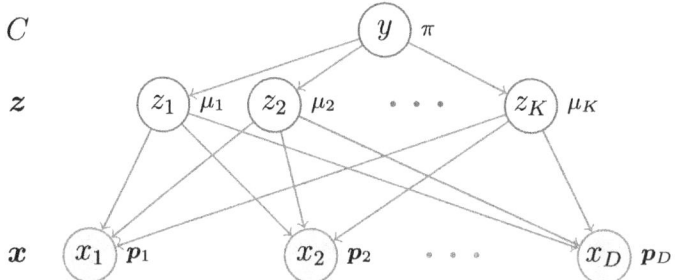

Fig. 3. Hierarchical Bernoulli Model.

4 A Hierarchical Extension

In general, the features for a class are likely to be correlated; therefore, a single model describing the instances' distribution may be inadequate when the assumption of conditional independence does not hold, leading to an inaccurate classifier.

This problem can be tackled by considering a distribution modeled as a mixture of (multivariate) Bernoullis. Then, introducing an intermediate K-dimensional layer z of latent binary indicator variables corresponding to the nodes $\{z_k\}_{k \in [1:K]}$, characterized by a distinct Bernoulli $P_k(x|z_k)$, a 2-tier model is defined whose structure is depicted in Fig. 3. This network, that will be referred to as *Hierarchical Bernoulli Model* (HBM), combines the mixture of multivariate Bernoullis (bottom-tier) with the former MBNB classifier (top-tier). Alternatively, this model can be also described in the form of a *Hierarchical Mixture of Experts* [9].

In this case, given the model parameters $\mathbf{\Pi} = \{\pi, \boldsymbol{\mu}, \boldsymbol{P}\}$, where $\mu_k = P(z_k = 1)$, $\boldsymbol{P} = [\boldsymbol{p}_k] \in [0,1]^{K \times D}$ with $\boldsymbol{p}_k = [p_{k1}, \ldots, p_{kD}]$, we can write:

$$P(\boldsymbol{x}|\mathbf{\Pi}) = \sum_{k=1}^{K} P(\boldsymbol{x}, z_k = 1|\mathbf{\Pi}) = \sum_k P(z_k = 1|\boldsymbol{\mu}) P_k(\boldsymbol{x}|z_k = 1; \boldsymbol{p}_k)$$
$$= \sum_k \mu_k \text{Ber}(\boldsymbol{x}|\boldsymbol{p}_k) \qquad (3)$$

The structure depends on the dimensionality of the mixture K, whose choice can be made in advance exploiting part of the training data, to maximize a score function, e.g., the BIC [15].

4.1 Classification with Hierarchical Bernoulli Models

To decide the membership to C for an input individual x with corresponding Boolean vector $\boldsymbol{x}$, using Eq. (3), the posterior is determined as:

$$P(y=1|\boldsymbol{x};\mathbf{\Pi}) = \frac{P(\boldsymbol{x}|y=1;\mathbf{\Pi})P(y=1)}{P(\boldsymbol{x}|\mathbf{\Pi})} = \frac{\pi_1 \sum_{k=1}^{K} \mu_k \text{Ber}(\boldsymbol{x}|\boldsymbol{p}_k)}{P(\boldsymbol{x}|\mathbf{\Pi})} \qquad (4)$$

IF C(x) (with prior π) THEN C_k(x) with $P(z_k = 1|y=1) = \mu_k$

IF C_k(x) THEN
    F_1(x) (with probability p_{k1})
    AND F_2(x) (with probability p_{k2})
    ...
    AND F_D(x) (with probability p_{kD})

Fig. 4. Rules extracted for C from the Hierarchical Model for $k \in [1:K]$.

The decision procedure is analogous to the one shown in Subsect. 3.1. Alternatively we could use disjunctive and conjunctive classification rules translating the hierarchical model.

4.2 Disjunctive Axioms and Rules

Given a HBM, and under the same OWA setting and positive-thresholding approach described previously, an axiom for class C may be extracted by defining the class in terms of the components:

$$C \sqsubseteq \bigsqcup_{\substack{k=1,\ldots,K \\ z_k=1}} C_k$$

which can be specified probabilistically indicating the class prior π and μ_k such that $z_k = 1$ or, alternatively, also as a *disjunctive classification rule* for C and a set of probabilistic rules for the C_k's as shown in Fig. 4.

Given a minimal cluster activation threshold θ_μ an approximate logic definition of target class C can be extracted from the model by considering the set $\mathcal{K} = \{j \in [1:k] \mid \mu_j > \theta_\mu\}$ indicating clusters positively correlated with the memberships to C and $\mathcal{F}_j = \{i \in [1:D] \mid p_{ji} > \theta_p\}$ indicating features positively correlated with cluster C_j. The approximate axiom is defined as:

$$C \sqsubseteq \bigsqcup_{j \in \mathcal{K}} C_j = \bigsqcup_{j \in \mathcal{K}} \bigsqcap_{i \in \mathcal{F}_j} F_i$$

This corresponds to an axiom defined as a disjunction of activated clusters, each represented by a conjunction of features positively correlated with it.

4.3 Fitting the Hierarchical Model

The network parameters can be determined using a *training set* $\mathbf{T} = \langle \mathbf{X}, \mathbf{y} \rangle$. The two tiers can be trained separately: the bottom one tackles an unsupervised learning task, while the top tier is essentially a MBNB classifier.

As regards the bottom-tier of the structure, latent variables and the parameters of the mixture model μ_j can be learned through a EM procedure.

In this case, the complete log-likelihood to be maximized is:

$$\mathcal{L}(\mathbf{\Pi}, \mathbf{Z}|\mathbf{X}) = \log \prod_{t=1}^{N} P(\bm{x}^t|\mathbf{\Pi}) = \sum_{t=1}^{N} \log \left[\sum_{k=1}^{K} \mu_k \mathrm{Ber}(\bm{x}^t|\bm{p}_k) \right] \quad (5)$$

Note that it also targets the latent variables $\bm{z}$.
The EM steps can be defined as follows:

- E-step: the responsibility of each component of the mixture is estimated as:

$$\hat{P}(z_k^t|\bm{x}^t) \leftarrow \frac{\hat{\mu}_k P_k(\bm{x}^t|\hat{\bm{p}}_k)}{\sum_{h=1}^{K} \hat{\mu}_h P_h(\bm{x}^t|\hat{\bm{p}}_h)};$$

- M-step: the parameters values are updated on the ground of the new estimates for $\hat{P}(z_k^t|\bm{x}^t)$ along the following rules:

$$\hat{\bm{p}}_k \leftarrow \frac{\sum_{t=1}^{N} \hat{P}(z_k^t|\bm{x}^t)\bm{x}^t}{\sum_{t=1}^{N} \hat{P}(z_k^t|\bm{x}^t)}; \quad \hat{\mu}_k \leftarrow \frac{1}{N} \sum_{t=1}^{N} \frac{\hat{P}(z_k^t|\bm{x}^t)}{\sum_{h=1}^{K} \hat{P}(z_h^t|\bm{x}^t)}.$$

In this work, we implement and compare three distinct approaches to learning the model parameters. The first is the classic Expectation-Maximization (EM) algorithm, which is detailed above and computes point estimates for the parameters iteratively. The second approach is a fully variational Bayesian method, which learns the posterior distribution for the parameters by placing Dirichlet priors over the mixture weights μ_k and Beta priors over the Bernoulli parameters $\boldsymbol{p}_k = [p_{k1}, \ldots, p_{kD}]$. The third method is based on stochastic gradient descent (SGD), which has been recognized as a form of approximate inference [10]. This approach uses direct optimization, whereby the Bernoulli parameters are passed through a sigmoid activation and the mixture weights are determined by a softmax layer to ensure they remain valid probabilities. This approach has the additional advantage of scalability with respect to the extent of the knowledge graphs (KGs) and the complexity of the model. This solution also enables incremental learning of the model, which is viable for distributed KGs.

5 Empirical Evaluation

First, we offer some details on how the models have been implemented. Subsequently, a detailed exposition of the experimental setup is provided, encompassing the datasets, target concepts and the configuration of hyperparameters. Finally, the results of this empirical evaluation are discussed.

5.1 Implementation

The prototypes of the models are implemented based on various facilities provided by Python libraries. Owlready2,[3] intended for ontology-oriented programming, was used to manage the KGs, including loading and storage. It relies on an embedded version of Pellet for reasoning services that are mainly used to initialize the binary encoding of the individuals in each ontology. PyTorch[4] was used for gradient descent based models, offering automatic differentiation for the parameters and various activation functions. Scikit-Learn[5] and SkLearn-Bayes[6] libraries offer various implemented models that can be extended, as well as facilities for organizing the experiments (e.g., measures, cross-validation) as described in the following.

All the models have been implemented in the Scikit-Learn framework, providing compatibility with its training and evaluation utilities. Specifically the MBNB model was implemented from scratch, following the training procedure provided in Subsect. 3.3. A general implementation of the Hierarchical Model is provided, using a generic Mixture as input for the unsupervised learning part (bottom tier of the hierarchical model, as described in Sect. 4). Three variants have been proposed: HB_{EM}, HB_{VB} and HB_{GD}, differing in the procedure used to estimate the parameters: Expectation Maximization, Variational Bayes, and Gradient Descent, respectively.

---

[3] https://pypi.org/project/Owlready2/.
[4] https://pypi.org/project/torch/.
[5] https://pypi.org/project/scikit-learn/.
[6] https://github.com/AmazaspShumik/sklearn-bayes.

5.2 Setup

Baselines. We compare our approach against three well-established simple classifiers to provide a broader context for the experimental results. We consider the classic *logistic regression* classifier [11] (LogReg) as an alternative to the MBNB model which is less interpretable being based on a linear combination of the features (including a regularization term). Then we use it also as an alternative top-tier for the presented hierarchical model (HLogReg). The third is a *decision tree classifier* [2] (Tree), constrained to a maximum depth of 3 and a minimum of 10 samples per leaf to limit model complexity, enhance interpretability and ensure a fair comparison with probabilistic models' expressivity. Note that we will use an implementation that learns trees usable as probabilistic classifiers.

Datasets. The KGs of four ontologies were selected to create problems and related datasets employed as a testbed: KRKZEROONE (a small ontology derived from a well-known UCI dataset), NEW TESTAMENT NAMES (NTNAMES), FINANCIAL, and an ontology that was generated using the LEHIGH UNIVERSITY BENCHMARK (LUBM). Ontologies, target classes, code and output files of the experiments are publicly available in the project repository.[7]

Features. For each ontology, basic features (minimal classes in the subsumption hierarchy) have been extracted, then classes formed as existential restrictions were also included, each involving one of the available object properties. However, to define the final set $\mathcal{F}$ and the encoding of the individuals for each dataset, a preliminary univariate *feature selection* phase was performed to pick the most informative ones, i.e. those that exhibited a higher variance, with respect to a cutoff threshold. Table 1 reports the numbers of classes and object properties selected per KG as well as the numbers of (generated/selected) features that were considered in the experiments.

Table 1. Numbers of defined classes and object properties per knowledge graph, generated and selected features, individuals

KGs	classes	obj. props.	valid fts.	selected fts.	individuals
KRKZEROONE	7	37	81	28	420
NTNAMES	47	27	74	19	676
FINANCIAL	59	16	75	13	1000
LUBM	43	25	68	13	1156

---

[7] https://github.com/ivandiliso/sphm4kg

Learning Problems. Artificial learning problems have been randomly created defining 10 new target classes for each ontology, based on their respective signatures. Two categories of target classes[8] of different complexity have been considered. The first, simpler category consists of 5 target classes, each defined as a disjunction of atomic concepts and existential restrictions. The second category comprises 5 target classes, that are defined as a disjunction of conjunctive classes and is intended for harder problems. To avoid trivial and imbalanced learning problems, we designed each target class to partition the set of individuals into meaningful subsets. Specifically, we sought to create splits that were as balanced as possible between instances with either label. The ground truth labels, i.e. the reference classification of all individuals in the ontology with respect to each problem[9] was determined using the reasoner and encoded in the respective target columns. Further details on the specific parameters used in the class creation, including the number of conjunctive and disjunctive terms used, the precise split thresholds and the OWL formalization of all the target classes for each ontology, are available in the project repository.

Training and Evaluation. For each problem, a *5-fold cross validation* was performed randomly splitting the examples (individuals labeled with 1 or 0 w.r.t. the target class) in a *stratified* fashion to preserve the proportions in each fold. The metrics that were measured are *precision, recall, F_1-measure*, and *Area Under the Curve* on binary problems.

Hyperparameters. The number of components for the Bernoulli mixture model was fixed to 5. In the subsequent axiom extraction phase, we introduced two additional hyperparameters: θ_μ, the threshold for including clusters in the disjunctive axiom, and θ_p, the threshold to determine which features participate in each cluster's rule based on their associated probability (this parameter is also used in the MBNB model rule extraction phase). These parameters were optimized for each model using a grid search with range $[0.1, 0.9]$. For the remaining implementation-specific parameters (see the Scikit-Learn), we adopted a conservative setup, e.g., limiting the number of random restarts to 10, as a trade-off between model effectiveness and training efficiency. A detailed list of all settings can be found in the project repository.[10]

5.3 Results

The outcomes of the tests in terms of the measures averaged over the various problems per KG are summarized in Tab. 2. More details and logs of each experiment on each fold and target are made available in the repository. As stated,

---

[8] Another category was also preliminarily considered that consisted exclusively of conjunctive classes. However, they proved to be quite easy to learn perfectly with all models.

[9] Note that all problems were run independently, hence all individuals were exploited as examples in each experiment, with the class-label depending on the target class.

[10] https://github.com/ivandiliso/sphm4kg.

each entry in the table represents the evaluation metric averaged across the 5 cross-validation folds and over the 10 artificial target concepts, summing up to a total of 800 different training phases (4 models, 4 datasets, 5 folds, 10 targets).

The "type" column in the table indicates the prediction model used for evaluating instance membership with respect to the target classes. The value "prob" denotes that the probabilistic model was directly used to compute the likelihood of membership. In contrast, the value "axiom" indicates a two-step process: deterministic axioms were extracted from the trained models using the previously described procedure (Subects. 3.2 and 4.2) based on thresholds θ_μ and θ_p. We then applied reasoning over these axioms to derive the set of individuals that satisfy them. The predicted membership was obtained from this inferred set and compared against the ground-truth labels to compute the evaluation metrics.

Model Performance. Across all datasets and metrics, probabilistic models (Prob) generally show superior performance compared to their logic counterparts (Axiom). This is especially true for the hierarchical model (HB) which maintains high precision, recall and F_1 scores, with near perfect AUCs. The stability of their performance (reflected in low standard deviations) further supports their robustness. This confirms that hierarchical probabilistic strategies, when used in their native probabilistic form, are highly effective in modeling complex concepts in KGs.

MBNB models also demonstrate solid performance, albeit lower than HB variants. This can be attributed to their simpler structure, which models target classes as conjunctions of concepts. Nevertheless, the high AUC indicates strong predictive performance and suggests that the decision boundary is less sharp compared to the HB models.

A steeper drop is observed when moving to axiom-based evaluation, particularly for MBNB. The decrease in F_1 and AUC (along with increased standard deviations) suggests that the deterministic nature of the extracted rules may oversimplify the underlying probabilistic model.

This is particularly evident for target classes defined as disjunctions of conjunctions since the axioms extracted from MBNBs are inherently mismatched in terms of expressiveness. Consequently, the performance of axioms from MBNBs is inferior to the HB models, which can capture such structures more accurately.

The performance of the baseline models (Trees, LogReg and Hierarchical LogReg) is notably weaker compared to the probabilistic models, particularly in terms of F_1 and AUC scores. While all models achieve competitive precision, their other metrics decrese significantly, especially on smaller datasets such as KRKZEROONE and NTNAMES. This suggests a tendency to overfit when training data is scarce, due to the limited expressiveness of these models. Interestingly, performance improves considerably on larger datasets like FINANCIAL and LUBM where the LogReg model achieves stronger performances. Overall, while the baseline models show improved performance with more data, they fall short in generalizing across different knowledge graphs and target classes. This reinforces the advantage of using hierarchical probabilistic models that combine per-

Table 2. Outcomes of the experiments with the models fitted using the various procedures, and evaluated with metrics: *Precision* (P), *Recall* (R), F_1-*measure* (F_1) and *Area Under the Curve* (AUC) ± standard deviation averaged over all the artificial classification problems per KG. In bold, the best results for each dataset and metric.

Models	Type	Metric	KGs			
			KRKZeroOne	NTNames	Financial	LUBM
MBNB	Prob	P	0.878 ± 0.060	0.932 ± 0.034	0.974 ± 0.039	0.942 ± 0.049
		R	0.849 ± 0.076	0.924 ± 0.034	0.969 ± 0.047	0.938 ± 0.051
		F_1	0.843 ± 0.080	0.924 ± 0.035	0.968 ± 0.049	0.937 ± 0.051
		AUC	0.978 ± 0.014	0.987 ± 0.023	0.995 ± 0.008	0.994 ± 0.009
	Axiom	P	0.861 ± 0.079	0.909 ± 0.067	0.874 ± 0.057	0.902 ± 0.032
		R	0.811 ± 0.147	0.874 ± 0.101	0.811 ± 0.122	0.873 ± 0.053
		F_1	0.793 ± 0.185	0.866 ± 0.110	0.790 ± 0.160	0.870 ± 0.055
		AUC	0.816 ± 0.131	0.863 ± 0.108	0.806 ± 0.113	0.868 ± 0.046
HB_{VB}	Prob	P	0.975 ± 0.016	0.984 ± 0.014	0.981 ± 0.025	0.989 ± 0.018
		R	0.975 ± 0.017	0.984 ± 0.014	0.979 ± 0.028	0.988 ± 0.019
		F_1	0.974 ± 0.017	0.984 ± 0.014	0.979 ± 0.028	0.988 ± 0.019
		AUC	0.995 ± 0.004	**0.997 ± 0.002**	0.996 ± 0.005	**0.999 ± 0.002**
	Axiom	P	0.922 ± 0.053	0.974 ± 0.026	0.977 ± 0.022	0.960 ± 0.034
		R	0.908 ± 0.067	0.971 ± 0.032	0.974 ± 0.025	0.954 ± 0.040
		F_1	0.907 ± 0.069	0.970 ± 0.033	0.974 ± 0.025	0.953 ± 0.041
		AUC	0.910 ± 0.066	0.969 ± 0.034	0.974 ± 0.024	0.948 ± 0.045
HB_{EM}	Prob	P	**0.981 ± 0.016**	**0.986 ± 0.013**	0.981 ± 0.024	**0.992 ± 0.015**
		R	**0.980 ± 0.016**	**0.986 ± 0.014**	0.979 ± 0.027	**0.991 ± 0.017**
		F_1	**0.980 ± 0.016**	**0.986 ± 0.014**	0.979 ± 0.028	**0.991 ± 0.017**
		AUC	**0.997 ± 0.003**	0.997 ± 0.003	0.996 ± 0.005	0.999 ± 0.002
	Axiom	P	0.918 ± 0.047	0.971 ± 0.032	0.979 ± 0.022	0.958 ± 0.035
		R	0.904 ± 0.057	0.967 ± 0.042	0.977 ± 0.026	0.952 ± 0.043
		F_1	0.903 ± 0.058	0.966 ± 0.044	0.977 ± 0.026	0.951 ± 0.044
		AUC	0.905 ± 0.055	0.966 ± 0.043	0.977 ± 0.025	0.946 ± 0.047
HB_{GD}	Prob	P	0.978 ± 0.016	0.981 ± 0.022	0.979 ± 0.027	0.991 ± 0.016
		R	0.978 ± 0.016	0.980 ± 0.024	0.977 ± 0.031	0.990 ± 0.017
		F_1	0.978 ± 0.016	0.980 ± 0.024	0.976 ± 0.031	0.990 ± 0.017
		AUC	0.996 ± 0.004	0.997 ± 0.004	**0.996 ± 0.005**	0.998 ± 0.005
	Axiom	P	0.930 ± 0.037	0.969 ± 0.032	0.979 ± 0.025	0.961 ± 0.040
		R	0.916 ± 0.046	0.964 ± 0.042	0.976 ± 0.029	0.954 ± 0.048
		F_1	0.915 ± 0.048	0.964 ± 0.043	0.976 ± 0.029	0.953 ± 0.049
		AUC	0.917 ± 0.046	0.964 ± 0.043	0.976 ± 0.028	0.948 ± 0.053
Tree		P	0.975 ± 0.020	0.982 ± 0.022	**0.982 ± 0.023**	0.988 ± 0.017
		R	0.974 ± 0.022	0.980 ± 0.026	**0.980 ± 0.026**	0.987 ± 0.019
		F_1	0.973 ± 0.022	0.980 ± 0.026	**0.980 ± 0.026**	0.987 ± 0.019
		AUC	0.973 ± 0.023	0.981 ± 0.026	0.980 ± 0.026	0.985 ± 0.023
LogReg		P	0.751 ± 0.002	0.848 ± 0.114	0.901 ± 0.038	0.915 ± 0.022
		R	0.524 ± 0.027	0.733 ± 0.209	0.871 ± 0.058	0.898 ± 0.032
		F_1	0.361 ± 0.031	0.639 ± 0.286	0.861 ± 0.070	0.895 ± 0.035
		AUC	0.500 ± 0.000	0.695 ± 0.239	0.908 ± 0.037	0.930 ± 0.026
HLogReg		P	0.751 ± 0.002	0.757 ± 0.009	0.912 ± 0.052	0.896 ± 0.033
		R	0.518 ± 0.024	0.551 ± 0.043	0.873 ± 0.107	0.864 ± 0.057
		F_1	0.354 ± 0.028	0.395 ± 0.053	0.856 ± 0.146	0.851 ± 0.075
		AUC	0.500 ± 0.000	0.516 ± 0.033	0.881 ± 0.111	0.898 ± 0.034

formances, interpretability and robustness, particularly in scenarios where data is limited or complexity of the target class is high.

Axiom Extraction and Interpretability. The effectiveness of axiom extraction hinges on the expressivity of the axiom format and the complexity of the target class. For MBNB, extracted axioms are inherently limited to conjunctions of atomic concepts, that are equivalent to HB models with a single cluster. While this format aligns well with some of the simpler target classes, it fails to capture more complex concept definitions. This structural mismatch results in lower average scores and higher variance.

By contrast, HB models can extract rules in the form of disjunction of conjunctions, making them more expressive and better aligned with the structure of the target classes. This is evident in the relatively small gap between the performance of the probabilistic models and the extracted axioms.

As a general observation on interpretability, the axioms are ultimately constructed from the Boolean features extracted from each KG (see Table 1). These features correspond to nodes in the input layer of the models and therefore comprise the vocabulary from which any axiom can be formed. The number of features D bounds the number of unique atomic units that can appear in any axiom. Thus, interpretability is directly linked to feature selection and representation. This highlights the importance of feature engineering, not just for predictive performance, but also for the quality and usability of symbolic outputs. This trend indicates that these models benefit substantially from more abundant training data, partially mitigating their inability to generalize from sparse observations. However, the high variance observed across metrics (especially in HLogReg) reflects a lack of robustness, and supports the hypothesis that these models are sensitive to data quantity and distribution.

Sample Axioms. In Fig. 5 we report sample approximated class definitions extracted from the hierarchical models for some realistic real-world targets generated for the LUBM ontology. In particular, we show the target concept C and its extracted approximations, denoted as C_{MB} when extracted using the Multivariate Bernoulli model, and C_{HB} when extracted using the Hierarchical Mixture Bernoulli model (in this example, trained using Variational Bayes).

Considering the first case, we observe how the model adapts to the data patterns of individuals, which is reflected in the predicted axioms. Although the original definition is logically valid, there are no individuals in the dataset which are both `FullProfessor` and participate in relation `tenured`. There is only one instance of `Chair` who is also the subject of a `headOf` relation. However, there are several `AssociateProfessor` individuals who `workFor` a department. This pattern explains the axiom extracted by the HB model: it correctly includes `AssociateProfessor` and the `worksFor` relation', while also adding other constraints that do not affect the resulting set of individuals. For example, in the dataset, all `AssociateProfessor` individuals hold a doctoral degree and all teach at least one course. With this axiom (excluding the single `Chair` individual) the axiom covers correctly the 99.5% of individuals in the dataset.

Analyzing the second target, a similar analysis can be performed. Examining the dataset, all individuals with a `masterDegreeFrom` relation also have a

$$\begin{aligned}
\text{SeniorAcademic} &\equiv (\text{FullProfessor} \sqcap \exists\,\text{tenured}.\top) \\
&\sqcup (\text{AssociateProfessor} \sqcap \exists\,\text{worksFor}.\text{Department}) \\
&\sqcup (\text{Chair} \sqcap \exists\,\text{headOf}.\text{Department}) \\
\text{SeniorAcademic}_{\text{MB}} &\sqsubseteq \text{Professor} \sqcap \exists\,\text{doctoralDegreeFrom}.\text{University} \\
&\sqcap \exists\,\text{memberOf}.\top \sqcap \exists\,\text{teacherOf}.\text{Course} \\
&\sqcap \text{worksFor}.\text{Department} \\
\text{SeniorAcademic}_{\text{HB}} &\sqsubseteq \text{AssociateProfessor} \sqcap \exists\,\text{doctoralDegreeFrom}.\text{University} \\
&\sqcap \exists\,\text{memberOf}.\top \sqcap \exists\,\text{teacherOf}.\text{Course} \\
&\sqcap \text{worksFor}.\text{Department}
\end{aligned}$$

$$\begin{aligned}
\text{DegreeHolder} &\equiv (\text{Person} \sqcap \exists\,\text{undergraduateDegreeFrom}.\text{University}) \\
&\sqcup (\text{Person} \sqcap \exists\,\text{masterDegreeFrom}.\text{University}) \\
&\sqcup (\text{Person} \sqcap \exists\,\text{doctoralDegreeFrom}.\text{University}) \\
\text{DegreeHolder}_{\text{MB}} &\sqsubseteq \text{Person} \sqcap \exists\,\text{undergraduateDegreeFrom}.\text{University} \\
&\sqcap \exists\,\text{memberOf}.\top \\
\text{DegreeHolder}_{\text{HB}} &\sqsubseteq (\text{Employee} \sqcap \exists\,\text{doctoralDegreeFrom}.\text{University} \\
&\sqcap \exists\,\text{memberOf}.\top \sqcap \exists\,\text{teacherOf}.\text{Course} \\
&\sqcap \exists\,\text{worksFor}.\text{Department}) \\
&\sqcup (\text{GraduateStudent} \sqcap \exists\,\text{advisor}.\text{Professor} \sqcap \exists\,\text{memberOf}.\top \\
&\sqcap \exists\,\text{takesCourse}.\text{Course})
\end{aligned}$$

$$\begin{aligned}
\text{TeachingStaff} &\equiv (\text{Lecturer} \sqcap \exists\,\text{teacherOf}.\text{Course}) \\
&\sqcup (\text{Professor} \sqcap \exists\,\text{teacherOf}.\text{Course}) \\
&\sqcup (\text{TeachingAssistant} \sqcap \exists\,\text{teachingAssistantOf}.\text{Course}) \\
\text{TeachingStaff}_{\text{MB}} &\sqsubseteq \text{Employee} \sqcap \exists\,\text{doctoralDegreeFrom}.\text{University} \sqcap \exists\,\text{teacherOf}.\text{Course} \\
&\sqcap \exists\,\text{memberOf}.\top \sqcap \exists\,\text{worksFor}.\text{Department} \\
\text{TeachingStaff}_{\text{HB}} &\sqsubseteq (\text{Lecturer} \sqcap \exists\,\text{doctoralDegreeFrom}.\text{University} \sqcap \exists\,\text{memberOf}.\top \\
&\sqcap \exists\,\text{worksFor}.\text{Department} \sqcap \exists\,\text{teacherOf}.\text{Course}) \\
&\sqcup (\text{GraduateStudent} \sqcap \text{TeachingAssistant} \sqcap \exists\,\text{teachingAssistantOf}.\text{Course} \\
&\sqcap \exists\,\text{advisor}.\text{Professor} \sqcap \exists\,\text{memberOf}.\top \sqcap \exists\,\text{takesCourse}.\text{Course})
\end{aligned}$$

Fig. 5. Samples of extracted axioms for LUBM problems

doctoralDegreeFrom relation, while most GraduateStudent individuals are linked via the advisor relation to some Professor. For this reason, in the axiom extracted from the HB model, the disjunction involving individuals with a masterDegreeFrom relation is omitted.

The case is different for the MB model, which, allowing conjunctive axioms only, includes solely the class with the majority of individuals, those in the undergraduateDegreeFrom relation. Nevertheless, it still achieves good results, as individuals with a doctoralDegreeFrom or masterDegreeFrom relation also have an undergraduateDegreeFrom relation.

These results suggest that with a larger and more populated dataset (where each concept contains a richer and more diverse set of individuals) it becomes possible to learn more complete and accurate definitions. This trend is also reflected in the evaluation, where we observe an increased performance for predictions with axioms in ontologies with greater numbers of individuals.

5.4 Additional Experimental Validation

To validate the performance of our models on large-scale, real-world datasets, we conducted experiments on subsets of the DBPEDIA and YAGO ontologies (24k and 90k individuals, respectively). The results for these datasets were consistent with the existing patterns. Additionally, to assess the statistical significance of the observed differences between the models, we performed non-parametric Friedman tests, followed by Nemenyi post-hoc analyses, on all metrics across all datasets. The Friedman test yielded p-values below 0.05 for all metrics and datasets, indicating overall significant differences among model distributions. Subsequent Nemenyi tests revealed that our models exhibited statistically significant differences from the LogReg and HLogReg baselines more often than those from the Tree baseline. The complete statistical test outputs (including analysis of the large-scale datasets), comparisons across all models and full evaluation tables for all datasets are available in the project repository.[11]

6 Conclusions and Possible Extensions

In order to better address the inherent incompleteness of the DL knowledge graphs, we extended the methods to generate simple probabilistic classifiers that leverage the semantics of basic logic features regarded as binary random variables. These models are especially suitable for problems related to incomplete data, which is the case of the DL KGs. Additionally, they can be converted into probabilistic rules or axioms with a straightforward interpretation in terms of the terminology employed by the KG, thereby enhancing the model interpretability. An experiment testing the effectiveness of these generative models, compared to a baseline of simple probabilistic classifiers, proved their effectiveness and potential for further investigation.

A number of limitations would require further attention. Knowledge graphs containing many classes and properties may provide numerous features for the initial, unsupervised feature selection phase. Supervised methods can then be used to identify a small subset of important features. Complex concept definitions may turn out to be harder to learn, especially when nested restrictions are considered, though such definitions are more rarely found in KGs. In its current implementation, the hierarchical model would require a more careful search for optimal values of other hyperparameters. This also calls for experiments involving larger datasets in terms of the number of individuals.

Based on related work on similar models, various extensions are possible along different lines. For example, one could incorporate existing rules or axioms into probabilistic models, consider different classification settings (including decision procedures that allow for rejection cases to better align with the original semantics), or use the proposed models in transductive semi-supervised approaches. Another possibility is integrating continuous (Gaussian) features to include restrictions on numerical data types in the model. Probabilistic models

---

[11] https://github.com/ivandiliso/sphm4kg.

could be applied to various other tasks, such as KG *debugging*, e.g. for anomaly detection, and *knowledge refinement*, e.g. using these models for axiom discovery.

Acknowledgments. This work was partially supported by the project FAIR - Future AI Research (PE00000013), spoke 6 - Symbiotic AI (https://futureai-research.it/) and the PRIN project HypeKG - Hybrid Prediction and Explanation with Knowledge Graphs (Prot. 2022Y34XNM, CUP H53D23003700006) under the PNRR MUR program funded by the European Union - NextGenerationEU.

References

1. Baader, F., Calvanese, D., McGuinness, D.L., Nardi, D., Patel-Schneider, P.F. (eds.): The Description Logic Handbook: Theory, Implementation and Applications. Cambridge University Press, 2nd edn. (2007). https://doi.org/10.1017/CBO9780511711787
2. Breiman, L., Friedman, J., Olshen, R., Stone, C.: Classification and regression trees. Chapman Hall/CRC (1984). https://doi.org/10.1201/9781315139470
3. d'Amato, C., Fanizzi, N., Esposito, F.: Query answering and ontology population: an inductive approach. In: Proceedings of ESWC 2008. LNCS, vol. 5021, pp. 288–302. Springer (2008). https://doi.org/10.1007/978-3-540-68234-9_23
4. Domingos, P.M., Pazzani, M.J.: On the optimality of the simple Bayesian classifier under zero-one loss. Mach. Learn. **29**(2–3), 103–130 (1997). https://doi.org/10.1023/A:1007413511361
5. Fanizzi, N., d'Amato, C.: Towards interpretable probabilistic classification models for knowledge graphs. In: Proceedings of SITIS 2022, pp. 25–31. IEEE (2022). https://doi.org/10.1109/SITIS57111.2022.00013
6. Fanizzi, N., d'Amato, C., Esposito, F.: Induction of robust classifiers for web ontologies through kernel machines. J. Web Semant. **11**, 1–13 (2012). https://doi.org/10.1016/j.websem.2011.11.003
7. Ghahramani, Z., Jordan, M.: Supervised learning from incomplete data via an EM approach. In: Proceedings of NIPS 1993, vol. 6, pp. 120–127. Morgan-Kaufmann (1993). https://doi.org/10.5555/2987189.2987205
8. Hogan, A., et al.: Knowledge graphs. ACM Comput. Surv. **54**(4), 1–37 (2021). https://doi.org/10.1145/3447772
9. Jordan, M., Jacobs, R.: Hierarchical mixtures of experts and the EM algorithm. In: Proceedings of IJCNN, vol. 2, pp. 1339–1344 (1993). https://doi.org/10.1109/IJCNN.1993.716791
10. Mandt, S., Hoffman, M.D., Blei, D.M.: Stochastic gradient descent as approximate bayesian inference. JMLR **18**(134), 1–35 (2017). https://dl.acm.org/doi/10.5555/3122009.3208015
11. McLachlan, G.J.: Discriminant Analysis and Statistical Pattern Recognition. Wiley (1992). https://doi.org/10.1002/0471725293
12. Minervini, P., d'Amato, C., Fanizzi, N.: Learning probabilistic description logic concepts: Under different assumptions on missing knowledge. In: Proceedings of SAC 2012, pp. 378–383. ACM (2012). https://doi.org/10.1145/2245276.2245349
13. Murphy, K.P.: Probabilistic Machine Learning: An introduction. MIT Press (2022)
14. Riefolo, C., Fanizzi, N., d'Amato, C.: Simple and interpretable probabilistic classifiers for knowledge graphs (2024). https://arxiv.org/abs/2407.07045

15. Schwarz, G.: Estimating the dimension of a model. Ann. Stat. **6**(2), 461–464 (1978)
16. Tresp, V., Hollatz, J., Ahmad, S.: Representing probabilistic rules with networks of Gaussian basis functions. Mach. Learn. **27**, 173–200 (1997). https://doi.org/10.1023/A:1007381408604
17. Wang, Q., Mao, Z., Wang, B., Guo, L.: Knowledge graph embedding: a survey of approaches and applications. IEEE Trans. Knowl. Data Eng. **29**(12), 2724–2743 (2017). https://doi.org/10.1109/TKDE.2017.2754499

Integrating Environmental Regulations into Autonomous Agricultural Robotics: A Case for Waterbody-Aware Fertilization

Guillaume Perution-Khili[1], Ahmad Kadi[2], Nikolas Müller[3], Akira Charoensit[1], David Carral[1(✉)], Pierre Bisquert[1,4], Federico Ulliana[1], Ansgar Bernardi[2], and Marie-Laure Mugnier[1]

[1] LIRMM, Boreal, Université Montpellier, Inria, CNRS, Montpellier, France
{Perution-Khili.Guillaume,Charoensit.Akira,Carral.David, Ulliana.Federico,Mugnier.Marie-Laure}@inria.fr
[2] Deutsches Forschungszentrum für Künstliche Intelligenz GmbH - DFKI, Trippstadterstr. 122, 67633 Kaiserslautern, Germany
{Kadi.Ahmad,Bernardi.Ansgar}@dfki.de
[3] Deutsches Forschungszentrum für Künstliche Intelligenz GmbH - DFKI, Hamburger Straße 24, 49084 Osnabrück, Germany
Müller.Nikolas@dfki.de
[4] IATE, Université Montpellier, INRAE, Institut Agro, Montpellier, France
Bisquert.Pierre@inrae.fr

Abstract. The operation of autonomous robots in the agricultural domain requires compliance with the regulatory aspects of the process. For instance, the improper spraying of chemicals near water bodies (e.g., pesticides or fertilizers) may cause significant environmental damage and, therefore, is strictly regulated at the legislation level. In this paper, we introduce a reasoning-enhanced framework to operate autonomous robots spreading chemicals near water bodies. Our framework leverages and extends semantic web vocabularies to integrate regulatory constraints and environmental conditions where the robot is operating. Then, it uses rules and reasoning to detect violations on real-time data generated by the autonomous robot. The inference of violations subsequently triggers actions controlling the robot behavior, but can also be transparently explained in our framework, thereby avoiding the robot to behave as a black-box to the supervising technician. Our approach has been implemented, and its feasibility showcased in a simulation environment.

Keywords: Logical Rules · Open Vocabularies · Autonomous Robots · Agriculture

1 Legislation-Aware Automatization in Agriculture

Competitive agriculture operating machines and robots for automation must also ensure that these behave in an ecologically sustainable manner. For instance,

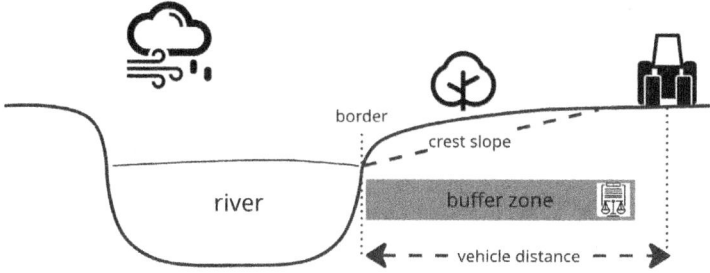

Fig. 1. Use-case: Legislation-Aware Chemical Spreading.

spreading plant protection agents and fertilizers near water bodies, like rivers, streams, or ponds, may cause significant environmental problems. Concretely, the sprayed chemicals can be washed by rain or irrigation, thus polluting the nearby water, with subsequent risks like eutrophication or groundwater contamination. In many European countries and regions, this practice is strictly regulated and must be operated in line with the current legislation. This is a challenging task, which gets even more complicated when operating autonomous robots.

For highly specialized robots, operating conditions for respecting a given legislation can be hard-coded, even as part of the used algorithms. But then, adjusting them to a certain environment becomes increasingly complex and error-prone. With increasing demand in more sophisticated autonomous machines, it makes more sense to handle knowledge about regulations in a *high-level declarative* way such that they are easily adaptable to various scenarios. Furthermore, using a declarative framework for expressing knowledge makes it able to explain the robot behavior to the operator (e.g., spraying at position x has been stopped to respect a precise regulation) thereby avoiding it to behave like a black-box.

A subtle aspect of operating a legislation-aware robot is that the legislation itself can vary from state to state, and even from region to region. For instance, France and Germany both apply European directives governing agriculture but implement them in different ways, hence have different national laws, e.g., for spraying fertilizers (our case study), and regions, like e.g., the Lower Saxony in Germany, specify additional regulation. With many regulations then comes the challenge of modeling the constraints they define in a unified manner.

Roughly speaking, the goal of a regulatory constraint is to define under which conditions spraying is allowed. As illustrated by Fig. 1, this is achieved by defining a *buffer zone*, that is, a protected area between the border of the water body and the spreading device, where the application of some products is prohibited. Buffer zones can be defined based on several types of conditions. First, environmental conditions on the land (e.g., higher river crest slopes increase the risk of pollutions due to running chemicals) and the type of water body (e.g., rivers with low streamflow are more at risk). Second, meteorological conditions such as rain and wind, which can cause runoff or dispersion of chemicals. Third, the composition of chemicals, the type and (real-time) position of the devices

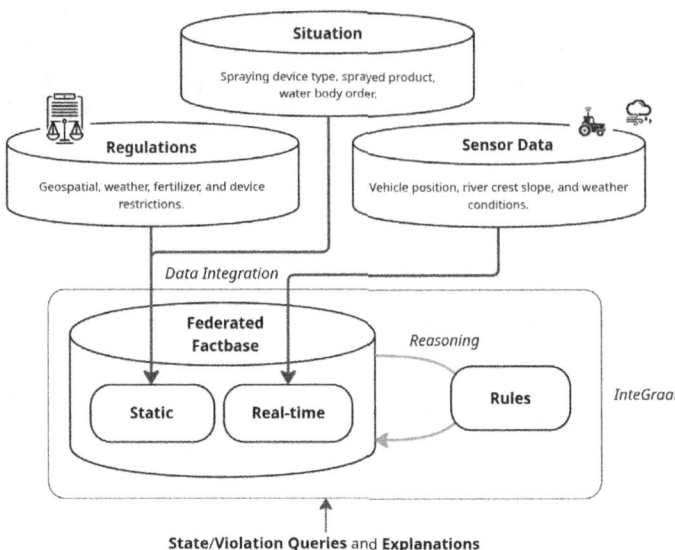

Fig. 2. Framework Architecture.

used for spraying (e.g., imprecise spreading devices are more subject to violate restrictions, even when the vehicle is at safe distance).

To perform this task and be able to make a decision on whether to stop spraying because a buffer zone may be at risk, an autonomous machine has to know the applicable regulatory constraints as well as to observe its environment to ensure with high certainty that those regulations are met. This requires to seamlessly integrate and reason on various data and knowledge, which is the issue we tackle in this paper.

Contributions. This paper introduces a framework using ontologies and rule-based reasoning for operating an agricultural autonomous robot dedicated to applying products potentially harmful to the environment - fertilizers in our case study - on a field that borders a water body. As a proof of concept, we assume that there is a single water body, however this assumption captures most real-life scenarios. We also point out, that beyond this case study, our approach could be applied to various applications in agriculture with autonomous mobile vehicles, where buffer zones have to be enforced according to regulatory constraints; for example, spraying pesticides near residential areas or navigating around wildlife corridors to protect biodiversity. However, the case of water body protection raises additional challenges, because the water level and the banks vary over the year, hence a static mapping of the water bodies is not adequate.

In our setting, we assume one or more moving vehicles that use different sensors to scan and build a spatial representation on the environment where they are operating; this sensed data is fused and interpreted, producing higher-level data such as the position of the spraying engine, the field slope gradient at this position, or the distance to the border of the water body. More specifically, we implemented a scenario where an unmanned ground vehicle (the spraying robot) and an unmanned aerial vehicle (a drone) are cooperating to provide background information. This scenario was simulated and tested on a physically based virtual environment (see Sect. 5).

The overall architecture of our framework is illustrated in Fig. 2. First, our framework makes use of RDF and open vocabularies (like SOSA [13], QUDT [11], PAM [10,26]) to model regulatory constraints. Importantly, the modeling of regulations is independent from the specific implemented use-case. One of the objectives was to make it easy to exchange and reuse in an automated way, hence the choice of standard semantic web formats and open vocabularies. Input information also includes data about the specific situation and real-time environment data where the robot is operating, which comes from the interpretation of sensor data. Second, this heterogeneous data is integrated into a first-order logic knowledge base, composed of a federated factbase resulting from data integration and a set of rules. Third, reasoning with this knowledge base allows to detect violations of regulations in real-time. Explanations can also be generated to support the decision to stop or resume spraying in accordance with the legislation, which can be useful for a post-spraying analysis of the robot's behavior.

The knowledge base and associated reasoning is managed by the InteGraal reasoning tool [2]. The whole workflow has been implemented and showcased (Sect. 5).

Related Work on Knowledge Processing in Agricultural Robotics. Handling of semantic knowledge in robotics has recently picked up due to robotics systems becoming more sophisticated and expanding to fields like agriculture [3,15,19] for autonomous fertilization [1] or explainable crop recommendation [24,27]. Such knowledge is often stored as an ontology [18,25], which describes the dynamic relations between semantic items [4,8,22,28], and is often used for navigation [14] and 3D mapping [12]. In particular, SEMAP [7-9] provides a spatio-semantic model for agricultural processes. It handles spatial information in an SQL database and semantic information in a knowledge base, and maintain a spatial map with explicit relationships between discrete objects. For our use-case, it is beneficial to leave the spatial map implicit and just acquire environmental measurements. Various other tools have been proposed to model [21] and analyze [29] agricultural processes and provide decision support under certain conditions [16,17]. Often used tools to handle knowledge are OpenEase [4] and KnowRob [28]. With respect to related work, our novelty is to propose a completely declarative framework, which allows to integrate various kinds of data in a principled way, including real-time data, and to reason about it. A clear distinction is made between the data layer (understood broadly, from raw data to more elaborated information) and the knowledge base layer, where reasoning is performed.

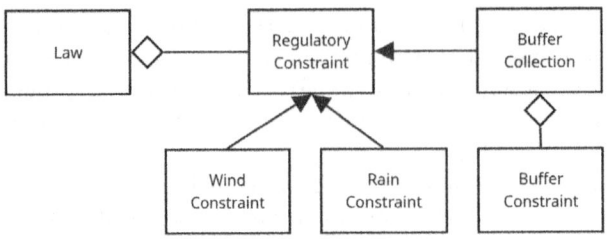

Fig. 3. UML of the Spraying Law Ontology.

2 An Ontology for Modeling Regulatory Constraints

The first step in our approach is to provide a setting for representing regulatory constraints as specified in legal texts. Its purpose is twofold. On the one hand, it allows experts to write and exchange a formal representation of the text laws, using open vocabularies and standards like RDF(S). On the other hand, it enables the automatic verification of such constraints by means of reasoning by integrating this data into a knowledge base.

In this work, we considered European laws for the application of pesticides and fertilizers near water bodies, with a particular focus on Germany and France. As already said, since regulations from national and regional legislation can vary considerably, it is imperative to structure them in a flexible schema to standardise and ensure interoperability. We introduce an ontology building on the PAM vocabulary [10,26] developed by a German project which serves the regulations related to applying plant protection agents near water bodies.[1] It includes a long list of commercial agents and their use, among others, with respect to restrictions related to nearby water bodies. This has been built on top of a database of plant protection agents offered by the Federal Office of Consumer Protection and Food Safety [5]. Our work goes beyond the modeling of regulations for German law for plant protection agents. We extended the PAM vocabulary in order to be able also to capture the French legislation as well as other agricultural practices, notably spraying fertilizers. Subsets of the legal texts have been manually translated into triples conforming to the ontology.[2] Figure 3 provides a high level presentation of the resulting ontology schema. Below, we illustrate its main concepts.

- A *Law* regroups a set of *regulatory constraints*, which can be of two types. The first type includes regulatory constraints that completely forbid the application of chemicals when certain conditions are met. This is the case, for instance, for wind and rain constraints; when they exceed a certain threshold, spraying is simply forbidden. The second type of constraints are more involved and impose minimal distances (we refer as "buffer zones" or simply "buffers") when certain conditions are met. In the ontology, these are called

---

[1] https://srv.ktbl.de/experimental/pam/sparql.
[2] This ontology is available at https://gitlab.inria.fr/boreal-artifacts/r4agri-artifacts.

buffer collections because they regroup a set of individual *buffer constraints*. The interest of having buffer collections is that they are used to regroup constraints that share a common set of conditions, as we illustrate later.
- A single *buffer constraint* can be seen as a tuple $(cond_1, \ldots, cond_n, v)$ capturing the fact that, when spraying is performed, if all conditions $cond_i$ are satisfied, then a distance of v from the water body bank must be respected. The conditions include for instance:
  - Geospatial conditions on the slope of the ground near the water body and the size and the stream order of the river.
  - Conditions on the fertilizer composition, such as the nutrient composition of the spread chemicals, particularly for nitrogen and phosphorus, as well as on the type of device used for spreading.
  - Conditions related to existence of perennial, continuous, unfertilized strip of grass or woodland along the river body.

Figure 4 illustrates the modeling of two articles from fertilization laws: the German Fertilizer Ordinance (article §5) and the Lower Saxony Water Law (article §58). The German Fertilizer Ordinance (article §5) defines buffer constraints in the case of different slopes up to the water body bank. This case of the legislation includes many buffer collections corresponding to different slope intervals; for concision, we report only two cases. In the first case (slope below 5%), the legislation sets a 1 m buffer for vehicles with precise spreading and 4 m distance for vehicles without precise spreading. In the second case (slope between 5–10%) the distance increases. As the example illustrates, property slv:bufferCategory is used to link a buffer constraint to the buffer collection where it is defined. It is important to note that the buffer collection expresses constraints (here, on the slope range) that are common to all constraints. The intended semantics is that every buffer constraint inherits the conditions of the buffer collection where it is defined. These two buffer collections model four buffer constraints of the form $(minSlope, maxSlope, preciseSpreading, safeDistance)$, i.e., $(0, 5, true, 1m)$, $(0, 5, false, 4m)$, $(5, 10, true, 3m)$, $(5, 10, false, 4m)$, that will be integrated in our framework. Finally, we made use of blank nodes (such as _:BufferConstraint1m and _:slopeOf5Percent) for concision to reuse quantities; these are expressed with their unit measure by using the QUDT vocabulary. Figure 4 also presents the Lower Saxony Water Law (article §58). This article includes three buffer collections, each setting a distance to respect according to the order of the river (the order of a river indicates its size and streamflow). Note that more constraints can apply at the same time, for instance here the two ordinances apply when spraying near by water bodies of a certain order and certain slope values.

Overall, the resulting ontology offers a means to experts to formalize regulatory constraints from text laws. This will be exploited in the subsequent stages of the framework.

```
@prefix rdfs: <http://www.w3.org/2000/01/rdf-schema#> .
@prefix slv: <http://dfki.de/data/SprayingLawVocabulary/> .
@prefix sli: <http://dfki.de/data/SprayingLawInstances/> .

sli:GermanFertilizerOrdinance5 a slv:FertilizationLaw ;

        slv:imposeBufferConstraint [
            a slv:BufferCollection ;
            rdfs:label "buffers when slope is below 5%" ;
            slv:smallerThan _:slopeOf5Percent;

            slv:bufferCategory [
                a slv:BufferConstraint ;
                rdfs:label "1m buffer when precise spreading" ;
                slv:preciseSpreading true;
                slv:bufferConstraint _:BufferConstraint1m ; ] ;

            slv:bufferCategory [
                a slv:BufferConstraint ;
                rdfs:label "4m buffer when no precise spreading" ;
                slv:preciseSpreading false;
                slv:bufferConstraint _:BufferConstraint4m ; ] ; ]

        slv:imposeBufferConstraint [
            a slv:BufferCollection ;
            rdfs:label "buffers when slope is between 5 - 10%" ;
            slv:greaterThan _:slopeOf5Percent ;
            slv:smallerThan _:slopeOf10Percent;

            slv:bufferCategory [
                a slv:BufferConstraint ;
                rdfs:label "3m buffer when precise spreading" ;
                slv:preciseSpreading true;
                slv:bufferConstraint _:BufferConstraint3m ; ] ;

            slv:bufferCategory [
                a slv:BufferConstraint ;
                rdfs:label "4m buffer when no precise spreading" ;
                slv:preciseSpreading false;
                slv:bufferConstraint _:BufferConstraint4m ; ] ; ]

sli:LowerSaxonyWaterLaw58 a slv:FertilizationLaw ;

        slv:imposeBufferConstraint [
            a slv:BufferCollection ;
            rdfs:label "10m buffer when nearby water body of 1st order";
            slv:nextToWaterBodyOfOrder 1 ;
            slv:bufferCategory [
                a slv:WaterConstraint ;
                slv:bufferConstraint _:BufferConstraint10m ; ] ; ]

        slv:imposeBufferConstraint [
            a slv:BufferCollection ;
            rdfs:label "5m buffer when nearby water body of 2nd order";
            slv:nextToWaterBodyOfOrder 2 ;
            slv:bufferCategory [
                a slv:BufferConstraint ;
                slv:bufferConstraint _:BufferConstraint5m ; ] ; ]

        slv:imposeBufferConstraint [
            a slv:BufferCollection ;
            rdfs:label "3m buffer when nearby water body of 3rd order";
            slv:nextToWaterBodyOfOrder 3 ;
            slv:bufferCategory [
                a slv:BufferConstraint ;
                slv:bufferConstraint _:BufferConstraint3m ; ] ; ]
```

Fig. 4. Modelling German Fertilizer Ordinance (article §5) and Lower Saxony Water Law (article §58).

3 Integrating Data and Knowledge for Decision Making

The second step in our approach is to integrate data and information that can support decision making for controlling the behavior of the autonomous robot.

As illustrated in Fig. 2 this is done through the means of a logical knowledge base (KB) [20] managed by the InteGraal tool [2]. More precisely, the KB is composed of several sets of facts, forming a so-called *federated factbase*, and a set of rules for detecting violations. In this section, we present the federated factbase built in this application.

The federated factbase is composed of different sets of facts, each acquired and processed in different ways.

1. Facts describing the *specific situation* where the robot is deployed. This includes the characteristics of the sprayed product and of the spraying device, the classification of the nearby water body order and references to the applicable regulations (which depends on the geographical location of the field). These are supposed to be provided by the supervising user, but could also be obtained from external sources (e.g. the characteristics of the sprayed product could be obtained from a database of authorized agricultural products).
2. Facts translating the *regulatory constraints*. The regulatory constraints described Sect. 2 are stored in an RDF triplestore. To integrate the regulatory constraints on our application, we used *mappings* from the triple store to a the KB. In a nutshell, mappings can be seen as rules where the body is a SPARQL query using the RDF vocabulary and the head is a conjunctive query on the KB vocabulary.
3. Facts coming from *sensor data* interpreted by the robot, giving the distance to the considered water body and the river crest slope at a given timestamp. These facts are built from a data stream coming from the robot.
4. Finally, facts containing measures of wind speed and rain intensity are collected through a *weather API*, at the rate permitted by the considered weather station[3].

Note that facts 1 and 2 are *static* (or *session parameters*), in the sense that they are specific to the working session, and do not change during this session. In contrast, facts 3 and 4 are *dynamic* as they are each associated with a timestamp. We now describe in more detail the construction of facts issued from regulatory constraints and from dynamic data.

Integrating Regulatory Constraints. One way of translating regulation constraints into facts consists in using a natural translation from RDF to first-order logic, with RDF classes and properties translated into unary and binary predicates, respectively. However, to avoid importing a lot of atoms that may not be relevant to the application, and for greater modularity, we followed a data-integration approach and used mappings as in ontology-based data access [23]. As illustrated in Fig. 5, the head of a mapping may contain new variables, i.e., variables that are not answer variables from the body query (variable C in the Figure). Such variables are existentially quantified: each time the mapping is applied, a new existential variable is created (classically called a named null in

---

[3] We used https://openweathermap.org/.

```
∃C.
  slopeBufferConstraint(C,RequiredDistance,MinSlope,MaxSlope),
  germanSlopeConstraintSessionParameters(C,Regulation,IsPreciseSpreading)            (1)
:-
  QuerySlopeConstraints(Regulation,RequiredDistance,MinSlope,MaxSlope,IsPreciseSpreading).
∃C.
  plainBufferConstraint(C,RequiredDistance),
  lowerSaxonyPlainBufferConstraintSessionParameters(C,Regulation,WaterBodyOrder),
  isApplicableAtAnyTime(C,RequiredDistance)                                          (2)
:-
  QueryWaterBodyOrderConstraints(Regulation,RequiredDistance,WaterBodyOrder).
```

Fig. 5. Mappings of the form (head :- body) where body is a SPARQL query.

databases). Such feature corresponds to the notion of (G)LAV mapping in data integration.

In our application, we have build one mapping for each type of regulatory constraint. Figure 5 illustrates the mappings for the buffer collections presented in Fig. 4. The body of the mapping is a SPARQL query that retrieves the values for the conditions that are common to the buffer collection as well as the value for the conditions at the level of the buffer constraints. These tuples of values are then used in the head of the mapping to build a new object C (an existentially quantified variable representing a regulatory constraint in the knowledge base) and some facts giving the safe distance imposed by C, as well as the dynamic and static (session) parameters defining the conditions under which C is applicable. When all the parameters are static, the constraint is said to be applicable at any timestamp, which is also recorded in a fact.

Facts Issued from Dynamic Data. The robot is equipped with LiDaR sensors and GPS localization, whose interpretation allows it to build an (implicit) spatial map. At each timestamp, the robot generates a message containing the estimated distance to the river and the slope gradient. Data issued from both the robot and the weather station are integrated by using the standard ontologies SOSA[4] (Sensor, Observation, Sample, and Actuator) and Qudt[5] (quantities and units). Figure 6 illustrates two sets of sensor data produced by the moving vehicle. The first sensor data represents the detection of a 4 m distance from the river border. The second sensor data shows the wind-speed data from the weather API. This RDF data is then translated into logical facts using a standard translation. Note that the measures of distance and slope come with an uncertainty, given as a standard deviation from a mean value, as illustrated in Fig. 6 for the distance (qudt:value is the mean value computed from sensor data fusion and qudt:standardUncertainty is the standard deviation). To be on the safe side of the regulation, the value retained for the translation into logical facts is the most restrictive one, i.e., the deviation is substracted from the distance value and added for the slope value.

---

[4] https://www.w3.org/TR/vocab-ssn/.
[5] https://www.qudt.org/.

```
ex:distance_100.03333855
    sosa:hasFeatureOfInterest ex:waterbody ;
    sosa:hasResult [ a qudt:Quantity ;
            qudt:standardUncertainty 1.759653e+00 ;
            qudt:unit unit:M ;
            qudt:value 4.070299e+01 ] ;
    sosa:madeBySensor ex:lidar ;
    sosa:observedProperty ex:distance ;
    sosa:resultTime "2024-01-10T14:11:07+00:00"^^xsd:dateTimeStamp .

:wind_1749642684.829681
    sosa:hasFeatureOfInterest ex:atmosphere ;
    sosa:hasResult [ a qudt:Quantity ;
            qudt:unit unit:M-PER-SEC ;
            qudt:value 1.34e+00 ] ;
    sosa:madeBySensor ex:anemometer ;
    sosa:observedProperty ex:windSpeed ;
    sosa:resultTime "2024-01-10T14:11:07+00:00"^^xsd:dateTimeStamp .
```

Fig. 6. Example of Sensor Measurement.

4 Reasoning and Explanations of Violations

Once the data integrated, the framework for operating the autonomous robot makes use of rule-based reasoning to take decisions controlling the robot behavior and ensuring that the relevant regulation is respected, in particular that no chemical is sprayed inside a buffer zone. This is one of the main interests of our approach, since the declarative nature of facts and rules within a KB, both the detection of violations and their explanations are not hard-coded or tied to a specific robotic software, making it modular, flexible, and easier to maintain and make evolve.

Rule Language Expressivity. In our framework, a knowledge base is constituted of facts and rules expressed with extensions of the Datalog language. Datalog has nowadays become a reference language in data management frameworks with reasoning capabilities, like e.g., DAtomic, Logica, or CozoDB.[6] While most of our rules are plain positive Datalog, some of them use built-in or user-defined predicates and functions, as well as stratified default negation. Functions are needed to transform values, like for instance rounding the precision of a timestamp from hundredths of a second (which is the precision given by the robot) to a second (which is the precision relevant to our application). It follows that, by applying this rounding, we may result with two distances measured for the same (rounded) timestamp. Default negation is then used to pick the minimum distance to the water body within a (rounded) timestamp. Similar processing is done about the slope, taking the maximum value for a (rounded) timestamp. Note that we do not need a more expressive language to deal with temporal information, as time-stamping dynamic facts is sufficient.

Reasoning on Dynamic Federated Factbases. Reasoning is performed in two stages, because of the distinction between static and dynamic facts we outlined before. The goal of the first stage is to infer which constraints are relevant to

---
[6] www.datomic.com/, https://logica.dev/, www.cozodb.org/.

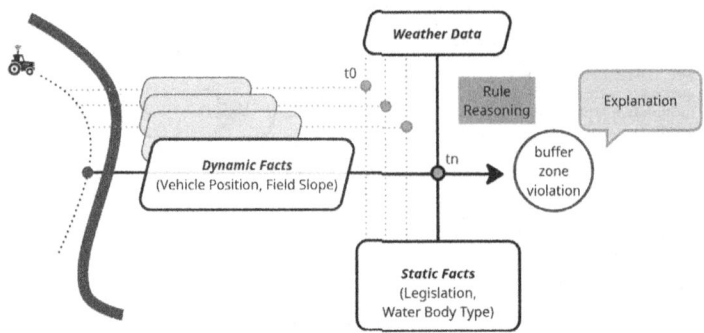

Fig. 7. Reasoning on Dynamic Federated Factbases.

the working session. This is done by applying rules to static facts concerning the session parameters and the legislation. As result, this yields a static saturated factbase, which can successively be combined with real-time dynamic facts. The goal of the second stage is to process the stream of dynamic facts acquired from sensor data. As this data is acquired in real-time, the factbase is dynamic. The specificity of this dynamic factbase is that it contains all observations made within a time window. In our case the size of the time window is set to 1 s. After reasoning is done on the time window $[t_i, t_{i+1s}]$, the facts sensed by the robot are discarded from the dynamic factbase, and the next window $[t_{i+1s}, t_{i+2s}]$ is processed. This is illustrated in Fig. 7.

Figure 8 presents some of the rules used to infer violations. These are of three types. The first type of rules are used to find regulatory constraints that are relevant to the current session. This is the case for instance for r_1 and r_2, inferring that the regulatory constraints on slope and water body order are relevant for the current session. The second type of rules are used to infer the constraints that are relevant at a given timestamp T. Rule r_3 presents the case of slope constraints. If a constraint C is session-relevant and the observed slope is within the range of the constraint at timestamp T, then the constraint is applicable at the same timestamp T. Rule r_4 presents the case of water body order constraints. This constraint is applicable at any time, and hence when a distance is observed at timestamp T then constraint is applicable at timestamp T. Finally, rule r_5 detects violations. If a constraint C is applicable at timestamp T requiring a distance D and the actual distance at T is D' with $D' < D$ then there is a violation due to distance D at timestamp T.

Explanations. An inherent feature of rule-based systems is that the reasoning is traceable and therefore explainable. Explanations in our framework again rely on InteGraal which provides a facility to enumerate the minimal subsets of the knowledge base that entail and answer to the violation query [6]. For a better interface with the user, such explanation could be further presented in natural language, as e.g.: "Article 5 from German Fertilizer Ordinance states the following constraint: when the slope is between 10% and 15%, the distance to a

```
% 1. Find constraints relevant to the session

isSessionRelevant(C) :-                                                    (r1)
    germanSlopeConstraintSessionParameters(C, Regulation, IsPreciseSpreading),
    session:applicableRegulation(Regulation),
    session:preciseSpreading(IsPreciseSpreading).

isSessionRelevant(C) :-                                                    (r2)
    lowerSaxonyWaterConstraintSessionParameters(C, Regulation, WaterBodyOrder),
    session:applicableRegulation(Regulation),
    session:waterBodyOrder(WaterBodyOrder).

% 2. Find constraints applicable at time T

isApplicable(C, TimeStamp, RequiredDistance) :-                            (r3)
    isSessionRelevant(C),
    slopeConstraint(C, RequiredDistance, MinSlope, MaxSlope),
    observed:slope(TimeStamp, ActualSlope),
    ActualSlope >= MinSlope,
    ActualSlope =< MaxSlope.

isApplicable(C, TimeStamp, RequiredDistance) :-                            (r4)
    isSessionRelevant(C),
    isApplicableAtAnyTime(C, RequiredDistance),
    observed:distance(TimeStamp, ActualDistance).

% 3. Find violations at time T

violation(TimeStamp, ActualDistance) :-                                    (r5)
    isApplicable(C, TimeStamp, RequiredDistance),
    observed:distance(TimeStamp, ActualDistance),
    ActualDistance < RequiredDistance.
```

Fig. 8. Rules to detect relevant constraints, applicability, and violations over time.

water body must be at least 4 meters; the slope at time $t100$ was 12%, hence this constraint was applicable; the vehicle was at 4 m from the water body at time $t100$, which violates this constraint".

5 Implementation and Validation

To test our approach, we simulated a land scenario in Isaac Sim[7] by procedurally generating the environment. More precisely, the generated land consists of a terrain with a river, some relief, a crop field and other vegetation (grass and trees), as illustrated in Fig. 9 (right). Then, we consider a UAV (flying drone) and a UGV (ground robot), each equipped with LiDaR sensors and provided with simulated GPS data for localization. The flying drone is first placed and scans the river to estimate its shape and surrounding terrain, building a spatial map. Then, the ground robot is launched within the terrain bounds and moves towards the river (Fig. 9, left), completing the spatial map and using it for estimating its current distance to the water body and the current slope of the field; this data is sent as a stream of ROS2[8] messages. The accuracy of the measures made by the

---
[7] https://developer.nvidia.com/isaac/sim.
[8] https://docs.ros.org/en/kilted/.

Fig. 9. Field and Autonomous Robot Movement Simulation.

robot was evaluated by comparison to the ground truth. The rest of the workflow has been implemented using the InteGraal library. The demonstration prototype is available at https://gitlab.inria.fr/boreal-artifacts/r4agri-artifacts: it provides a docker with a full integration of the workflow from running the simulation environment to the detection of violations.

Regarding the issue of autonomous fertilization, the limitation that we identified in our approach comes from the sensor data interpretation made by the robot. The distance to the river is accurately estimated and is provided with a high certainty. This is related to the high precision of the GPS localization. The slope of the field is also mostly correctly estimated, however in some cases it is provided with a high uncertainty. This arrives when the robot moves between a tree (i.e., a high object) and the river. Then, the robot has difficulties to distinguish between the terrain and the tree, which leads to a high uncertainty about the slope value, hence a high overestimation in the generated facts. Note that objects in the (implicit) spatial map built by the robot are not distinguished using semantics.

One way of mitigating this problem would be to put safeguards in place at the level of the rule-based reasoner, by discarding measurements that are judged to be aberrant: maximum values can be set for slope values and their differences between two timestamps, and when a measurement received at time t does not respect these constraints, the measurement taken at time t-1 is taken again for time t. A more robust way of doing would be to integrate semantics already into the map built by the robot, to distinguish objects, which would allow to deliver more accurate, or more certain, measurements in heavily vegetated zones. We believe this to be an interesting issue for future work.

6 Conclusion

Focusing on a use-case in agriculture, we presented a rule based framework for operating an autonomous robot according to regulatory constraints. We showed how open vocabularies can be used to integrate both knowledge about the legislation and data sensed by the robot. We showed the use of rules to reason on real-time data and decide when to stop spreading as well as a valuable explanation tool for the supervising person. Our approach has been implemented and tested on a simulation environment. As future direction, we plan to investigate how to inject semantics into the interpretation of sensor data for building a more reliable map of the environment.

References

1. Abhiram, R., Megalingam, R.K.: Autonomous fertilizer spraying mobile robot. In: 2022 IEEE 19th India Council International Conference (INDICON), pp. 1–6. IEEE (2022)
2. Baget, J.F., et al.: InteGraal: a tool for data-integration and reasoning on heterogeneous and federated sources. In: Proceedings of the Conference BDA'2023. Montpellier, France (2023). https://hal-lirmm.ccsd.cnrs.fr/lirmm-04304601
3. Bai, Y., Zhang, B., Xu, N., Zhou, J., Shi, J., Diao, Z.: Vision-based navigation and guidance for agricultural autonomous vehicles and robots: a review. Comput. Electron. Agric. **205**, 107584 (2023)
4. Beetz, M., Tenorth, M., Winkler, J.: Open-ease. In: 2015 IEEE International Conference on Robotics and Automation (ICRA), pp. 1983–1990. IEEE (2015)
5. BVL: Online-datenbank pflanzenschutzmittel. https://www.bvl.bund.de/DE/Arbeitsbereiche/04_Pflanzenschutzmittel/01_Aufgaben/02_ZulassungPSM/01_ZugelPSM/01_OnlineDatenbank/psm_onlineDB_node.html (2023). Accessed 20 Jun 2025
6. Charoensit, A., Carral, D., Bisquert, P., Rouquette, L., Ulliana, F.: Rule-aware datalog fact explanation using group-SAT solver. In: RuleML+RR'24: Companion Proceedings of the 8th International Joint Conference on Rules and Reasoning. Bucarest, Romania (2024). https://hal.science/hal-04706324
7. Deeken, H., Wiemann, T., Hertzberg, J.: A spatio-semantic model for agricultural environments and machines. In: Recent Trends and Future Technology in Applied Intelligence: 31st International Conference on Industrial Engineering and Other Applications of Applied Intelligent Systems, IEA/AIE 2018, Montreal, QC, Canada, June 25-28, 2018, Proceedings 31, pp. 589–600. Springer (2018)
8. Deeken, H., Wiemann, T., Hertzberg, J.: A spatio-semantic approach to reasoning about agricultural processes. Appl. Intell. **49**(11), 3821–3833 (2019). https://doi.org/10.1007/s10489-019-01451-2
9. Deeken, H., Wiemann, T., Lingemann, K., Hertzberg, J.: SEMAP-a semantic environment mapping framework. In: 2015 European Conference on Mobile Rrobots (ECMR), pp. 1–6. IEEE (2015)
10. Estel, S., et al.: 62. Deutsche Pflanzenschutztagung ; Online-Veranstaltung ; 2021.09.21-23: Der produktionsmittel-anwendungs-managers (pam) – ein exemplarisches beispiel für verteilte internetbasierter dienste in der digitalen landwirtschaft (2021). https://doi.org/10.5073/20210721-093221, https://www.openagrar.de/receive/openagrar_mods_00074078
11. Hodgson, R., Mekonnen, D., Price, D., Hodges, J.E.M., Cox, S.J.D., Ray, S.: Quantities, units, dimensions and types (QUDT) schema (2025). http://qudt.org/doc/2025/05/DOC_SCHEMA-QUDT.html, topQuadrant Inc
12. Igelbrink, F., et al.: Online knowledge integration for 3D semantic mapping: a survey. arXiv preprint arXiv:2411.18147 (2024)
13. Janowicz, K., Haller, A., Cox, S.J., Le Phuoc, D., Lefrançois, M.: SOSA: a lightweight ontology for sensors, observations, samples, and actuators. J. Web Semant. **56**, 1–10 (2019)

14. Joo, S., et al.: A flexible semantic ontological model framework and its application to robotic navigation in large dynamic environments. Electronics **11**(15), 2420 (2022)
15. Ju, C., Kim, J., Seol, J., Son, H.I.: A review on multirobot systems in agriculture. Comput. Electron. Agric. **202**, 107336 (2022)
16. Kuntke, F., Kaufhold, M.A., Linsner, S., Reuter, C.: GeoBox: design and evaluation of a tool for resilient and decentralised data management in agriculture. Behav. Inf. Technol. **43**(4), 764–786 (2024)
17. Leroux, C., et al.: Geofis: an open source, decision-support tool for precision agriculture data. Agriculture **8**(6), 73 (2018)
18. Manzoor, S., et al.: Ontology-based knowledge representation in robotic systems: a survey oriented toward applications. Appl. Sci. **11**(10), 4324 (2021)
19. Moysiadis, V., Tsolakis, N., Katikaridis, D., Sørensen, C.G., Pearson, S., Bochtis, D.: Mobile robotics in agricultural operations: a narrative review on planning aspects. Appl. Sci. **10**(10), 3453 (2020)
20. Mugnier, M.L., Thomazo, M.: An introduction to ontology-based query answering with existential rules. In: Reasoning Web. Reasoning on the Web in the Big Data Era: 10th International Summer School 2014, Athens, Greece, September 8-13, 2014. Proceedings 10, pp. 245–278 (2014)
21. Palma, R., et al.: Agricultural information model. In: Information and Communication Technologies for Agriculture—Theme III: Decision, pp. 3–36. Springer (2022)
22. San Emeterio de la Parte, M., Lana Serrano, S., Muriel Elduayen, M., Martínez-Ortega, J.F.: Spatio-temporal semantic data model for precision agriculture IoT networks. Agriculture **13**(2), 360 (2023)
23. Poggi, A., Lembo, D., Calvanese, D., De Giacomo, G., Lenzerini, M., Rosati, R.: Linking data to ontologies. J. Data Seman. X, 133–173. Springer (2008)
24. Razak, S.F.A., Yogarayan, S., Sayeed, M.S., Derafi, M.: Agriculture 5.0 and explainable ai for smart agriculture: a scoping review. Emerging Sci. J. **8**(2), 744–760 (2024)
25. Renz, J., Nebel, B.: Qualitative spatial reasoning using constraint calculi. In: Handbook of spatial logics, pp. 161–215. Springer (2007)
26. Scheiber, M., et al.: Pflanzenschutz-anwendungs-manager (pam): Automatisierte berücksichtigung von abstandsauflagen. praktische vorführung und feldtestergebnisse. In: Informatik in der Land-, Forst-und Ernährungswirtschaft 2016, pp. 177–180. Gesellschaft für Informatik eV (2016)
27. Shams, M.Y., Gamel, S.A., Talaat, F.M.: Enhancing crop recommendation systems with explainable artificial intelligence: a study on agricultural decision-making. Neural Comput. Appl. **36**(11), 5695–5714 (2024)
28. Tenorth, M., Beetz, M.: Knowrob—knowledge processing for autonomous personal robots. In: 2009 IEEE/RSJ International Conference on Intelligent Robots and Systems, pp. 4261–4266. IEEE (2009)
29. Wisnubhadra, I., Kamal Baharin, S.S., Herman, N.S.: Open spatiotemporal data warehouse for agriculture production analytics. Int. J. Intell. Eng. Syst. **13**(6) (2020)

SPARQL in N3: SPARQL CONSTRUCT as a Rule Language for the Semantic Web

Dörthe Arndt[1,2(✉)], William Van Woensel[3], and Dominik Tomaszuk[4]

[1] Computational Logic Group, Technische Universität Dresden, Dresden, Germany
[2] ScaDS.AI, Dresden/Leipzig, Germany
doerthe_arndt@tu-dresde.de
[3] Telfer School of Management, University of Ottawa, Ottawa, Canada
[4] University of Bialystok, Bialystok, Poland

Abstract. Reasoning in the Semantic Web (SW) commonly uses Description Logics (DL) via OWL2 DL ontologies, or SWRL for variables and Horn clauses. The Rule Interchange Format (RIF) offers more expressive rules but is defined outside RDF and rarely adopted. For querying, SPARQL is a well-established standard operating directly on RDF triples. We leverage SPARQL CONSTRUCT queries as logic rules, enabling (1) an expressive, familiar SW rule language, and (2) general recursion, where queries can act on the results of others. We translate these queries to the Notation3 Logic (N3) rule language, allowing use of existing reasoning machinery with forward and backward chaining. Targeting a one-to-one queryrule mapping improves exchangeability and interpretability. Benchmarks indicate competitive performance, aiming to advance the potential of rule-based reasoning in the SW.

Keywords: SPARQL · Notation3 · Rule-based reasoning

1 Introduction

In our experience, most reasoning on the Semantic Web (SW) relies on Description Logics (DL) in the form of OWL2 DL [26] ontologies. DL is less expressive than first-order logic, and expressing the desired (e.g., rule-based) logic can be challenging. SWRL [24] extends OWL interpretations with variables and Horn-like rules, but operates on OWL rather than RDF, and cannot generate blank nodes. The more expressive Rule Interchange Format (RIF) offers 3 dialects to cover the different needs of rule systems. However, it is defined outside of the RDF data model, and is, to the best of our knowledge, not widely adopted. We thus argue that the potential of logic SW reasoning has not been realized.

On the other hand, when it comes to querying RDF data, SPARQL [19] is an expressive and well-established standard, with native support for RDF triples. Notably, since SPARQL CONSTRUCT queries are closed, i.e., RDF graphs are used as both input and output, they can be used to represent logical rules: if the WHERE clause holds, then the query template can be inferred. The expressivity and popularity of SPARQL can be leveraged to express logic rules on the SW. Moreover, this adds general recursion in SPARQL: i.e., when executed as rules, CONSTRUCT queries can operate on the results of other CONSTRUCT queries. In this work, we support SPARQL 1.1 query patterns, filters, and the SELECT and CONSTRUCT forms.

Others have proposed using SPARQL as a logic rule language. Two types of approaches exist: (a) translating SPARQL into a non-SW logic rule language, namely Datalog [3,18,29], so that rule engines can be used for reasoning; and (b) extending an existing query engine with reasoning capabilities [25,31]. However, Datalog does not follow SW principles; and while query engines allow dealing with large datasets and many joins, they lack backward reasoning capabilities.

We propose a translation of SPARQL into the Notation3 (N3) [13,37] logic rule language, called SiN3 (SPARQL-in-N3). This allows leveraging the existing rule machinery (eye [38], cwm [12], jen3 [36]) for implementing backward and forward reasoning. Moreover, as N3 follows SW principles, translations are not restricted to local use and can be exchanged on the SW. A "runtime" set of rules, which is novel in the literature on SPARQL to rule translation, allows (1) translating a single query into a single rule, which makes it easier to exchange, and even manually tweak, translations; and even (2) a true cross-fertilization, by also allowing SPARQL features to be used in N3. To illustrate its meta-reasoning capabilities, we used N3 itself to translate from a triple-based SPARQL (SPIN [25]) to N3 rules. Our evaluation shows a competitive performance for our preliminary work. A demo paper was previously published about this work [6].

Contributions. (1) We translate SPARQL into the SW-compliant N3 rule language; (2) In doing so, we add general recursion to SPARQL, a feature that is still lacking [3,31]; (3) We provide correctness results for our mapping; (4) We evaluate and compare our approach to other similar systems, using large datasets from the literature. As far as we know, this is the first effort to translate SPARQL into a SW rule language, with a one-to-one mapping between queries and rules.

Paper Organization. Sect. 2 introduces the overall idea of our approach. Section 3 discusses related work. Sections 4 and 5 explain SPARQL, and N3, respectively. Section 6 describes our translation of SPARQL queries into N3 rules, including complex constructs and runtime rules. Section 7 evaluates the performance of our method. Finally, Sect. 8 concludes the paper.

All formal proofs are provided in the online appendix accompanying this paper [9], the code for the technical experiments is available on github [8].

2 Motivation

To motivate our choice for logic rule language, we provide examples of SPARQL and N3 which illustrate how closely these two frameworks are related.

SPARQL and N3 both operate on RDF triples like for example:[1]

$$\text{:John a :Researcher.} \tag{1}$$

---
[1] For brevity, we omit prefixes if they are not relevant or well-known.

With SPARQL we can query for patterns on sets of triples and retrieve variable bindings (SELECT) or create new graphs (CONSTRUCT). Applying the query

$$\text{CONSTRUCT } \{?x \text{ a :Person . }\} \text{ WHERE } \{?x \text{ a :Researcher . }\} \qquad (2)$$

on a graph containing triple 1 results in:

$$:\text{John a :Person.} \qquad (3)$$

Since a new graph is being constructed from the original graph, this is comparable to the application of the following N3 rule

$$\{?x \text{ a :Researcher .}\} \Rightarrow \{?x \text{ a :Person .}\} \qquad (4)$$

where => is a logical implication; the conclusion (second clause) is inferred if the premise holds (first clause). Applying rule 4 on triple 1 also yields triple 3.

An important difference between executing rule 4 and query 2, however, is that N3 applies rules recursively: triple 3 becomes part of the knowledge, and other rules can be applied on this derivation. In contrast to that, SPARQL is a query language and only produces triple 3 to provide it as output to the user.

When choosing a logic rule language, the close relation in terms of syntax between SPARQL and N3 makes the latter a good candidate: users coming from SPARQL, while they will likely not be N3 experts, will be better able to understand and—if needed—tweak the N3 translation. To further facilitate such manual editing, as well as the exchange of translations on the Web, we translate each query to exactly one N3 rule. Users can also combine these rules with existing, "native" N3 rules from other sources to suit their needs (e.g., OWL2 RL [17], OWL-P [34] and L2 [16] inferencing).

3 Related Work

Below, we review approaches that utilize SPARQL to perform reasoning.

3.1 SPARQL Translation to Rule Languages

Polleres [29] first translated SPARQL into Datalog, with negation as failure based on Answer Set Programming (ASP). It allows blank node-free CONSTRUCT queries to act as a recursive rule language over RDF. Gottlob et al. [18] target general recursion in SPARQL by developing TriQ-Lite 1.0 based on Warded $Datalog^{\exists,\neg sg,\perp}$. The authors translate SPARQL queries under the OWL2 QL entailment regime into TriQ-Lite 1.0. Angles et al. [5] present SparqLog, a SPARQL translation engine built on Vadalog [11]. Similar to Gottlob et al., they rely on Warded Datalog, and both support OWL2 QL entailment. However, recursive querying is not directly supported; queries are translated using overlapping predicate names, and without referring to the results of other queries.

In general, we point out that Datalog does not follow SW principles, such as the use of IRIs for resource identification, and using triples as atomic formulas. Hence, translations are not easily exchangeable, and there is an impedance mismatch as RDF triples first need to be translated into predicates.

3.2 Extensions to SPARQL Engines

Reutter et al. [31] propose recSPARQL, which introduces a fixed-point operator, similar to the one from SQL:1999, into SPARQL. Using CONSTRUCT queries, a temporal graph is iteratively populated until reaching the least fixed point (forward reasoning). The authors focus on CONSTRUCT queries without blank nodes in the template part, and require them to have fixed points. A restriction to linear recursion [31] means an iteration can only rely on the original data and triples from the prior iteration. The system was implemented on top of Apache Jena [4] (ARQ module). SPIN [25] (SPARQL Inferencing Notation) allows representing rules and constraints in RDF using SPARQL. The spinrdf [2] library supports reasoning with SPARQL CONSTRUCT queries, It also uses a fixed point (forward reasoning) algorithm and is also implemented on top of Apache Jena.

Hogan et al. [23] introduce SPARQAL, which combines graph querying with analytical operations, including DO...WHILE loops. Corby et al. [15] extend SPARQL with LDScript, an imperative language that introduces functions and loops. While these loops may allow for recursion on query results, it requires an imperative extension that we consider outside the scope of this paper. Atzori et al. [10] propose a SPARQL function for resolving recursive expressions.

4 SPARQL

In this section, we give a short introduction to the main features of SPARQL. Our definitions follow the work of Pérez et al. [28] and extend them to accommodate the features introduced in SPARQL 1.1, drawing on related works [30,32]. A more detailed introduction can be found there.

4.1 Syntax

Atomic terms in SPARQL are taken from the sets I, B, L, and V, representing IRIs, Blank Nodes, RDF literals, and Variables, respectively. A filter condition R is a (logical) formula which depends on a (possibly empty) set of atomic terms. The set of filter conditions contains the formulas $\top$ (true) and $\bot$ (false).

We recursively define the set GP of graph patterns as follows:
(1) If $P \subset (I \cup L \cup V) \times (I \cup V) \times (I \cup L \cup V)$, then $P \in GP$. We call P a Basic Graph Pattern (BGP)[2],
(2) If $P, P_1, P_2 \in GP$ and R is a filter condition, then:

- AND(P_1, P_2), UNION(P_1, P_2), MINUS$(P_1, P_2) \in GP$
- FE(P_1, P_2), FNE$(P_1, P_2) \in GP$,
- OPT$(P_1, P_2, R) \in GP$,
- FILTER$(P, R) \in GP$.

---

[2] In practice, BGPs also allow blank nodes in subject and object position. We omit them here to keep the semantics concise. Note that our translation in Sect. 6.1 also works if we allow blank nodes in BGPs as these are locally scoped in N3.

Note that we define FILTER EXISTS (FE) and FILTER NOT EXISTS (FNE) as separate graph patterns even though they are special cases of the FILTER condition. This is because their evaluation depends on both the variable bindings and the graph the query is evaluated against, while all other filter conditions only depend on the former [19, Section 17.4.1.4]. We still assume that the translation form concrete SPARQL syntax into the algebra [19, Section 18.2] treats FE and FNE as filters when producing the algebra expression OPT for the OPTIONAL operator. Here, we also remind the reader that if there is no FILTER condition occuring on the second argument of an OPTIONAL expression in conrete syntax, $\top$ is added as filter argument during the translation.

4.2 Semantics

Let $T = I \cup B \cup L$ be the set of nonvariable terms. The semantics of SPARQL graph patterns rely on partial mappings from V to T. The domain of a mapping μ, denoted $dom(\mu)$, is the set of variables where μ is defined. Two mappings, μ_1 and μ_2, are compatible, written as as $\mu_1 \sim \mu_2$, if, for any $x \in dom(\mu_1) \cap dom(\mu_2)$, $\mu_1(x) = \mu_2(x)$. Below, we consider mappings as sets of pairs and therefore use the union operator $\cup$ to combine them.

Given sets of mappings Ω_1 and Ω_2, we define:

- $\Omega_1 \bowtie \Omega_2 = \{\mu_1 \cup \mu_2 \mid \mu_1 \in \Omega_1, \mu_2 \in \Omega_2 \text{ and } \mu_1 \sim \mu_2\}$,
- $\Omega_1 \cup \Omega_2 = \{\mu \mid \mu \in \Omega_1 \text{ or } \mu \in \Omega_2\}$,
- $\Omega_1 \setminus_M \Omega_2 = \{\mu \in \Omega_1 \mid \text{for all } \mu' \in \Omega_2 : \mu \not\sim \mu' \text{ or } dom(\mu) \cap dom(\mu') = \emptyset\}$.

We apply a mapping μ to a BGP or filter condition Q, denoted by $Q\mu$, by replacing all variables $v \in dom(\mu)$ occurring in Q by $\mu(v)$. If $R\mu = \top$ for a filter condition R and a mapping μ, we also write $\mu \models R$

Evaluation of SPARQL Graph Patterns. The evaluation of graph patterns over an RDF graph G produces a set of mappings. The function $[\![P]\!]_G$ denotes the evaluation of a graph pattern P on G, and is defined as follows:

(1) If P is a BGP, then $[\![P]\!]_G = \{\mu \mid dom(\mu) = var(P) \text{ and } P\mu \subseteq G\}$,
(2) If P is AND(P_1, P_2), then $[\![P]\!]_G = [\![P_1]\!]_G \bowtie [\![P_2]\!]_G$,
(3) If P is OPT(P_1, P_2, R), then

$$[\![P]\!]_G = \{\mu_1 \cup \mu_2 \mid \mu_1 \in [\![P_1]\!]_G, \mu_2 \in [\![P_2]\!]_G, \mu_1 \sim \mu_2 \text{ and } \mu_1 \cup \mu_2 \models R\}$$
$$\cup \{\mu_1 \in [\![P_1]\!]_G \mid \nexists \mu_2 \in [\![P_2]\!]_G, \mu_1 \sim \mu_2 \text{ and } \mu_1 \cup \mu_2 \models R\},$$

(4) If P is UNION (P_1, P_2), then $[\![P]\!]_G = [\![P_1]\!]_G \cup [\![P_2]\!]_G$,
(5) If P is MINUS (P_1, P_2), then $[\![P]\!]_G = [\![P_1]\!]_G \setminus_M [\![P_2]\!]_G$,
(6) If P is FE (P_1, P_2), then $[\![P]\!]_G = \{\mu \in [\![P_1]\!]_G \mid [\![P_2\mu]\!]_G \neq \emptyset\}$,[3]
(7) If P is FNE (P_1, P_2), then $[\![P]\!]_G = \{\mu \in [\![P_1]\!]_G \mid [\![P_2\mu]\!]_G = \emptyset\}$,

---
[3] Note that in our definition, the term $[\![P_2\mu]\!]_G$ in the evaluation of FE and FNE could be undefined as μ could map variables occurring in P_2 to blank nodes which we excluded. In that case we treat the blank nodes as constants. Here, we deviate from SPARQL 1.1 [19] to address the known issues related to the EXISTS pattern [1].

(8) If P is FILTER (P_1, R), then $[\![P]\!]_G = \{\mu \in [\![P_1]\!]_G \mid \mu \vDash R\}$.

The domain of a solution mapping is called its scope [33, 18.2.1]. As the definitions later in this paper will rely on it, we formally introduce it and define the function sv which retrieves the scope of each query pattern.

Let $var : GP \to 2^V$ be a function which maps a graph pattern to the set of variables occurring in it. The function $sv : GP \to 2^V$ is defined as follows:

(1) If P is a BGP t, then $sv(P) = var(t)$,
(2) If $P = X(P_1, P_2)$, with $X \in \{\text{AND}, \text{UNION}\}$ then $sv(P) = sv(P_1) \cup sv(P_2)$,
(3) If $P = \text{OPT}(P_1, P_2, R)$, then $sv(P) = sv(P_1) \cup sv(P_2)$
(4) If $P = X(P_1, P_2)$, with $X \in \{\text{MINUS}, \text{FE}, \text{FNE}\}$ then $sv(P) = sv(P_1)$,
(5) If $P = \text{FILTER } (P_1, R)$, then $sv(P) = sv(P_1)$.

Evaluation of SPARQL Queries. SPARQL queries normally also come with a query form, that is, a query is written as

$$(n\ x) \text{ WHERE } P$$

where P is a graph pattern and the pair (n, x), called query form, consists of a name $n \in \{\text{SELECT}, \text{CONSTRUCT}\}$, and argument x. The latter is either a list of variables or an asterisk if $n = \text{SELECT}$, or a pattern $Q \subset (I \cup L \cup V \cup B) \times (I \cup V) \times (I \cup L \cup V \cup B)$, if $n = \text{CONSTRUCT}$. For all $\mu \in [\![P]\!]_G$ the evaluation of SELECT retrieves the variable bindings, the evaluation of CONSTRUCT retrieves instantiated version $Q\mu$ of Q, where $Q\mu$ stands for the pattern retrieved by replacing each x occurring in Q by $\mu(x)$ and each blank node b by a blank node b_μ such that b_μ does not occur in G and $b_\mu \neq b'_\mu$ if $b \neq b'$.

With the current definition, it can happen, that μ leaves variables in Q unbound. This is the case if Q contains "new" variables, that is if $var(Q) \setminus sv(P) \neq \emptyset$, or if Q contains variables which are instantiated through an OPT pattern which sometimes does not retrieve a result. For the former case, the SPARQL query does not lead to a result - for the remainder of the paper we exclude this case from our considerations[4] - in the latter case, we assume that unbound variables will be replaced by a term indicating their unboundness (in our concrete implementation that will be a special kind of blank node).

5 Reasoning in N3

This section focuses on the aspects of Notation3 Logic relevant for this paper, and refers to the full specification provided by the W3C community group [37].

5.1 Syntax

The syntax of SPARQL and N3 is closely related (Sect. 2). In fact, BGPs can be directly used as premises and conclusions of N3 rules, but N3 allows for extra patterns. We thus define N3 Graph Pattern (N3GP) as an extension of BGP.

Given the sets I, B, L, and V, representing IRIs, Blank Nodes, RDF literals, and Variables, respectively, we define the set $T_{N3} := AT \cup GT \cup LT$ of N3 terms:

---

[4] Note that we can easily check before evaluation whether $var(Q) \setminus sv(P) = \emptyset$.

- $AT := I \cup B \cup L \cup V$ is the set of *atomic terms*,
- $GT := \{G \mid G \in N3GP\}$ is the set of *graph terms* (N3GP is defined below),
- $LT := \{(t_1, \ldots, t_n) \mid n \geq 0, t_1, \ldots, t_n \in T_{N3}\}$ is the set of *list terms*.

We call a tuple of form $T_{N3} \times T_{N3} \times T_{N3}$ an *N3 triple*. An *N3 graph pattern* (N3GP) is a finite set of N3 triples. Note that $BGP \subset N3GP$.

We call graph terms *closed* if they, and their possibly nested subgraphs, do not contain variables, and denote their set by GT_c. If lists, and their possible nested sublists, only contain elements of $I \cup L \cup GT_c$, we call them *closed*. We denote the set of closed lists by LT_c and define the set of closed terms as $T_c := I \cup L \cup GT_c \cup L_c$. We call a set of *closed* triples $G \subset T_c \times T_c \times T_c$ a *closed* graph.

5.2 Semantics

As the syntax reveals, N3 is rather expressive as it supports lists and graph terms. We present a simplified version of its semantics, focusing on the aspects relevant to this work (see the Community Group Report [7] for more details).

Base Semantics. N3 semantics extends RDF simple entailment [21]. Given a closed N3 graph, N3's basic interpretation function $\mathfrak{I}$ maps closed terms into the domain of discourse. The domain of discourse contains normalised syntactic representations of graph terms and canonical representations of lists, and $\mathfrak{I}$ maps graph terms and lists to their representations. For all other ground terms, it corresponds to RDF's interpretation function I. Relations are interpreted using RDF's function $IEXT$ and a triple $\langle t_1, t_2, t_3 \rangle$ is true iff $(\mathfrak{I}(t_1), \mathfrak{I}(t_3)) \in IEXT(\mathfrak{I}(t_2))$. A closed graph is true iff all its triples are true.

Closed triples are those which are not (implicitly) quantified on the graph level. They are the N3 counterpart of the RDF graphs containing blank nodes. To interpret non-closed N3 graph patterns, we rely on mappings for blank nodes and variables. In N3, these mappings can be seen as a mixture of RDF's mapping function A, which maps blank nodes to the domain of discourse, and the variable mappings found in the SPARQL semantics (Sect. 4.2). We use mappings of the form $A : X \to D \times T_c$, where $X \subseteq B$ or $X \subseteq V$, and D is the domain of discourse and T_c as defined before. For each $A(x) = (A_1(x), A_2(x))$, we have $\mathfrak{I}(A_2(x)) = A_1(x)$. If a variable is found in a graph term, or any of its nested subgraphs, then it is first grounded using $A_2(x)$ and then the resulting closed graph is interpreted. Otherwise, A_1 is used to directly map the variable into the domain of discourse. Variables are universally quantified and blank nodes are existentially quantified. With some exceptions we will discuss later the scope of variables is global, the scope of blank nodes is local to the graph term. If a triple or graph g is true under $\mathfrak{I}$, we also write $\mathfrak{I} \models_b g$. We further write $\mathfrak{I}[A]$ for the interpretation that uses a mapping A to interpret variables or blank nodes.

Log Semantics. Logical operations like impl in N3 are expressed by built-in predicates, whose special meaning is not covered by the base semantics. For the logical built-in predicates which we collect in the set LP we define the log semantics as an extension of base semantics.

We say that an interpretation $\mathfrak{I}$ is log model for a graph g, written as $\mathfrak{I} \models_l g$, iff $\mathfrak{I} \models_b g$ and for each triple $\langle s, p, o \rangle \in g$ with $p \in LP$, the triple fulfills extra conditions which depend on the particular p. We give these conditions for the predicate impl. $\mathfrak{I} \models_l \langle s, \text{impl}, o \rangle$ iff (**1**) $\mathfrak{I} \models_b \langle s, \text{impl}, o \rangle$, and (**2**) if for $A: V \to D \times T_c$ it holds that $\mathfrak{I}[A] \models_b \langle s, \text{impl}, o \rangle$ and $\mathfrak{I}[A](s), \mathfrak{I}[A](o) \in GT$ then $\mathfrak{I}[A] \models_l o$ if $\mathfrak{I}[A] \models_l s$.

The semantics of the other built-in predicates is defined in a similar way. We only list those which are relevant for this work. For the predicate log:includes (or "incl" for brevity) we have that $\mathfrak{I} \models_l \langle s, \text{incl}, o \rangle$ if $\mathfrak{I} \models_b \langle s, \text{incl}, o \rangle$ and if for $A: V \to D \times T_c$ it holds that $\mathfrak{I}[A] \models_b \langle s, \text{incl}, o \rangle$ and $\mathfrak{I}[A](s), \mathfrak{I}[A](o) \in GT$ then there exists a mapping μ from the blank nodes occurring in o to $T_C \cup B$ such that $\mathfrak{I}[A](o)\mu \subseteq \mathfrak{I}[A](s)$. The predicate has one peculiarity: if $\langle s, \text{incl}, o \rangle$ occurs in an asserted triple and s or o are graph terms containing variables, then these variables are treated as blank nodes. If the triple occurs in the premise of a rule and s or o are graph terms containing variables which do not occur anywhere else in the same rule, then these variables are as well treated as locally existentially quantified. The base interpretation will map the graph term containing these local variables to a normalised representation where these are replaced by blank nodes. For incl, we have a special case if the subject of the triple is not specified. If we write $\langle \_, \text{incl}, o \rangle^5$, subject gets instantiated by the deductive closure $close(F)$ of the input graph F, that is by a graph term containing all triples which can be derive from F (note that in N3 the input graph also includes the rules). $\mathfrak{I} \models_l \langle \_, \text{incl}, o \rangle$ if $\mathfrak{I} \models_b \langle close(F), \text{incl}, o \rangle$ and if for $A: V \to D \times T_c$ it holds that $\mathfrak{I}[A] \models_b \langle close(F), \text{incl}, o \rangle$ and $\mathfrak{I}[A](o) \in GT$ then there exists a mapping μ from the blank nodes occurring in o to $T_C \cup B$ such that $\mathfrak{I}[A](o)\mu \subseteq close(F)$.[6] In short that means that $\mathfrak{I}[A](o)$ can be derived from F. $\mathfrak{I} \models_l \langle s, \text{notIncl}, o \rangle$ iff $\mathfrak{I} \not\models_l \langle s, \text{incl}, o \rangle$. N3 furthermore contains predicates to produce a copy of a graph term with renamed variables (log:copy, "copy" for brevity), e.g., $\{\langle ?x, p, o \rangle\}$ becomes $\{\langle ?x_{new}, p, o \rangle\}$ and to produce a conjunction, i.e. the union, of two graphs (log:conjunction, "conj" for brevity).

5.3 Forward and Backward Reasoning

Reasoners implement the semantics presented above using different execution strategies; some reasoners (notably EYE [38]) even enable the user to specify how rules will be applied. Forward reasoning presents a bottom-up approach: given a set of initial facts, the reasoner applies rules to infer new conclusions; these are then used as extra input into the rules, leading to more conclusions. This process continues until no other conclusions can be drawn. Backward reasoning is a top-down approach that begins with a given query, such as ?x a :Person. The reasoner searches for rules with conclusions that may satisfy the query, and then

---

[5] In concrete syntax, we would use an arbitrary variable.
[6] Note that N3 does normally not allow for infinite graph terms.

checks whether the premises of those rules hold, by searching for matching facts or other rules with matching conclusions. Here, the process ends if all premises can be matched to facts. While the execution strategies clearly differ, both can be considered equivalent in terms of expressivity. Our evaluation illustrates how backward reasoning can have a distinct benefit in case of large search spaces.

6 From SPARQL to N3

In this section, we define the actual mapping between SPARQL and N3 following the idea presented in Sect. 2. Provided with a query

$$(n\ x)\ \text{WHERE}\ P$$

we define a mapping m from SPARQL graph patterns to N3 graph patterns (Sect. 6.1) and a mapping h from the whole query to N3 graph patterns (Sect. 6.2) such that our translated rule is

$$m(P) \rightarrow h((n\ x), P)$$

With this setup, we ensure that each SPARQL query is represented by one single N3 rule. However, this requires the direct translation of SPARQL concepts to equivalent N3 constructs, which cannot be done for UNION and OPTIONAL. To implement these concepts as N3-native constructs, we require an extra "runtime" set of rules. That is, the translated queries $m(P) \rightarrow h((n\ x), P)$ always need to be combined with a fixed set of rules. We explain these rules in Sect. 6.3. The proofs for the lemmas provided below can be found in our online appendix [9].

6.1 From SPARQL Graph Patterns to N3 Premises

Before proceeding, we need to define an auxiliary function to cope with the MINUS operator. In the SPARQL semantics (Sect. 4.2) this is evaluated as the mapping-difference between the sets of mappings $\Omega_1 \setminus_M \Omega_2 = \{\mu \in \Omega_1 \mid$ for all $\mu' \in \Omega_2 : \mu \not\sim \mu'$ or $\text{dom}(\mu) \cap \text{dom}(\mu') = \emptyset\}$. For our translation, that means that we have to cover two cases: (M1) the solution mappings are not compatible and (M2) the domains of the solution mappings are disjoint.

Regarding MINUS, case (M2) can be easily checked without even knowing the data graph; given $\text{MINUS}(P_1, P_2)$, if the scopes $sv(P_1)$ and $sv(P_2)$ are disjoint, then we can simply proceed with P_1. If they are not disjoint, we need to distinguish between shared and local variables (case (M1)).

To illustrate the complexity of MINUS, we provide an example. In Listing 1 we display a MINUS query with a nested FILTER EXISTS query in its second argument. In our notation from above, the query pattern can be written as $P = \text{MINUS}(\{\langle?x,p,?n\rangle\}, \text{FE}(\{\langle?x,q,?m\rangle, \langle?m,r,?n\rangle\}))$. As the domains of P_1 and P_2 are not disjoint, case (M2) from above is not relevant. To check case (M1), we evaluate the query on graph $G = \{\langle s,p,o\rangle, \langle s,q,a\rangle, \langle a,r,b\rangle\}$. The first argument

```
1  SELECT * WHERE {
2    ?x :p ?n . MINUS { ?x :q ?m . FILTER EXISTS {?m :r ?n}}}
```

Listing 1. Example query demonstrating the behavior of variable scoping for MINUS with a nested FILTER EXISTS.

$P_1 = \{\langle ?x, p, ?n\rangle\}$ of MINUS matches the first triple from G and we get the solution mapping $[\![P_1]\!]_G = \{\{(?x,s), (?n,o)\}\}$. To evaluate the second argument, we first evaluate $P_{2,1} = \{\langle ?x, q, ?m\rangle\}$ and retrieve $[\![P_{2,2}]\!]_G = \{\{(?x,s), (?m,a)\}\}$. Then, we apply the mapping $\mu = \{(?x,s), (?m,a)\}$ on $P_{2,2} = \{\langle ?m, r, ?n\rangle\}$, i.e., $P_{2,2}\mu = \{\langle a, r, ?n\rangle\}$. Next, when evaluating $P_{2,2\mu}$ on the data, triple $\langle a, r, b\rangle$ allows us to unify $?n$ with b, yielding a non-empty solution mapping for this expression and thus $[\![P_2]\!]_G = \{\{(?x,s), (?m,a)\}\}$. As the solution mappings of P_1 and P_2 are compatible, we get $[\![P_{2,2}]\!]_G = \emptyset$.

We observe that, during evaluation, two different values were assigned to the variable $?n$: once with o while evaluating P_1, and once with b while evaluating $P_{2,2\mu}$. This is not a problem in SPARQL, as no actual binding of variables in the second argument of FE (here, $P_{2,2\mu}$) occurs, and there is thus no conflict. However, we aim to translate one SPARQL query to one single N3 rule, and N3 does not allow two different bindings for the same variable in the same premise (the scope of variables is global in N3; Sect. 5.2). We thus have to relabel the second occurrence of variable $?n$. We do that with the function $rl : N3GP \times 2^V \to N3GP$ that relabels all variables found in the first argument, *except* those given as the second argument, by "fresh" variables that neither occur in the first nor second argument. An example relabeling for $P_{2,2}$ is $rl(P_{2,2}, \{?x, ?m\}) = \{\langle ?m, r, ?n_{new}\rangle\}$. Note that this relabeling does not influence the result of the query pattern as $P' = \text{MINUS}(\{\langle ?x,p,?n\rangle\}, \text{FE}(\{\langle ?x,q,?m\rangle\}, \{?m, r, ?n_{new}\}))$ retrieves the exact same bindings as P.

We use scoping and relabeling functions to define our translation function from SPARQL query patterns to N3 graph patterns. Let Q be a graph pattern and let ft a function which translates a filter expression to its N3GP translation. We define the premise mapping $m : GP \to N3P$ recursively as follows:

- if Q is a BGP P, then $m(Q) = P$,
- if Q is $\text{AND}(Q_1, Q_2)$, then $m(Q) = m(Q_1) \cup m(Q_2)$,
- if Q is $\text{OPT}(Q_1, Q_2, R)$, then $m(Q) = \{\langle m(Q_1), \text{opt}, (m(Q_2) \cup ft(R))\rangle\}$,
- if Q is $\text{UNION}(Q_1, Q_2)$, then $m(Q) = \{\langle m(Q_1), \text{union}, m(Q_2)\rangle\}$,
- if Q is $\text{MINUS}(Q_1, Q_2)$, then

$$m(Q) = \begin{cases} m(Q_1), & \text{if } sv(Q_2) \cap sv(Q_1) = \emptyset \\ m(Q_1) \cup \{\langle \_, \text{notIncl}, rl(m(Q_2), (sv(Q_2) \cap sv(Q_1)))\rangle\}, & \text{else,} \end{cases}$$

- if Q is $\text{FNE}(Q_1, Q_2)$, then $m(Q) = m(Q_1) \cup \{\langle \_, \text{notIncl}, m(Q_2)\rangle\}$,
- if Q is $\text{FE}(Q_1, Q_2)$, then $m(Q) = m(Q_1) \cup \{\langle \_, \text{incl}, m(Q_2)\rangle\}$,
- if Q is $\text{FILTER}(Q_1, R)$, then $m(Q) = m(Q_1) \cup ft(R)$.

We do not detail the function ft provided in the above definition because the exact translation depends on the filter element. In most cases, there exist N3 built-in functions that behave identically to SPARQL's filter functions. E.g., the filter expression ?m < ?n becomes the N3 triple ?m math:lessThan ?n.

Note that the translation simply converts UNION and OPTIONAL patterns to corresponding N3 triples with custom "union" and "optional" predicates. For these two predicates, we define our run-time rules (Sect. 6.3).

For the MINUS, note that we relabel all variables in Q_2, *except* for those that occur in the scope of Q_1 and Q_2. Intuitively, we thus only relabel variables that are *not* relevant to the outside, and should thus not conflict with "outside" variables. Coming back to our example from Listing 1, the variables excluded from relabeling are $sv(\langle ?x,p,?n\rangle) \cap sv(\text{FE}(\{\langle ?x,p,?m\rangle,\langle ?x,q,?n\rangle\})) = \{?x,?p\} \cap \{?x,?m\} = \{?x\}$, leading to the application of the relabeling function $rl(m(Q_2),\{?x\})$, i.e., all variables except ?x are relabeled. This ultimately leads to $m(P) = \{\langle ?x,p,?n\rangle, \langle \_, \text{notIncl}, \{\langle ?x,q,?m_{new}\rangle, \langle \_, \text{incl}\langle ?m_{new},r,?n_{new}\rangle\rangle\}\rangle\}$, which solves the issue of multiple bindings per variable in N3.

It still remains to show that the mapping we defined works correctly. We do that for RDF ground graphs which do not contain any built-in IRI of N3. We call these graphs proper RDF graphs, We limit our consideration to ground graphs to avoid extra difficulties with N3's local scoping. Otherwise we could not consider the rule premise in isolation. As the translation function for the filter is out of scope in this paper and the runtime rules for the predicates "opt" and "union" will only be discussed in Sect. 6.3, we rely on the following assumption:

Assumption Given an RDF ground graph G for each mapping $\mu : X \to I \cup L$ we have that $\mu \models R$ iff $G \models_l ft(R)\mu$, $G \models_l m(\text{OPT}(P_1,P_2,R))\mu$ iff $\mu \in [\![\text{OPT}(P_1,P_2,R)]\!]_G$, and $G \models_l m(\text{UNION}(P_1,P_2))\mu$ iff $\mu \in [\![\text{UNION}(P_1,P_2)]\!]_G$.

Under the above assumption we show:

Lemma 1. *Given a proper RDF graph G, a SPARQL graph pattern P, and a mapping $\mu : sv(P) \to I \cup L$, then the following holds:*

$$\mu \in [\![P]\!]_G \text{ iff } G \models_l m(P)\mu.$$

6.2 From Queries to Consequences

Given a SPARQL query $(n\ x)$ WHERE P, we define the function h which takes the query form $f = (n\ x)$ and the SPARQL graph pattern P as input and produces an N3 graph pattern as output.

Let F be the set of query forms and "tl" a function which, provided with a set of variables V, produces an ordered list of these. We define the head function $h : F \times GP \to N3P$ as follows:

$$h(f,P) = \begin{cases} Q, \text{ if } f = (\text{CONSTRUCT},Q), \\ \{\langle \_, \text{result}, l\rangle\}, \text{ if } f = (\text{SELECT},l), \text{ if } l \neq *, \\ \{\langle \_, \text{result}, \text{tl}(sv(P))\rangle\}, \text{ if } f = (\text{SELECT},*). \end{cases}$$

where _ stands for an arbitrary blank node. Note that we use the scoping function sv from above to resolve the asterisk.

For our example query P with its concrete realisation in Listing 1, our mapping produces the consequence[7]

$$h((SELECT, *), P) = \{\langle \_, \text{result}, \text{tl}(sv(P))\rangle\} = \{\langle \_, \text{result}, (?x?n)\rangle\}. \quad (5)$$

Combining the results from applying the functions m and n to the query in Listing 1 we get the following N3 rule as a translation:

$$\{\langle ?x, p, ?n\rangle, \langle \_, \text{notIncl}, \{\langle ?x, q, ?m\rangle, \langle ?m, r, ?n_{new}\rangle\}\rangle\} \rightarrow \langle \_, \text{result}, (?x\ ?n)\rangle$$

We can use Lemma 1 to prove the following:

Lemma 2. *Given a query* (CONSTRUCT Q)WHERE P *and a proper RDF graph* G : *If* $\mu \in \llbracket P \rrbracket_G$, *then* $G \cup \{m(P) \rightarrow h((\text{CONSTRUCT } Q), P)\} \models_l Q\mu$

With the lemma we can apply a single translated rule to a ground RDF graph and obtain the same triples the original query provides. When applying the rules recursively, we rely on N3 semantics. Note that the result can easily be extended to RDF graphs containing blank nodes as N3 rules never change the scoping of blank nodes in plain RDF graphs and these are quantified on graph level.

6.3 SPARQL Concepts in N3

Our goal is to map one SPARQL query to one N3 rule, however, some SPARQL concepts do not have an equivalent N3 construct. To address this mismatch, we introduce a dedicated set of auxiliary *runtime rules*, expressed in native N3, which must be evaluated alongside the translated rules to achieve the intended results. These runtime rules can also be integrated with native N3 rules, providing direct support for SPARQL-specific features such as UNION, OPTIONAL, and property paths within N3; thus providing a true cross-fertilization. We explain the rules for UNION and OPTIONAL below.[8]

For UNION, a single translated N3 rule will include a triple `<a> union <b>`. This triple will be resolved by the following runtime rules:

$$\langle x, \text{union}, y\rangle \leftarrow \langle \_, \text{incl}, x\rangle \qquad \langle x, \text{union}, y\rangle \leftarrow \langle \_, \text{incl}, y\rangle \quad (6)$$

---

[7] In our implementation, the result triple also includes the original SELECT variable names as strings, so query results are returned in a way similar to SPARQL.
[8] To make the assumption in Sect. 6.1 true, we need to provide a proof that the rules work exactly like their corresponding SPARQL pattern. We only provide an explanation here to at least make the rules plausible to the reader. The main reason for omitting the proof is that the rules for OPTIONAL are defined using the predicate copy. This predicate has no model theoretic semantics yet. We plan to provide a formalisation and a proof in future work.

```
SELECT * {
  :x1 :p ?v . OPTIONAL { :x2 :q ?w .
    OPTIONAL { :x3 :p ?v }}}
```

Listing 2. Example query demonstrating the behavior of OPTIONAL.

These rules are evaluated using the subject <a> and object <b> of the union triple, and succeeds if at least one of the corresponding subgoals is satisfied. By that, we mimic disjunction. Note that we also support property paths but consider them out of scope for this paper; we address them in future work.

The rules for OPTIONAL are more complicated. We show them in Fig. 1. As with the MINUS, we illustrate the complexity of the OPTIONAL applying an example query (Listing 2) to a data graph $G = \{\langle x1, p, 1\rangle, \langle x2, q, 2\rangle, \langle x3, p, 3\rangle\}$.

Here, the variable ?v will be bound twice with different values; once with 3 in the most deeply nested OPTIONAL clause, and once with 1 in the mandatory clause. For that reason, SPARQL considers the variable bindings of the mandatory and nested OPTIONAL as non-compatible, and only the former are returned. Similar as with the MINUS, however, N3 does not allow different bindings for the same variable in the same premise. We again solve the problem by relabelling variables: we represent each $X \in N3GP$ as a pair (X_P, X_I), where X_P is the pattern with the original variables, and X_I is a copy of X_P with "fresh" variables to be instantiated. We then use the latter to find matches in the data without variable conflicts. We use the N3 "copy" predicate to create X_I from X_P.

The OPTIONAL in SPARQL is implemented using a nested left join. On the left-hand side, the first rule first invokes the predicate "eval", which retrieves the final pattern (X_P) and instantiation (X_I) of the solution. Here, the next triple with predicate "incl" will instantiate the variables in X_P using the values from X_I[9]. The last two rules with the "unest" predicate deal with nested OPTIONAL clauses, and thus implement the recursive nature of the left join. On the right-hand side, the rules implement the actual left join. Before binding variables, they use the "copy" N3 builtin to create copies X_I of patterns as described above. They further rely on the "incl" and "notIncl" predicates as described earlier. Here, we consider three cases: (1) Solution mappings for both OPTIONAL arguments are compatible and fulfill the filter condition; (2) There is a solution mapping for the first argument, but not for the second; or, the union of both mappings does not fulfill the filter condition; (3) There is no solution mapping for the first argument, in which case an empty solution pattern is retrieved.

7 Evaluation

We implemented the above SPARQL-in-N3 (SiN3) translation and compare its performance with state-of-the-art systems. All code is available on github [8], including an online demo of the Zika screening use case (see below).

---

[9] Note that this predicate thus also binds variables in the argument graphs.

$\langle M, \text{opt}, O \rangle$
$\leftarrow \langle (M, O), \text{eval}, (X_P, X_I) \rangle, \langle X_P, \text{incl}, X_I \rangle$

$\langle (M, O), \text{eval}, (Z_P, Z_I) \rangle$
$\leftarrow \langle M, \text{unest}, (X_P, X_I) \rangle,$
$\langle O, \text{unest}, (Y_P, Y_I) \rangle,$
$\langle ((X_P, X_I), (Y_P, Y_I)) \text{leftjoin}, (Z_P, Z_I) \rangle$

$\langle X, \text{unest}, (Y_P, Y_I) \rangle$
$\leftarrow \langle X, \text{equalTo}, \langle M \text{ opt } O \rangle \rangle,$
$\langle (M, O), \text{eval}, (Y_P, Y_I) \rangle$

$\langle X, \text{unest}, (X, \{\}) \rangle$
$\leftarrow \langle X, \text{notEqualTo}, \langle M \text{ opt } O \rangle \rangle$

$\langle ((M_P, M_I), (O_P, O_I)), \text{leftjoin}, (R_P, R_I) \rangle$
$\leftarrow \langle (M_P, O_P), \text{conj}, R_P \rangle,$
$\langle R_P, \text{copy}, R_I \rangle, \langle \_, \text{incl}, R_I \rangle,$
$\langle R_I, \text{incl}, M_I \rangle, \langle R_I, \text{incl}, O_I \rangle$

$\langle ((M_P, M_I), (O_P, O_I)), \text{leftjoin}, (M_P, R_I) \rangle$
$\leftarrow \langle M_P, \text{copy}, R_I \rangle, \langle \_, \text{incl}, R_I \rangle,$
$\langle (M_P, O_P), \text{conj}, C_P \rangle, \langle C_P, \text{copy}, C_I \rangle,$
$\langle C_I, \text{incl}, R_I \rangle, \langle \_, \text{notIncl}, C_I \rangle$

$\langle ((M_P, M_I), (O_P, O_I)), \text{leftjoin}, (\{\}, \{\}) \rangle$
$\leftarrow \langle \_, \text{notIncl}, M_P \rangle$

Fig. 1. Runtime rules for OPTIONAL.

7.1 Evaluation Setup

Datasets and queries
Our evaluation covers the following use cases:

LMDB and YAGO. We apply a similar setup as recSPARQL [31], which used the *LMDB* (Linked Movie Database), an RDF dataset about movies and actors [20] (6,148,121 triples); and *YAGO* (Yet Another Great Ontology), RDF data including people, locations, and movies [27] (3,000,006 triples). Movie-related recursive CONSTRUCT queries were formulated on both datasets:

Bac1. Searches for actors with a finite "Bacon number", i.e., they co-starred in the same movie with Kevin Bacon or another actor with such a number.

Bac2. Searches for actors with a finite Bacon number whereby all collaborations were done in movies with the same director.

Bac3. Searches for actors connected to Kevin Bacon through movies where the director is also an actor (not necessarily in the same movie).
They further formulated the following queries on the YAGO dataset:

Geo. Searches for places in which the city of Berlin is (transitively) located.

MarrUs. Searches for people who are transitively related to someone through the *isMarriedTo* relation, who owns property within the United States. Hence, these queries mostly calculate the transitive closure of a given relation.

Zika Screening. We base ourselves on a prior healthcare use case on Zika screening [6]. Using CONSTRUCT queries, we implemented the CDC testing guidance for Zika, which determine whether a patient should be tested for Zika, based on a series of factors. We expand on this test case with randomly generated datasets, different versions of the used HL7 FHIR vocabulary [22], and reasoning over a biomedical ontology, i.e., SNOMED [35].

Availability. All datasets and queries are in our git repository [8].

Evaluated Systems
We evaluate our SPARQL-in-N3 translation, labelled *sin3*, using the EYE v10.24.10 reasoner [38], which can perform both forward and backward reasoning. Our prior demo paper [6] outlines the implementation of *sin3*, including

the different execution steps and rulesets involved. We compare with two other systems that utilize CONSTRUCT queries for rule-based reasoning, namely *spinrdf* [2] and *recSPARQL* [31]. The work by Polleres [29] was implemented using an older version of dlvhex which we found to no longer be compatible with modern OS. As far as we know, the work by Gottlob et al. [18] was not implemented; and, as mentioned, the SparqLog [3] does not support recursive querying.

Hardware. The experiments were conducted on a MacBook Pro with an Apple M1 Pro processor, 32 GB of RAM, and a 1 TB SSD, running macOS Sonoma 14.6.1. Each experiment was executed 5 times and results were averaged.

Compliance. Regarding compliance with the SPARQL 1.1 specification [19], we currently lack support for the HAVING clause, named graphs, expressions in BIND and SELECT clauses, and LIMIT clauses in subqueries. We currently support only the CONSTRUCT and SELECT query forms.

7.2 Results

Table 1. Execution times for LMDB and YAGO queries (times in seconds).

Query	sin3				spinrdf			recSPARQL	
	Load	Gen SPIN	Gen N3	Exec	Load	Gen SPIN	Exec	Load (TDB)	Exec
LMDB									
Bac1	31	0.58	0.10	20.1	26.9	0.06	12	75.4	65.7
Bac2		0.58	0.08	2.4		0.02	3.9		18.4
Bac3		0.58	0.08	9.0		0.02	19.5		24.5
YAGO									
Bac1	36.1	0.58	0.08	14.3	44.9	0.02	7.5	113686	50.2
Bac2		0.57	0.08	1.5		0.003	0.01		3.2
Bac3		0.57	0.08	5.0		0.003	2.8		22.4
Geo		0.57	0.07	0.4		0.003	0.004		14.4
MarrUs		0.57	0.08	12.3		0.003	5.1		83.2

We only show and discuss the results for the *LMDB* and *YAGO* experiments for space considerations. Our git repository [8] details the *Zika* experiment.

Both *sin3* and *spinrdf* involve converting input SPARQL queries into SPIN code (Gen SPIN). Subsequently, *sin3* converts the SPIN code into N3 rules (Gen N3). We observe that Gen SPIN takes much longer for *sin3* than *spinrdf*, as the former requires starting a separate JVM for generating SPIN code. *Sin3* and *spinrdf* load the dataset into memory (Load), whereas *recSPARQL* pre-creates a persistent Jena Triple DataBase (Load TDB). *Sin3* is competitive regarding reasoning performance (Exec): for the LMDB dataset, on average, *sin3* takes ca. 10.5 s, *spinrdf* ca. 11.8 s, and recSPARQL ca. 36.2 s. For the Yago dataset, on average, *sin3* takes ca. 6.7 s , *spinrdf* ca. 3.1 s, and recSPARQL ca. 34.7 s. Hence, we note that *spinrdf*, which uses a query engine (Jena), performs much better for the Yago dataset. We revisit this in future work.

A benefit of rule languages is that both forward- and backward reasoning strategies can be used. To illustrate this, we used the Deep Taxonomy (DT)[10], a CONSTRUCT query that implements the OWL2 RL *cax-sco* rule [14], and a custom query requesting all instances of class A2. Backward reasoning has an advantage here, as only a small part of the transitive closure has to be searched; forward reasoning has to materialize the entire transitive closure. Indeed, after translating the OWL2 RL query to a backward-chaining N3 rule, *eye* takes avg. 34 ms, while *spinrdf* does not return results after 1h (results not shown in table).

8 Conclusions

We argue that the full potential of logic reasoning on the SW has not been realized. Given that SPARQL is a well-established standard for SW querying, one way to meet this potential is to use SPARQL CONSTRUCT queries to express logic rules. We implemented reasoning over CONSTRUCT queries by translating them into N3. As N3 natively operates on RDF triples and follows SW principles, translations can be exchanged between parties. Our translation maps 1 query to 1 rule, enabled by the novel concept of "runtime" rules, making the translations easier to exchange and manually tweak. The runtime rules further allow using SPARQL features, namely UNION and OPTIONAL, directly within "vanilla" N3 rules. In fact, in the long term, we foresee the line between N3 and SPARQL syntax becoming blurred, and this translation is a first step in that direction. Our evaluation shows a competitive performance compared to state-of-the-art systems, and the benefits of having both forward and backward reasoning.

Future Work. We aim to implement the missing SPARQL 1.1 features (see Sect. 7.1). We will formalize our translation of property paths and are currently investigating their efficient evaluation, for instance, by generating partially grounded, forward-chaining rules. The experiments showed that our rule translations are at a disadvantage for complex data structures (i.e., requiring many joins). Future work involves the optimization of rule-based reasoning in such a setting; e.g., rule engine optimizations, and combining forward with backward reasoning. Finally, we plan to extend the cross-fertilization between N3 and SPARQL, by supporting SPARQL expressions (e.g., FILTER) in N3 rules.

References

1. SPARQL Exists report. W3C community group report, W3C (2019). https://w3c.github.io/sparql-exists/docs/sparql-exists.html
2. Andy Seaborne, M.J.: Spinrdf (2019). https://github.com/spinrdf/spinrdf

---

[10] https://eulersharp.sourceforge.net/2009/12dtb/.

3. Angles, R., Gottlob, G., Pavlovic, A., Pichler, R., Sallinger, E.: SparqLog: a system for efficient evaluation of SPARQL 1.1 queries via datalog. Proc. VLDB Endow. **16**(13), 4240–4253 (2023). https://www.vldb.org/pvldb/vol16/p4240-sallinger.pdf
4. Apache: Apache Jena (2021). https://jena.apache.org/
5. Arenas, M., Gottlob, G., Pieris, A.: Expressive languages for querying the semantic web. ACM Trans. Database Syst. **43**(3) (2018). https://doi.org/10.1145/3238304
6. Arndt, D., Van Woensel, W., Tomaszuk, D.: SiN3: scalable inferencing with SPARQL CONSTRUCT queries. In: Fundulaki, I., Kozaki, K., Garijo, D., Gómez-Pérez, J.M. (eds.) Proceedings of the ISWC 2023 Posters, Demos and Industry Tracks: From Novel Ideas to Industrial Practice co-located with 22nd International Semantic Web Conference (ISWC 2023), Athens, Greece, November 6-10, 2023. CEUR Workshop Proceedings, vol. 3632. CEUR-WS.org (2023). https://ceur-ws.org/Vol-3632/ISWC2023_paper_469.pdf
7. Arndt, D., Champin, P.A.: Notation3 semantics. W3C community group report, W3C (2023). https://w3c.github.io/N3/reports/20230703/semantics.html
8. Arndt, D., Van Woensel, W., Tomaszuk, D.: SPARQL in N3 github repository. https://github.com/domel/research-paper-2025
9. Arndt, D., Van Woensel, W., Tomaszuk, D.: SPARQL in N3: SPARQL construct as a rule language for the semantic web (extended version). https://doi.org/10.48550/arXiv.2508.13041
10. Atzori, M.: Computing recursive SPARQL queries. In: 2014 IEEE International Conference on Semantic Computing, pp. 258–259. IEEE (2014)
11. Bellomarini, L., Sallinger, E., Gottlob, G.: The vadalog system: datalog-based reasoning for knowledge graphs. Proc. VLDB Endow. **11**(9), 975–987 (2018). https://doi.org/10.14778/3213880.3213888
12. Berners-Lee, T.: Cwm (2000–2009). http://www.w3.org/2000/10/swap/doc/cwm.html
13. Berners-Lee, T., Connolly, D., Kagal, L., Scharf, Y., Hendler, J.: N3Logic: a logical framework for the World Wide Web. Theory Pract. Logic Program. **8**(3), 249–269 (2008). https://doi.org/10.1017/S1471068407003213
14. Calvanese, D., et al.: OWL2 web ontology language profiles (second edition): OWL2 RL. W3c recommendation, W3C (2012). https://www.w3.org/TR/2012/REC-owl2-profiles-20121211/
15. Corby, O., Faron-Zucker, C., Gandon, F.: LDScript: a linked data script language. In: International Semantic Web Conference, pp. 208–224. Springer (2017)
16. Fischer, F., Unel, G., Bishop, B., Fensel, D.: Towards a scalable, pragmatic knowledge representation language for the web. In: Perspectives of Systems Informatics: 7th International Andrei Ershov Memorial Conference, PSI 2009, Novosibirsk, Russia, June 15-19, 2009. Revised Papers 7, pp. 124–134. Springer (2010)
17. Fokoue, A., Horrocks, I., Motik, B., Grau, B.C., Wu, Z.: OWL 2 web ontology language profiles (second edition). W3C recommendation, W3C (2012), https://www.w3.org/TR/2012/REC-owl2-profiles-20121211/
18. Gottlob, G., Pieris, A.: Beyond SPARQL under OWL 2 QL entailment regime: Rules to the rescue. In: Twenty-Fourth International Joint Conference on Artificial Intelligence (2015)
19. Harris, S., Seaborne, A.: SPARQL 1.1 query language. W3C recommendation, W3C (2013). https://www.w3.org/TR/2013/REC-sparql11-query-20130321/
20. Hassanzadeh, O., Consens, M.P.: Linked movie data base. In: LDOW (2009)
21. Hayes, P., Patel-Schneider, P.F.: RDF 1.1 Semantics. W3c recommendation, W3C (2014). https://www.w3.org/TR/rdf11-mt/

22. HL7 International: HL7 Fast Health Interop Resources (FHIR). https://www.hl7.org/index.cfm
23. Hogan, A., Reutter, J., Soto, A.: Recursive SPARQL for graph analytics. arXiv preprint arXiv:2004.01816 (2020)
24. Horrocks, I., Patel-Schneider, P.F., Boley, H., Tabet, S., Grosof, B., Dean, M.: SWRL: a semantic web rule language combining owl and ruleml. Tech. rep., W3C (2004). https://www.w3.org/submissions/SWRL/
25. Knublauch, H., Hendler, J.A., Idehen, K.: SPIN - overview and motivation. https://www.w3.org/submissions/spin-overview/
26. Motik, B., Patel-Schneider, P., Grau, B.C.: OWL 2 web ontology language direct semantics (second edition). W3C recommendation, W3C (2012). https://www.w3.org/TR/2012/REC-owl2-direct-semantics-20121211/
27. Pellissier Tanon, T., Weikum, G., Suchanek, F.: YAGO 4: a reason-able knowledge base. In: Harth, A., et al. (eds.) ESWC 2020. LNCS, vol. 12123, pp. 583–596. Springer, Cham (2020). https://doi.org/10.1007/978-3-030-49461-2_34
28. Pérez, J., Arenas, M., Gutierrez, C.: Semantics and complexity of SPARQL. ACM Trans. Database Syst. (TODS) **34**(3), 1–45 (2009)
29. Polleres, A.: From SPARQL to rules (and back). In: Proceedings of the 16th International Conference on World Wide Web, pp. 787–796 (2007)
30. Polleres, A., Wallner, J.P.: On the relation between SPARQL 1.1 and answer set programming. J. Appl. Non-Classical Logics **23**(1-2), 159–212 (2013)
31. Reutter, J., Soto, A., Vrgoč, D.: Recursion in SPARQL. Seman. Web **12**(5), 711–740 (2021)
32. Salas, J., Hogan, A.: Semantics and canonicalisation of SPARQL 1.1. Seman. Web **13**(5), 829–893 (2022)
33. SPARQL Working Group: SPARQL 1.1 Query Language (2013). https://www.w3.org/TR/sparql11-query
34. Tomaszuk, D.: Inference rules for OWL-P in n3logic. In: FedCSIS (Communication Papers), pp. 27–33 (2018)
35. U.S. National Library of Medicine: SNOMED CT. https://www.nlm.nih.gov/healthit/snomedct/index.html
36. Van Woensel, W.: Jen3. https://github.com/william-vw/jen3
37. Van Woensel, W., Arndt, D., Champin, P.A., Tomaszuk, D., Kellogg, G.: Notation3 language. W3C community group report, W3C (2023). https://w3c.github.io/N3/reports/20230703/
38. Verborgh, R., De Roo, J.: Drawing conclusions from linked data on the web: the EYE reasoner. IEEE Softw. **32**(5), 23–27 (2015)

Positioning LLM-Enabled Agents as Legal Compliance Aides for Data Pipelines

Adela Nedisan Videsjorden[1(✉)], Nikolay Nikolov[1], Carl-Henrik Lien[2], Arda Goknil[1,3], Sagar Sen[1], Hui Song[1], Ahmet Soylu[4,6], and Dumitru Roman[1,5]

[1] SINTEF Digital, Oslo, Norway
adela.videsjorden@sintef.no
[2] University of Oslo, Oslo, Norway
[3] Oslo Metropolitan University, Oslo, Norway
[4] Kristiania University of Applied Sciences, Oslo, Norway
[5] Bucharest University of Economic Studies, Bucharest, Romania
[6] Seoul National University, Seoul, South Korea

Abstract. Ensuring the legal compliance of data pipelines with evolving EU legislation, such as the AI Act, presents a significant challenge due to the complexity of both technical infrastructures and regulatory texts. This paper explores the potential of Large Language Models (LLMs) to support automated compliance assessment of data pipelines, and proposes an approach that leverages LLM-based agents to extract, label, and assess data pipeline artifacts against relevant legal requirements, guided by the actor's role and the system's risk level. By decomposing the assessment process into modular agent tasks, we mitigate token limitations and enable fine-grained analysis of regulatory obligations. The approach is supported by a prototype implementation that integrates outputs from SIM-PIPE, a tool for simulating and analyzing big data pipelines, with a structured interpretation of the regulatory document, e.g., the AI Act. The implementation demonstrates the feasibility of intelligent, scalable compliance auditing and highlights key challenges related to trust, context interpretation, and output validity. We argue that such LLM-powered tools can play a critical role in advancing compliance-by-design practices for legally aligned data-driven systems.

Keywords: Legal Compliance · Large Language Models · Data Pipelines · Legal Automation · Agent-Based Reasoning

1 Introduction

The regulation of AI and large-scale data processing systems has become a critical focus in the European Union's digital strategy. With the adoption of the Artificial Intelligence Act (AI Act) [3], the EU has introduced a comprehensive legal framework that imposes explicit requirements on AI systems and their underlying data pipelines, particularly those categorized as high-risk. These requirements span a wide range of obligations, from data governance, transparency, and traceability to human oversight, accuracy, and cybersecurity. When taken together with existing regulations, such as the General Data Protection Regulation (GDPR) [1] and the Data Governance Act (DGA) [2], the legal landscape for AI development and deployment is both ambitious and complex.

At the same time, data- and AI-enabled systems increasingly rely on automated, distributed, and heterogeneous data pipelines [9,10] to ingest, transform, and model vast quantities of data. These pipelines often span multiple services, tools, and infrastructure layers, making them difficult to trace, audit, or align with legal requirements. The dynamic nature of such systems further complicates regulatory enforcement: compliance is no longer a static certification step but a continuous obligation that must be monitored and maintained across the system's lifecycle. Ensuring legal compliance in this context is a multidisciplinary challenge, requiring tight coordination between legal experts, software engineers, data scientists, and system architects. In practice, however, this coordination is often lacking. Legal norms are written in natural language and require interpretation in light of specific technical artifacts and deployment contexts. Engineers, on the other hand, may lack the legal expertise to determine which system components are subject to which legal provisions. The result is a costly and error-prone process where compliance checks are reactive, fragmented, and difficult to scale. Manual audits are inefficient for modern AI pipelines, and static checklists quickly become obsolete in evolving systems.

This paper argues that Large Language Models (LLMs), as typically used for language understanding, reasoning over structured inputs, and bridging knowledge domains, offer a promising foundation for addressing this gap. Specifically, we explore how LLMs can be used to automate key aspects of compliance analysis by interpreting legal texts and evaluating whether a given data pipeline provides the necessary documentation, controls, or evidence required by regulation. In this context we outline an agent-based approach in which multiple LLM agents collaborate to evaluate the compliance of a data pipeline against relevant regulatory requirements. The core idea is to combine outputs from a data pipeline simulations with a structured representation of regulatory document, and to orchestrate a set of LLM-based agents that perform a modular, article-by-article compliance evaluation.

Besides motivating the need for scalable legal compliance solutions, this paper highlights key challenges, limitations, and future research directions for integrating LLM-based approaches for data pipelines compliance (Sect. 2), and contributes with an LLM-enabled agents approach for compliance of data pipelines, supported by a proof of concept prototype (Sect. 3). While this approach remains at an experimental level, it illustrates the feasibility of using LLMs to support regulatory reasoning and compliance auditing. It also raises important questions about the trustworthiness, validity, and governance of LLM-driven legal assessments, highlighting the need for future work on validation strategies, human-in-the-loop mechanisms, and robust error-handling to ensure reliability and accountability in high-stakes legal contexts (Sect. 4). Finally Sect. 5 provides a summary and outlook.

2 Legal and Technical Context for Automating Data Pipeline Audits

The automation of compliance audits for data pipelines requires a solid understanding of both the legal frameworks that govern AI systems and the technical characteristics of the infrastructures being audited. This section outlines the regulatory obligations introduced by the EU and the structural and operational complexities of modern data pipelines that challenge compliance efforts. It also introduces the potential of LLMs and agent-based decomposition as enabling technologies for scalable, intelligent compliance assessments. We also introduce SIM-PIPE [13], a simulation framework used to model and analyze data pipelines, which generates the technical artifacts for compliance assessment in our proposed approach.

2.1 Legal Landscape for AI and Data Pipelines in the EU

The European Union has introduced a comprehensive regulatory framework to govern AI and data-intensive systems, with key instruments including the AI Act, GDPR, the DGA, and the Data Act. These regulations impose detailed obligations on AI systems, especially those classified as high-risk, such as those used in healthcare, infrastructure, or law enforcement.

The AI Act introduces a risk-based classification and mandates that high-risk systems comply with requirements for data governance, risk management, documentation, human oversight, and robustness. These obligations apply across the entire data pipeline, not just the AI model. Furthermore, the AI Act differentiates responsibilities based on actor roles, providers, deployers, and others, with specific duties ranging from documentation to post-deployment monitoring.

The GDPR continues to govern personal data usage, requiring principles such as data minimization and accountability. The DGA and Data Act further promote secure, fair, and ethical data sharing and access, especially in cross-border and cross-sectoral contexts.

Together, these instruments emphasize a compliance-by-design approach, requiring legal obligations to be embedded within the system development lifecycle. However, translating legal provisions into actionable, system-specific checks is complex, especially for distributed and evolving data pipelines. This challenge underscores the need for automated and intelligent compliance tools, motivating the use of LLMs to bridge legal and technical domains.

2.2 Characteristics and Challenges of Data Pipelines

Modern AI systems and data-driven applications rely heavily on *data pipelines*, automated sequences of processes that extract, transform, move, and load data across various components. These pipelines serve as the operational backbone for tasks such as data cleaning, feature extraction, model training, monitoring, and inference. In large-scale systems, data pipelines are *distributed, heterogeneous, and highly dynamic*, often spanning multiple tools, environments, and organizational boundaries.

Typical data pipelines consist of multiple interconnected stages, including data ingestion from sensors or APIs, preprocessing and transformation through cleaning and normalization routines, model integration, and output dissemination to downstream services or users. Each stage may be implemented using different technologies (e.g., Spark, Kafka, Docker, Kubernetes), deployed in different environments (e.g., cloud, edge, on-premises), and maintained by different teams. This heterogeneity increases both complexity and opacity, making it difficult to reason about the pipeline as a coherent whole.

Their *complexity and dynamism* pose significant challenges for regulatory compliance. Artifacts relevant to legal obligations, such as logs, configurations, and documentation, are often scattered and poorly integrated. Pipelines evolve rapidly, leading to *outdated or incomplete compliance evidence*, and runtime behaviors such as scaling or versioning complicate traceability. Legal accountability is further fragmented across roles (e.g., data providers, pipeline developers, deployers), each with distinct responsibilities under regulations like the AI Act and GDPR. Ensuring compliance requires a holistic view of the entire pipeline, not just the AI model.

Addressing these challenges requires tools that can *automatically extract, structure, and interpret pipeline artifacts in alignment with legal requirements*. Such capabilities are essential for enabling scalable, regulation-aware development of AI systems.

2.3 Large Language Models for Compliance Reasoning

LLMs such as GPT and BERT have shown significant potential in legal and compliance tasks, including legal document analysis, contract review, and regulatory compliance checking [6,12]. These models excel at parsing complex legal language, identifying relevant clauses, and mapping unstructured text to formal requirements. Key advantages for compliance reasoning include:

- *Requirement extraction and mapping:* LLMs can automatically identify and classify legal obligations within dense regulatory texts and relate them to specific artifacts or policy documents.
- *Structured output through prompting:* With techniques like few-shot learning and chain-of-thought prompting, LLMs can be guided to produce structured assessments, e.g., listing regulatory requirements and marking whether they are met [5,6,14].
- *Hybrid semantic-graph approaches:* Advanced systems combine vector-based retrieval with knowledge graphs to support traceable reasoning and reduce hallucinations, crucial for compliance accuracy.

However, such forms of compliance reasoning come with notable limitations:

- LLMs are prone to hallucination or generating outputs without real grounding, which poses a risk in legal auditing [14].

- Their reasoning tends to rely on semantic pattern matching, lacking deeper principled reasoning needed for legal rigor [14,16].

Recent research introduced purpose-built compliance LLMs, such as LegiLM [16], which is fine-tuned on GDPR datasets and achieves high accuracy in identifying regulatory breaches and offering legal explanations. However, best practice emphasizes combining careful prompt engineering, agentic orchestration, and human oversight to mitigate limitations and ensure reliability [4,8,14].

2.4 Agent-Based Decomposition for Managing LLM Context Limitations

LLMs are increasingly used in complex reasoning tasks, but their effectiveness is often constrained by *context window limitations*. Most LLMs can only process a fixed number of tokens at a time, making it difficult to handle long documents, multi-step tasks, or system-level compliance assessments that require integrating information from many sources. This limitation is particularly problematic in regulatory contexts, where legal texts and system artifacts are both long and structurally complex.

One emerging solution is to decompose such tasks into smaller subtasks handled by specialized LLM agents, each operating within a constrained context. This approach enables scalable processing of long-context inputs by dividing responsibility among multiple agents and coordinating their outputs through structured workflows. The Chain-of-Agents (CoA) framework proposed by Zhang et al. [15] demonstrates how multiple LLM agents can collaborate to process long-context tasks by dividing the input into segments and assigning each agent a distinct portion to analyze. A manager agent then synthesizes their outputs into a coherent final answer. This strategy improves performance on tasks such as long-document question answering, summarization, and code reasoning. Similarly, ReadAgent, introduced by Lee et al. [7], mimics human reading by creating "gist memories" of document segments, allowing an agent to navigate and recall information efficiently while keeping the context manageable. It shows strong results across multiple reading comprehension benchmarks.

These studies demonstrate that agent-based decomposition is a viable and increasingly adopted strategy for overcoming context length constraints in LLM applications. It allows for modular reasoning, traceability, and scalability, making it especially suitable for legally grounded tasks like compliance auditing, where structured outputs and interpretability are essential.

2.5 SIM-PIPE for Data Pipeline Simulation and Artifact Extraction

SIM-PIPE [13] is a dry-run testing and simulation tool designed to evaluate container-based big data pipelines in isolated environments prior to deployment. Developed to address the high cost and complexity of testing pipelines on production infrastructure, SIM-PIPE executes each pipeline step sequentially using representative sample data in a sandbox environment. It collects resource usage metrics, e.g., CPU, memory, and execution time, for each step, enabling developers to analyze performance bottlenecks and functional correctness without relying on historical execution data or expensive infrastructure.

The tool supports pipelines defined using a domain-specific language (DSL) and encapsulates each processing step in a software container, ensuring portability and reproducibility across Edge-Cloud infrastructures. SIM-PIPE outputs logs, resource profiles, and intermediate artifacts for each pipeline step, which can be repurposed for system diagnostics, deployment planning, and, critically in our case, legal compliance assessment. By generating structured, labeled artifacts, SIM-PIPE serves as a bridge between pipeline execution and downstream compliance analysis using LLM-based agents.

3 Our Approach: LLM-Orchestrated Compliance Auditing with SIM-PIPE

We present an experimental agent-based approach in which multiple LLM agents collaborate to evaluate the compliance of a data pipeline against relevant regulatory requirements. Our approach, illustrated in Fig. 1, integrates legal and technical inputs to determine whether a given data pipeline meets the obligations of regulatory document, e.g., AI Act. It takes two primary inputs:

- The *full text of the regulatory document*, parsed into a machine-readable dictionary of articles and annexes.
- The *output generated by SIM-PIPE*, which simulates the pipeline and collects artifacts related to execution, resource usage, and data flow.

A modular, agent-based architecture is employed to traverse these inputs step by step, minimizing context overload while ensuring granular compliance checks:

- *Artefact structuring:* An agent parses the deployment configuration and functional and performance evaluations, extracts all technical outputs, and labels them semantically (e.g., "training data", "logging configuration", etc.).
- *Article filtering:* Based on the manually specified risk level and actor role (e.g., pipeline provider or deployer), the system selects a subset of applicable provisions (articles) from the regulatory framework.
- *Information requirement inference:* For each relevant article, an agent determines what information would be required from the pipeline artifacts to verify compliance.
- *Gap analysis:* Another agent compares the required information to the available artifacts, identifying missing elements and annotating them with references to specific provisions (e.g., "(9.1) No evidence of a documented risk management system").
- *Compliance assessment:* A final set of agents evaluates each article individually, assessing whether the pipeline satisfies the corresponding legal requirement using the mapped artifacts.

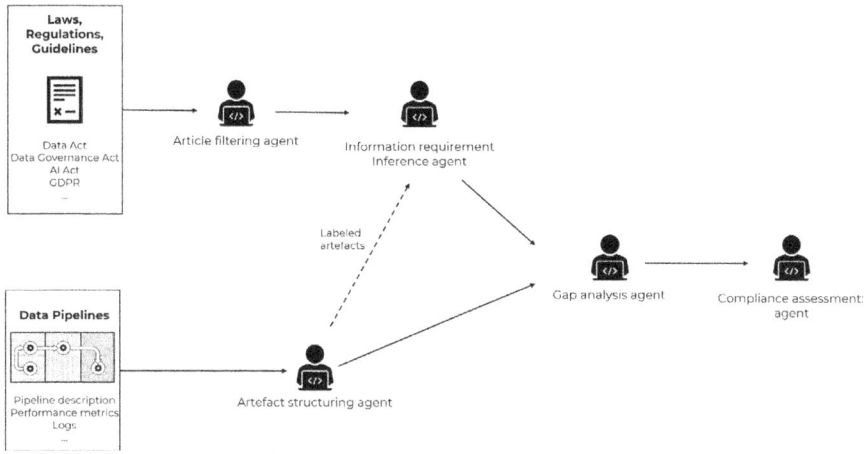

Fig. 1. LLM-enabled compliance workflow. Artefacts produced by SIM-PIPE's deployment simulation are evaluated against a dictionary of provisions by an LLM agent system, yielding a structured compliance assessment for the data pipeline.

A key advantage of this modular, agentic architecture is that it mitigates *context length limitations*, a major constraint in LLMs, by decomposing the compliance task into sequential, interpretable subtasks. Each agent operates on a focused slice of the overall process, allowing the system to scale to larger pipelines and legal corpora without overwhelming the model context.

3.1 Artifact Extraction and Structuring

The process begins with an agent that recursively traverses the SIM-PIPE output directory. All relevant artifacts, such as configuration files, logs, metrics, and step outputs. Are parsed and stored in a structured Python dictionary. The agent organizes and semantically labels each artifact (e.g., "training_data", "pipeline_log", "risk_analysis_output"), providing a standardized representation of the technical evidence base.

3.2 Legal Scope Identification

Before proceeding with compliance checks, the user specifies the risk level of the system (e.g., high-risk) and the actor role (e.g., provider or deployer). Based on this input, the system filters regulatory document to extract only the relevant articles for the specified context. This step ensures that compliance is evaluated only against applicable obligations.

3.3 Information Requirement Inference

For each selected article, an agent reads its content and generates a list of required information elements necessary to assess compliance. For example, Article 9 may require evidence of a documented risk management system, while Article 10 demands traceability of training data and data governance practices.

3.4 Gap Analysis

Another agent performs a gap analysis by comparing the list of required elements to the available artifacts (each truncated to 1000 characters to stay within context limits). For each missing or incomplete requirement, the system annotates the output with a reference to the specific legal provision (e.g., "(10.2) No evidence of dataset bias monitoring").

This step is essential for identifying missing documentation or implementation gaps that prevent a full compliance assessment. It can also guide organizations in improving their documentation or tooling.

3.5 Article-by-Article Compliance Evaluation

For each relevant article, the system spawns a dedicated agent to perform an in-depth assessment. The agent matches labeled artifacts to the legal content of the article and reasons whether the artifact supports, contradicts, or fails to address the compliance requirement. Assessments are recorded in a structured format and linked to their corresponding legal citations. This modular, article-specific assessment strategy improves scalability and traceability, enabling targeted re-evaluation when specific parts of the pipeline are updated.

3.6 Output and Traceability

The final output consists of a structured compliance report indicating (i) which articles were assessed, (ii) which requirements were fulfilled or missing, (iii) which artifacts were used as evidence, and (iv) where additional documentation is required. This report can support internal audits, external reviews, and documentation for regulatory filings.

4 Future Directions and Research Opportunities

This work lays the foundation for leveraging agent-based LLM systems to support legal compliance auditing of data pipelines, but several promising directions remain for further development and exploration.

One critical avenue is the *scalability of the approach*, especially in handling complex legal texts and increasingly elaborate data pipeline configurations. As the volume of legal documentation and pipeline metadata grows, the coordination between LLM agents will need to become more efficient. Optimizing agent collaboration to handle larger workloads and enabling parallel reasoning across independent legal provisions may help scale the approach better without compromising accuracy or energy efficiency.

Although our approach leverages LLM agents for legal compliance auditing, we recognize *inherent limitations such as hallucinations and reliance on pattern matching*. To reduce these risks, we design modular agents that separate factual extraction from interpretation. Still, legal applications demand high trust, and our approach would benefit from complementary validation layers, such as rule-based checks or human oversight, to ensure consistency, correctness, and accountability. Future work must prioritize the *development of formal guarantees, uncertainty quantification, majority voting, prompt ensembles, and provenance tracking* to bolster trustworthiness in legal reasoning tasks.

A further direction involves enhancing the *domain-awareness and legal sophistication of the agents*. By incorporating structured legal knowledge (such as ontologies, taxonomies of regulatory obligations, or precedent-based reasoning), the system can better contextualize its outputs. This could reduce hallucinations, improve grounding in legal doctrine, and support more nuanced assessments of vague or conditional obligations.

In parallel, attention must be paid to the *explainability, auditability, and transparency* of the agents' decisions. Although LLMs are capable of generating plausible compliance judgments, their black-box nature may limit trust and legal defensibility. Future versions of the framework could combine natural language explanations with symbolic justifications or rule-based validation layers to increase traceability and confidence for legal professionals.

Finally, while this study focuses on the AI Act and its intersection with data pipeline artifacts, *future applications should generalize the method to a wider range of EU and international regulatory frameworks*. These may include the GDPR (for personal data protection), the Data Governance Act (for data access and reuse), the Digital Services Act, and sector-specific standards (e.g., medical, financial, or energy sectors).

5 Outlook

This paper proposed a novel approach for automating the legal compliance assessment of data pipelines by combining simulation outputs from SIM-PIPE with agent-based orchestration of LLMs. The method enables structured, article-level reasoning over regulatory texts and pipeline artifacts, supporting scalable and interpretable compliance audits. By modularizing the assessment process, this approach advances compliance-by-design practices and opens new directions for intelligent, regulation-aware infrastructure, which we will investigate in the DataPACT project [11].

Acknowledgments. The work is funded through the projects DataPACT (HE 101189771), UPCAST (HE 101093216), enRichMyData (HE 101070284), ENFIELD (HE 101120657) INTEND (HE 101135576), CauseFinder (PNRR 760049), and NRF RS-2023-00268071.

References

1. General data protection regulation, regulation - 2016/679 - EN - gdpr - EUR-Lex (2016). https://eur-lex.europa.eu/eli/reg/2016/679/oj
2. Data governance act, regulation - 2022/868 - EN - EUR-Lex (2022). https://eur-lex.europa.eu/eli/reg/2022/868/oj/eng
3. Artificial intelligence act, regulation - EU - 2024/1689 - EN - EUR-Lex (2024). https://eur-lex.europa.eu/eli/reg/2024/1689/oj/eng
4. Ferrag, M.A., Tihanyi, N., Debbah, M.: From LLM reasoning to autonomous AI agents: A comprehensive review. arXiv preprint arXiv:2504.19678 (2025)
5. Guha, N., et al.: LegalBench: a collaboratively built benchmark for measuring legal reasoning in large language models. Adv. Neural. Inf. Process. Syst. **36**, 44123–44279 (2023)
6. Hassani, S., Sabetzadeh, M., Amyot, D., Liao, J.: Rethinking legal compliance automation: opportunities with large language models. In: 2024 IEEE 32nd International Requirements Engineering Conference (RE), pp. 432–440. IEEE (2024)
7. Lee, K.H., Chen, X., Furuta, H., Canny, J., Fischer, I.: A human-inspired reading agent with gist memory of very long contexts. arXiv preprint arXiv:2402.09727 (2024)
8. Li, H., et al.: LegalAgentBench: Evaluating LLM agents in legal domain. arXiv preprint arXiv:2412.17259 (2024)
9. Munappy, A.R., Bosch, J., Olsson, H.H.: Data pipeline management in practice: challenges and opportunities. In: Morisio, M., Torchiano, M., Jedlitschka, A. (eds.) PROFES 2020. LNCS, vol. 12562, pp. 168–184. Springer, Cham (2020). https://doi.org/10.1007/978-3-030-64148-1_11
10. Raj, A., Bosch, J., Olsson, H.H., Wang, T.J.: Modelling data pipelines. In: 2020 46th Euromicro Conference on Software Engineering and Advanced Applications (SEAA), pp. 13–20. IEEE (2020)
11. Roman, D., Konstantinidis, G., Palmonari, M., Musidlowska, M., Prodan, R.: DataPACT: compliance by design of data/AI operations and pipelines. Selected Papers of HybridAIMS and CAI Workshops (2025)
12. Siino, M., Falco, M., Croce, D., Rosso, P.: Exploring LLMs applications in law: A literature review on current legal NLP approaches. IEEE Access (2025)
13. Thomas, A., Nikolov, N., Pultier, A., Roman, D., Elvesæter, B., Soylu, A.: SIMPIPE DryRunner: an approach for testing container-based big data pipelines and generating simulation data. In: 2022 IEEE 46th Annual Computers, Software, and Applications Conference (COMPSAC), pp. 1159–1164. IEEE (2022)
14. Wang, J., et al.: LLM-based HSE compliance assessment: Benchmark, performance, and advancements. arXiv preprint arXiv:2505.22959 (2025)
15. Zhang, Y., Sun, R., Chen, Y., Pfister, T., Zhang, R., Arik, S.: Chain of agents: large language models collaborating on long-context tasks. Adv. Neural. Inf. Process. Syst. **37**, 132208–132237 (2024)
16. Zhu, L., Yang, L., Li, C., Hu, S., Liu, L., Yin, B.: LegiLM: a fine-tuned legal language model for data compliance. arXiv preprint arXiv:2409.13721 (2024)

Learning to Contest Argumentative Claims

Emanuele De Angelis[1]✉, Maurizio Proietti[1], and Francesca Toni[2]

[1] IASI-CNR, Rome, Italy
{emauele.deangelis,maurizio.proietti}@iasi.cnr.it
[2] Imperial College London, London, UK
ft@ic.ac.uk

Abstract. Contestability is a highly desirable property for human-centric AI, ensuring that the outcomes of an AI system can be challenged, and possibly changed, when interacting with humans and/or other AI systems. In this paper we study contestability of *argumentative claims* obtained from Assumption-Based Argumentation (ABA) frameworks, a unifying formalism for various non-monotonic reasoning methods that can be used for explainable AI systems. Specifically, we focus on ABA frameworks that are learnt with *ABA Learning*, a recent approach to symbolic learning from positive and negative examples, given a background knowledge . We formally define a notion of contestation when desirable claims are rejected or undesirable claims are accepted in learnt ABA frameworks. We also show that ABA Learning can be adapted to redress issues raised by contestation so that the desirable claims are accepted and the undesirable claims are rejected. This is naturally achieved by extending the learnt ABA framework without restarting from scratch, and instead preserving as much as possible thereof by considering some of its rules defeasible. We conduct several experiments with a variety of tabular datasets to demonstrate the computational advantages of our *contestable ABA Learning* in comparison with re-learning from scratch.

Keywords: Symbolic learning · Argumentation · Contestability

1 Introduction

As the use of AI in society grows, the need for accountability, safety, security and alignment with human values of AI models also increases. Towards these ends, contestability is perceived by several as a highly desirable property for AI [20], and a crucial functionality for human-centric AI. In a nutshell, contestability amounts to ensuring that the outcomes of AI systems can be challenged, and possibly changed, if these outcomes are deemed inadequate or inappropriate by humans and/or other AI systems. For illustration, an AI system aiding a bank manager to decide on loan applications, may suggest that a specific applicant should not be granted their request if they have had career breaks in recent years;

the manager or the applicant may want to contest the AI system on unfairness grounds, if the applicant's career breaks were due to parental leave.

In this paper, we study the contestability of *argumentative claims* obtained from Assumption-Based Argumentation (ABA) frameworks [1,10,29]. ABA frameworks are systems of *rules* that generalise many non-monotonic, rule-based formalisms, including (non-stratified) logic programs with negation as failure [1, 4,23]. The rules in ABA frameworks may admit *assumptions* amongst their premises. These render the rules defeasible, by means of derivations for the *contraries* of the assumptions. In this setting, an argument is simply a derivation (i.e., a deduction) of a claim (i.e., a sentence) constructed via rules.

Continuing the earlier loan illustration, an ABA framework may include, for applicant jo, rules $loan(jo) \leftarrow employed(jo), nobreaks(jo)$ and $breaks(jo) \leftarrow onleave(jo)$, where $nobreaks(jo)$ is an assumption with contrary $breaks(jo)$, as well as rules (with true premises, i.e., *facts*) $employed(jo) \leftarrow$ and $onleave(jo) \leftarrow$. To determine whether claims are accepted, arguments need to be constructed and defended against attacks, according to some ABA semantics [1,10]. In the illustration, the claim $loan(jo)$ is *not accepted* (i.e., it is *rejected*), no matter which ABA semantics is adopted: an argument for $loan(jo)$ can be constructed from the rules, but it needs to rely upon the assumption $nobreaks(jo)$, and this is attacked by an argument with claim $breaks(jo)$ which cannot be attacked.

Specifically, in this paper we focus on ABA frameworks that are learnt with *ABA Learning* [6,7,22,28], a recent approach to symbolic learning from positive and negative examples (e.g., about applicants who received or not a loan in the past), given a background knowledge (e.g., knowledge about applicants). We formally define a notion of *contestation* when given desirable claims are rejected or given undesirable claims are accepted in learnt ABA frameworks. We also define a notion of *redress* of issues raised by contestation so that given desirable claims are accepted and undesirable claims are rejected. The notions of contestation and redress take into account the positive and negative examples that led to the learnt ABA framework and that still need to be accepted and rejected, respectively. Redress can be naturally achieved by extending the learnt ABA framework without restarting from scratch, and instead preserving as much as possible thereof while considering some of its rules defeasible.

Overall, we make the following contributions: (1) we define novel notions of contestation and redress in the context of ABA Learning (Sect. 3); (2) we define algorithmic counterparts of these notions, based on a modification of the forms of ABA Learning studied in [6,7] (Sect. 4); (3) we implement our algorithms as part of the ABALearn tool; and (4) we conduct several experiments with a variety of tabular datasets to demonstrate the computational advantages of our *contestable ABA Learning* in comparison with re-learning from scratch.

Related Work. The need for contestable AI is advocated by several (e.g., see the recent survey in [20]) but only a handful of algorithmic solutions exist. Amongst these, [25] propose a novel approach to fine tune neural models when they are contested on the basis of having learnt causal dependencies deemed inappropriate by subject matter experts. Furthermore, [11] develop an argumentation-based model for contestable AI, but focusing on verification of claims in natural language with large language models and based on argumentation frameworks and semantics of a different kind than for ABA. Both [11] and our work in this paper align with the vision of [20], also adopted by [8], that argumentation should play a crucial role in achieving contestable AI.

In [20], three forms of contestability are identified, for a given AI model M: (1) outputs by M for individual inputs are deemed undesirable, e.g., $y = M(x)$ for input x is deemed the wrong classification; (2) how M determines outputs for specific inputs is deemed undesirable, e.g., the way M uses a particular rule is deemed inappropriate; and (3) the full model M is contested without reference to any specific input, e.g., a rule in M could be the object of contestation. In this paper we focus on case (1) only, leaving the other two to future work.

Several other approaches to symbolic learning exist, besides ABA Learning that we rely upon. Some of these other approaches are also based on argumentation [3,9,14], while others [16,27,30] are based on learning exceptions to defeasible rules (via negation-as-failure) similarly to the case of ABA learning (which however uses assumptions). Other approaches to symbolic learning are based on abductive reasoning [15], which is closely related to the use of assumptions similarly to ABA, or answer set programming (ASP) [18,19,26], which is related to ABA as some forms of ASP can be mapped to ABA frameworks, and ASP can be used to determine acceptability of claims in ABA as we do in ABA Learning [6]. None of these approaches accommodates (forms of) contestability.

Amongst symbolic learning systems, IncrementalLAS [17] can be seen as accommodating a form of contestability (also of the first kind) by seeing learning as an incremental process. A formal and empirical comparison between our approach and IncrementalLAS requires a formal mapping between their learning and contestability problems and is thus left to future work.

2 Background

2.1 Assumption-Based Argumentation (ABA)

An *ABA framework* (as originally proposed in [1], but presented here following [4,10,29]) is a tuple $\langle \mathcal{L}, \mathcal{R}, \mathcal{A}, \overline{} \rangle$ such that:

- $\langle \mathcal{L}, \mathcal{R} \rangle$ is a deductive system, where $\mathcal{L}$ is a *language* and $\mathcal{R}$ is a set of *(inference) rules* of the form $s_0 \leftarrow s_1, \ldots, s_m$ ($m \geq 0, s_i \in \mathcal{L}$, for $1 \leq i \leq m$);
- $\mathcal{A} \subseteq \mathcal{L}$ is a (non-empty) set of *assumptions*;[1]
- $\overline{}$ is a *total mapping* from $\mathcal{A}$ to $\mathcal{L}$, where $\overline{a}$ is the *contrary* of a, for $a \in \mathcal{A}$ (also denoted as $\{a \mapsto \overline{a} \mid a \in \mathcal{A}\}$).

Given a rule $s_0 \leftarrow s_1, \ldots, s_m$, s_0 is the *head* and $s_1, \ldots, s_m$ is the *body*; if $m=0$ then the rule is called a *fact* (represented as $s_0 \leftarrow$). In this paper, we focus on

---

[1] The non-emptiness requirement can always be satisfied by including in $\mathcal{A}$ a *bogus assumption*, with its own contrary, neither occurring elsewhere [29].

flat ABA frameworks, where assumptions are not heads of rules[2]. Elements of $\mathcal{L}$ can be any sentences, but in this paper we focus on ABA frameworks where $\mathcal{L}$ is a finite set of ground atoms. However, we will use *schemata* for rules, assumptions and contraries, using variables, similarly to logic programs, to represent compactly all instances over some underlying universe $\mathcal{U}$. In particular, we will write a fact $p(a) \leftarrow$, with a a tuple of constants, as $p(X) \leftarrow X = a$, with X a tuple of variables.

Example 1. The following ABA framework $\langle \mathcal{L}, \mathcal{R}, \mathcal{A}, \overline{} \rangle$ represents the strategy used by a bank for granting loans: a loan is approved if the applicant has been employed for a certain period without breaks. Let the universe $\mathcal{U}$ be the set $\{$ *jo, bob, claudia, diana*$\}$ of constants.

$\mathcal{L} = \{loan(X), employed(X), nobreaks(X), breaks(X), onleave(X) \mid X \in \mathcal{U}\}$
$\mathcal{R} = \mathcal{R}_1 \cup \mathcal{R}_2$ where[3]
  $\mathcal{R}_1 = \{\rho_1.\ employed(X) \leftarrow X = jo, \quad \rho_2.\ employed(X) \leftarrow X = bob,$
      $\rho_3.\ employed(X) \leftarrow X = claudia,$
      $\rho_4.\ onleave(X) \leftarrow X = jo, \quad \rho_5.\ onleave(X) \leftarrow X = bob,$
      $\rho_6.\ maternity(X) \leftarrow X = jo, \quad \rho_7.\ maternity(X) \leftarrow X = diana\}$
  $\mathcal{R}_2 = \{\rho_8.\ loan(X) \leftarrow employed(X), nobreaks(X),$
      $\rho_9.\ breaks(X) \leftarrow onleave(X) \mid X \in \mathcal{U}\}$
$\mathcal{A} = \{nobreaks(X) \mid X \in \mathcal{U}\}$
$\overline{nobreaks(X)} = breaks(X)$, for all $X \in \mathcal{U}$.

where the assumption $nobreaks(X)$ renders rule ρ_8 defeasible: the rule can be applied only if $breaks(X)$ cannot be derived.

In the remainder, by $vars(E)$ we denote the set of variables occurring in atom, rule, or rule body E (e.g. $vars(onleave(X) \leftarrow X = jo) = \{X\}$). We will assume that variables range over the universe $\mathcal{U}$ of the individual constants occurring in $\mathcal{L}$, without, however, mentioning $\mathcal{U}$ explicitly. We will also often leave $\mathcal{L}$ implicit, and use $\langle \mathcal{R}, \mathcal{A}, \overline{} \rangle$ to stand for $\langle \mathcal{L}, \mathcal{R}, \mathcal{A}, \overline{} \rangle$.

In this paper, the semantics of (flat) ABA frameworks (to determine accepted/rejected claims) is given by *stable extensions*, defined below for arguments and attacks as follows [4,10,29]:

- An *argument* for (the claim) $s \in \mathcal{L}$ *supported by* $A \subseteq \mathcal{A}$ and $R \subseteq \mathcal{R}$ (denoted $A \vdash_R s$, or simply $A \vdash s$, when R is immaterial) is a finite tree with nodes labelled by sentences in $\mathcal{L}$ or by *true*, the root labelled by s, leaves either *true* or from A, and non-leaves s' with, as children, the elements of the body of some rule in R with head s' (and all rules in R are used in the tree).
- Argument $A_1 \vdash_{R_1} s_1$ *attacks* argument $A_2 \vdash_{R_2} s_2$ iff $s_1 = \overline{a}$ for some $a \in A_2$.

Let $Args$ be the set of all arguments and $Att = \{(\beta, \gamma) \in Args \times Args \mid \beta$ attacks $\gamma\}$, for 'arguments' and 'attacks' defined as above. Then, $\Delta \subseteq Args$ is a *stable extension* iff (i) $\nexists \beta, \gamma \in \Delta$ such that $(\beta, \gamma) \in Att$ (i.e. Δ is *conflict-free*) and (ii)

---

[2] Flat ABA frameworks of the form considered here can be mapped onto logic programs, where assumptions are replaced by the negation as failure of their contraries.
[3] We use identifiers ($\rho_1, \ldots, \rho_9$ in the example) for rules, for ease of reference.

$\forall \gamma \in Args \setminus \Delta, \exists \beta \in \Delta$ such that $(\beta, \gamma) \in Att$ (i.e. Δ "attacks" all arguments it does not contain, thus pre-emptively "defending" itself against attacks).

We say that an ABA framework is *satisfiable* if it admits at least one stable extension, and *unsatisfiable* otherwise. We will write $\langle \mathcal{R}, \mathcal{A}, \overline{} \rangle \models_\Delta s$ to denote that Δ is a stable extension of $\langle \mathcal{R}, \mathcal{A}, \overline{} \rangle$ and $s \in \mathcal{L}$ is the claim of an argument in Δ; we also say that s is a *credulous consequence* of $\langle \mathcal{R}, \mathcal{A}, \overline{} \rangle$.

Example 2. Given the ABA framework presented in Example 1, we can construct, amongst others, the following arguments:

β_1: $\{nobreaks(jo)\} \vdash loan(jo)$
β_2: $\{nobreaks(bob)\} \vdash loan(bob)$
β_3: $\{nobreaks(claudia)\} \vdash loan(claudia)$
β_4: $\emptyset \vdash breaks(jo)$
β_5: $\emptyset \vdash breaks(bob)$

Arguments β_1, β_2 are attacked by arguments β_4, β_5, respectively. β_3 is not attacked by any argument. The unique stable extension of the ABA framework of Example 1 contains $\beta_3, \beta_4, \beta_5$, but not β_1, β_2 (and thus the claims $loan(jo)$ and $loan(bob)$ are rejected while claim $loan(claudia)$ is accepted).

2.2 ABA Learning via Transformation Rules

We define the problem of learning an ABA framework from a *background knowledge* (i.e., any satisfiable ABA framework), and *positive and negative examples*, following [6,7,22]. By $pred(E)$ we denote the set of predicate symbols occurring in E, where E is an atom, a rule, a set thereof, or an ABA framework.

Definition 1. *Given a satisfiable background knowledge $F = \langle \mathcal{R}, \mathcal{A}, \overline{} \rangle$, positive examples $\mathcal{E}^+$ and negative examples $\mathcal{E}^-$, with $\mathcal{E}^+ \cup \mathcal{E}^- \subseteq \mathcal{L}$ and $\mathcal{E}^+ \cap \mathcal{E}^- = \emptyset$, and a set $\mathcal{T}$ of learnable predicates, with $\mathcal{T} \cap pred(\mathcal{A}) = \emptyset$[4] and $pred(\mathcal{E}^+ \cup \mathcal{E}^-) \subseteq \mathcal{T}$, the goal of (credulous, a.k.a. brave) ABA Learning is to construct $F' = \langle \mathcal{R}', \mathcal{A}', \overline{}' \rangle$ such that: (i) $\mathcal{R} \subseteq \mathcal{R}'$, (ii) for each $H \leftarrow B \in \mathcal{R}' \setminus \mathcal{R}$, $pred(H) \cap pred(F) \subseteq \mathcal{T}$, (iii) $\mathcal{A} \subseteq \mathcal{A}'$, (iv) $\overline{\alpha}' = \overline{\alpha}$ for all $\alpha \in \mathcal{A}$, (v) F' is satisfiable and admits a stable extension Δ, such that:*

1. *for all $e \in \mathcal{E}^+$, $F' \models_\Delta e$, i.e., all positive examples are covered in Δ*
2. *for all $e \in \mathcal{E}^-$, $F' \not\models_\Delta e$, i.e., no negative example is covered in Δ.*

F' is called a solution based on Δ *of the ABA Learning problem $(F, \langle \mathcal{E}^+, \mathcal{E}^- \rangle, \mathcal{T})$ (we also say that F' credulously entails $\langle \mathcal{E}^+, \mathcal{E}^- \rangle$). A solution F' is* intensional *when $\mathcal{R}' \setminus \mathcal{R}$ is made out of rule schemata without any occurrence of individual constants in the universe $\mathcal{U}$.*

Intensionality is a notion that captures the generality of a rule, as it enforces that the rule makes no explicit reference to the underlying universe.

---
[4] Recall that we consider flat ABA frameworks, and thus an assumption cannot appear in the head of a learnt rule.

To solve ABA learning problems, we follow an approach based on the following *transformation rules* [22] .

R1. Rote Learning. Given atom $p(t) \in \mathcal{L}$, with $p \in \mathcal{T}$, add $\rho \colon p(X) \leftarrow X = t$ to $\mathcal{R}$. Thus, $\mathcal{R}' = \mathcal{R} \cup \{\rho\}$.

We can use R1 either to add facts from positive examples or facts for contraries of assumptions.

R2. Folding. Given distinct rules $\rho_1 \colon H \leftarrow B_1, B_2$ and $\rho_2 \colon K \leftarrow Eqs, B_1$, where Eqs are equalities with $vars(Eqs) \cap vars(H \leftarrow B_2) = \emptyset$, replace ρ_1 by $\rho_3 \colon H \leftarrow Eqs, K, B_2$. Thus, $\mathcal{R}' = (\mathcal{R} \setminus \{\rho_1\}) \cup \{\rho_3\}$.

We can use R2 to generalise the body of a rule.

R3. Assumption Introduction. Replace $\rho_1 \colon H \leftarrow B$ in $\mathcal{R}$ by $\rho_2 \colon H \leftarrow B, \alpha(X)$, where X is a tuple of variables in ρ_1 and $\alpha(X)$ is a (possibly new) assumption with contrary $c\_\alpha(X)$. Thus, $\mathcal{R}' = (\mathcal{R} \setminus \{\rho_1\}) \cup \{\rho_2\}$, $\mathcal{A}' = \mathcal{A} \cup \{\alpha(X)\}$, $\overline{\alpha(X)}' = c\_\alpha(X)$, and $\overline{\beta}' = \overline{\beta}$ for all $\beta \in \mathcal{A}$.

R3 can be used to render a rule defeasible and introduces a contrary that defines the exceptions to that rule.

R4. Fact Subsumption. Let $\rho \colon p(X) \leftarrow X = t$ be a rule in $\mathcal{R}$ such that $\langle \mathcal{R} \setminus \{\rho\}, \mathcal{A}, \overline{} \rangle$ credulously entails $\langle \mathcal{E}^+, \mathcal{E}^- \rangle$. Then, $\mathcal{R}' = \mathcal{R} \setminus \{\rho\}$.

Example 3. Let us consider, as background knowledge, $F = \langle \mathcal{R}_1, \mathcal{A}, \overline{} \rangle$ as per Example 1.

$\mathcal{E}^+ = \{loan(claudia)\} \quad \mathcal{E}^- = \{loan(bob)\}$

We consider *loan* as the unique learnable predicate, i.e., $\mathcal{T} = \{loan\}$. It can be shown that $F' = \langle \mathcal{R}_1 \cup \mathcal{R}_2, \mathcal{A}, \overline{} \rangle$ is an intensional solution of the ABA learning problem $\langle F, \langle \mathcal{E}^+, \mathcal{E}^- \rangle, \mathcal{T} \rangle$. It can be seen that these two rules be derived by using the transformation rules R1–R4. In particular, rule ρ_8 can be obtained by rote learning $loan(X) \leftarrow X = claudia$ from the positive example $loan(claudia)$ (i.e., applying transformation rule R1), then folding this rule with ρ_3 (i.e., applying transformation rule R2), and finally using the assumption $nobreaks(X)$ via R3.

To support contestability, we will rely upon various algorithms and implementations of the transformation-based approach to ABA learning [6,7,28].

3 Contestation and Redress

Suppose that we have learnt an ABA framework F' from a background knowledge F, positive and negative examples $\langle \mathcal{E}^+, \mathcal{E}^- \rangle$, and learnable predicates $\mathcal{T}$. Given a claim c, not appearing amongst the examples in $\langle \mathcal{E}^+, \mathcal{E}^- \rangle$, we will define the contestation of F' according to the request that c is covered or not in a stable extension, say Δ, of F'. We also require that Δ continues to be a solution to the given ABA learning problem, and thus all positive examples $\mathcal{E}^+$ are covered in Δ and no negative examples in $\mathcal{E}^-$ are covered in Δ. The existential quantification on stable extensions is consistent with the credulous reasoning approach we follow in this paper.

Definition 2 (Contestation). *Let F' be a solution of an ABA learning problem $(F, \langle \mathcal{E}^+, \mathcal{E}^- \rangle, \mathcal{T})$. Let $c \notin \mathcal{E}^+ \cup \mathcal{E}^-$ be a claim in $\mathcal{L}$ whose predicate belongs to $\mathcal{T}$. Then*

1. *F' is contested by want of c iff there is no stable extension Δ of F' such that (i) $\mathcal{E}^+ \cup \{c\}$ are covered in Δ, and (ii) $\mathcal{E}^-$ are not covered in Δ;*
2. *F' is contested by want of not c iff there is no stable extension Δ of F' such that (i) $\mathcal{E}^+$ are covered in Δ, and (ii) $\mathcal{E}^- \cup \{c\}$ are not covered in Δ.*

In the definition of contestation, the background knowledge F is not used at Points 1 and 2. However, F is relevant for the related definition of incremental redress (Definition 3) to partition the set of rules between those that can be modified (i.e., the learnt rules) and those that cannot (i.e., the rules in F).

Example 4. Let $\mathcal{E}^+ = \{p(1)\}$, $\mathcal{E}^- = \{p(2)\}$ and $c = p(3)$. Let F' admit two stable extensions, Δ_1, Δ_2 such that
$$F' \models_{\Delta_1} p(1), \quad F' \not\models_{\Delta_1} p(2), p(3), \quad \text{and} \quad F' \models_{\Delta_2} p(1), p(3), \quad F' \not\models_{\Delta_2} p(2).$$
F' is a solution based on any of the two extensions, but the want of (not) c may restrict the choice between Δ_1 and Δ_2. Indeed, F' is not contested by want of c, because of the existence of Δ_2, and F' is not contested by want of not c, because of the existence of Δ_1. If instead
$$F' \models_{\Delta_1} p(1), p(3), \quad F' \not\models_{\Delta_1} p(2), \quad \text{and} \quad F' \models_{\Delta_2} p(1), p(2), \quad F' \not\models_{\Delta_2} p(3),$$
then F' is a solution based on Δ_1 only, and thus F' is contested by want of not c, while not being contested by want of c (due to Δ_1). Finally, if
$$F' \models_{\Delta_1} p(1), \quad F' \not\models_{\Delta_1} p(2), p(3), \quad \text{and} \quad F' \models_{\Delta_2} p(3), \quad F' \not\models_{\Delta_2} p(1), p(2),$$
then, again, F' is a solution based on Δ_1 only, and thus F' is contested by want of c, while not being contested by want of not c (due to Δ_1).

Note that our choice of semantics of stable extensions enforces that, for every c, F' is either not contested, or contested by want of c, or by want of not c, but cannot be contested by want of both.

Proposition 1. *Let F' be a solution of an ABA learning problem $(F, \langle \mathcal{E}^+, \mathcal{E}^- \rangle, \mathcal{T})$, and $c \in \mathcal{L}$. F' cannot be contested by both want of c and want of not c.*

Proof. Let F' be a solution of $(F, \langle \mathcal{E}^+, \mathcal{E}^- \rangle, \mathcal{T})$ based on stable extension Δ. Either c is covered in Δ or not. If c is covered in Δ, then all claims in $\mathcal{E}^+ \cup \{c\}$ are covered in Δ and no claim in $\mathcal{E}^-$ is covered in Δ and F' is not contested by want of c. If c is not covered in Δ, then all claims in $\mathcal{E}^+$ are covered in Δ and no claim in $\mathcal{E}^- \cup \{c\}$ is covered in Δ and F' is not contested by want of not c. □

When a solution F' of an ABA Learning problem $(F, \langle \mathcal{E}^+, \mathcal{E}^- \rangle, \mathcal{T})$ is contested, the ABA framework should be redressed to resolve the contestation. If F' is contested by want of c, with predicate in $\mathcal{T}$, then the goal of redress consists in deriving a new ABA framework F'' such that c is covered in at least one stable extension of F''. Analogously, if F' is contested by want of not c, with predicate in $\mathcal{T}$, then the goal of redress consists in deriving a new ABA framework F'' such that c is not covered in a stable extension of F''. In both cases all examples of $\mathcal{E}^+$ and $\mathcal{E}^-$ should be still be covered and not covered, respectively.

There is a trivial form of redress: we can start from the original ABA Learning problem and add c to the positive examples, in the case of want of c, or to the negative examples, in the case of want of not c. Thus, redressing reduces to forgetting F' and solving one of the two ABA Learning problems: $(F, \langle \mathcal{E}^+ \cup \{c\}, \mathcal{E}^- \rangle, \mathcal{T})$ or $(F, \langle \mathcal{E}^+, \mathcal{E}^- \cup \{c\} \rangle, \mathcal{T})$. We call this form *redress from scratch*.

Clearly, it is undesirable to redress a learnt ABA framework from scratch, if contestation is expected to happen often. In this scenario it is highly desirable to enforce an *incremental redress*, that is, a redress that starts from F' and modifies it as little as possible.

Example 5. Let us consider the ABA framework F' that is a solution of the ABA Learning problem $\langle F, \langle \mathcal{E}^+, \mathcal{E}^- \rangle, \mathcal{T} \rangle$ from Example 3. Suppose now that F' is contested by want of $loan(jo)$, which is not covered by any stable extension of F'. Intuitively, one would like that the claim $loan(jo)$ is accepted. We can incrementally modify F' by applying the transformation rules presented in Sect. 2.2 as follows. By R3 we introduce a new assumption $\alpha(X)$, with contrary $c\_\alpha(X)$, and transform rule ρ_9 into:

ρ_{10}. $breaks(X) \leftarrow onleave(X), \alpha(X)$

Then, by R1, we get the rule:

ρ_{11}. $c\_\alpha(X) \leftarrow X = jo$

as $c\_\alpha(jo)$ is a positive example that we want to learn. Finally, by folding ρ_{10} with ρ_6, we get

ρ_{12}. $c\_\alpha(X) \leftarrow maternity(X)$

Intuitively, the learnt rules enforce that a loan is granted to an applicant who is employed unless she/he has had a career break, excluding maternity leaves. Now $loan(jo)$ is covered in the unique stable model of the ABA framework $F'' = \langle \mathcal{R}'', \mathcal{A}'', \overline{}'' \rangle$, where: $\mathcal{R}'' = \mathcal{R}_1 \cup \{\rho_8, \rho_{10}, \rho_{12}\} = \{\rho_1, \ldots, \rho_7, \rho_8, \rho_{10}, \rho_{12}\}$, $\mathcal{A}'' = \{nobreaks(X), \alpha(X)\}$, $\overline{nobreaks(X)}'' = breaks(X)$, $\overline{\alpha(X)}'' = c\_\alpha(X)$.

This example suggests that an incremental redress of a solution F' of an ABA Learning problem $(F, \langle \mathcal{E}^+, \mathcal{E}^- \rangle, \mathcal{T})$ can be realised by: (1) selecting (some of) the rules in F' that have been learnt from F and making them defeasible by assumption introduction, thus deriving $(F'_{ai}, \langle \mathcal{E}^+, \mathcal{E}^- \rangle, \mathcal{T}')$, where $\mathcal{T}'$ is obtained by adding the contraries of the new assumptions, and then (2) solving one of the ABA Learning problems (2.1) $(F'_{ai}, \langle \mathcal{E}^+ \cup \{c\}, \mathcal{E}^- \rangle, \mathcal{T}')$, if F' is contested by want of c, or (2.2) $(F'_{ai}, \langle \mathcal{E}^+, \mathcal{E}^- \cup \{c\} \rangle, \mathcal{T}')$, if F' is contested by want of not c.

We define incremental redress in the presence of multiple contestations.

Definition 3 (Incremental Redress). *Let $F' = \langle \mathcal{R}', \mathcal{A}', \overline{}' \rangle$ be a solution of an ABA Learning problem $\langle F, \langle \mathcal{E}^+, \mathcal{E}^- \rangle, \mathcal{T} \rangle$, where $F = \langle \mathcal{R}, \mathcal{A}, \overline{} \rangle$. Let $\langle \mathcal{E}_C^+, \mathcal{E}_C^- \rangle$ be two sets of claims such that: (i) the predicates of $\mathcal{E}_C^+ \cup \mathcal{E}_C^-$ belong to $\mathcal{T}$, and (ii) $(\mathcal{E}^+ \cup \mathcal{E}_C^+) \cap (\mathcal{E}^- \cup \mathcal{E}_C^-) = \emptyset$. Given a rule $(H \leftarrow B) \in \mathcal{R}' \setminus \mathcal{R}$, we define:*

$$(H \leftarrow B)_{ai} = \begin{cases} H \leftarrow B & \text{if an assumption } \alpha(X) \in \mathcal{A} \text{ occurs in } B \\ H \leftarrow B, \alpha(X) & \text{otherwise,} \\ & \text{where } \alpha(X) \text{ is an assumption not in } \mathcal{A}' \\ & \text{and } X = vars(H \leftarrow B), \end{cases}$$

Let F'_{ai} be $\langle \mathcal{R}'_{ai}, \mathcal{A}'_{ai}, \overline{(.)}'_{ai} \rangle$, where $\mathcal{R}'_{ai} = \mathcal{R} \cup \{\rho_{ai} \mid \rho \in \mathcal{R}' \setminus \mathcal{R}\}$, $\mathcal{A}'_{ai} = \mathcal{A}' \cup \{\alpha(X) \mid \alpha(X) \text{ is an assumption occurring in } \rho_{ai} \text{ for some } \rho \in \mathcal{R}' \setminus \mathcal{R}\}$, and $\overline{\alpha(X)}'_{ai} = \overline{\alpha(X)}'$, for $\alpha(X) \in \mathcal{A}'$. An *incremental redress* of F' with respect to $\langle \mathcal{E}^+_C, \mathcal{E}^-_C \rangle$ is any (intensional) solution of the ABA Learning problem $(F'_{ai}, \langle (\mathcal{E}^+ \cup \mathcal{E}^+_C), (\mathcal{E}^- \cup \mathcal{E}^-_C) \rangle, \mathcal{T}'_{ai})$, where $\mathcal{T}'_{ai} = \mathcal{T}' \cup \{\overline{\alpha(X)} \mid \alpha(X) \in \mathcal{A}'_{ai}\}$.

Example 6. Let us consider the following example, which is a variant of an example in [9]. F is a background knowledge with the following set $\mathcal{R}$ of rules:

$\rho_1.\ bird(X) \leftarrow X=r,\quad \rho_2.\ bird(X) \leftarrow penguin(X),\quad \rho_3.\ robin(X) \leftarrow X=r,$
$\rho_4.\ gull(X) \leftarrow X=g,\quad \rho_5.\ penguin(X) \leftarrow X=p1,$
$\rho_6.\ penguin(X) \leftarrow superpenguin(X),\quad \rho_7.\ superpenguin(X) \leftarrow X=p2,$
$\rho_8.\ ostrich(X) \leftarrow X=o,\quad \rho_9.\ cat(X) \leftarrow X=c,\quad \rho_{10}.\ bat(X) \leftarrow X=b$

The sets of positive and negative examples are, respectively:

$\mathcal{E}^+ = \{flies(r), flies(g)\} \quad \mathcal{E}^- = \{flies(p1), flies(c)\}.$

We consider *flies* as the unique learnable predicate, i.e., $\mathcal{T} = \{flies\}$. An intensional solution F' of the given ABA learning problem can be constructed by deriving the following two rules:

$\rho_{11}.\ flies(X) \leftarrow bird(X), \alpha 1(X) \quad \rho_{12}.\ c\_\alpha 1(X) \leftarrow penguin(X)$

Thus, the rules of the learnt framework F' are $\mathcal{R}' = \mathcal{R} \cup \{\rho_{11}, \rho_{12}\}$ (it can be shown that these two rules can be derived by using R1–R4 – see [22] for a similar derivation). Let us now assume that F is contested by want of *flies(p2)* and *flies(b)* and by want of not *flies(o)*. We construct F'_{ai} by assumption introduction. In particular, by R3, rule ρ_{12} is transformed into $(\rho_{12})_{ai}$, that is:

$\rho_{13}.\ c\_\alpha 1(X) \leftarrow penguin(X), \alpha 2(X)$

and $\mathcal{R}'_{ai} = \mathcal{R} \cup \{\rho_{11}, \rho_{13}\}$. Now, incremental redress consists in solving the new ABA Learning problem: $(F'_{ai}, \langle \mathcal{E}^+ \cup \{flies(p2), flies(b)\}, \mathcal{E}^- \cup \{flies(o), \{flies, c\_\alpha 1, c\_\alpha 2\})$. By R1, we learn:

$\rho_{14}.\ c\_\alpha 1(X) \leftarrow X=o \quad \rho_{15}.\ c\_\alpha 2(X) \leftarrow X=p2 \quad \rho_{16}.\ flies(X) \leftarrow X=b$

Now, by folding, we get:

$\rho_{17}.\ c\_\alpha 1(X) \leftarrow ostrich(X) \quad \rho_{18}.\ c\_\alpha 2(X) \leftarrow superpenguin(X)$
$\rho_{19}.\ flies(X) \leftarrow bat(X).$

The new ABA framework with rules $\mathcal{R} \cup \{\rho_{11}, \rho_{13}, \rho_{17}, \rho_{18}, \rho_{19}\}$ is an intensional solution of the ABA Learning problem with background knowledge F'_{ai}, and hence it is an incremental redress of F' relative to the new positive examples $\{flies(p2), flies(b)\}$ and negative examples $\{flies(o)\}$.

Theorem 1. *Let F'' be the incremental redress of an ABA framework F' with respect to $\langle \mathcal{E}^+_C, \mathcal{E}^-_C \rangle$. Then, F'' is not contested by want of c, for any claim $c \in \mathcal{E}^+_C$, and F'' is not contested by want of not c, for any $c \in \mathcal{E}^-_C$.*

Proof. Directly from the definitions of solutions of an ABA Learning problem (Definition 1) and of contestation of a learnt ABA framework (Definition 2). □

It might be impossible to redress an ABA framework, simply because there are ABA Learning problems that cannnot be solved.

Example 7. The ABA Learning problem $(\langle \mathcal{R}, \mathcal{A}, \overline{}\rangle, \langle \mathcal{E}^+, \mathcal{E}^-\rangle, \mathcal{T})$, where: $\mathcal{R} = \{p \leftarrow q\}$; $\mathcal{A} = \emptyset$; $\mathcal{E}^+ = \{q\}$; $\mathcal{E}^- = \{p\}$; $\mathcal{T} = \{p, q\}$, has no solution.

We now show that redress from scratch of a learnt ABA framework with respect to a pair $\langle \mathcal{E}_C^+, \mathcal{E}_C^-\rangle$ is possible if and only if incremental redress is possible. This property holds also under the further requirement that ABA frameworks are constructed by applying the transformation rules R1–R4.

Theorem 2. *Let $F' = \langle \mathcal{R}', \mathcal{A}', \overline{}'\rangle$ be a solution of an ABA Learning problem $\langle F, \langle \mathcal{E}^+, \mathcal{E}^-\rangle, \mathcal{T}\rangle$, where $F = \langle \mathcal{R}, \mathcal{A}, \overline{}\rangle$. Let $\mathcal{E}_C^+, \mathcal{E}_C^-$ be two sets of claims such that: (i) the predicates of $\mathcal{E}_C^+ \cup \mathcal{E}_C^-$ belong to $\mathcal{T}$, and (ii) $(\mathcal{E}^+ \cup \mathcal{E}_C^+) \cap (\mathcal{E}^- \cup \mathcal{E}_C^-) = \emptyset$.*
(1. If incremental redress succeeds, then redress from scratch succeeds.)
If F'' is an incremental redress of F' with respect to $\langle \mathcal{E}_C^+, \mathcal{E}_C^-\rangle$, then F'' is a solution of the ABA Learning problem $\langle F, \langle (\mathcal{E}^+ \cup \mathcal{E}_C^+), (\mathcal{E}^- \cup \mathcal{E}_C^-)\rangle, \mathcal{T}\rangle$. Furthermore, if F' is an intensional solution derived by R1–R4 and F'' is an intensional solution derived from F'_{ai} by R1–R4, then F'' can be derived by R1–R4.
(2. If redress from scratch succeeds, then incremental redress succeeds.)
If F'' is a solution of the ABA Learning problem $\langle F, \langle (\mathcal{E}^+ \cup \mathcal{E}_C^+), (\mathcal{E}^- \cup \mathcal{E}_C^-)\rangle, \mathcal{T}\rangle$, then there exists an incremental redress of F' with respect to $\langle \mathcal{E}_C^+, \mathcal{E}_C^-\rangle$. Furthermore, if F'' is an intensional solution derived from F by R1–R4, then an incremental redress F''' of F' with respect to $\langle \mathcal{E}_C^+, \mathcal{E}_C^-\rangle$ can be derived by R1–R4.

Proof. (Sketch) (1) It is easy to see that if incremental redress succeeds, then redress from scratch also succeeds. Indeed, a solution of the ABA learning problem $(F'_{ai}, \langle (\mathcal{E}^+ \cup \mathcal{E}_C^+), (\mathcal{E}^- \cup \mathcal{E}_C^-)\rangle, \mathcal{T}'_{ai})$ shown in Definition 3 is also a solution of $(F, \langle (\mathcal{E}^+ \cup \mathcal{E}_C^+), (\mathcal{E}^- \cup \mathcal{E}_C^-)\rangle, \mathcal{T})$. Moreover, if F' is derived from F by applying the transformation rules R1–R4, and also the ABA framework F'' resulting from incremental redress is derived from F'_{ai} by applications of R1–R4, then F'' can be derived from F by R1–R4. Indeed, F'_{ai} is derived by applying R3 to F'. An analogous property holds if we consider intensional solutions, instead of simply solutions.
(2) We only consider that more difficult case where we use the transformation rules R1–R4 for ABA Learning. Suppose that we derive, by R1–R4, a solution F' of the ABA Learning problem $(F, \langle (\mathcal{E}^+), (\mathcal{E}^-)\rangle, \mathcal{T})$, and we also derive, by R1–R4, a solution F' of the ABA Learning problem $(F, \langle (\mathcal{E}^+ \cup \mathcal{E}_C^+), (\mathcal{E}^- \cup \mathcal{E}_C^-)\rangle, \mathcal{T})$. Then, from F', by repeated applications of R3, we can compute the ABA framework F'_{ai} with set of rules $\mathcal{R}'_{ai}$ as shown in Definition 3. Now, each rule in $\mathcal{R}'_{ai}$ is of the form $H \leftarrow B', \alpha(X)$ and, without loss of generality (by possibly renaming predicates), we can assume that $\alpha(X)$ is new assumption, that is, an assumption in $\mathcal{A}' \setminus \mathcal{A}$, whose contrary $\overline{\alpha(X)}$ does not occur in $\mathcal{R}$. We assume that (again, without loss of generality), there exists a predicate, say dom with a rule $dom(X) \leftarrow X = a$ for each constant a occurring in the universe $\mathcal{U}$. For each $\overline{\alpha(X)}$, by rote learning (R1) and folding (R2), we can add a rule $\overline{\alpha(X)} \leftarrow dom(X)$ and derive a new set $\mathcal{R}'_{ai} \cup \hat{\mathcal{R}}$ of rules. Let us now consider the subset $\mathcal{R}_l$ of the rules of F'', which,

by hypothesis, have been derived from $\mathcal{R}$ by R1–R4. By the same sequence of applications of the transformation rules, we can derive a new ABA framework F''' with rules $\mathcal{R}_l \cup \mathcal{R}'_{ai} \cup \hat{\mathcal{R}}$. Only arguments constructed by using rules in $\mathcal{R} \cup \mathcal{R}_l$ can be accepted by a stable extension of F''', as all others would be attacked by a rule in $\hat{\mathcal{R}}$, which cannot be attacked. Thus, there is a one-to-one mapping ϕ from the stable extensions of F'' and F''' such that, for every claim c in their common language (including the examples), $F'' \models_\Delta c$ iff $F''' \models_{\phi(\Delta)} c$. □

Notice that, in the proof of Point (2) Theorem 2, we introduce rules $\overline{\alpha(X)} \leftarrow dom(X)$ that can be used for attacking all arguments supported by the assumption $\alpha(X)$. This derivation step allows us to use, instead, the rules that, by hypothesis, can be obtained by a derivation from scratch. Obviously, this is not effective in practice, and indeed our redress algorithm of Sect. 4 learns suitable rules $\overline{\alpha(X)} \leftarrow p(X)$ such that $p(a)$ can be derived for a *minimal* set of constants in $\mathcal{L}$. For instance, in Example 6, we learn rules ρ_{17}, ρ_{18}, instead of rules of the form $\overline{c\_\alpha N(X)} \leftarrow animal(X)$, where $animal(X) \leftarrow X = a$ is a fact, for all constants a occurring in the language.

4 An ASP-Based Algorithm for Incremental Redress

Algorithm 1 implements a strategy, called *RASP-ABAlearn*, to perform the incremental redress of a solution $F' = \langle \mathcal{R}_0, \mathcal{A}_0, \overline{}^{\,0} \rangle$ of the ABA Learning problem $(F, \langle \mathcal{E}^+, \mathcal{E}^- \rangle, \mathcal{T})$ with respect to a pair $\langle \mathcal{E}_C^+, \mathcal{E}_C^- \rangle$ of positive and negative examples. Algorithm 1 orchestrates the application of the transformation rules R1–R4 presented in Sect. 2.2 and takes advantage of a mapping between ABA frameworks under the stable extension semantics and ASP programs [2,13]. This mapping, formalised by Definition 4, reduces some reasoning tasks required by R1 and R4 to computing answer sets of an ASP program.

Definition 4. *Let* dom(t) *hold for all tuples* t *of constants of* $\mathcal{L}$. *We denote by* $ASP(\langle \mathcal{R}_0, \mathcal{A}_0, \overline{}^{\,0} \rangle, \langle \mathcal{E}^+, \mathcal{E}^- \rangle, \langle \mathcal{E}_C^+, \mathcal{E}_C^- \rangle, \mathcal{T})$ *the following ASP program* P.

(a) Each rule in $\mathcal{R}_0$ is a rule of P (rewritten in the ASP syntax)
(b) Each $\alpha \in \mathcal{A}_0$ is encoded in P by the rule α :- dom(X), not c_α. ,
    where c_α *is an ASP atom encoding $\overline{\alpha}$, and $vars(\alpha) =$* X
(c) Each $e \in (\mathcal{E}^+ \cup \mathcal{E}_C^+)$ is encoded in P as :- not e.
(d) Each $e \in (\mathcal{E}^- \cup \mathcal{E}_C^-)$ is encoded in P as :- e.
(e) Each atom $p(X)$ with $p \in \mathcal{T}$ is encoded in P as
    p(X) :- newp(X). #minimize{1,X: newp(X)}.
(e.1) If $p \in pred(\overline{\alpha(X)})$ with $\alpha(X) \in \mathcal{A}$ and B is the body in which $\alpha(X)$ occurs, then P has the choice rule { newp(X) } :- b., *where* newp *is a new predicate name and* b *is the conjunction of the non-assumption atoms in B such that $vars(X) \cap vars(b) \neq \emptyset$, and*
(e.2) If $p \in pred(\mathcal{E}_C^+)$, then P has the choice rule { newp(t_1);...;newp(t_n) }.,
    where $\{newp(t_1), \ldots, newp(t_n)\} = \{newp(t) \mid p(t) \in \mathcal{E}_C^+\}$.

Point (a) is a straightforward ASP translation of the rules in $\mathcal{R}_0$. Point (b) introduces an ASP rule for each assumption in $\mathcal{A}_0$ stating that an assumption α holds if its contrary $\bar{\alpha}$ does not (i.e., any assumption holds by default). Points (c) and (d) introduce integrity constraints stating that positive examples are supported by the rules and negative examples are not. Point (e) specifies how to generate atoms that represent positive examples and contraries of assumptions. These atoms constitute the ground truth through which R1 introduces new rules into $\mathcal{R}_0$ and R4 decides to ignore examples that are already supported by rules in $\mathcal{R}_0$. In particular, the choice rules at points ($e.1$) and ($e.2$) generate a set of atoms representing contraries and positive examples, respectively, and the optimization statement at point (e) enforces this set to be minimal. The optimization statement aims at reducing the number of rules required to redress a solution.

Algorithm 1 consists of two procedures: $RoLe()$ and $Gen()$.

$RoLe()$ is responsible for repeatedly applying rule R1 (Rote Learning). It extends the background knowledge with a minimal set of facts to get a (non-intensional) solution to the input redress problem. $RoLe()$ checks whether the ASP encoding of the learning problem P at line 4 has a solution. If P has no solution, then $RASP$-$ABAlearn$ fails. Otherwise, it uses an answer set of P (line 8) to apply R1 (line 10). It has the same structure of $RoLe()$ used in ASP-$ABAlearn_B$ [6], but it makes use of the new ASP encoding (Definition 4) to deal with redress.

$Gen()$ is responsible for repeatedly applying rules R4 (Fact Subsumption), R2 (Folding), R3 (Assumption Introduction) and R1 (Rote Learning) to transform the non-intensional solution produced by $RoLe()$ into an intensional solution. In contrast to ASP-$ABAlearn_B$ [6], it combines R2 and R3 to make the learnt rules defeasible by construction (specifically, by introducing an assumption to every rule obtained by folding). This mechanism guarantees that any solution produced by $Gen()$ has the form required by F'_{ai} in Definition 3, and can therefore be used as input in a subsequent run of $RASP$-$ABAlearn$ to redress a solution. In particular, $Gen()$ takes any fact ρ introduced by $RoLe()$ (line 14) and applies rule R4 to check whether it is subsumed by the rules in $\mathcal{R}_l$ (line 16). If that is not the case, it invokes $FoldingWAsmIntro(\rho)$ which applies rule R2 (lines 27-29) and R3 (lines 30-40) as follows. A repeated application of R2 transforms a non intensional rule ρ into an intensional one by using the *greedy* folding strategy presented in [7]. Then, R3 introduces an assumption in the body of ρ either (i) by using an assumption in $\mathcal{A}$ introduced in a previous application of R3 or (ii) by creating a fresh new assumption to be added to $\mathcal{A}$, thereby adding the new rule ρ_g to $\mathcal{R}_l$. Finally, $Gen()$ applies R1 to learn a minimal set of facts for the contrary of the assumption occurring in ρ_g.

Algorithm 1 makes also use of two subsidiary functions: (i) $as(P)$ that returns any answer set of the ASP program P, and (ii) $sat(P)$ that returns *true* if P is satisfiable (it has at least one answer set), and *false* otherwise.

By using the properties of the transformation rules R1–R4 [6], we can extend the soundness and termination results for ASP-$ABAlearn_B$ to the incremental redress algorithm $RASP$-$ABAlearn$. We omit the proofs for lack of space.

Algorithm 1: $RASP\text{-}ABAlearn$

Input: $(\langle \mathcal{R}_0, \mathcal{A}_0, \overline{}^0 \rangle, \langle \mathcal{E}^+, \mathcal{E}^- \rangle, \langle \mathcal{E}_C^+, \mathcal{E}_C^- \rangle, \mathcal{T})$: redress problem
Output: $\langle \mathcal{R}, \mathcal{A}, \overline{} \rangle$: incremental redress relative to $\langle \mathcal{E}_C^+, \mathcal{E}_C^- \rangle$

1 $\mathcal{R} := \mathcal{R}_0;\quad \mathcal{A} := \mathcal{A}_0;\quad \overline{} := \overline{}^0;\quad \mathcal{R}_l := \emptyset;$
2 $RoLe();\quad Gen();\quad \textbf{return } \langle \mathcal{R}, \mathcal{A}, \overline{} \rangle;$
3 **Procedure** $RoLe()$
4      $P := ASP(\langle \mathcal{R}, \mathcal{A}, \overline{} \rangle, \langle \mathcal{E}^+, \mathcal{E}^- \rangle, \langle \mathcal{E}_C^+, \mathcal{E}_C^- \rangle, \mathcal{T});$
5   **if** $\neg sat(P)$ **then**
6 | fail;
7   **else**
8          $S := as(P);$
        // R1. Rote Learning
9   **foreach** $\texttt{newp(t)} \in S$ **do**
10 | $\mathcal{R}_l := \mathcal{R}_l \cup \{p(X) \leftarrow X = t\};$
11   **end**
12   **end**
13 **Procedure** $Gen()$
14   **foreach** $\rho : (p(X) \leftarrow X = t) \in \mathcal{R}_l$ **do**
15         $\mathcal{R}_l := \mathcal{R}_l \setminus \{\rho\};$
        // R4. Fact Subsumption
16   **if** $\neg sat(ASP(\langle \mathcal{R} \cup \mathcal{R}_l, \mathcal{A}, \overline{} \rangle, \langle \mathcal{E}^+, \mathcal{E}^- \rangle, \langle \mathcal{E}_C^+, \mathcal{E}_C^- \rangle, \emptyset))$ **then**
            // R2 w/ R3. Folding with Assumption Introduction
17             $\langle \rho_g, \alpha(X), C_\alpha \rangle := FoldingWAsmIntro(\rho);$
18             $\mathcal{R} := \mathcal{R} \cup \{\rho_g\};$
19             $\mathcal{A} := \mathcal{A} \cup \{\alpha(X)\};$
20             $\overline{\alpha(X)} := c\_\alpha(X);$
            // R1. Rote Learning
21   **foreach** $\texttt{c\_}\alpha\texttt{(t)} \in C_\alpha$ **do**
22 | $\mathcal{R}_l := \mathcal{R}_l \cup \{c\_\alpha(X) \leftarrow X = t\};$
23   **end**
24   **end**
25   **end**
26 **Function** $FoldingWAsmIntro(\rho)$
    // R2. Folding
27   **while** $foldable(\rho, \mathcal{R})$ **do**
28 | $\rho := fold(\rho, \mathcal{R});$
29   **end**
    // R3. Assumption Introduction
30   Let ρ be $H \leftarrow B;\ X := vars(B);$
31   **if** there exists $\alpha(X) \in \mathcal{A}$ relative to B **then**
32         $\rho_g := H \leftarrow B, \alpha(X);\quad C_\alpha := \emptyset;$
33   **if** $\neg sat(ASP(\langle \mathcal{R} \cup \{\rho\}, \mathcal{A}, \overline{} \rangle, \langle \mathcal{E}^+, \mathcal{E}^- \rangle, \langle \mathcal{E}_C^+, \mathcal{E}_C^- \rangle, \emptyset))$ **then**
34 | fail;
35   **end**
36   **else** // introduce an assumption $\alpha(X)$, with a new predicate α
37         $\rho_g := H \leftarrow B, \alpha(X);$
38         $F := \langle \mathcal{R} \cup \{\rho\}, \mathcal{A} \cup \{\alpha(X)\}, \overline{} \cup \{\alpha(X) \mapsto c\_\alpha(X)\}\rangle;$
39         $C_\alpha := \{c\_\alpha(X) \mid c\_\alpha(X) \in as(ASP(F, \langle \mathcal{E}^+, \mathcal{E}^- \rangle, \langle \mathcal{E}_C^+, \mathcal{E}_C^- \rangle, \{c\_\alpha\}))\};$
40   **end**
41   **return** $\langle \rho_g, \alpha(X), C_\alpha \rangle;$

Theorem 3 (Soundness). Let $F' = \langle \mathcal{R}_0, \mathcal{A}_0, \overline{}^0 \rangle$ be a solution of the ABA Learning problem $(F, \langle \mathcal{E}^+, \mathcal{E}^- \rangle, \mathcal{T})$. If Algorithm 1 with input $(F', \langle \mathcal{E}^+, \mathcal{E}^- \rangle, \langle \mathcal{E}_C^+, \mathcal{E}_C^- \rangle, \mathcal{T})$ terminates with success, then its output is an incremental redress of F' with respect to $\langle \mathcal{E}_C^+, \mathcal{E}_C^- \rangle$. Also, the output is an intensional ABA framework.

Similarly to ASP-ABAlearn$_B$, Algorithm RASP-ABAlearn may terminate with failure, even if redress is possible. However, if we admit that FoldingWAsmIntro may return a non-intensional rule, then we get the following result.

Theorem 4 (Weak Completeness). For all inputs $(F', \langle \mathcal{E}^+, \mathcal{E}^- \rangle, \langle \mathcal{E}_C^+, \mathcal{E}_C^- \rangle, \mathcal{T})$, Algorithm 1 terminates and returns a, possibly non-intensional, ABA framework, if an incremental redress of F' with respect to $\langle \mathcal{E}_C^+, \mathcal{E}_C^- \rangle$ exists.

5 Experimental Evaluation

This section presents the experimental evaluation to assess the effectiveness and efficiency of RASP-ABAlearn.

Learning Problems. We have formalized six ABA learning problems (reported in the first column of Table 1) from standard datasets included in the UC Irvine (UCI) Machine Learning Repository [21,30] by translating the features of each tuple into facts of the background knowledge and considering such tuple as denoting a positive or negative example according to its classification.

Implementation. We have implemented Algorithm 1 as a module of the ABALearn tool [5]. In particular, we have (i) extended ABALearn to deal with the new formalization of the learning problem, and (ii) we have implemented the *greedy* folding strategy presented in [7]. The implementation is based on the SWI-Prolog [31] system (v9.2.9) and the Clingo [12] ASP solver (v5.7.1). The tool and the datasets are available at https://github.com/ABALearn/aba_asp.

Experimental Processes. We have considered the two variants of redress presented in Sect. 3: (S) Redress from scratch and (R) Incremental redress. The experimental process consists in running Algorithm 1 with input $(F, \langle \emptyset, \emptyset \rangle, \langle \mathcal{E}_C^+, \mathcal{E}_C^- \rangle, \mathcal{T})$, where $\mathcal{E}_C^+$ and $\mathcal{E}_C^-$ include 90% of the tuples classified as positive and negative examples, respectively. Then, we have performed 10 additional executions of (S) and (R) each using a randomly selected new example.

Technical Resources. Experiments have run on an Apple M1 with 8 GB of RAM.

Results. Table 1 shows the results of the experimental evaluation. Column 'Problem' describes the ABA learning problem: (i) the name of the problem, (ii) the size (number of facts) of the background knowledge, and (iii) the number of positive and negative examples used for the first run of Algorithm 1. The remaining columns report the results of each run of Algorithm 1: column '0' is standard ABA Learning (by setting $\langle \mathcal{E}^+, \mathcal{E}^- \rangle = \langle \emptyset, \emptyset \rangle$); columns from '1' to '10' report the results of the 10 additional runs each using a randomly selected new example. For each problem, Table 1 includes five rows: the first row gives whether

Table 1. Column 'Problem' reports: (i) the *name* of the learning problem, (ii) the size (number of facts) of the background knowledge, and (iii) the number of positive and negative examples $\langle |\mathcal{E}_C^+|, |\mathcal{E}_C^-| \rangle$ (90% of the tuples classified as positive and negative examples) used for the first run of Algorithm 1 (i.e., with input $(F, \langle \emptyset, \emptyset \rangle, \langle \mathcal{E}_C^+, \mathcal{E}_C^- \rangle, \mathcal{T})$). Column '0' reports the results of the first run. Columns from '1' to '10' report the results of the 10 additional runs each using a randomly selected new example. For each learning problem, the first row gives whether the randomly selected example to redress is positive (+) or negative (−); rows 'T_S' and 'T_R' report the times in milliseconds (sum of the CPU and System time) taken by our tool to perform a *redress from scratch* (S) and an *incremental redress* (R), respectively; rows 'S_S' and 'S_R' report the number of rules of the learnt ABA frameworks generated by performing (S) and (R), respectively.

Problem		0	1	2	3	4	5	6	7	8	9	10
			+	−	−	−	−	+	−	+	+	+
acute	T_S	39	31	32	31	32	32	37	41	38	40	39
495	T_R	36	2	3	3	2	4	7	2	3	2	3
$\langle 54, 55 \rangle$	S_S	501	501	501	501	501	501	503	503	503	503	503
	S_R	501	501	501	501	501	501	502	502	502	502	502
			+	+	+	−	+	−	−	−	−	+
autism	T_S	13524	14427	14552	15004	14985	15252	15048	15114	15246	15097	15329
6568	T_R	12741	970	905	999	44	1126	47	46	44	44	1144
$\langle 171, 464 \rangle$	S_S	6953	6954	6955	6956	6956	6958	6958	6958	6958	6958	6961
	S_R	6953	6954	6955	6956	6956	6957	6957	6957	6957	6957	6958
			+	−	−	−	−	+	−	+	+	+
breastw	T_S	8371	8749	9061	9258	9208	9082	9039	9086	9061	9235	9318
6325	T_R	8482	36	430	35	36	36	36	35	35	37	418
$\langle 216, 400 \rangle$	S_S	6519	6519	6520	6520	6520	6520	6520	6520	6520	6520	6521
	S_R	6519	6519	6520	6520	6520	6520	6520	6520	6520	6520	6521
			−	−	−	+	+	+	−	−	+	−
krkp	T_S	40595	42557	42250	42173	42357	41985	42417	42673	42321	41987	42910
33210	T_R	40475	111	1711	106	106	108	106	1682	1189	107	106
$\langle 1503, 1374 \rangle$	S_S	33409	33409	33410	33410	33410	33410	33410	33411	33412	33412	33412
	S_R	33409	33409	33410	33410	33410	33410	33410	33411	33412	33412	33412
			+	−	−	−	−	+	−	−	+	+
mushroom	T_S	555525	559972	471200	469676	474180	552260	552583	579530	513419	551619	472482
33868	T_R	471191	300	11338	280	11680	11409	279	279	280	281	279
$\langle 214, 1587 \rangle$	S_S	34762	34762	34763	34763	34764	34763	34763	34763	34763	34763	34763
	S_R	34762	34762	34763	34763	34764	34765	34765	34765	34765	34765	34765
			+	+	−	+	+	−	−	+	−	+
voting	T_S	663	663	675	670	669	705	707	664	664	666	667
2172	T_R	664	11	12	12	12	70	10	185	11	12	12
$\langle 98, 112 \rangle$	S_S	2230	2230	2230	2230	2230	2233	2233	2229	2229	2229	2229
	S_R	2230	2230	2230	2230	2230	2231	2231	2234	2234	2234	2234

the additional randomly selected example used to redress is positive or negative (columns '1'-'10'); rows 'T_S' and 'T_R' report the times in milliseconds (sum of the CPU and System time) taken by our tool to perform the experimental processes

(S) and (R), respectively; rows 'S_S' and 'S_R' report the number of rules of the learnt ABA frameworks generated by performing (S) and (R), respectively.

The times demonstrate the computational advantages of performing incremental redress (S) compared to redress from scratch (R): the time to redress is always lower than the time to re-learn from scratch. Moreover, the results also show that the sizes of the learnt ABA framework are comparable, as incremental redress preserves most rules and does not add many new ones. However, in this paper we do not present any formal result characterising the relationships between the ABA frameworks re-learnt from scratch (S) and the ones obtained by incremental redressing via *RASP-ABAlearn* (R). They could even admit different stable extensions. The only guarantee is that they are (possibly different) solutions of the same ABA learning problem, and thus each of them admits a stable extension that covers all specified positive examples and does not cover any specified negative example.

6 Conclusions

We have studied the issue of contestability for ABA frameworks learnt from a given background knowledge and sets of positive and negative examples. We have proposed a method for incremental redress when sets of claims are subject to contestation, either because one wishes to accept or reject them, in contrast to the current version of the framework. In essence, we view redressing as a way of learning from additional positive or negative examples, and hence we can use a form of ABA Learning [6,7,22] to realise it. The most important properties we use for obtaining incrementality is the ability to learn defeasible rules and to manipulate these rules through transformations. Our experiments show that incremental redress is indeed much more efficient, in terms of computation time, than re-learning from scratch, and also that the number of rules learnt incrementally is comparable with the number of rules learnt from scratch.

This work can be extended in several directions. Here we have assumed that contestation targets claims that are accepted or rejected by the learnt ABA framework, but they are consistent with the examples from which learning had been performed. We believe that our approach can be adapted to the case where new examples are in contrast to previous ones, that is, the (human or AI) agents that provide the examples may "change their mind". We could also relax the assumption that the original background knowledge is fixed, and instead allow the addition of new background knowledge together with a contestation. For instance, continuing the loan example, an applicant could support her contestation by also providing the extra fact that she owns real estate. Another interesting issue is the contestation of rules, rather than claims, as proposed in [20].

Finally, we would like to make a formal complexity analysis of the redressing problem and also perform further experimental evaluation to assess the practicality of our method. We have only considered tabular datasets, and it would be interesting to make experiments on datasets where the background knowledge consists of a set of rules, besides facts. It would also be interesting to construct a mapping between the learning problems studied here and those considered by IncrementalLAS [17], the incremental version of FastLAS [18], so as to be able to make a comparison between that system and our *RASP-ABAlearn*.

Acknowledgments. We thank support from the Royal Society, UK (IEC\R2\ 222045). Toni was partially funded by the ERC (grant agreement No. 101020934) and by J.P. Morgan and the RAEng, UK, under the Research Chairs Fellowships scheme (RCSRF2021\11\45). De Angelis and Proietti were supported by the MUR PRIN 2022 Project DOMAIN funded by the EU NextGenerationEU (2022TSYYKJ, CUP B53D23013220006, PNRR, M4.C2.1.1), by the PNRR MUR project PE0000013-FAIR (CUP B53C22003630006), and by the INdAM - GNCS Project *Argomentazione Computazionale per apprendimento automatico e modellazione di sistemi intelligenti* (CUP E53C24001950001). De Angelis and Proietti are members of the INdAM-GNCS research group. Finally, we would like to thank the anonymous reviewers for their constructive remarks.

References

1. Bondarenko, A., Dung, P.M., Kowalski, R.A., Toni, F.: An abstract, argumentation-theoretic approach to default reasoning. Artif. Intell. **93**, 63–101 (1997). https://doi.org/10.1016/S0004-3702(97)00015-5
2. Brewka, G., Eiter, T., Truszczyński, M.: Answer set programming at a glance. Commun. ACM **54**(12), 92–103 (2011). https://doi.org/10.1145/2043174.2043195
3. Cocarascu, O., Stylianou, A., Cyras, K., Toni, F.: Data-empowered argumentation for dialectically explainable predictions. In: Proceedings of ECAI 2020. FAIA, vol. 325, pp. 2449–2456. IOS Press (2020). https://doi.org/10.3233/FAIA200377
4. Cyras, K., Fan, X., Schulz, C., Toni, F.: Assumption-based argumentation: disputes, explanations, preferences. FLAP **4**(8) (2017). http://www.collegepublications.co.uk/downloads/ifcolog00017.pdf
5. De Angelis, E., Proietti, M., Toni, F.: Code and data for "Learning Brave Assumption-Based Argumentation Frameworks via ASP". Zenodo (2024). https://doi.org/10.5281/zenodo.13330013
6. De Angelis, E., Proietti, M., Toni, F.: Learning brave assumption-based argumentation frameworks via ASP. In: Proceedings of ECAI 2024. FAIA, vol. 392, pp. 3445–3452. IOS Press (2024). https://doi.org/10.3233/FAIA240896
7. De Angelis, E., Proietti, M., Toni, F.: Greedy ABA learning for case-based reasoning. In: Proceedings of AAMAS 2025, pp. 556–564 (2025)
8. Dignum, V., Michael, L., Nieves, J.C., Slavkovik, M., Suarez, J., Theodorou, A.: Contesting black-box AI decisions. In: Proceedings of AAMAS 2025, pp. 2854–2858 (2025)
9. Dimopoulos, Y., Kakas, A.: Learning non-monotonic logic programs: learning exceptions. In: Lavrac, N., Wrobel, S. (eds.) ECML 1995. LNCS, vol. 912, pp. 122–137. Springer, Heidelberg (1995). https://doi.org/10.1007/3-540-59286-5_53
10. Dung, P., Kowalski, R., Toni, F.: Assumption-based argumentation. In: Argumentation in Artificial Intelligence, pp. 199–218. Springer (2009). https://doi.org/10.1007/978-0-387-98197-0_10

11. Freedman, G., Dejl, A., Gorur, D., Yin, X., Rago, A., Toni, F.: Argumentative large language models for explainable and contestable claim verification. In: Proceedings of AAAI-25, pp. 14930–14939. AAAI Press (2025). https://doi.org/10.1609/AAAI.V39I14.33637
12. Gebser, M., Kaminski, R., Kaufmann, B., Schaub, T.: Multi-shot ASP solving with clingo. TPLP **19**(1), 27–82 (2019). https://doi.org/10.1017/S1471068418000054
13. Gelfond, M., Lifschitz, V.: The stable model semantics for logic programming. In: Proceedings of ICLP 1988, pp. 1070–1080. MIT Press (1988)
14. Gould, A., Paulino-Passos, G., Dadhania, S., Williams, M., Toni, F.: Preference-based abstract argumentation for case-based reasoning. In: Proceedings of KR 2024, pp. 394–404 (2024). https://doi.org/10.24963/kr.2024/37
15. Inoue, K., Haneda, H.: Learning abductive and nonmonotonic logic programs. In: Abduction and Induction: Essays on their Relation and Integration, pp. 213–231. Kluwer Academic (2000). https://doi.org/10.1007/978-94-017-0606-3_14
16. Inoue, K., Kudoh, Y.: Learning extended logic programs. In: Proceedings of IJCAI 1997, pp. 176–181. Morgan Kaufmann (1997)
17. Law, M., Broda, K., Russo, A.: Search space expansion for efficient incremental inductive logic programming from streamed data. In: Proceedings of IJCAI 2022, pp. 2697–2704. ijcai.org (2022). https://doi.org/10.24963/IJCAI.2022/374
18. Law, M., Russo, A., Bertino, E., Broda, K., Lobo, J.: FastLAS: scalable inductive logic programming incorporating domain-specific optimisation criteria. In: Proceedings of AAAI 2020, pp. 2877–2885. AAAI Press (2020). https://doi.org/10.1609/AAAI.V34I03.5678
19. Law, M., Russo, A., Broda, K.: Inductive learning of answer set programs. In: Fermé, E., Leite, J. (eds.) JELIA 2014. LNCS (LNAI), vol. 8761, pp. 311–325. Springer, Cham (2014). https://doi.org/10.1007/978-3-319-11558-0_22
20. Leofante, F., et al.: Contestable AI needs computational argumentation. In: Proceedings of KR 2024, pp. 888–896 (2024). https://doi.org/10.24963/kr.2024/83
21. Kelly, M., Longjohn, R., Nottingham, K.: The UCI machine learning repository. https://archive.ics.uci.edu
22. Proietti, M., Toni, F.: Learning assumption-based argumentation frameworks. In: Proceedings of ILP 2022. LNCS, vol. 13779, pp. 100–116. Springer (2024). https://doi.org/10.1007/978-3-031-55630-2_8
23. Rapberger, A., Ulbricht, M., Toni, F.: On the correspondence of non-flat assumption-based argumentation and logic programming with negation as failure in the head. In: Proceedings of NMR 2024. CEUR Workshop Proceedings, vol. 3835, pp. 112–121 (2024)
24. Ray, O.: Nonmonotonic abductive inductive learning. J. Appl. Log. **7**(3), 329–340 (2009). https://doi.org/10.1016/j.jal.2008.10.007
25. Russo, F., Toni, F.: Causal discovery and knowledge injection for contestable neural networks. In: Proceedings of ECAI 2023. FAIA, vol. 372, pp. 2025–2032. IOS Press (2023). https://doi.org/10.3233/FAIA230495
26. Sakama, C.: Induction from answer sets in nonmonotonic logic programs. ACM TOCL **6**(2), 203–231 (2005). https://doi.org/10.1145/1055686.1055687
27. Shakerin, F., Salazar, E., Gupta, G.: A new algorithm to automate inductive learning of default theories. TPLP **17**(5–6), 1010–1026 (2017). https://doi.org/10.1017/S1471068417000333
28. Tirsi, C., Proietti, M., Toni, F.: ABALearn: an automated logic-based learning system for ABA frameworks. In: Proceedings of AIxIA 2023. LNCS, vol. 14318, pp. 3–16. Springer (2023). https://doi.org/10.1007/978-3-031-47546-7_1

29. Toni, F.: A tutorial on assumption-based argumentation. Argument Comput. **5**(1), 89–117 (2014). https://doi.org/10.1080/19462166.2013.869878
30. Wang, H., Shakerin, F., Gupta, G.: FOLD-RM: a scalable, efficient, and explainable inductive learning algorithm for multi-category classification of mixed data. TPLP **22**(5), 658–677 (2022). https://doi.org/10.1017/S1471068422000205
31. Wielemaker, J., Schrijvers, T., Triska, M., Lager, T.: SWI-Prolog. TPLP **12**(1–2), 67–96 (2012)

Author Index

A
Adams, Zekeri 137
Amato, Claudiad' 176
Anthony, Peter 137
Arndt, Dörthe 209
Arp, Daniel 137

B
Balogh, Štefan 137
Bernardi, Ansgar 194
Bhatt, Mehul 156
Bisquert, Pierre 194

C
Calvanese, Diego 119
Carral, David 194
Charbonnier, Léa 36
Charoensit, Akira 194

D
De Angelis, Emanuele 237
Diliso, Ivan 176
Dimitrakos, Theo 54

F
Fanizzi, Nicola 176
Feremans, Len 90

G
Galadima, Kefas Rimamnuskeb 137
Ghasemi, Amin 108
Giustozzi, Franco 36
Goethals, Bart 90
Goknil, Arda 227

H
Homola, Martin 137

K
Kadi, Ahmad 194
Kalala, Kalonji 18
Kargl, Frank 54
Kiringa, Iluju 18
Kowalski, Robert 1
Krontiris, Ioannis 54

L
Li, Chengkai 108
Lien, Carl-Henrik 227
Liu, Heng 72

M
Monsen, Julius 156
Mugnier, Marie-Laure 194
Müller, Nikolas 194

N
Nikolov, Nikolay 227

O
Onoja, Monday 137
Ouattara, Koffi Ismael 54

P
Perution-Khili, Guillaume 194
Petrovska, Ana 54
Proietti, Maurizio 237

R
Roman, Dumitru 227

S
Saunier, Julien 36
Sen, Sagar 227

Shirvani-Mahdavi, Nasim   108
Song, Hui   227
Soylu, Ahmet   227
Suchan, Jakob   156

T
Ternovska, Eugenia   72
Tomaszuk, Dominik   209
Toni, Francesca   237

U
Ulliana, Federico   194

V
Van Woensel, William   209
Videsjorden, Adela Nedisan   227

W
Wandji, Romuald Esdras   119
Wingfield, Devin   108

Y
Yeap, Tet   18

Z
Zanni-Merk, Cecilia   36

Made in the USA
Monee, IL
03 May 2026